Paul Jay Bowman M.D.
160 Brandon Way
Fort Bragg Calif
April 9 - 1978

SHRUBS, TREES AND CLIMBERS

Other Books by Sima Eliovson:

South African Wild Flowers for the Garden
The Complete Gardening Book
Discovering Wild Flowers in Southern Africa
Proteas for Pleasure
Bulbs for the Gardener
Gardening the Japanese Way
Namaqualand in Flower

SHRUBS, TREES AND CLIMBERS

Sima Eliovson

M

This edition first published in 1975
by
MACMILLAN SOUTH AFRICA (PUBLISHERS)
Johannesburg
Associated companies in London, New York, Dublin,
Madras and Melbourne

ISBN 0 86954 011 4

First edition 1952
Second edition 1953
Third edition 1956
Fourth revised edition 1962
Fifth edition 1965
Sixth edition 1969
Seventh edition 1971
Eighth edition, Enlarged and Reset, 1975

Photographs and Lay-out of Plates by Sima Eliovson

Filmset in Monophoto Bembo by
Asco Trade Typesetting Limited, Hong Kong

Printed in Hong Kong by
Dai Nippon Printing Co., (H.K.) Ltd.

Endpapers: Flame-Tree, *Brachychiton acerifolium*

The burgeoning forest
pulsating growth
welcome shade
glinting sunlight
flash of flowers
fire of autumn leaves
erupting of buds—

all these convey an excitement of life that goes beyond
a mere appraisal of the marvellous diversity of shapes,
patterns and colours,
stirring the emotions,
affirming the way of nature—
ever alive and changing
yet ever changeless in its rhythm—

an inexhaustible source of renewal,
ensuring a sense of balance
and uplifting the spirit.

FOREWORD BY PROFESSOR R. H. COMPTON
Former Director of National Botanic Gardens, Kirstenbosch, Cape Town

I have read the manuscript with admiration and am most impressed with the very beautiful photographs which will adorn it. It seems to me by far the best thing ever published on its subject—a subject of the greatest interest to garden lovers in South Africa. It is packed full of information, and always tells you exactly what you want to know from the grower's point of view. Obviously it has been written from the basis of direct knowledge and experience in growing the plants themselves, and this gives it a special value. It is amazing to find that so many shrubs and trees, coming from very diverse climates, can grow successfully in South Africa.

One of the surprises of recent years is the adaptability of so much of the Cape flora to high-veld conditions and I am glad to see that the author has giken prominence to the Leucospermums, Proteas *and many other of the distinctive shrubs and trees of the Cape coastal belt, some of which are among the best garden subjects in the world. I am specially gratified, too, that she mentions the part played by Kirstenbosch in making these plants available for gardens, and that she has advised membership of the Botanical Society of South Africa as a means both of supporting the work of Kirstenbosch and of obtaining seeds of indigenous plants unprocurable elsewhere.*

Shrubs and trees are an essential feature in every garden and occupy so much space as well as time in growing, that more thought than usual is necessary in choosing suitable subjects, picking the right position, preparing the ground, and so on. This is where this book will be so valuable and I think that everyone with a new garden to make or an old one to overhaul will be very well advised to possess a copy and consult it freely. I like it very much indeed, it is just what is wanted, and I am sure it will be a great success.

FOREWORD TO THE EIGHTH EDITION

Man's present concern about his environment has highlighted the vital role that vegetation and the individual plants of which it is composed play in our lives. Most of the African veld in all its fascinating variations and complexity is composed of two main elements, grass and trees. Grass, the staff of life, feeds us and our domestic animals and clothes the veld in a summer's cloak of green fading to the pale gold of winter. Trees are the structure, the bones, of our savanna, bush and forest. They too are woven tapestry of our lives as they give us shelter shade and food. Little wonder therefore that most people feel an affinity to trees and that imaginative gardeners through the ages have used them, together with grass and other plants, to create a beauty in gardens which has supplemented nature itself. Gardeners strive after beauty and it is for them that this book is written. In these pages the tools for the creation of more verdant and peaceful gardens in our cities and on our farms are supplied.

I have long been interested in plants, particularly grasses and trees and therefore it gives me special pleasure to comply with the request to write the foreword to this edition of Shrubs, Trees and Climbers.

Sima Eliovson's name has become synonymous with gardening and garden plants in South Africa. No other author has done as much as she to stimulate the interest of the man in the street in gardening and garden plants. In these ventures there has always been a close and cordial relationship between the Botanical Research Institute and herself. It began twenty-two years ago with the preparation of the first edition of Flowering Shrubs and Trees. Since then six subsequent editions have seen the light. Whereas each of these editions was to some extent revised and added to, the eighth edition is virtually a new book. It has been greatly expanded and all the photographs have been retaken. The arrangement of the information has, however, been maintained.

Like all the other books by Sima Eliovson this volume is aesthetically pleasing and at the same time eminently useful and practical, thus bearing witness to her deep personal knowledge of her subject.

Since the first edition of this work our knowledge of trees, shrubs and climbers suitable for growing under tropical and subtropical conditions has increased greatly. This book contains much that is new and should prove most useful, not only in Southern Africa but also in other parts of our hemisphere.

I believe that this book will become a standard handbook which will contribute much to the development of the gardens of the future. By the production of this book Sima Eliovson has yet again increased the debt that we owe her.

Dr. B. de Winter
Botanical Research Institute, Pretoria
1975

CONTENTS

MEASUREMENTS

Following international scientific publications, centimetres have been used throughout this book.

For the convenience of gardeners, the following conversion table will cover any measurements referred to in this text, and may be found useful.

3 mm	= approximately $\frac{1}{8}$ inch
1 cm	= approximately $\frac{3}{8}$ inch
5 cm	= approximately 2 inches
30 cm	= approximately 1 foot
1 metre	= approximately 1 yard

LIST OF ILLUSTRATIONS

ACKNOWLEDGEMENTS

It gives me pleasure to acknowledge the help I have received over the years since this book was first published.

There will always be the special remembrance of my late husband, Ezra, who took the photographs for the first edition and gave me the encouragement needed to write the book at the time. The practical help from botanists who helped me to establish the correct names of the plants, especially at the beginning when these were little known in this country, will always be remembered with appreciation. Not to be forgotten are the late Mrs. M. Moss and the late Dr. H.B. Gilliland, both at the University of the Witwatersrand.

Dr. R.A. Dyer, Dr. L.E.W. Codd and the staff of the Botanical Research Institute, Pretoria, have always afforded me the greatest assistance with indigenous plants of South Africa, while Mrs. L. du Toit was especially helpful with the taxonomy of the exotic plants in the first edition. The benefits of my long association with Professor H.B. Rycroft and the staff of the National Botanic Gardens, Kirstenbosch, have also been reflected in the information needed for this book.

On the horticultural side, there are people like Mr. Ernest Thorp and the staff of the Durban Botanical Gardens, as well as nurserymen and gardeners too numerous to mention, whose friendly co-operation in allowing me to take photographs of their plants helped to make this book a reality. My special thanks are due to Richard Pope, Snr. for giving me two beautiful photographs taken at Cypress Gardens, Florida, U.S.A., *Pyrostegia ignea* and *Rhododendron* "Duchess of Cypress".

Finally, I am deeply grateful to Professor R.H. Compton, former Director of the National Botanic Gardens, Kirstenbosch, for very kindly writing the foreword to the first edition, as well as to Dr. B. de Winter, Chief of the Botanical Research Institute, Pretoria, for consenting to write the foreword to this revised, enlarged edition.

INTRODUCTION

The 8th edition of this book is virtually a new one. This was my first gardening book, written 20 years ago, which has been revised with every edition and many new colour pictures added in the sixth. All these changes took place within the limits of the printed book and had to be fitted in carefully. When the last edition went out of print, it was decided to reset the text and remake all the pictures as for a new book. The pleasure of being able to make numerous additions was tempered by the shock of discovering that the original transparencies were no longer usable and that I would have to re-photograph everything from scratch. Although this task led me to one of the most active periods of my life, in which I took more than two and a half thousand photographs within a year, I found that it added a new dimension to my experience and that I revelled in recapturing the beauty of flowers and trees that I have admired for many years, reaffirming their attractions. During the pursuit, I have been rewarded by coming across many new beauties and photographing them for the first time, so that a disadvantage ultimately became an advantage. The photographs give me special pleasure as they recall the gardens of friends and the many places I visited in order to find good specimens.

The format of the book is new and the pictorial grouping should make it simpler for the reader to select plants, as well as study the text with easy reference to the pictures of the relevant plants in alphabetical order.

The Scope of this Book

Although written primarily for use in Southern Africa, this book is equally applicable to Australia, New Zealand and South America. It could be used in the temperate and warmer parts of the northern hemisphere, provided that the seasons are changed by six months, July being equivalent to December and so on.

There are three chief climatic zones in South Africa that have parallels in Australia and South America. The east and south coasts of South Africa have a mild, sub-tropical climate and plants thriving here will do equally well at the coast near Sydney, Australia, or in Brazil, South America. The variations in temperature are not important as the main factors of warmth and humidity, especially in summer, govern these areas.

The winter-rainfall area of the S.W. Cape has its parallels in the area around Perth, S.W. Australia, Chile, parts of Southern California and the western Mediterranean. Plants that grow well in the S.W. Cape also thrive in New Zealand.

The dry interior of South Africa, with a dormant period in winter often accompanied by frost, has its rain mainly in summer. The cold highveld areas which experience frost are kept distinct from lower altitudes, which are generally hotter in summer and milder in winter, so that many sub-tropical plants thrive in the lowveld at altitudes of about 1000 metres. Comparisons may be made to higher altitudes in Brazil, around Brazilia and Belo Horizonte, as well as in the Argentine, where the climate is more temperate, and the interior of Australia.

Suffice it to say that gardeners are never deterred by climatic difficulties and will try growing everything, often with surprisingly good results. With a little shelter in winter one can grow many sub-tropical plants on the highveld. Altitude is usually the governing factor in the temperate zones of the world, where one can grow an amazing variety of subjects from both hemispheres. The African Flame Tree (*Spathodea*) from tropical Africa does as well in Cuernavaca, Mexico, as it does in the warmer parts of South Africa, while the shrubs from Japan do well in all the cool mountain areas where there is high rainfall. One can, therefore, seldom make hard and fast rules, indicating only the natural needs of plants so that gardeners can give them these requirements and thus adapt them to the conditions in one's own garden.

The Names

The bugbear of every horticultural writer is to keep up with research on the changing botanical names, particularly with regard to plants from countries other than one's own. It would be easy if botanists were to agree or if various scientific dictionaries would not have such confusing descriptions that botanists themselves cannot always identify unknown species with certainty. The botanists of Great Britain sometimes have different opinions from those of America or Japan, so that the writer must make a decision as to which botanist to follow before going into print. Plant geography should be the guide and in deciding which names are valid it is best to follow the botanists who are nearest to the country of origin of the plants in question. In any case, it is not actually incorrect to refer to a plant by the name used formerly, remembering always that this is the more recent name. The valid name to be retained is the older name, while the "new" name which must be "sunk" may be remembered by referring to it in parenthesis. One does this when names are so well-known that it adds to the confusion to leave out all reference to them.

Botanical names are simply a guide to obtaining the species wanted and one should not make a fetish of keeping up with the "latest" names if this is used as a discouragement to those who have no access to botanical institutes, which are labouring themselves to keep up-to-date. The knowledge of the latest name changes should not be used to denigrate less-informed gardeners, but studied in order to acknowledge and accelerate the work of botanical research, since the use of common names is generally unsatisfactory because they are unstable and vague. The study of botanical names should not deter one from the main objective, which is to grow and learn to discover plants for their own worth.

The layman often complains about the changing names, but this can be explained by the accidents of human discovery. When two explorers found the same plant independently, each giving it a different name, it was important to eliminate confusion by deciding which name to retain. This is the work of the taxonomist who investigates which person named the plant first and decides which name is valid. Some of the tales behind unravelling the names make fascinating reading. The famous Jacaranda tree that throws its blue veil over Pretoria and Johannesburg in October, for instance, was originally described by two botanists in different publications that appeared on the same day in 1822, by extraordinary coincidence. Both descriptions were made from flowers growing in the private botanic garden of the Compte and Comtesse de Vandes, at Bayswater. The name *J. mimosifolia*, given by D. Don, was given preference over that of *J. ovalifolia*, given by Robert Brown, as he found them to be one and the same species in the following year. The tree came originally from north-west Argentina, bringing yet another argument into focus regarding a species from Peru, *J. acutifolia*. This had been the name given to *J. mimosifolia* in the *Flora Brasiliensis* and the Peruvian taxonomist, Dr. J. Feyrerra, still believes that this is the correct name for the cultivated tree, but some botanists believe that it is a different species, supporting this belief with sound reasons. If botanists do not agree, the layman indeed has a problem.

Insistence on the correct botanical name does not mean that one should avoid using common names, especially if these are unique. I have often invented common names where none existed in order to popularise certain plants and also because their botanical names may be too difficult to remember. I have been happy that names I published years ago are now being used familiarly for plants like the Marmalade Bush, Pompon Tree, Oxford and Cambridge Bush, Gold-Tips, Knobkerrie Bush, Rose Cockade, Fire-Dart Bush, Peanut-Butter Cassia, Karoo Gold and others. Red Meg seems an easy common name, too, for *Megaskepasma erythroclamys*.

The Choice

It has been gratifying to note the ever-increasing number of species of flowering tree and shrubs that have been introduced to horticulture in this country from all over the world since this book was first written. Yet it has required some discipline to limit the choice of trees and shrubs to the most attractive or useful that may be recommended to the gardener.

In choosing plants for this volume, the problem was to select woody shrubs, trees and climbers without cluttering the book with large permanent plants that do not fall into this category. Distinctive plants like Bamboos, Grasses, Aloes, Pelargoniums and New Zealand Flax, (*Phormium*) may grow to the size of shrubs and trees, but are unique plants that form groups of their own, many in the nature of perennials. There are so many outstanding species of woody plants that there is no need to include such special plants in a book dealing with the vast subject in hand. Nevertheless, a few sub-shrubs or shrubby perennials have been included, mainly because of the wish to include several attractive indigenous plants that may be grown or treated as shrubs.

It is almost impossible to separate some shrubs from trees or rambling shrubs from climbers. Size does not indicate the categories in which they should be placed, as they grow to different sizes in differing climates and it is a matter of personal decision to think of a species as either a large shrub or as a small tree. One is inclined to imagine that a shrub is a bushy rounded plant and that a tree has a main trunk, but these are overlapping distinctions. Similarly, a rambling shrub can become a climber if it strikes a support on which to mount. It is, therefore, impracticable to separate trees, shrubs and climbers into different sections, as these are flexible. One must assess each plant individually if one is to provide an honest guide for the gardener.

The primary motive behind writing this book is to stimulate interest in the fantastic range of marvellous flowering trees, shrubs and climbers that may be incorporated into our gardens. Local nurseries are excellent in the wide selection they offer and continue to introduce as time goes on, needing new material in order to inspire their clients. Some trees and shrubs obviously have more horticultural merit than others and one is hard put to restrain oneself from becoming purely a collector of new introductions instead of choosing what is most aesthetically pleasing to oneself, or even curious or simply useful for a special purpose.

The amazing number of species from all over the world that will grow in the many climates of southern Africa have only to be tried to prove themselves. The plants described in this book are all available, but there is no limit to those which may prove successful in the future. The deciduous trees from the cold climates of the northern hemisphere grow easily in the highveld interior with its cold winters, yet summers are warm and sunny enough to enable tropical shrubs to flourish side by side with them, provided that they can be brought through the few frosts of winter by skilful placing and protection. Deciduous trees will not grow easily in the sub-tropical coastal districts but succeed in the cooler south-western coastal area, which is, by nature, a climate for evergreens. As the fun of gardening is to try plants that might not grow, there is a challenge for all.

A few famous trees of the world have been included even though they are difficult to grow, as it would indeed be an achivement and a conversation piece to have them in the country and see them for oneself without travelling half-way around the world in order to do so. Their inclusion will surely prompt some enterprising gardener to succeed with them sooner or later. If one simply cannot have what has been dubbed the most beautiful tree in the world—*Amherstia nobilis*—and marvel at the texture of its graceful candelabra of bloom, then one might as well enjoy a glimpse of it through a photograph. The curious and beautiful flower of the Cannon-ball tree—*Couropita*—falls into the same category. Looking at pictures of beautiful trees is like reading mouth-watering recipes or studying seed-catalogues—they give the plant-lover a vicarious thrill.

The advice to people who are planting a garden, nevertheless, is always to choose plants that will grow easily, no matter how commonly seen. Once having created a lovely setting with trees and shrubs that act as a background and shelter, one can then dabble and try the plants that challenge curiosity and horticultural skill.

The joys of getting to know trees, shrubs and climbers will overflow the limits of one's own garden, extending to the admiration of one's own neighbourhood when beautiful trees are in bloom and enlarging one's horizons while discovering them on one's travels at home or abroad, for flowering trees and shrubs are valued features in every country of the world. The love for these plants, that will increase with familiarity, must surely prompt us to appreciate the beauty of the world's natural forests or woodland and try to preserve them for their aesthetic qualities as well as for their importance towards life on earth. To visit even the fringes of primeval forests and see flowering trees growing wild in all their grandeur is to experience·the thrill of the explorer. Every traveller's journeys are enhanced by the trees of the area. The bare rocks of the Corcovado would be nothing without the approach through the forest below it, nor could a Caribbean cruise be enjoyed without the rich greenery and colourful trees to be seen. Special trips to New England or Japan to see the brilliant blaze of falling forest leaves are considered worthwhile by the most blasé of travellers, while Cherry Blossom time in Japan is world renowned. Table Mountain without its skirt of silvery trees rippling in the breeze would be deprived of glory. Safaris to the game reserves of Africa would be souless without the background of unique trees that make up its parklands and form the canopy that protects both animal and bird life.

It is interesting to note where the majority of beautiful shrubs and trees in gardens grow in their wild state. The greatest treasure-house is acknowledged to be in south-east Asia, chiefly in China and Japan, followed closely by the riches of Central America, especially in Brazil and Peru. Lucky is the traveller who can fly over these forests or stand beneath them in awe, for the majority must be content with being armchair travellers. The gardener can bring the world into his garden by growing trees and shrubs from other lands. These are suitably, as well as scientifically, described as "exotic". When contemplating their flowers, form or foliage brought to successful maturity, one can be transported into other worlds and achieve the thrill that is the stuff of dreams. In such involvement can be found the true importance of a garden, which releases tension in the reflective enjoyment of nature, consequently inducing tranquillity.

Cultivating exotic plants does not mean that one should not also grow the beautiful plants of one's own country. A garden should not be limited by geographical boundaries or chauvinism, but should be eclectic, mingling the plants of the world in harmony, interweaving their attractions aesthetically and reflecting the personality of the owner in their selection and arrangement.

We need trees. To grow them in our gardens is but a step in the direction of appreciating them more and more. Few people think of creating a forest in their own gardens, although this could be an answer to trouble-free gardening. Instead of planting trees in borders, one could cover a large area with a grove of trees, as in a forest. The ground could be carpeted with shade-loving shrubs and perennials or ground-covers, as on the floor of a forest, with pathways between so that one could take a walk in one's own piece of woodland. A garden does not have to be large in order to plant a forest. One has only to study the gardens of Japan in order to see how to create the illusion of forest within a small area. A grove of small trees that resembles the edge of a forest, with a path leading into it and disappearing behind a bush, so that one must travel further into it in one's own imagination, is an easy way to make the garden appear larger than it is and create the atmosphere of woodland.

Many of these passing thoughts repeat what has already been written in the body of this book, but they bear repetition if they can stimulate interest in flowering trees, shrubs and climbers beyond mere cultivation. In these days of the awareness of the importance of ecology, it behoves us to cherish and protect the trees in the woods and forests of the world, while appreciating their beauty. Our concern for them will reward us with a visual pleasure-ride through life, ever-increasing in fascination, bringing us friends everywhere, as this great interest has done for me.

1

2

3

4   ↓ 5

PLATE 1

1 Glossy Abelia,
   Abelia grandiflora,
   will grow almost
   anywhere. It
   makes a pretty
   hedge.

2 *Abutilon mega-*
   potamicum is a
   trailing plant that
   is seen above as a
   grafted standard.

3 Yellow *Abutilon,*
   known as Chinese
   Lanterns, is a
   bushy evergreen.
   There are many
   other hybrids with
   rose, red or orange
   flowers.

4 This variegated
   Abutilon is valued
   for its decorative
   foliage.

5 Copperleaf,
   Acalypha hybrids,
   come in a variety
   of colours that
   make impressive
   landscape shrubs
   for the sub-tropics.
   They tolerate
   coastal wind and
   humidity.

The bright bobbles of numerous Acacias or Wattles enliven winter and spring.
1   Pearl Acacia, *A. podalyriaefolia,* has distinctive rounded grey leaves and blooms in mid-winter.
2   Knife-leaf Wattle, *Acacia cultriformis*, has massed flowers in spring.

3   Sydney Golden Wattle, *Acacia longifolia*, has finger-like flower spikes in spring. ↑
4   Prickly Acanthus, *Acanthus pubescens*, has dense flower-spikes from mid-winter to spring, needing room to spread.

Japanese Maples, *Acer palmatum*, have dainty leaves with fiery autumn colours, at their best in cool mountain conditions (right). Numerous garden varieties include the *dissectum* group, with 7–11 deeply cut lobes. (below).

2

3

↓4

PLATE 3

1 The spreading flat-topped Silk-Tree, *Albizia julibrissin*, blooms in early summer.

2 A dwarf succulent shrub, *Adenium obesum*, has striking flowers. The variety *multiflorum* blooms profusely on bare stems in late winter.

3 *Alberta magna* is an evergreen shrub with scarlet tubular flowers in spring, followed by scarlet bracts that persist throughout summer.

4 Giant Allamanda, *Allamanda cathartica* var. *hendersonii*, is a sub-tropical evergreen climber with gorgeous trumpets tumbling in a golden cascade down a slope or over a wall.

↓4

PLATE 4

A challenge to the tropical gardener, *Amherstia nobilis* bears metre-long chandeliers of graceful flowers, each like a delicate orchid, in early summer. This rounded evergreen tree was said to be the most beautiful in the world.

The Coral-Vine, *Antigonon leptopus* (left) flowers gaily in late summer, draping gracefully over fences and walls.

Even more floriferous, *Antigonon guatamalense* is rarer and requires sub-tropical warmth (below, left).

The Strawberry Tree, *Arbutus unedo*, has tiny white urn-like flowers, with decorative fruits in autumn, but grows slowly.

PLATE 5

1 Giant Dutchman's Pipe, *Aristolochia gigantea,* is a large evergreen climber with immense flowers.

2 The Banksias of Australia form an interesting group of evergreen trees and shrubs. *Banksia baxteri* is a shrub with broad triangular leaves and a globe of yellow flowers.

3 *Banksia speciosa* forms a striking accent with its long narrow serrated leaves and silvery cone of flowers.

4 *Banksia ericifolia* has long flower-spikes amongst needle-like leaves on a tall bush.

5 Giant Trumpet Climber, *Beaumontia grandiflora*, is a spreading evergreen climber that needs a strong support. It blooms in early spring, at its best in hot frost-free areas.

1

2

3

4

↓5

PLATE 6   ↑   3   The magnificent Hong Kong Orchid Tree, *Bauhinia blakeana*, blooms during winter in mild areas and at intervals in spring, summer and autumn.

1/2/4   The Orchid Tree, *Bauhinia variegata*, is a delightful street tree in warm areas, with pretty pink or white flowers (above and top row).

5   The White Camelsfoot, *Bauhinia corniculata*, grows very easily. ↓

6   Pride-of-de Kaap, *Bauhinia galpinii*, is a rampant, spreading bush that is covered with bloom in late summer. ↓

PLATE 7   Shrimp Flower, *Beloperone guttata*, is in bloom throughout the year in warm situations. The rust colour is typical, but variations graduate to lime yellow (right).

Wintergreen Barberry, *Berberis julianae*, is a hardy evergreen shrub with bright flowers and autumn leaves.

Madame Galen is a hybrid of *Campsis radicans*. Being deciduous, it is best grown against a wall.

The Lipstick Tree, *Bixa orellana*, is attractive in flower and fruit (below). The variety at right has more brilliant burrs than the species.

PLATE 8

Bougainvillea is the most adaptable of climbers, obtainable in many brilliant or pale hues, "double" or single forms. The plants bloom when small and colours may be selected at the nursery.

It will drape gracefully over walls and posts or cover ground with billowing colour. It may be trained to grow in pots, an especially useful attribute when it is difficult to find warm sunny walls in cool winter areas.

1

2

↓3

PLATE 9

1 *Bouvardia* hybrids are small, evergreen shrubs that fit into sheltered corners in tiny gardens, flowering in sun or partial shade.

2 The Flame Tree, *Brachychiton acerifolium*, is wreathed with loose clusters of brilliant tiny bells in early summer.

3 Queensland Lacebark, *Brachychiton discolor*, has striking flowers like pink velvet on leafless branches. The leaves drop shortly before the tree blooms in early summer.

Breynia nivosa, Snow-Bush, comes from the South Sea Islands and needs a semi-tropical climate or greenhouse conditions. It enjoys shade.

Burchellia bubalina, known as Wild Pomegranate, is splendid in shade and flowers brightly in summer.

4

↓5

1

↓2

↓3

PLATE 10

Brunfelsias are lovely scented shrubs.

1 Large-flowered *Brunfelsia calycina*
   var. *macrantha*

2 Yesterday, Today and Tomorrow,
   Brunfelsia calycina var. *eximia*

3 Lady-of-the-Night, *Brunfelsia
   americana.*

4 Winter-flowering Sage Wood,
   Buddleia salvifolia, is strongly
   scented.

5 Butterfly-Bush, *Buddleia davidii,*
   has scented flowers of many hues
   in spring.

6 Flame-of-the-Forest, *Butea superba*
   is an enormous climber for large,
   sub-tropical gardens, flowering in
   early summer.

↓4

↓5

6↓

1

↓ 3

2

4 ↑

↓ 5

↓ 6

PLATE 11

1 Bird of Paradise, *Caesalpinia gilliesii*, a hardy shrub, is bright when little else blooms.

2 Peacock Flower, *Caesalpinia pulcherrima*, needs sub-tropical warmth.

3 *Caesalpinia peltophoroides*, Sibipiruna, is a tall tree.

4 *Calliandra selloi*, Shuttlecock Flower, blooms at intervals.

5 *Calliandra surinamensis* has forked leaflets in pairs.

6 Red Powderpuff, *Calliandra haematocephala*, is spectacular in warm districts.

1

2

↓3

4

↓5

↓6

PLATE 12

1 Weeping Bottlebrush, *Callistemon viminalis,* is a graceful small tree.

2 Tree Bottlebrush, *Callistemon speciosus,* is hardy and decorative.

3 Net-bush, *Calothamnus quadrifidus,* is a drought-resistant evergreen shrub.

4 Japanese Beauty-Berry, *Callicarpa japonica,* prefers cool, moist gardens and has attractive bead-like berries in late autumn.

5 Cape Chestnut, *Calodendrum capense,* is a tender evergreen tree with large flower clusters in summer.

6 Carolina Allspice, *Calycanthus floridus,* has apple-scented flowers. A hardy, deciduous shrub, it needs moist, rich soil.

1

↓2

3 ↑

↓4

PLATE 13

↓5

↓6

1/2 Evergreen *Camellia japonica* never fails to excite admiration when it blooms in winter or spring. There are numerous hybrids and forms.

3 Graceful *Cantua buxifolia*, Flower-of-the Incas, is a semi-evergreen shrub that is arresting in bloom. This is the bi-coloured form.

4 *Ceanothus dentatus* provides a welcome note of blue in early summer.

5 Autumn is enriched by Wonder-of-Peru, *Centradenia grandiflora*, a shrub with flowers of several hues.

6 A rounded evergreen tree, the Moreton-Bay Chestnut, *Castanospermum australe*, does best in warm situations.

1

2

3

4

5

↓ 6

PLATE 14

Cassias or Shower Trees are numerous and eye-catching.
1 Candlestick Senna, *Cassia alata*, is a tender shrub.
2 Silver Cassia, *Cassia artemesioides*, is a low shrub.
3 Pudding Pipe Tree, *Cassia fistula*, is gorgeous in sub-tropics.
4 *Cassia speciosa* is golden in autumn.
5 Peanut Better Cassia, *C. didymobotrya*, has brown buds.
6 *Cassia multijuga* has narrow leaflets.
7 Pink Cassia, *C. nodosa*, from N. Brazil, is similar to *C. javanica* from Java.

↓ 7

1

2

PLATE 15

1 *Cecropia palmata*, Snakewood Tree, has magnificent silvery foliage.

2 *Ceratopetalum gummiferum*, Australian Christmas Bush, makes a tall evergreen tree.

3 *Ceratostigma wilmottianum* grows easily and seeds freely.

4 *Cercis siliquastrum*, the Judas Tree, blooms in springtime.

5/6 Red Cestrum, *C. fasciculatum*, is a graceful, adaptable shrub.

7 *Cestrum diurnum* is fragrant.

8 *Cestrum aurantiacum* will flower in the shade.

3

5   ↓ 6   ↓ 7

4   ↓ 8

↓ 4

PLATE 16

1 *Chamaelaucium uncinatum,* Geraldton Wax Flower, is a dainty evergreen shrub that forms a cloud of bloom in early spring.

2 Hardy Japanese Flowering Quince, *Chaenomeles lagenaria,* flowers on bare stems in late winter, providing beautiful flowers for arrangements. There are several colour varieties and forms.

3 Golden Cypress, *Chamaecyparis lawsoniana* var. *lutea,* needs full sunshine in order to preserve its golden tips.

4 *Chamaecyparis pisifera* var. *filifera aurea* is a dwarf False-Cypress with golden branchlets.

5 The Fringe-Tree, *Chionanthus retusa,* is a hardy shrub, needing rich, moist soil.

6 Flame Pea, *Chorizema cordatum,* is a small evergreen suitable for the rockery or pot-culture.

7 *Cienfuegosia sturtii,* Sturt's Desert Rose, is a drought-resistant, long-flowering, evergreen shrub from Australia. ↓

1

2

3

↓ 5   6 ↓

PLATE 17

1/2 Tall *Chorisia speciosa*, Floss-Silk Tree, is glorious in full bloom in autumn, especially if the leaves have dropped. ↑

3 *Clematis jackmannii* is a hybrid climber for the connoisseur. ↓

4 Yellow Daisy-Bush, *Chrysanthemum frutescens*, is a sub-shrub that blooms from mid-winter to spring. ↓

↓ 5   ↓ 6

5 *Cistus villosus* Rock-Rose, is a drought-resistant evergreen Mediterranean shrub.

6 *Cistus purpureus* is a hybrid of the White Rock-Rose, which is also known as "Brilliancy". It forms an evergreen, spring-flowering shrub.

PLATE 18

1 *Clerodendron bungei,* Lilac Glory Bower, is a slender, easily-grown shrub.

2 *Clerodendron splendens,* Climbing Scarlet Clerodendron, is a magnificent evergreen climber for warm places.

3 *Clerodendron thompsoniae* var. *balfourii* is a tender climber for shady places.

4 *Clerodendron ugandense,* Oxford and Cambridge Bush, is a shrub which needs a sheltered spot.

5 The rich blue, double form of the slender Butterfly Pea Vine, *Clitoria ternata*, which is suitable for frost-free areas.

6 Evergreen *Clytostoma callistegioides,* commonly called Mauve Bignonia or Argentine Trumpet Vine, is fairly hardy in areas with cold winters.

PLATE 19

Gorgeous white Camellia-like flowers on a rounded evergreen tree attract attention to *Clusia grandiflora* and the rose-coloured *Clusia hilariana.* The seed-pod is like a sunburst and no less striking. The Brazilian name, Onion-of-the-Forest, refers to the buds.

1

Brilliant foliage of many forms characterise the hybrids of sub-tropical *Codiaeum variegatum,* commonly called Crotons.

↓ 2

↓ 3

The Confetti Bush, *Coleonema pulchrum,* flowers all through winter and spring.

A soft-wooded shrub for shady places, *Colquhounia mollis* comes from the Himalayas.

Spectacular flower-spikes in early summer make the rambling *Combretum jacquinii,* from Brazil, desirable.

1

2

PLATE 20

1 *Coprosma baurii* var. *picturata,* the Looking-Glass Plant, has polished leaves and will thrive at the sea as well as inland.

2 Velvet Congea, *Congea tomentosa,* forms a huge spreading climber in sub-tropical areas.

3 *Cordia sebestena*, Geiger Tree, a tender evergreen shrub, flowers almost continuously.

4 *Cornus florida,* Dog-Wood, a small hardy tree, is wreathed in ethereal blossoms in spring.

5 *Couroupita guianensis,* the Cannon-Ball Tree, is a challenge to the grower in a sub-tropical area.

↓ 5

3   ↓ 4

PLATE 21

Bright berries in autumn attract birds and last well in vases, especially if stripped of their leaves.

Cotoneaster serotinus, (above) is a tall graceful evergreen with large clusters of berries, excellent for picking.
Cotoneaster horizontalis (centre) has "fish-bone" branches that will lie flat against a wall.
Crotolaria agatiflora, Bird Flower, (below) is useful for wilder corners, needing scant attention.

Hardy deciduous *Crataegus phaenopyrum*, Washington Thorn (above) has shining berries and comes true from seed.

Crataegus lavallei, Lavalle Hawthorn, (centre) and *Crataegus stipulacea*, Mexican Hawthorn (below) are both hardy and decorative small trees.

PLATE 22

1 Colville's Glory, *Colvillea racemosa*, is a spectacular sub-tropical tree that blooms in autumn. Its magnificent pendant flower-sprays are mainly at the top.

2 *Colvillea* buds open into puffs of stamens.

3 Cigarette Flower, *Cuphea platycentra*, is a small sub-shrub, useful for autumn colour.

4 The Tree Tomato, *Cyphomandra betacea*, has edible, decorative fruits in autumn.

5 The Pompon Tree, *Dais cotinifolia*, massed with bloom in early summer, is a dainty tree for any garden and makes a good street tree.

1

↓2   ↓4

↓5

↓3

PLATE 23

The Flamboyant, *Delonix regia*, native to Madagascar, is one of the world's most spectacular trees. It is suitable for frost-free areas. There are several colour variations, including yellow tipped with flame (above).

Moonflowers are graceful shrubs with large fragrant flowers that make striking accents. *Datura candida plena* (left) is popular. *Datura mollis*, from Equador, is more tender (above).

PLATE 24

1   *Dichorisandra thyrsiflora*, known as Blue-Flowered Bamboo, is a tender sub-shrub for shady places and may be grown in a greenhouse.

2/3   Hardy Japanese Persimmon, *Diospyros kaki*, has large, decorative fruits together with brilliant autumn foliage. Modern hybrids are eaten when crisp, and, unlike the species, do not need to become soft before losing their astringency.

4   *Distictis riversii* is a large evergreen climber that blooms freely in summer.

5   Golden Cats Claw Creeper, *Doxantha unguis-cati*, will curtain a large area, clinging by means of tiny claw-like hooks.

1 ↓4 2 ↓3

↓5

PLATE 25

Dombeya burgessiae, Wedding Flower, has white or pink flowers which dry to beige, on a large rounded shrub.

Pink Dombeya has been developed from *Dombeya burgessiae* and improved hybrids are constantly being selected for form and colour.

Dombeya macrantha, introduced from Madagascar, is a large, furry shrub.

Echium fastuosum, Pride-of-Madeira, flowers in spring.

Embothrium wickhami, the Fire Tree from Queensland, is a half-hardy evergreen that blooms in spring.

PLATE 26 Ericas are among the showiest and long-flowering of evergreen shrubs. Of the 600 species, three of the best for gardens are Red Signal Heath, *Erica mammosa* (top left), Knysna Heath, *Erica densifolia* (above) and the bi-coloured form of Bridal Heath, *Erica bauera* (below)

Escallonia macrantha (left) is a dense evergreen shrub, useful for screening. Daintier hybrids include the graceful *Escallonia langleyensis* (below) and *Escallonia* Apple Blossom (bottom left

1

PLATE 27

Some of the world's most exciting trees occur among the *Erythrina* group, thrilling the traveller and gardener alike.

1 The Tambookie Thorn, *Erythrina acanthocarpa*, is a small hardy shrub suitable for most gardens, with spectacular flowers in spring.

2 The Kaffirboom, *Erythrina lysistemon*, is a rugged, drought-resistant tree, with crested compact flower-heads on bare stems.

3 The Coast Kaffirboom, *Erythrina caffra*, is a tender tree from the eastern coast of S. Africa. The flowers are more spreading than in *E. lysistemon*. There are many colour variations.

4 The Coral Tree, *Erythrina crista-gallii*, flowers in early summer together with the leaves.

5 Flattened flower-heads in autumn and spring distinguish *Erythrina coralloides* from Mexico.

6 Hume's Kaffirboom, *Erythrina humeana*, is a deciduous shrub which blooms in mid-summer. ↓

2

3

4

↓5

1   2   ↓ 5   3   4   ↓ 6

PLATE 28   1 Brush-Cherry, *Eugenia myrtifolia*, is an evergreen tree with edible, attractive fruits.
              2 *Eucalyptus torquata*, Coral Gum, is one of the best for gardens, growing to about 6 metres.
              3 *Eucalyptus preissiana*, Bell Fruit Mallee, is a large shrub that blooms in spring and early summer.
              4 *Eucalyptus kruseana*, Kruse Mallee, is a shrub with attractive foliage.
              5 Red-flowering Gum, *Eucalyptus ficifolia*, is a magnificent tree, with red, rose, salmon or white flowers.
              6 Florist's Gum, *Eucalyptus cinerea*, is valued for its silvery foliage and quick slender growth.
       7/8 Christ-thorn, *Euphorbia milii* var. *splendens*, is a low-growing spiny shrub from Madagascar,
                flowering most profusely in early spring. A long-leaved form is seen below, right.

↓ 7   ↓ 8

1

2

↓ 4

PLATE 29
1 Poinsettias, *Euphorbia pulcherrima*, are magnificent shrubs for warm areas.
2 A "double" form.
3 Hybrid "Ecke's Flaming Sphere", has pendent, spherical heads.
4 Dwarf hybrid, "Paul Ecke", is grown in pots and makes a compact bush in the garden.
5 White Lace Euphorbia, *Euphorbia leucocephala*, is a cloud of white in autumn.
6 Bronze Euphorbia, *Euphorbia cotinifolia*, has decorative foliage and seeds itself freely. ↓

3

↓ 5

PLATE 30

1/2 Spindle-Trees, *Euonymus japonicus*, are useful evergreen shrubs in cold gardens. The variegated form (left) is grown for its foliage, but needs bright light so as to keep its yellow markings. The plain green species will tolerate shade and bears fascinating split berries in winter.

1

3

4

5 ↓6

3 Giant Ageratum, *Eupatorium sordidum*, likes partial shade and needs mild winter conditions.

5 Shade-loving Fuchsias are among the most graceful of small shrubs and their drooping habit makes them most effective in garden design. They will grow in pots and ma be trained to form standards.

4 *Fuchsia fulgens* is a vivid, floriferous species.

6 There are innumerable *Fuchsia* hybrids, both single and double, and collecting these can be fascinating. They grow easily from cuttings.

PLATE 31

1 Graceful, weeping branches of Chile-Heath, *Fabiana imbricata*, are covered with small white flowers in early summer.

2 Pineapple-Guava, *Feijoa sellowiana*, has soft pink flowers in early summer, followed by edible fruits.

1

2

Golden-Bells, *Forsythia intermedia*, flower during winter and spring and may be grown in shade.

Gardenia thunbergia, Wild Gardenia, has long-tubed fragrant flowers.

Galphimia glauca, a small evergreen shrub, flowers freely in mild districts.

Gardenia jasminoides var. *plena*, Double-White Gardenia, is a favourite neat evergreen laden with perfumed flowers in summer.

PLATE 32

1 *Gingko biloba*, Maidenhair Tree, has glorious autumn foliage.
2 *Grevillea biternata* is a billowing mass of bloom.
3 *Grevillea banksii* is a striking landscape shrub.
4 *Grevillea juniperina* has dainty blooms and foliage.
5 *Greyia sutherlandii*, Mountain Bottlebrush, has fascinating flowers that last well in the vase.
6 *Grevillea barkleyana*, a spreading evergreen bush, has ''toothbrush'' flowers.

1

2

1–6 Chinese Hıbiscus, *Hibiscus rosa-sinensis,* is a glamorous shrub, tolerant of drought as well as humidity. The numerous hybrids vary in colour and form. Pink Butterfly is popular as a standard (2 and 5).

3

4

↓7

5

↓9

6

↓8

PLATE 33

7 *Hibiscus mutabilis* flowers change colour each day.

8 This Hawaiian hybrid of *Hibiscus schizopetalus* is hardier than the species.

9 Syrian Hibiscus, *H. syriacus,* is deciduous and withstands cold. There are several forms and colours.

PLATE 34

1 Lilac-Vine, *Hardenbergia comptoniana*, needs little attention, tolerating drought and heat.

2 *Hebe speciosa*, a small evergreen shrub that flowers for long periods, has many forms and colours.

3 The rich purple form of Heliotrope, *Heliotropium peruvianum,* may be grown in a tub on a shady verandah.

4 Gold Flower *Hypericum sinense*, is a cheerful shrub that is easy to grow.

5 Red Chinese-Hat Plant, *Holmskioldia sanguinea*, is a half-hardy evergreen shrub which is covered with flowers in late autumn. There are several other colours.

← A delightful slender evergreen tree, *Hymenosporum flavum* is a graceful accent in almost any sized garden.

PLATE 35

Hydrangeas are favourite garden shrubs that are adaptable to cold or warm areas. They require plenty of moisture during summer and need shade in hot dry climates.

1 *Hydrangea macrophylla* will grow on a sunny bank in a humid atmosphere.

2 Pink *Hydrangea macrophylla* likes slightly acid to neutral soil.

3 Blue Hydrangeas retain their colour only when soil is very acid.

4 *Hydrangea quercifolia* has serrated leaves that bronze before falling.

5 Peegee Hydrangea, *H. paniculata grandiflora*, is tall and hardy.

1

2

↓ 3

4

↓ 5

PLATE 36

1 *Iboza riparia*, Misty Plume Bush, will grow in partial shade.

2 *Ilex verticillata*, Winterberry, likes cold winters and should be planted in groups for good berrying.

3 The berries of English Holly, *Ilex aquifolium*, redden in winter.

4 Tree Convolvulus, *Ipomoea arborescens*, blooms in autumn.

5 An improved form of the tropical evergreen shrub, *Ixora coccinea*.

6 *Ixora coccinea* and yellow *Ixora lutea*.

7 *Ixora macrothyrsa*, from Sumatra, has larger leaves and flowers.

8 *Jacobinia carnea*, Pink Jacobinia, will grow in pots and semi-shade.

9 *Jacobinia umbrossa* is an excellent shrub for shade in sub-tropical areas.

PLATE 37 Few trees can rival the splendour of a Jacaranda in full bloom, especially in dry-winter areas where the leaves drop completely before flowering. A carpet of fallen flowers adds to the spectacle.

One of several white-flowered Jasmines, *J. multipartitum* is a shrub native to S. Africa.

Chinese Jasmine, *Jasminum polyanthum*, is a popular climber.

Primrose Jasmine, *J. primulinum* forms a billowing shrub.

1

2

3

4

↓ 5

6

↓ 7

PLATE 38

1 *Jatropha hast*
Peregrina, is a
tender evergreen
shrub.

2 Coral-Plant,
Jatropha multifi
forms a filigree
of ornamental
foliage in a
sub-tropical gar

3 The sculpture
leaves of *Jatrop*
podagrica, Guat
mala Rhubarb,
make this shrub
attractive accent
for pot or rockery

4 *Kunzea baxte*
is an evergreen,
drought-resistar
shrub.

5 *Kolkwitzia*
amabilis is a har
deciduous sprin
flowering shrub.

6 Junipers are
valued as hardy
evergreens. Here
a purple-foliage
variety of *Juni-*
perus horizontal
borders *Juniper*
chinensis aurea.

7 Blue Tube
Flowers,
Jochroma
tubulosum,
is an easy-
to-grow shrub.

PLATE 39

1 Pride of India, *Lagerstroemia indica*, is a favourite shrub for cold and warm climates.
2 Queen Crepe-Myrtle, *Lagerstroemia speciosa*, needs the sub-tropics.
3 *Lagunaria pattersonii*, Pyramid Tree, tolerates sea air.
4 *Kerria japonica florepleno*, Globe Flower, is hardy.
5 *Lantana montevidensis* is excellent for overhanging low walls and window-boxes.
6 Yellow *Lantana* Drap D'Or is a hybrid that grows from cuttings.

3

1

↓ 2

↓ 5

4

↓ 6

PLATE 40

1 *Leonotis leonurus*, Lion's Ear, a sub-
shrub that blooms brightly in autumn,
should be cut down after flowering.

2 Mountain-Devil, *Lambertia formosa*, is an
Australian shrub belonging to the Protea
family.

3 *Leea coccinea* will grow in dense shade
and makes a good foliage plant in a tub.

4/5 The Tea-Tree, *Leptospermum nicholsii* var.
scoparium, a winter-flowering shrub with
many beautiful varieties, flowers while small.

1

2

3

PLATE 41

1 The flaming autumn colours of the American Sweetgum, *Liquidambar styraciflua*, make this a desirable tree for cool areas.

2 Gold-Tips, *Leucadendron salignum*, formerly known as *L. adscendens*, has erubescent leaves at the top in winter, spring and early summer.

3 Silver Tree, *Leucadendron argenteum*, is valued for its silvery foliage, even when young.

4 Nodding Pincushion, *Leucospermum cordifolium*, is one of the finest of landscape shrubs, with hundreds of long-lasting flowers for picking.

5 Rocket Pincushion, *Leucospermum reflexum*, forms an immense, noble bush.

6 *Leucospermum tottum*, Firewheel Pincushion, blooms in mid-summer.

4

5

↓ 6

1

2

PLATE 42

1 The strongly fragrant flowers of the lovely Pink Swa, *Luculia gratissima*, appear in late autumn and last well when picked.

2 Giant Honeysuckle, *Lonicera hildebrandiana*, is spectacular in both garden and vase.

3 Variegated Japanese Honeysuckle, *Lonicera japonica* var. *aureo-reticulata*, makes a bright yellow curtain for a sunny bank.

4 Scarlet Honeysuckle, *Lonicera sempervirens*, needs a warm, sheltered position.

5 *Mackaya bella* is a beautiful shade-loving shrub that makes a good tub-plant. ↓

3

↓ 4

1

2

↓ 3

↓ 5

↓ 4

PLATE 43

Magnolias have the most noble and exquisite blooms, treasured by everyone.

1 *Magnolia soulangeana*, Purple or Tulip Magnolia, is a hybrid that is festooned with huge blooms in spring in cold countries, but starts flowering in autumn in the southern hemisphere, continuing through winter and spring in sheltered gardens.

2 One of the many variations of *Magnolia soulangeana*, which blooms earlier than the Purple Magnolia.

3 White Laurel Magnolia, *Magnolia grandiflora*, has majestic fragrant flowers in mid-summer.

4 Star Magnolia, *Magnolia stellata*, a low-growing shrub, needs a moist, cool climate for best display.

5 Holly Mahonia, *Mahonia aquifolium*, has attractive foliage and grows easily in shade or sun.

PLATE 44

1 Flowering Crab-Apples (*Malus floribunda*), are a delight in the spring, providing shade for other plants in summer. They need sunshine, moist soil and cold winters.

2 *Malus aldenhamensis* is a hybrid with purplish-red blossoms and fruits.

3 *Malus eleyi* is a similar hybrid with rosier blossoms.

4 Fire-Dart Bush, *Malvaviscus mollis*, is a cheerful, drought-resistant shrub, suitable for sun and shade.

5 *Malvaviscus penduliflorus*, Giant Fire-Dart, makes a luxuriant hedge in frost-free areas. It comes in sealing-wax red or shell pink.

1

↓ 2

3

PLATE 45

1/2 Pink *Mandevilla splendens*, formerly known as *Dipladenia*, needs a warm, sheltered position in cool-winter areas and the support of a trellis.

3 Fragrant White *Mandevilla suaveolens*, from Chile, is not so tender and will flower well in the shade.

4 Shade-loving *Medinilla magnifica* is a tropical evergreen shrub that needs a greenhouse in cold areas.

4

↓ 5

↑ *Manihot utilissima* var. *variegata*, Bitter Cassava, is suited to sub-tropical gardens.

5 Red Meg, *Megaskepasma ethrochlamys*, is a tender shrub that likes shade and spreads over a large area in hot, humid places.

PLATE 46

Melaleucas are drought-resistant, evergreen trees and shrubs. Their flowers have long colourful stamens.

1 *Melaleuca hypericifolia* is a shrub.

2 *Melaleuca linariifolia*, Flax-Leaf Paperbark, a rounded tree when mature, has fluffy flowers.

3 *Melaleuca armillaris*, Bracelet Honey-Myrtle, is smaller, with bottle brush flower spikes.

4 *Melaleuca nesophila*, Tea-Myrtle, is a tall tree.

5 *Melia azedarach*, China-Berry, is a useful shade tree, easy to grow.

6 *Mimetes cucullatus*, Red Bottlebrush, enjoys acid, well-drained soil at the coast, needing shelter from frost inland.

PLATE 47

The Flag-Bushes, *Mussaenda*, are spectacular shrubs in sub-tropical places.

1. White Flag-Bush, *Mussaenda frondosa*, is a showy landscape shrub.

2 Donna Aurora Flag-Bush, *Mussaenda philippica* var. *Donna Aurora*, has large balls of bracts and there are several hybrids in pink and red.

3 Red Flag-Bush, *Mussaenda erythrophylla,* is brilliant through summer and autumn.

4 Tree Daisy, *Montanoa bipinnatifida*, blooms in autumn.

5 Tapeworm Bush, *Muehlenbeckia platyclados*, is an interesting evergreen.

PLATE 48 1 *Mucuna nova-guineensis*, commonly called Scarlet Jade Vine or New Guinea Creeper, is a stunning climber for a pergola in a sub-tropical area.

2 *Millettia grandis*, Umzimibiti, is a frost-tender tree with erect flowers in mid-summer.

3 *Nymania capensis*, called Klapperbos or Chinese Lanterns, is a desert-type evergreen shrub.

4 *Ochna atropurpurea*, Carnival Bush, is a delightful evergreen shrub, colourful all through the year.

5 Oleander, *Nerium oleander*, though commonplace, can be relied upon for ease-of-growth, screening and masses of colour in summer.

1

2

↓ 4   3   ↓ 5

1

2

3

↓ 4

↓ 5

PLATE 50

1 *Passiflora vio-lacea* is a hardy Passion Flower. There are many beautiful species, including the Granadilla.

2 Royal *Paulownia tomentosa* is a large spreading hardy tree that blooms in early summer.

3 A small tender shrub, *Pavonia multiflora* may be grown in greenhouses in cold areas.

4 Hardy and self-clinging, Virginia Creeper, *Parthenocissus tricuspidatus*, has brilliant autumn tints.

5 *Pentas* are soft evergreen shrubs that need protection from frost.

1

2

↓ 3

↓ 4

PLATE 51
1 Purple Wreath, *Petrea volubilis*, is a magnificent climber that needs warmth for best performance and flowers while small.
2 *Pereskia aculeata* var. *godseffiana* is the most attractive of the Lemon Vines, but has sharp spines.
3 *Persoonia pinifolia*, Geebung, is a cheerful evergreen shrub, an Australian member of the Protea family.
4 Few evergreen climbers can rival the Mexican Blood-Trumpet, *Phaedranthus buccinatorius*, still called *Bignonia cherere* by gardeners.

1

2

3

4

5

PLATE 52

1 Snail Vine, *Phaseolus caracalla*, grows easily from seed.

2 *Photinia davidsoniae* is a large evergreen shrub, useful for screening.

3 Pink Rice-Flower, *Pimelia ferruginea*, a small evergreen shrub, blooms in early summer.

4 *Pittosporum viridiflorum*, Bosboekenhout, is a small evergreen tree with orange berries.

5 Rosewood, *Physocalymma scaberrima*, is a dainty tree that blooms early in summer.

6 Ever-popular Frangipani, *Plumeria rubra* var. *acutifolia*, is fragrant. There are several colours.

7 Forest Spur-Flower, *Plectranthus fruticosus*, is a sub-shrub for shady places.

↓6

↓7

PLATE 53

1/2 Proteas are evergreen shrubs with fabulous flowers for picking. They vary from plate-sized King Protea, *Protea cynaroides*, to plum-sized *Protea nana*. These two species are small enough for any garden.

1

3 The True Sugarbush, *Protea repens*, forms a large bush.

4 *Protea neriifolia*, Oleander-Leaved Protea, has hundreds of flowers in winter and spring.

5 Giant Woolly-Beard, *Protea barbigera*, needs well-drained soil.

6 *Protea eximia*, Ray-flowered Protea, grows easily.

7 *Protea aristata*, Ladismith Protea, blooms in mid-summer.

3   4   ↓ 5   ↓ 6   ↓ 7

1

2

↓ 3

4

↓ 5

PLATE 54

1 Silver Lace-Vine, *Polygonum aubertii*, will climb rapidly in one season.
2 Sweetpea Bush, *Podalyria calyptrata*, is a large shrub with scented spring flowers.
3 *Polygala myrtifolia*, a bushy evergreen, blooms most of the year.
4 Port St. Johns Creeper, *Podranea ricasoliana*, is a billowing evergreen climber.
5 Dwarf Pomegranate, *Punica granatum* var. *nana*, is attractive in flower or fruit and may be grown in a tub.
6 Plumbago, *P. auriculata*, is a spreading evergreen shrub that is popular everywhere.

↓ 6

1   ↓3   2   ↓4

            ↓5   ↓6

LATE 55

Brown-leaved Plum, *Prunus cerasifera* var. *atropurpurea*, often flowers in winter.

Double Flowering Peach, *Prunus persica flore-pleno*, is glorious for only a few weeks, but remains in the memory throughout the year.

Flowering Almond, *Prunus glandulosa*, is a shrub that flowers in late spring.

Japanese Flowering Cherry, *Prunus serrulata* ''Kanzan'' is a splendid spherical form.

A Weeping Cherry, *Prunus pendula*, the epitome of grace, in Japan. It is called *P. subhirtella pendula* in England.

Cherry Trees have beautiful bark and brilliant autumn foliage.

PLATE 56

1 *Pyrostegia ignea*, variously called Golden Shower, Flame Vine or Cracker Vine, is popular. It is one of the most useful as well as brilliant of large creepers, being drought-resistant, free-flowering and quick. It requires a warm sunny aspect in places which have frost.

2 *Pyracantha angustifolia*, Orange Fire-thorn, is a hardy, drought-resistant evergreen shrub.

3 The Mahogany Castorbean, *Ricinus communis* var. *purpureus*, has bronze-purple leaves at all times.

1

↓ 2

↓ 3

1

PLATE 57

1   *Raphiolepis umbellata*, Yeddo
    Hawthorn, is a hardy, evergreen shrub.

2/3   Deciduous *Rhododendron
      japonicum*, Japanese
      Azalea, also known as
      Azalea mollis, has hybrids
      in orange, salmon, rose or
      red. The golden-yellow kinds
      stem from the deciduous
      Chinese species, *Rhododen-
      dron molle*.

4   *Rhigozum obovatum*, Karoo Gold, is a drought-
    resistant, hardy evergreen shrub that flowers in
    spring.

5   *Reinwardtia indica*, Yellow Flax, is a small shrub that
    flowers brightly in mid-winter.

2   ↓ 3

↓ 4

↓ 5

1

2

4

PLATE 58

Few evergreen shrubs can equal Evergreen Rhododendrons for sheer spectacle in spring. There are innumerable species and hybrids, best chosen when in bloom.

1 *Rhododendron simsii*, previously known as Indian Azalea, is popular.

2 Variations of *R. simsii*.

3 Early-flowering "Duchess of Cypress" forms a massed display.

4 A large-leaved Rhododendron hybrid, "Pink Pearl".

5 Rhododendrons make good companion plants to Camellias.

6 A hybrid known as "Blue Diamond".

7 Kurume Azalea, *Rhododendron obtusum*, is a compact, hardy species which is popular as a pot plant as well as in gardens. There are many hybrids.

3

↓ 6

PLATE 59

1 *Rondeletia amoena*, a shrub for warm areas, has posies of flowers with old-fashioned charm.

2/3 *Rothmannia capensis*, Scented Cups, has masses of fragrant flowers in summer and tolerates dryness in winter.

4 The hardy Wax Tree, *Rhus succedanea*, becomes a vivid flame in late autumn.

5 Rosemary, *Rosemarinus officinalis*, is an aromatic, hardy shrub for every garden.

6 *Russelia equisetiformis*, Coral-Bell Bush, is a tender shrub with dainty pendent stems.

1

2

3

↓5   4

↓6

1

PLATE 61

1   The gorgeous, scented chalice of Cup-of-Gold, *Solandra guttata*, rivets attention on this spreading evergreen.

2/3   The Blushing Bride, *Serruria florida*, is a dainty bush grown for its enchanting, delicately tinted flowers, blooming in, mid-winter. Plants should be replaced every seven years.

4   The yellow cascade of the Canary Creeper, *Senecio tamoides*, is a gay sight in the autumn.

5   *Sophora japonica*, Pagoda Tree, is a medium, dainty shade or street tree, blooming in summer.

2   ↓ 3

↓ 4

↓ 5

1

2 ↓ 4

3 ↓ 5

PLATE 62

1 Spanish Broom, *Spartium junceum*, is fragrant and easily grown.

2 *Solanum mammosum*, Pig's Ears, a prickly shrub, has fascinating fruits, prized in floristry.

3 Potato Tree, *Solanum macranthum*, has flowers that change colour against dramatic sub-tropical foliage.

4 Mauve Potato Creeper, *Solanum wendlandii*, bears splendid heads of bloom in sun or shade.

5 The brilliant flowers of the Firewheel Tree, *Stenocarpus sinuatus*, emblazon the dark, striking foliage.

1

PLATE 63

/2 *Spathodea campanulata*, Fiery-Torch Tree, African Flame or Nandi Flame, lifts gorgeous lanterns up to tropical skies the world over. The name Nandi Flame pin-points its origin in Kenya.

2

Bridal-Wreath May, *Spiraea prunifolia* var. *plena*, has a shower of dainty flowers in winter and early spring, acting as an excellent foil to scarlet Japanese Flowering Quince.

Popular Cape May, *Spiraea cantoniensis*, forms a rounded shrub, most effective beneath colourful spring-flowering Peaches or Lucky Bean Trees.

Red May, *Spiraea bumalda* var. *Anthony Waterer*, a dwarf, hardy shrub for summer flowering, will fit into any small nook.

Fragrant *Stephanotis floribunda* may be trained around a pole in a warm garden or grown in a greenhouse.

3

↓ 5

4

↓ 6

1

2

3

↓4

PLATE 64

1 Large puffs of saffron stamen highlight the evergreen foliag of this half-hardy small tree, *Stifftia chrysantha*.

2 Palm like, with large, dramat leaves, *Strelitzia nicolai* creat a sub-tropical effect of architectural value.

3 The Crane Flower, *Strelitzia reginae*, forms a clump of canna-like leaves, above wh soar the bird-like flowerhead

4 Golden Vine, *Stigmaphyllon ciliatum*, is a tender twiner w dainty ruffled flowers.

5 Variegated Indian-Currant, *Symphoricarpus orbiculatus* var. *variegatus*, is a hardy sh with ornamental foliage.

↓5

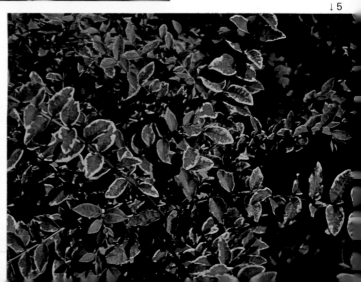

PLATE 65

1 The sensational flowers of the Jade Vine, *Strongylodon macrobotrys*, produce gasps of admiration, especially as two hundred long trusses may dangle from a pergola to sway gently in the sub-tropical breeze. Once established, it blooms for most of the year, at its best in summer. Seen here as the treasured feature in a small courtyard garden, it has the limelight.

2 *Strophanthus petersianus*, Corkscrew Flower, is a slender vine with curious small flowers, suited to a greenhouse or a warm garden. All parts are poisonous.

3 Glorious in spring, the Marmalade Bush, *Streptosolen jamesonii*, needs a warm situation and can be shaped or allowed to billow.

4 *Sutera grandiflora*, Wild Phlox, is a dainty sub-shrub that flowers most of the year, especially during autumn and winter.

↓2   1   ↓3   ↓4

1

2

↓ 4

3

5 ↓

PLATE 66

1 Scented English Lilac, *Syringa vulgaris*, in man varieties, will bloom satisfactorily only if given cold, moist situation.

2 *Syringa villosa* is a fragrant species that flowers easily.

3 *Tabebuia ipe*, Pink Trumpet Tree, flowers spectacularly on bare stems in winter or spring.

4 Mexican Pue, *Tabebuia pentaphylla* (*T. rosea*) massed with bloom in autumn, as well as at intervals during winter and spring.

5 Yellow Tabebuia, *Tabebuia chrysotricha*, is breath-taking in its intensity of colour.

6 Balloon-Pea, *Sutherlandia frutescens*, is a har sub-shrub, valued for its winter flowering. ↓

1   2

PLATE 67   1/2   Drought-resistant Tamarisks have dainty appeal, whether it be the Spring-flowering *Tamarix parviflora* (left) or Late Tamarisk, *T. pentandra* (right).

              3   Yellow Bush Tecoma, *Tecoma stans*, grows quickly and blooms gaily in autumn.

              4   Hardy Swamp Cypress, *Taxodium distichum*, has feathery foliage with russet autumn tints.

              5/6   Cape Honeysuckle, *Tecomaria capensis*, is a rambling shrub that makes a bright spectacle in autumn. Normally orange-flowered (left), there are yellow and orange varieties and deeper red forms. (below, right).

3   ↓ 5   4   ↓ 6

1

2

3
↓5 4

PLATE 68

1 The huge leaves of the Rice-Paper Plant, *Tetrapanax papyrifera*, make a dramatic impact.

2 *Thevetia peruviana*, Yellow Oleander, needs a warm situation in areas with cold winters.

3 A quick-growing shade tree, *Tipuana tipu* provides colour after the Jacaranda.

4 Hardy *Thuya orientalis* var. *aurea*, a conifer of 2 metres, makes a good accent

5 The Waratah, *Teleopea speciosissima*, has a sumptous head of flowers in springtime.

PLATE 69

1 The magnificent
   pendent sprays
   of the Mysore
   Trumpet Vine,
   *Thunbergia
   mysorensis*, are
   best appreciated
   when falling
   from a pergola.
   They both rival
   and complement
   the Jade Vine,
   when grown as
   companions,
   and bloom
   almost continuously
   throughout the year.

2 *Thunbergia
   grandiflora,* the
   Bengal Trumpet
   Vine, has huge
   flattish flowers,
   resplendent
   against the
   luxuriant foliage
   in autumn. It
   grows quickly,
   but needs a
   warm situation.

1

↓2

PLATE 70

1/2 The regal
splendour of
*Tibouchina
granulosa* com-
pels attention,
befitting the
common name,
Purple Glory Tree
There are several
colours forms of
this rounded sub
tropical tree.

3/4 Pink Glory Tre
*Tibouchina
granulosa* var.
rosea, is a colour
variety.

5 A popular ever-
green shrub, the
Brazilian Glory
Bush, *Tibouchin
semidecandra*,
needs a warm
position in cold
areas.

6 Small-leaved
Glory Bush,
*Tibouchina
elegans*, has
flowers that
change colour.

PLATE 71

Masses of fragrant flowers in spring and early summer draw one to the hardy Star-Jasmine, *Trachelospermum jasminoides*, a rambling evergreen.

Uncarina sakalava is an evergreen shrub from the dry parts of Madagascar.

Viburnum carlesii is a hardy spring-flowering deciduous shrub.

The Guelder Rose, *Viburnum opulus*, has small heads of flowers followed by red berries.

The Snowball Bush, *Viburnum opulus* var. *sterile* has no berries, but the ball-like flowerheads are larger and more spectacular.

Double-File Viburnum, *V. tomentosum*, has gorgeous flowers in spring, with several varieties.

The evergreen Keurboom, *Virgilia oroboides*, has scented flowers and grows very quickly.

1

2

4

3   ↓ 6

5   ↓ 7

PLATE 72

1 The Candy Corn Vine, *Wagatea spicata*, is a billowing evergreen climber for sub-tropical places, needing plenty of space.

2 *Wigandia caracasana* is a spreading shrub for the wild corner, with large plumes of flowers in spring and huge leaves.

3 Dainty *Weigela florida* is a beautiful deciduous shrub with branches that last in the vase, but must be trimmed after flowering.

4 *Weigela* Eva Rathke is one of several hybrids worth cultivating.

5/6 Whether grown as a standard (left) or over a rustic fence, the graceful Wistaria, *Wisteria sinensis*, lifts the heart in springtime.

CHAPTER I

CLIMATE, AND THE WAY IT AFFECTS THE SHRUBS WE GROW

When writing a book on flowering shrubs and trees for South Africa, it must be remembered that South Africa is a huge country which has no fewer than four climates within its shores. It has a sub-tropical climate along the Eastern shore and on the lowveld; a temperate climate with winter rainfall as in the Cape; dry grasslands with summer rainfall as in the highveld of the Transvaal, and semi-desert conditions such as are found in parts of the Karoo.

It follows, therefore, that many shrubs will be found growing vigorously in parts of the country which will not survive in others. This applies to indigenous shrubs, meaning those found growing wild in the country, as well as to those imported shrubs which started life in China, Japan, England or America and have been grown all over the world without many people knowing or caring about the country of their origin. This fact really concerns only the botanist or naturalist, but it is also valuable to the average gardener in so far as it gives a clue on how to treat each shrub, by trying to imitate conditions found in its natural home and so giving it an opportunity to flourish in any garden anywhere in the world.

There are several basic differences in climate which make it difficult for shrubs and trees to survive where they do not have what they need. Temperature, moisture and light are the three most important influences in the life of a plant. Soil conditions are important too, but do not hold first place and do not come in at this stage while we are discussing climate. When considering temperature, we must note whether the plant is used to a hot climate or a cold, and whether too much of either extreme will affect it in such a way that it will not be able to survive. This is where the all-important question of frost crops up. A tender shrub, such as Poinsettia, which thrives in warm Natal, will not survive the frost of the highveld, even if it has grown vigorously all the year round, unless the gardener takes some precaution in giving it a sheltered spot where the frost will not kill it altogether. In this case, therefore, it is possible to take a plant from the sub-tropical climate and grow it successfully in the frost area, provided that one knows the weakness of the plant that tends to succumb to cold and frost and protects it accordingly.

Light plays an important part in the life of many plants. Numbers of shrubs can be planted anywhere in the garden but there are many that will thrive best in the shade, such as Fuchsia, and those that will do well only in the open sun, such as Erythrina. Naturally the exceptions can always be found, but on the whole one gets the best results if one knows which are the shade-loving shrubs and plants them in the shade and vice versa. This knowledge also helps in planning the garden, when one can make a point of placing shade-loving plants under the shade of trees and can make them a feature of the landscape.

Moisture is the third important element to be considered. In a generally dry country like South Africa, this might almost be all-important, but it is possible to give certain shrubs too much moisture. Sometimes this point is over-done and people warn the amateur gardener about the dreadful results of overwatering, such as mildew and rot. Unfortunately, most gardeners underwater in any case, so that these sad results are seldom evident. In the case of annual plants, over-watering can wreak havoc, but the beauty of growing shrubs is that they can take overwatering very well and revel in it. One has only to see the growth put on by many shrubs and trees during a rainy spell to prove this point. As a general rule, the indigenous shrubs and trees can survive with very little water, as they are used to thirst in this parched land of ours, but even they respond to cultivation and good watering, and outstrip their veld sisters in size and flowering.

This discussion on the climatic requirements of shrubs does not mean that it is only possible to grow those which do well in your own area. Besides, as one becomes more and more interested in gardening, it is inevitable that one will want to grow those shrubs which do not do well in one's own area, but come from different provinces and are rare in one's own home town. The old story of forbidden fruit holds good and it becomes much more exciting to grow a tender, rust-coloured Bougainvillea that might not survive the winter in a cold area than the ordinary hardy purple Bougainvillea that spreads in a wealth of colour in the summer.

This story was told to me by a friend who was gardening in Switzerland with the help of an old French gardener. The garden, although beautiful in a rambling way, had been neglected and she had ordered Tulips and Daffodils from Holland as well as Ixias and Freesias from South Africa. The old gardener was horrified and said that his garden was not for luxury flowers. In spite of his protests, how-ever, he had been imbued with the spark, for she later found him burning large piles of Dahlia bulbs which he declared to be weeds, as they grew too easily. After that, it was all she could do to stop him from pulling up everything that grew too easily and which he looked down upon as resembling a weed.

It is not necessary to go to the extreme of the old French gardener, and one should definitely grow those shrubs which do well in your area as well as those which need particular requirements. The gardener must first know what those *special requirements* are and then *do his best to provide them*. It is certainly easy to plant a *shade-loving shrub* in the shade, whether complete shade or filtered sunlight, under a tree such as a Syringa. Other shrubs that do not care particularly for shade can be planted anywhere in the open sun of the garden. *Moisture* too, can be controlled to a large extent. In the dry winter of the Transvaal, a shrub that comes from the winter rainfall area of the Cape should be well watered in winter, so as to simulate the shrub's natural home or habitat. *Humidity* plays an important part in the amount of moisture available. Hydrangeas are usually grown in the shade in the Transvaal and given a great deal of water during the summer months. In Durban and Cape Town, however, the humidity of the atmosphere near the sea keeps the fleshy leaves turgid and does not allow rapid transpiration or loss of moisture through the leaves, so that one often sees Hydrangeas growing right out in the open sun without wilting, as they would do in a dry atmosphere. In dry areas on a very hot day, it often helps to spray plants such as Hydrangeas and Azaleas with the hosepipe, in order to retard transpiration from the leaves, which may or may not show signs of wilting. Proper watering makes it possible for shrubs to grow even in the semi-desert areas, provided that one can obtain the water for gardening.

One of the biggest enemies of moisture is *the wind*, for this dries the leaves rapidly so that they lose more moisture by evaporation than they can absorb through their systems from their roots. The consequence is that the leaves, not having enough moisture in them, become wilted, and the plant will suffer if this is not remedied, as the leaves are the breathing organs of the plant, converting the sunlight and air into nourishment. In windy weather, therefore, the gardener should pay extra attention to the watering of shrubs, particularly if it is also hot at the same time. Here again it helps to spray the leaves. In the case of shrubs that dislike wind, see that they are protected from the wind by other shrubs, trees or even a wall.

The battle against frost, however, is not so easy. One can try to prevent the ravages of frost, but this cannot be as easy as controlling the requirements of light and moisture. Frost comes in winter, though not every winter, to the gardens of the highveld. It does not come to the coastal belt of Natal or the Cape as a rule, unless the altitude is very high.

Normally there is a very short period of frost, which comes for a few nights, but this is enough to cause the death of many tender plants, unless they are protected. Frost accompanied by wind is called a "black frost", so called because the affected plants are found next morning, dead and blackened, flaccid and rotten, burnt beyond all chance of recovery. In the case of particularly tender shrubs, the whole shrub is affected and cannot recover, but in many cases, after the blackened parts are cut away, the shrub will send out new growths in the spring. Each year, unless there is no frost, the cycle will be repeated, so that one need not lose the shrub completely. Also, a slight frost might not affect them, whereas a hard frost would. Such shrubs can be called "half-hardy". A "hardy" shrub, on the other hand is one that will endure the hardest frost and is the gardener's joy, particularly on the highveld. "Tender" shrubs are so-called because they cannot endure frost, although no strict rules can be laid down as to whether these will be completely annihilated by frost or merely have their tender young growth affected.

The gardener can *plant shrubs in special positions* in order to protect them from the frost, by finding warm spots for those plants which come from a hot climate. In South Africa, a north-facing wall is the warmest spot in winter, and one should try to plant all very tender shrubs in front of a north-facing wall, hedge or even a clump of other hardier shrubs.

One must really understand what frost is, before realising why simply facing north is not always good enough. When a plant is affected by frost it is burnt. It is burnt by the sun, on the morning following the night after the frost or dew has settled, which thaws the cold frost off and in so doing burns the tender growth, much in the same way as a human being gets frost-bite if he places his frozen hand into hot water or near a fire. So we can understand why it is necessary to protect the tender shrub from the morning sun. The shrub should have shade in the early morning so that the frost can thaw slowly by itself, and receive the sun at midday and in the afternoon to give it heat once more. In other words, a tender shrub should not be placed facing east if possible. Hibiscus, for example, will do better if it is placed in a corner against the house where one wall faces north and the other west, than if it is merely placed facing due north and receives the early morning sun. Even a position simply facing west is preferable to that facing east, but here there should be some protection from cold south winds if the shrub is to do well.

Walls retain the heat of the sun and that is why they are the warmest spots for some tender shrubs, but others, although they like warmth, prefer a position where there is more circulation of air than is found against a wall. Protected nooks can be found or made in any garden. A section of the garden, about 10 metres long, can be a sheltered spot if it has a screen of trees or shrubs on its south side and a few hardy shrubs east and west, roughly forming the 3 sides of a box. A split pole fence overgrown with creepers, or a low garden wall, can also form one of the sides of this rough "box", which should certainly not be too symmetrical, for the sake of appearance.

A popular method of protection against frost is "covering" the shrubs for the winter. The danger here is that many shrubs are often suffocated and die from lack of air instead of from the frost. This usually happens when the unfortunate shrubs are swaddled in hessian, which is tied right up against the body of the plant, so that there is no circulation of air. The best material for covering the shrub is conveniently found growing in the veld just before winter when it is time to cover them. This is the long grass which is already dry and brownish and should be cut off as long as possible (it is usually a metre in length).

A framework of pliable, bared twigs should be made first around each shrub. The branches of the Wattle Tree are very suitable and stakes should be cut off to the required length with all leaves removed. Place 4 or 5 stakes around each shrub, which, when tied together at the top are at least 25 cm higher than the tip of the shrub. Then tie two or three horizontal rows of pliable twigs on to these stakes, so that the framework crudely resembles the framework of a Red–Indian tent. The long grass is stacked in bundles against this framework and tied right around with several pieces of string. Leave air-spaces here and there, particularly on the western side of the "tent". The grass will meet at the top and prevent the frost from settling on the shrub. This covering should be put on at the beginning of winter and left until all danger of frost has passed. It permits a free circulation of air around the shrub, without which it cannot live. Watering should continue as before.

One can cover tender plants with a sheet of cloth or polythene film on cold nights, but be careful not to let the polythene touch the leaves in case it is left on during the day and causes sun–scorch.

A simple way to cover small special shrubs, such as Proteas, is to place an up–turned cardboard box over each plant at night, removing it at about 9 o'clock in the morning so that the plant can receive plenty of air and the sunshine that is often present on winter days.

It is a fact that a shrub which has been planted in the open and has been covered for the first 3 or 4 winters, will finally grow very big and strong and be so well established that it is unnecessary, and even inconvenient, to continue with the covering. At most, only the new young growth will be affected by a hard frost and this can be trimmed off without further ill effects. It is for the gardener to judge the vigour and size of his shrub and decide when to stop covering in winter.

In spite of all these precautions against frost, however, losses often occur, so that frost remains the great leveller, and whether the shrub is tender to frost or not, is the most important thing to consider when choosing new shrubs for a garden which is situated in an area where heavy frost falls in winter. Once the larger trees have grown to shelter a garden, one will find it possible to grow tender plants that one was not able to grow when the garden was new.

It can be seen, therefore, that any shrub can be tried or planted anywhere in South Africa, provided that one learns in advance what are the ideal requirements for each shrub and is willing to provide them to the best of one's ability. This sort of knowledge prevents many disappointments on the part of the average gardener. It prevents the disappointment of loss when a shade-loving plant cannot survive in a sunny spot, a moisture-loving plant does not thrive in a dry spot or when a favourite tender shrub is lost during winter simply because it had no protection. The hardiest sun-loving shrub which can survive the coldest winter will also prove a disappointment to the gardener if it is planted in a shady spot. Even though it will live and grow, it will do neither vigorously, and the beauty of its flowering will be spoiled, so that the gardener will take a dislike to it and think that it was not a good shrub to have grown. Half an hour spent in locating a good position for each shrub will be rewarded with extra weeks of attractive flowering each year and a healthy bush which forms an indispensable part of the landscape.

On the other hand, the gardener need not be too discouraged by this task, as shrubs, like human beings, can withstand a great deal of buffeting and will survive many risks. It is often the neglected fig tree behind the servant's quarters that bears the most abundant figs.

The best way to ensure that delicate and "difficult" shrubs will do well in your area is to grow them from seed. If they grow up knowing no other climate, then they will acclimatise themselves and adjust themselves gradually. Some shrubs, such as Bauhinia, grow very easily and rapidly from seed, but others are slow and plants must be bought from the nurserymen, unless the gardener has infinite time and patience or is willing to take cuttings. When buying shrubs in tins try, as far as possible, to buy from a nursery near by, so that your own climatic conditions will resemble those to which the plant is accustomed.

In all parts of South Africa it must be realised that climate varies between the shortest distances in the same province, and even in the same town. Johannesburg and Pretoria, whilst only 56 kilometres apart, represent vastly different climates, so that *Petrea*, which is rarely seen growing as a very large bush in Johannesburg, reaches magnificent proportions in Pretoria and is much showier. Even in Johannesburg itself, one part of the town is cooler than another, and in many suburbs flowerings of various shrubs takes place at different times. It is interesting to note that the climate around the city of Durban is quite different from that of Kloof, which is only about 30 kilometres away. This is because one ascends steeply into Kloof, which is about 600 metres above sea-level and consequently has less humidity, heat and wind than is experienced at sea-level itself. Study your local conditions, therefore, and give your shrubs and trees the very best positions that it is within your powers to do.

Within the area of one's own garden there are different little pockets of climate. This may be seen when two similar trees, planted a little distance away from each other, often grow unevenly. The gardener must use his own judgement, therefore, about placing the shrubs and trees that require different climatic conditions, and decide for himself which are the warm, cool, protected or exposed positions in his own garden. This will enable him to grow a large variety of shrubs which will respond to suitable conditions with healthy, vigorous growth and abundant flowers.

CHAPTER II

THE CONDITION OF THE SOIL

The condition of the soil is of the utmost importance if shrubs and trees are to be grown successfully. The wrong type of soil will never give good results, but it is very easy to create the right type of soil. The ideal thing would be for the gardener to prepare a large piece of ground and improve all the ground and its drainage, but this is not always practicable. The gardener, however, can do a great deal for his shrubs by simply changing the soil in the small area which each shrub will occupy.

Good garden soil is recognised as having a rich, dark brown colour and a soft crumbly texture, which has neither too much clay to make it stiff nor sand to make it poor. It can be presumed that such a soil is fairly rich in organic matter, particularly if there are earthworms present, since they exist only in a soil which contains organic matter. In time, they further improve the soil by consuming it and passing it out of their bodies in the form of worm casts. These casts are rich in food value and have a fine texture. The earthworm also aerates the soil by burrowing through the earth, as deeply as 2 metres, and lining these burrows with a substance rich in plant foods.

The aim is to supply a good garden soil which is a copy of the fertile soil in which the shrubs grow in their wild state. Fertile soil is rich in organic matter such as leaves and manures which have accumulated and decomposed over the centuries. Man's imitation of this is the manufacture of compost and the addition of this to the soil. Not only is it possible to increase the fertility of the soil by the use of manure and compost, but there is another requirement in the soil to be considered, which varies with the different shrubs, and is known as the acid reaction of the soil. Both of these essentials must be discussed in detail, for the gardener is able to change his soil to suit his shrubs, provided that he is acquainted with what they want.

Manure or Compost?

The question is often asked, "Why use manure if compost can supply all that is required in the soil?" The fact is that compost should really contain manure, for in uncultivated land the manure dropped by wild animals becomes part of the humus formed by decomposing leaves. It is important to use both compost and manure, for each plays a very definite part in both gardening and farming.

A natural phenomenon known as *mycorrhizal association* has been studied in England by Dr. M. C. Rayner, who has written pamphlets and books and carried out numerous experiments on the subject, and her findings throw a new light on the importance of compost. (See "The Living Soil" by E.B. Balfour).

Myco means "fungal" and *rhiza* means "root". Growing trees have been found to have a fungus growing at the roots which inter-connects the soil and the growing system of the tree. This is not a parasitic fungus, but one that plays an important part in the life of the tree. *Mycorrhiza* is the name used to describe the tree root plus its thread-like fungi or *mycelium*.

It is agreed that soil fungi break down complex substances that are otherwise not available to shrubs and trees and that they also excrete substances that stimulate growth. *Mycorrhizal association* suggests that many plants benefit from *specific* soil fungi. Dr. Rayner proves that in some cases (Heaths or Orchids) normal seedling development depends on the presence of the fungus, or growth can be stopped without it. Now vigorous fungal activity is dependent on a sufficient supply of humus or compost, and the fungi cannot live in soil without it, so that the addition of compost is of paramount importance when planting a tree or shrub.

Compost does not act directly by supplying nourishment in itself, but it acts indirectly by stimulating the activity of the soil fungi. The action of these fungi, in association with the tree roots, stimulate growth in a remarkable way, sur-passing results obtained by using inorganic chemicals, and in addition improving the health and strength of the tree and its powers of resisting disease. Also, shrubs growing on compost-treated soil are more likely to survive hard winters.

Compost is, therefore, essential when planting shrubs and trees. When trans-planting trees, particularly indigenous specimens, as much as possible of the soil in the area in which the tree has been growing should be taken with it, and a good "ball" of earth should be taken (See Chapter III). Compost also improves the texture of the soil. A stiff clay clay will be made porous and a sandy soil held together by the addition of compost.

Manure supplies nutrients to the roots direct. When planting a shrub, it is customary to add manure to the lower half of the hole which is prepared for it, so that, after a season, when the shrub has established itself, its roots will reach the now very well-rotted manure and grow vigorously. Manure is not only a food but a stimulant, and the shrub seems to spring forward in growth when its roots reach it, deep down. There are those who say that it is unnecessary to add manure to the sub-soil since it has been proved that only the top 15 cm of the soil contains the mass of organic matter and the bacteria which are essential to plant life. As one digs lower, the bacteria decrease considerably. This is true, but from the gardener's point of view it is highly desirable to improve the sub-soil. The gardener who gets a thrill out of seeing his shrubs do well will find it a pleasure to do something practical to hasten the best results. It seems obvious that one should try and improve the sub-soil as well as the top-soil when planting a shrub for permanent enjoyment in the garden, rather than leave the sub-soil in its original state of unfriendly hardness. Then, too, there is the question of drainage to be provided at the bottom of the hole, so that while one is in the process of digging out the sub-soil, one should add the manure which will later be of benefit to the shrub.

Make Your Own Compost

Compost is composed of decayed plant material, and there is no doubt that its addition to the soil works wonders. The case for compost is unopposed, and the only question that occupies gardeners is that of how the compost should be made. There have been books written on the subject of compost, which is a complete study in itself, and there are many theories and methods of making it which have been and are being perfected by experts.

The main thing is that the gardener should have a continuous supply of compost all the year round. Every time he wants to plant a shrub, there should be a fresh supply on hand, and this can also be used as a top dressing around one's shrubs as well as all over the garden. Compost must be properly made if it is to do its work successfully, and should include some product of animal origin since compost does not nourish the plant direct but stimulates the fungi in the soil.

Briefly, these are the methods used in making compost. The old, enormous pit, which is now outmoded as a means of making compost, was a convenient dump for rubbish but had many disadvantages. In addition to the many months one had to wait for compost, there was usually a bad smell from these pits as the vegetable matter was putrefying and not decomposing correctly. Also, there was no air for the bacteria which bring about the decomposition of the compost.

There are three popular methods of making compost, two above ground and one below the surface. When making compost above ground, one may build heaps or make the compost with the aid of a box or frame. Here the living organisms which break down the vegetable matter are able to breathe. The decomposition creates heat which should be kept in by the use of earth or sacks, which also help to keep out excess moisture such as storm-water, which might exclude the air by saturation.

Any heap that is well made will eventually turn into good compost, but it has been found that the addition of activators will speed up the whole process of making compost in quite a remarkable way (by stimulating or activating the micro-organisms). Fresh manure is the ideal and natural activator and other organic activators are dried blood, sewage sludge, papaw pips crushed with water and untreated tobacco dust or leaves. Commercial activators are sold by seedsmen and are very good if they are made up of organic material. Experiments in England tend to prove that although chemical activators rot the vegetable matter quickly, organic matter used as an activator produces a greater degree of disease resistance in plants. Apart from this consideration, animal residues such as farmyard manure, dried blood or sewage sludge should be included in compost, since the fungi in the soil feed on compost and require a mixed diet of animal and vegetable matter.

The details of building up the compost are the same whether you make an open heap or build it up in a frame or box.

The heaps are about 2 metres square and 1 metre high. The heat will evaporate too readily from smaller heaps and larger ones are too difficult to handle. The boxes or frames vary in size from 1 to 2 metres square according to one's needs, and are made of planks or split poles on 4 sides but not at the bottom. They have removable fronts and are covered by a lid or sack.

In both cases the materials are added in layers, starting with a 15 cm layer of green matter, followed by a 5 cm layer of manure and then a thin covering of good soil. A sprinkling of agricultural lime is then added and then another 15 cm layer of green matter. The layers are built up in this way to the desired height.

While building the heap, 2 or more stakes should be placed upright near the centre so that when the layers are completed, these may be withdrawn to provide air vents. Ready prepared activators are usually poured in solution down these holes. Cover the last layer with soil and then with sacks in order to keep the heat in. The finished heap should be watered but not saturated. The heaps should be turned over twice, at intervals of about a month, so that every part of the compost has a chance of being in the centre where the greatest heat is concentrated.

Making compost in bins or heaps is very successful in those part of the country which have a moist atmosphere such as at the coast, but in dry atmospheres it is very difficult for the gardener to keep the heaps in the ideal state of moisture. Exposed as they are to the air, they will dry out rapidly and thus slow down the whole process, so that one should use these methods only when conditions of humidity prevail.

In the dry atmosphere inland, there is yet another method of making compost which has been used with great success. It is easy to prepare, maintain and handle, and can be used in the small garden as well as on large estates. This method also ensures a continuous supply of compost and is known as the three-pit-system.

Three shallow pits are dug side by side. They are each 45 cm deep and about 1,5 metres square. The green matter is put into the first pit, together with the manure or other activator, soil and a sprinkling of lime. Make several layers and allow the top to protrude slightly above the ground as it will sink down while decomposing. Water it and cover with soil or sacks. After three weeks, throw it all into the second pit, and after another three weeks, throw it into the third. At the same time recommence the process in the first pit. At the end of about 10 weeks you will have excellent compost, and if you follow up the routine in the other 2 pits, you will have a continuous supply throughout the year. The compost may be sifted before using and the residue put back into the first pit.

This is a good method since it enables one to use up the garden rubbish as it accumulates continuously. It is also easy and inexpensive and requires very little labour, for the smallness of the pits makes the compost easy to handle when throwing it from one pit to the other, a task which turns it at the same time. It seems to be the common-sense method which would appeal to all gardeners. All compost should be used as soon as possible after it is ready.

Shredding machines that mince up vegetable matter hasten compost making, since they expose larger areas to bacteria for decomposition. A hammer mill is useful for this purpose.

Dried leaves should not be added to compost material as they take a year or more to decompose. They may be collected in autumn and stacked neatly in cages made of chicken wire, held in place by four stakes to make a square. Water the leaves so that they pack down and begin decomposition. If the leaves are shredded into tiny pieces and sprinkled lightly with activators and soil, or urea in pill form, they will decompose within a few weeks and may be used in the garden or mixed with other compost.

THE MYSTERY OF THE SOIL

Acidity and Alkalinity of the Soil

It sometimes happens that despite a carefully chosen position, as well as adequate feeding and watering, a shrub will not thrive. It may start off by simply not flowering, and later die back slowly. This is often a great puzzle to the gardener. Many a gardener has bought a beautiful flowering Rhododendron (Azalea) and found to his great disappointment that the following year masses of promising looking buds will turn brown and wither, so that not a single flower will be produced. After a year or two of watering carefully, not too much and not too little, without success, he gives up and imagines that Azaleas are difficult.

What is the "mystery" that makes them do well in some gardens? Is it the "green-finger" of the gardener who has some secret handed down from generation to generation? Very often this mystery of the soil can be solved very scientifically in the study of the acidity and alkalinity of the soil.

This need not be as difficult or complicated as it sounds because modern research supplies the answer quite easily. A sample of your soil can be sent to any Agricultural College or Government Agricultural department and they will give you a report on your soil. Any analytical chemist will also be able to supply the same information and there are also some very simple soil-testing kits from America which are available to gardeners.

It is necessary to understand what the report means in scientific terms. The degree of acidity or alkalinity is referred to as the pH value of the soil. For a neutral soil the pH is 7. Numbers from 7 to 14 indicate the degree of alkalinity and numbers from 7 back to 0 indicate the degree of acidity of the soil. Research stations determine the exact pH preferences of each plant or shrub, and special plant lists are made and given out by soil-testing laboratories.

The exact pH preferences need not be followed strictly by the amateur gardener, but they do give an idea of the requirements of the different plants and can be consulted for accuracy where plants are not doing well. In other words, the reaction of the soil is of the greatest importance and the modern gardener should consider the pH preference of his shrubs in the same way as he considers the positions in which they are to be planted. Also, in the same way that the gardener improves the fertility of poor soil with compost and manure, so can he make a soil more acid or more alkaline.

It is easy to make a soil more alkaline or "sweeter" by adding agricultural lime. One simply sprinkles it over the surface of the ground, lightly forking it in and following by a good watering.

In South Africa one always hears the saying that the ground in sour (acid) and can never have too much sweetness—in the form of lime. Lime assists in making available more readily the essential ingredients of the soil, but if the soil is over-limed, as it is when the pH of the soil is raised above 8, then these essential mineral nutrients (iron, phosphates and minor elements such as copper, zinc and manganese) cannot be released and the shrub will be deficient in these elements and eventually prove a failure. Thus one should lime only when it is known that a plant is particularly fond of lime and can "take" any amount of it, or when there is proof that the soil lacks lime. Lavender, for example, makes a lovely little hedge in the garden but has an annoying habit of dying out. A good application of lime will end this seemingly mysterious habit.

There are various methods of making the soil more acid, in order to benefit acid-loving plants. *An ideal good garden soil is always very slightly acid*, the pH being slightly above 6. Many shrubs prefer a soil that is very acid, with a pH as low as 4, and should be grown together in a separate portion of the garden or can be treated individually.

One of the quickest methods is the use of aluminium sulphate, which is a powder that can be obtained from the chemist. This must be used sparingly but in sufficient quantity to maintain the required degree of acidity. On the average, this should be used on ordinary garden soils at the rate of two handfuls to the square yard. Where soils are strongly alkaline, a larger quantity is required. Sprinkle this powder around the base of the shrub and water it in. Wait for several weeks and repeat the procedure. Even if this is done only a couple of months before the flowering season, the results of the readjustment of the soil can often be seen, and in the case of the once barren Rhododendron, which likes an acid soil, a sheet of bloom will appear once more in the spring. Other inorganic chemicals which will render the soil more acid are iron sulphate, iron chelate, ammonium sulphate, ammonium phosphate and soil sulphur (flowers of sulphur).

Another successful chemical is commercial tannic acid which has the added advantage of being organic material. It is made chiefly from the bark of Wattle Trees, is manufactured in Natal and can be bought quite cheaply in blocks. A readily available form of tannic acid, which should appeal to all gardeners, is present in used tea-leaves. After the gardener has enjoyed his cup of tea, he should pour the contents of the pot at the base of his acid-loving shrubs. In order to save up the precious tea-leaves without always running out into the garden, a stone jar should be kept in the kitchen, into which all the dregs should be thrown. As this is filled, the gardener can transfer it to the shrubs. The tea-leaves dry up and also act as a mulch to the shrub. This can be done almost continuously to the short list of known acid-loving shrubs such as Azaleas, Camellias, Gardenias, Magnolias and *Leptospermum*. A friend of mine, who gave this treatment to his purple Magnolia, was amazed at the way the hitherto small, stunted shrub grew long vigorous stems with large, healthy green leaves in a single season. He thereupon coined a phrase, which amusingly sums up the whole situation, "It's always tea-time for Magnolias."

Other mulches of organic materials which contain acid may be used around the base of acid-loving shrubs. These include certain leaves, particularly those of the Oak and the Sumac Trees, as well as Pine-needles. Other suitable materials for acid mulches are the rotted bark of trees such as Chestnuts, Oaks, Gums, Pines and Wattles; well-rotted sawdust or ground acorns. All these mulches should be replaced or added to from time to time, as the acid is leached out by watering. Some acid-loving shrubs such as Rhododendrons, need a permanent mulch of leaves, at least 10 cm thick, around the base in order to keep the roots from drying out. Most acid-loving shrubs like a light, porous soil, and, as a general rule, should be planted with masses of compost which has been made without lime.

It is interesting to note that the colours of Hydrangeas can be changed by readjusting the pH of the soil. Pink Hydrangeas like a very slightly acid soil (pH 6) while blue Hydrangeas like a strongly acid soil (pH 4-5). The addition of lime will turn them pink and the addition of aluminium sulphate will turn them blue. In both cases water the roots with a weak solution of the powder about once a month.

Acid-loving shrubs should not be planted up against the lime-washed walls of a house, as an accumulation of lime washed down by the rains into the bed might cause deterioration of the shrub.

All these methods of making the soil more acid or more alkaline should be repeated at least once or twice a year, as many things, such as rainwater and earthworms, tend to alter the soil reaction and the soil loses its acidity or alkalinity in time.

Unless the soil is known to be actively alkaline, as in districts which have "chalk" soils, the majority of gardens have slightly acid soil and most shrubs will thrive in these conditions. There is no need to keep juggling with pH values if shrubs are growing well, but only if they are not doing so. The plants that must have very acid soil are limited to a few genera and these should be avoided in districts with decidedly alkaline soil, where it proves too difficult to change the soil permanently or to improve drainage. In such cases, it is best to grow one's favourites in large tubs of specially prepared soil, which cannot be altered by the surrounding earth, and, in special cases, to water them with rainwater.

CHAPTER III

PROPAGATION AND PLANTING

"We can build a garden quickly in South Africa"

We are lucky in a sunny land like South Africa in the way in which our shrubs and trees grow so quickly. An almond tree will take 9 years to grow to a height of 4 metres in England, but will reach that height in South Africa in about 4 years. For the amateur gardener and the possessor of a new garden, this fact has a very definite advantage in that it is possible to build up a garden that looks quite well established in a third of the time that it would take in Europe. The gardener can do many things to hasten growth and that well-established look by careful attention to watering and general care as well as by planting sizeable shrubs and trees from nurseries.

Methods of Raising Shrubs and Trees

The idea of *growing a shrub or tree from seed* seems very laborious to the home gardener, but in fact, it is very often easy and quick. Some trees do much better when they are grown from seed and planted out when quite small. This is true of *Bauhinia variegata* which grows a long tap root very rapidly and is best planted out while only a seedling and easy to handle. It very often flowers in the third year of planting, attains a height and spread of 3 metres in 4 years and has a much more natural and compact shape if grown from seed than if bought in a tin, where it is usually grown with a long stem.

On the other hand it is really too much for the gardener to expect to grow Ericas, which are particularly difficult, or any other slow growing shrub from seed, as it takes a number of years for the plant to reach the size at which it can be bought from the nursery at quite a low figure. The average shrub costs no more than a tray of annual plants, and when one considers the everlasting value of the former it is surprising that the average garden does not have more shrubs in it.

Our indigenous South African shrubs and trees grow very easily from seed and in fact can be grown almost without exception from seed. Growing them from seed enables them to acclimatise themselves in different parts of the country away from their natural home. The Silver Tree, which grows on Table Mountain, can be grown readily from seed and adjusts itself to the cold winter of the Transvaal, whereas it seldom survives transplanting. It will reach a size of 2 metres in about 3 years, particularly if it is pampered by lots of water during winter (to simulate the winter rainfall of the Cape) and has some protection from frost in the way of a sheltering wall or rock, in the early stages of growth.

The National Botanic Gardens at Kirstenbosch supply seeds of many indigenous shrubs, trees and plants of all descriptions. These seeds are unobtainable from ordinary seed shops and are supplied only to members. Membership is very inexpensive, and in return for subscriptions paid, packets of seed, which can be chosen from a seed list issued each year, are supplied to members annually. Every garden lover should belong to Kirstenbosch, for apart from his personal gains, he will be helping to maintain the gardens, which depend to a large extent on the support of the public. The botanists at Kirstenbosch are helping to preserve the natural flora which gives pleasure to gardeners all over the world. Many treasures are available to us through their efforts and the gardens at Kirstenbosch represent a beautiful example of how our natural heritage is being nurtured, so that the enemies of the plants, in the shape of forest fires and vandalism, can be combated.

Some nurseries supply South African shrubs and there are a few in particular that devote all their efforts to supplying indigenous or native bulbs and plants as well as seeds, so that the busy gardener need not bother to plant seeds at all.

A great number of shrubs and trees can be grown from seed without much trouble, however, and in much the same way as ordinary annuals. Prepare tins in the same way as they are prepared for flower seeds, with holes and small stones for drainage at the bottom and filled with a mixture of good soil and compost. The addition of vermiculite mixed with the soil aids water retention and makes the germination of seeds almost always successful. Large seeds should be planted in individual tins as this makes them much easier to handle for transplanting.

Very large, hard-skinned seeds can be forced to germinate more quickly in a number of ways. They can be soaked in water for several days or until their skins split and then planted out, although there is a danger here that they might rot. Some, such as the Acacia seeds, need to be softened in boiling water. They can also be scratched slightly with a razor blade on the smooth side, but one must be very careful not to damage the scar which marks the point where the seedling emerges.

The golden rule of covering any seed with a layer of soil not thicker than its own diameter applies to the seeds of trees or shrubs. The tins should be covered with a piece of hessian which is removed only when watering, and removed completely when the seedling has emerged.

One disadvantage of growing shrubs and treeds from seed is that the improved varieties often revert back to the original parent and the new characteristics are often lost. Also it is not always likely that the flowers will be the same colour as those of the parent plant, so that if one wants to obtain the identical plant, the best way to do so is to take cuttings.

Cuttings

These are often easy to take. Success varies with the individual species and it is always interesting to experiment for oneself depending on the patience of the grower. Some trees, such as the Willow, strike so easily from cuttings that if their twigs are used to make a "fence" to keep the dogs off a bed in the garden, they will often produce leaves and begin to grow. The time to take cuttings is in spring or autumn.

A cutting can be cut from a fairly firm stalk of a shrub near the tip. A piece of roughly 20 cm is a good length to cut, although this length may vary considerably. The main requirement is that it should be cut cleanly at a point immediately below the junction of a leaf with the stem. Another way to taking a cutting is to break off a short side branch in such a way that a heel or piece of the main stem is left on it. Cuttings can also be made of very soft young wood at the growing tip, in which case the cut should also be made just below the junction of a leaf and stem.

All leaves except the top ones should be pulled off and two-thirds of the cutting should be inserted into a tin containing damp river sand. This should be kept damp and preferably in the shade. When the leaves show signs of growing or, alternatively, the cutting has been pulled out and seen to have grown roots, it may be planted out like any ordinary seedling. This usually takes anything from 4 to 8 weeks. Sometimes, as in the case of Poinsettia, the cuttings may be planted directly into the position where they are to grow and not disturbed any further. Other cuttings, such as those of Rosemary, can be handled as above.

Layers are formed when a branch of a shrub is bent over and kept in contact with ground, by means of either a peg or stones, and which will grow roots at that point. When it has grown roots the branch can be cut away from the parent plant and will grow as a separate plant. Sometimes a plant will do this naturally if its branches grow along the ground, as is the case with *Cotoneaster horizontalis*. This method does require attention, however, and is not as quick or easy as taking a cutting.

Grafting and Budding are two methods of propagation best left to the nursery-man or the really enthusiastic gardener who wishes to make a study of this art. It is complicated, and needs a great deal of attention, knowledge and experience. *Propagation by division* is an easy method of acquiring a new plant from a friend. This can only be done when a shrub increases sideways and produces many stalks at the base as in the case of *Cestrum*. One or more stalks, together with their roots, are dug out of the ground, in the autumn, winter or spring, in the same way as many perennials are increased by division. This method is usually completely successful.

Size to Plant Out

Tree roots grow rapidly so that trees should be planted out as young as possible. If you have grown your own tree or shrub from seed, it follows that you will transplant it into the garden when it is much younger than any tree that you may buy.

When buying shrubs which are established in tins, they may be planted at any size as their roots are confined to the tin. It is always best not to plant trees that are too big as their roots may be pot-bound and badly tangled. It usually takes a large tree at least two seasons to establish itself and begin to fill out its foliage, so that there is not really much gain in time. Some trees, such as *Melia azedarach* (Syringa) grow more rapidly if planted when small. A large one is apt to remain static in growth for many years, while a younger one will outstrip it and also form a better shape.

The only time that it is a definite advantage to buy large specimens in tins is when they are very slow growing, and one can save a number of years, as in the case of Magnolias. But here again the shrub must not be too large in proportion to its roots.

When to Plant and Transplant

There are two definite sets of rules which apply to the planting out or trans-planting of shrubs and trees. One rule applies to *evergreen trees*, which do not lose their leaves in winter, and another rule to *deciduous trees*, which lose their leaves during the winter months.

Neither of these rules applies to trees and shrubs which are bought established in tins from nurseries, for these may be planted out at any time of the year without danger of loss. Early spring is the best time to plant any shrub, for that is the time when all growth begins and the newly planted shrub will grow and establish itself well before the following winter. Spring is the best time to plant all tender shrubs, when all danger of cold and frost is over, and they may have a whole season in which to establish themselves before the cold weather comes again.

The rules for planting out evergreens or deciduous trees apply to trees and shrubs which are being moved from the open ground, that is, when they are not in tins.

Transplanting Deciduous Trees

Many nurseries supply *deciduous trees* from the open ground. This is done only at one time of the year, in mid-winter or late winter when the sap is at its lowest and the trees are leafless and dormant. It is cheaper to buy trees from the open ground as the nurseries are saved the expense of tins and storage and pass this benefit on to the customer. Losses often occur when planting trees from the open ground when people are careless about one simple requirement. The roots must not be allowed to dry out even for a half-hour, nor must the wind or air be allowed to get at them, or they may never recover. Do not buy a tree from the open ground, therefore, unless the hole has been prepared and is waiting for the tree, or when you will not have time to plant it on arrival. Also see that the roots are covered with a wet sack until you are ready to plant. Immediately on planting, water copiously.

When transplanting deciduous trees from one part of the garden to the other, the same procedure should be followed. Before removing the tree, tie a handkerchief to mark a branch of the tree which faces north, and be sure to plant the tree in its new position with the same branch facing north. This will help to keep constant the position of the tree in relation to the sun. In transplanting, extra care is needed to dig out the tree. If the ground is very hard, water it well the day before so that it will be softened. Then dig a narrow trench around the base of the tree at a distance from the trunk, varying from 50 cm to 1 metre according to the size of the tree. In this way it is possible to see how far the roots of the tree have spread. If they are very large, the circle should be made bigger. One will have to sever some roots and it is best to cut them off cleanly with a sharp cutter. When the trench is finished the tree will remain standing with a ring of earth around it. One should now try to dig underneath this earth in order to lift the whole "ball" of earth together with the tree without disturbing it. Some soil will naturally fall away, but provided that one keeps the part immediately around the centre of the root intact, there is no danger of loss. If the roots of the tree are deep, the trench will have to be deepened, but it is nearly always necessary to sever the main roots so that the tree can be handled easily, and this can usually be done with safety.

The nurseries usually cut back the branches of the tree to balance the cutting back of the roots, and this serves the double purpose of allowing root growth to compete with leaf growth in the spring and to allow for easy transport and storage. In one's own garden, however, this need not be done, as it frequently spoils the shape. Only very small twiggy growths need be removed, unless the tree is really very big, in which case it can be cut back more severely.

Transplanting Evergreens

Evergreen trees are never supplied by nurserymen from the open ground in South Africa, as they would never survive. In moist countries like Japan or in coastal areas of the northern hemisphere, large evergreen trees are uprooted and replanted with the aid of special machinery. They are generally prepared for a year or two in advance by trenching and root-pruning in stages, then boxing or balling the roots before the tree is finally severed from the earth at the base. In very moist places such as parts of Florida, U.S.A., it is unnecessary to make preparations in advance for transplanting. If evergreens are to be transplanted from one part of the garden to the other, this should be done in spring or early summer and during rainy weather, and they should not be too large.

After transplanting, evergreens require even more water than deciduous trees as the fact that the leaves are always on the tree makes them lose water more rapidly. It has been proved that the leaves pull up water from the roots like a magnet, and that this is not pumped up from below. Also the leaves "transpire" or lose their water by evaporation. During normal growth the leaves draw up as much water as they need, but the transplanted root system is not able to continue this flow uninterruptedly, for it must first establish itself. In the short time that it takes for the root system to start performing its work efficiently once more, the leaves may wither and die, and not being there to draw up the sap, the sap may die down too. Unless the plant is watered copiously, it may die altogether.

It is important, therefore, to slow up evaporation from the leaves so that they do not demand a great deal of water from the root system, at least for a while until the shrub has established itself. The moisture in the air during the rainy weather, as well as the falling rain, will slow up evaporation. In addition, the leaves can be sprayed with water when the rain stops, but most important of all, the shrub should be given a continuous supply of water trickling from the hosepipe, for 24 hours at a stretch if necessary. The soil should be saturated to a considerable depth. This treatment should be continued until one can see an obvious sign that the shrub has "taken". This may be seen by the growth of a new leaf. Scratching the bark to see whether the tree is green underneath is definitely a sign of life but in the case of evergreens, one must wait until a leaf grows before ceasing one's vigilance.

Frequently the leaves of evergreens will wither or die in a day or two as there has not been enough food supply, but one must continue to water copiously until the shrub has taken. Do not pull out a transplanted evergreen when it looks as if it has died. Care for it for several months, or even a complete season, and eventually you may encourage the sap to rise and it may send out a new strong shoot from the base. There is nothing like a number of days of rain to help an evergreen to re-establish itself in a new environment.

When transplanting evergreens, as with deciduous trees, the same system of digging around the trunk should be employed. Here, however, it is so important to retain the ball of earth around the roots, that this should be wrapped with hessian which is preferably dampened, and tied securely with string before digging underneath the tree. As the root is severed at the bottom, and the tree is tipped over to one side, more hessian should be wrapped around the base in order to prevent the soil from falling away. The tree is now "balled", and can be planted with the hessian around it. The hessian will rot in time and the tree roots will grow through it, but this does help to prevent any dislodging of the delicate root hairs which are so necessary for the absorption of water through the roots. With evergreens, it is all a question of how quickly the tree can establish its normal routine of water absorption.

Cutting back of evergreens is usually recommended so that there will be fewer leaves to supply with food and water, and there will, therefore, be less of a strain on the root system. There is a danger in cutting back evergreens indiscriminately, as many evergreens, such as Magnolias, thoroughly dislike pruning and one can do more harm by cutting back such a shrub than not. Stripping off most of the leaves would be a better idea in such cases.

Nothing gives the gardener a greater thrill than to transplant a tree or shrub successfully, but one should be prepared for the risks involved. As trees become older and larger, it becomes increasingly difficult to transplant them. The size at which one can transplant varies with each tree. A Eucalyptus should not be transplanted when it has grown larger than 1 metre, while an Oak tree can be transplanted up to 5 metres or more. Generally speaking, one can transplant deciduous trees almost up to any size, while evergreens are best transplanted when small. Some trees which have deep taproots will not transplant unless they are very tiny, while fibrous-rooted trees are quite easy to handle. One can see, there-fore, that there is a risk involved in transplanting, which should not be done unless it is absolutely necessary, for even the most expertly transplanted tree will suffer a setback and slow down in growth for a while until it is completely established. It is always safer to transplant established shrubs from tins as this ensures no loss.

How to Plant

The ground should always be well prepared before planting.

Preparing the Ground

There is a controversy about digging holes for trees and shrubs as some say that this disturbs the sub-soil. Where the soil is known to be rich and deep, then one can dig small holes, but if the ground is hard, gravelly, consists of shale, rocks or poor soil, it seems ridiculous not to prepare the ground so that the tree can thrive for the first few years of its life until its root system grows beyond the limits of the hole prepared for it and can carry on growing from there. It is surprising what small roots some trees do have. I transplanted an 8-year-old Oak, and found the root span to be only 1,5 metres and the depth 60 cm. Some people believe that square holes are better than round holes as this encourages the roots to penetrate into the corners and out into the surrounding area, instead of encircling the main root in a round hole. The shape of the hole is not of great importance if the soil is reasonably good and not rock hard.

The hole should be prepared with compost which is always excellent. Manure can also be used at the bottom of the hole. In the case of fast growing trees, this may be foolish according to some, but at least it carries the young tree through the first few years and stimulates faster growth.

The size of the hole varies with the gardener's energy. The site for this particular Oak tree was rocky and poor, so we dug a hole nearly 3 metres square and 2 metres deep and removed all the rocks. Then we filled up with sub-soil, manure and good top-soil mixed with compost. After planting the tree we put the hose-pipe on it for 2 days, night and day, until the ground was saturated. We continued to water twice a week for several hours at a stretch until the tree put on its first leaves in the spring and for a month afterwards. Later we reduced the time of watering, merely filling the large "basin" made around the tree twice a week. This may sound extreme, but the Oak thrived and bore acorns where before, neglected and never watered, it had never done. This treatment shows the extreme to which the gardener will go to pamper his treasures.

The average hole should be at least 1 metre across and the same depth. *Drainage* should be provided at the bottom in the form of a layer of small stones several inches thick. There are some who say that this is unnecessary as the water cannot drain further. It is true that one could make a perfectly drained spot by constructing a bank, several feet high, built on a foundation of rubbish and stones, but this is not always possible. For practical purposes, we should try and provide a certain amount of drainage, which, even if it is useful only for the first few years of the shrub's life, will have helped towards its establishment. This is especially important if the soil is not well-drained naturally.

The bottom half of the hole should be filled with soil and manure mixed. Use the sub-soil if it is not too poor and gravelly, otherwise substitute with ordinary garden soil. The manure will enrich the bottom soil and stimulate the shrub when its roots reach it in the following seasons. The top half of the hole should consist of good garden soil mixed generously with compost.

Planting

First put down a 10 cm layer of the mixture of compost and soil on top of the manured soil, so that the shrub roots will not come in contact with the manure for some time, and then pile the centre of the soil into a small mound. Place the shrub or tree on top of this mound with its roots spreading outwards and downwards and cover with a layer of soil mixed with compost. Press this well down so that soil enters into all the spaces between the roots. It must be remembered that the roots absorb water through their tiny root-hairs, and these must be in close contact with the earth, or they will shrivel in a vacuum of air. Then begin to fill up the hole with the remaining soil and compost, stopping half-way to tramp the soil well down all around and up to the base of the stem. The tree will now be firmly planted in the ground and it will not be possible to dislodge its position easily. Finish off with the soil level at the top.

Do not plant the shrub deeper than it was planted before. The mark on the stem where the soil reached before is quite easily seen, for the bark is a different colour. Trees and shrubs planted too deeply might die months or even years after planting.

See that the soil level of the hole is slightly below that of the surrounding soil or lawn. This forms a "basin" in which the water can collect and aids watering.

Immediately after planting, without losing any time, the shrub must be thoroughly soaked with water. The equivalent of 2 buckets of water must be given and, in the case of a transplanted tree, the hosepipe should be left to trickle slowly into the hole for several hours.

This applies to trees planted out from the open ground or transplanted. When shrubs are bought from the nursery already established in tins, the procedure is slightly different. Prepare the hole in exactly the same way as before, with the manured soil in the bottom half of the hole. Meanwhile soak the tin with water so that it is thoroughly damp. This is most important as no amount of watering afterwards will penetrate the solid block of soil and really soak it. This also prevents tearing the delicate roots away from the sides of the tin. Then cut away the tin with a sharp pair of tin-snips or a tin opener. Cut down all 4 corners of the tin, so that the sides can be opened flat, being careful not to damage the roots of the plant. Plants are often supplied in black plastic containers that may be torn apart easily.

Then lift the complete "ball" of earth gently and place it on top of the layer of soil and compost, trying not to let any of it crumble off. Fill up all round with the remaining soil and compost as before, tramping it down firmly in the same way. There is no need to worry about the level of planting, as the level of the soil in the tin should be the correct level. Let the hosepipe trickle into the hole as before, until the ground is thoroughly saturated.

There is practically no risk of losing a shrub planted out in this way as the root system is not disturbed. It is only when the roots are roughly handled and not well watered that a shrub is lost. Some shrubs such as *Leptospermum*, the Australian Tea-Tree, so dislike their roots to be handled, that many people merely cut off the bottom of the tin and plant the shrub with the sides of the tin encasing its roots. In time the tin will rot and the roots will grow through it, but if the few simple instructions above are carried out, there need be no risk of loss.

Watering

Although the soil should be soaked thoroughly at the beginning, the top surface must be allowed to dry out before watering the young shrub again, otherwise the tiny air spaces in the soil will be filled with water instead of oxygen, so that the roots will rot and the plant will die. Always allow the top surface to dry out before applying water once more. Keep the surface from drying out by placing a mulch over it. (see Chapter IV)

Where soil conditions are very dry, and where water supplies and labour are limited, one can insert a wide hollow pipe into the hole when planting the tree, so that the top projects above ground and the base rests on a few stones and does not become clogged with soil. A bucket of water can be poured down the pipe so as to benefit the roots directly and economically.

Staking

Any shrub or small tree that has a slender stem should be staked at first. The stake should be placed in the ground at the same time as the tree is planted, for it might damage the roots if driven into the ground at a later date. Place the stake alongside the tree before the roots are covered with soil. Then fill in the soil firmly around both the tree and the stake. In this way the stake will be as firmly planted in the earth as the tree and will not bend in the wind.

Do not tie the stake closely to the stem of the young tree, for as it grows, the twine will cut into the bark and cut off the supply of food to the leaves, so that the tree may die eventually. More suddenly, the tree will snap off in a strong wind, the stem being literally sawn off by the twine. Wrap a piece of hessian around the stem and tie a piece of twine around it. Then tie the other end of the twine around the stake, keeping the stem erect. All too often people see that the stake, and not the stem of the tree, is erect. One should remove the hessian every 6 months and re-tie it in a different spot. This enables the trunk to grow evenly and prevents damage to the bark which may leave an entry for disease. As soon as the trunk thickens and the tree is sturdy enough to stand by itself, remove the stake altogether.

Two or 3 stakes, at a small distance apart on the one side of the tree, are often necessary when the tree is tall or top-heavy. Take particular notice of the prevailing winds and support the tree so that the wind cannot bend it over, by placing the stakes on the same side as the direction from which the wind blows. Many people allow their trees to grow in their natural bushy form without forming a "standard" and these trees will seldom require staking.

CHAPTER IV

GENERAL CARE

"Shrubs are easy"

A friend of mine once said, "Every time I plant a shrub, I know that there is another spot in the garden that I don't have to worry about." This may be a little extreme, but it is perfectly true that one could almost forget about a shrub and that it will survive.

It is amazing how much neglect a shrub can stand and still manage to survive. A gardener I met recently, showed me her 2-metre-high *Tecoma stans*, and comparing it with another one on the other side of the house which stood 6 metres high, said, "I'm afraid that it is rather slow. We found it this size when we bought the house and it has hardly grown since." I asked a simple question, "Do you water it much?" "Why, no!" came the surprised answer. "I don't think that we've ever given it a drop of water!" We both smiled, for further comment was unnecessary.

The most important time to look after a shrub is when it is first planted, and for a few years afterwards until it is completely established. It is easy to see the difference between a neglected and a continuously well-cared-for shrub, and this care makes all the difference between a pleasing garden and an unattractive one.

Shrubs ask for very little. They ask to be planted in the right position, whether it be in the sun or in the shade; they ask for sufficient water and they would appreciate a little extra feeding once or twice a year. Some need to be pruned occasionally and they rarely suffer from pests and diseases. Some have extra requirements, such as an acid soil, which are easy to provide.

In return, they are inexpensive to buy and to maintain. They give the gardener the biggest value for his money in the garden, for once they are bought they are permanent and there is no further expense attached to them. Their value as far as beauty is concerned, and the fact that they take up space which would otherwise have to be filled with annuals, perennials, and other features, is inestimable. No garden is complete without shrubs.

The success of a shrub really depends on the care given to it and its position in the garden. There is no mystery about the successful gardener, and "green-fingers" are only attributed to those who study what each shrub needs and go to the trouble of providing it. That there is an art in planting will not be denied, but a few simple rules carried out will ensure success, and are well worth the trouble when one obtains a beautiful and healthy shrub.

WATERING

The secret of a garden that boasts healthy and luxuriant growth, is good, deep watering. It is a necessity, and no amount of fertiliser or manure can compensate for the lack of it.

Proper watering means watering in imitation of a big, soaking rain. It is useless to sprinkle the top 5 cm of the soil, or the roots which are deep down will turn upwards seeking for water, and the plant will eventually die through inability to "take root" as well as through actual lack of moisture.

When watering, give each shrub at least two large buckets of water. Let the one sink in, and then pour over the other bucket. The water will really sink down to root level and keep the earth below damp for a few days. If one must water with a hosepipe, let the hosepipe fill each bucket before you pour it over the base of the shrub, so as to give you an idea of how much water is required. Alternatively, while busy working elsewhere in the garden, allow the hosepipe to trickle slowly into the "basin" around each shrub until it is full to overflowing and then change the hosepipe to the next shrub.

It is essential to see that each shrub has a "basin" consisting of a rim of earth made around it, so that the water collects in one spot and then sinks down into the earth, and is not allowed to trickle away over the surface. It is essential to see that these basins are always maintained, as most of our gardens are watered by untrained or inexperienced gardeners, and this ensures that each shrub or tree is peoperly watered.

As a general rule, each shrub should receive this type of watering twice a week, especially before it has grown to full size. If it is impossible to water twice a week then once a week will do, provided that it is a very deep watering. In times of drought and heat, however, every effort should be made to water twice a week in this way. When the shrub has grown to full size, it may require less water if its roots are deep and it can find the moisture that usually lingers in the earth where the sun's rays cannot penetrate. Shrubs and trees have been known to survive with scarcely a watering, depending on the rainfall to carry them through, but these are generally poor specimens and wear an air of neglect. Even if one cannot water shrubs regularly throughout the year, one should always try and water them when they make their buds and when they flower. This will prolong the flowering time and give them water when they need it most.

Mulching

One can keep the soil moist for long periods by placing thick *mulches* of various kinds on the surface around the shrubs. This keeps the roots cool and helps to withstand drought. The mulches should be 10 cm thick in order to be really effective and consist of dry leaves, decayed grass cuttings, rough compost, husks, sawdust or other organic materials. Always add nitrogen to damp soil before putting down these half-decayed organic mulches, as they will rob the plants of oxygen while breaking down themselves. Inert materials like black plastic strips covered with a layer of stones may be used, but stone mulches are rather forbidding in appearance. It is important to choose a mulch which looks attractive.

Shrubs which are planted in the lawn require special attention. It has been proved that the grass deprives the shrub of water as well as oxygen. One can help those shrubs which are set in the lawn to overcome any harmful effects by being particularly careful to water them very heavily, and at least twice a week if possible. Also one should cut a ring out of the lawn so that the soil is not covered over and suffocated by the grass. A circle of about 60 cm in diameter is large enough for most shrubs, and can be made larger in proportion to the size and spread of the shrub. This circle must be maintained and clipped constantly, or the grass will grow over it very quickly.

FEEDING

Further care means keeping weeds down and keeping the ground around your shrubs fresh and clean. Loosening soil around the shrubs in a good way of letting in moisture and air, but this is dangerous in the case of surface-rooting shrubs such as Rhododendrons, which will be killed by digging around their roots. Special selective weedkillers may be used for such special plants.

The best way to keep the soil moist, cool and in good condition is to put a thick mulch of compost around the base of each shrub. This can be administered several times throughout the year. The compost helps to improve the soil, as well as conserve moisture. Other mulches are also effective.

Once a year, usually at the end of winter, place half a wheel-barrow of well-rotted manure around the base of each tree and water it in. This can be repeated in mid-summer if possible. Do not allow the manure to touch the bark of the tree. Compost containing manure may be used instead.

A mature tree that has been neglected can be given a new lease of life by applying a balanced chemical fertilizer to the whole root area. Punch holes, 45 cm deep, in well dampened soil under the branches of the tree, with the aid of an iron bar, spacing them about 60 cm apart and keeping them 60 cm away from the trunk. Use 1 kilogram of fertiliser to each 2,5 cm of the trunk's diameter and pour it in equal amounts into the holes. Fill the holes with water and then with compost or good soil.

PRUNING

Pruning is the subject of a book in itself, but the average gardener needs to know only a few simple things about it in order to keep his shrubs and trees in trim.

Why to Prune

One must know the reasons for pruning before proceeding further. The practice of pruning fruit trees and rose bushes in order to improve fruit and flowers is well-known, but it is also possible to improve the flowers on many shrubs by pruning. An obvious example is the Buddleia which, left unpruned, produces miserable flowers and deteriorates rapidly in appearance, even in a single season. This happens to be one of those shrubs which likes to be pruned very severely. Here the number of flowers will not necessarily be increased, but the quality will be excellent and the growth will also be vigorous, so that the flowers will really be numerous as well. Pruning stimulates the growth of new branches as well as flowers. A shrub that has remained static in growth will sometimes spring up after pruning.

Dead branches in trees are Nature's way of providing light and air for new growth, so that by thinning out superfluous growth we can give the shrub a better chance to grow vigorously. At the same time we prevent unsightliness caused by tangled and untidy growth, especially in winter when there are no leaves to hide the bare branches.

Pruning helps to keep the shape of the bush by checking uneven or straggling growth. By cutting off the bottom branches of certain shrubs, one can form a standard or trunk instead of allowing the shrub to bush out from the ground. This is, of course, a matter of taste, but in many cases lack of space dictates that shrubs should be trained upwards with a standard, while in others this is definitely desirable.

Pruning helps to keep size in check and prevent some shrubs from overgrowing others. In this case it would have been better not to plant a large shrub where it is not wanted, but sometimes a shrub will outgrow one's expectations and must be kept in check. Continual trimming is necessary here rather than a complete cutting back.

Pruning removes parts that will not flower again in some shrubs. Weigela, for example, always flowers on new growth, so that the old previous year's growth should be cut away after flowering, as it only looks hideous in winter and prevents those beautiful long flowering branches from forming. Pruning also assists us in training creepers to grow where we wish them to. The vigorous stems can be encouraged to grow in a set pattern while the superfluous growth is always cut away. Creepers can be trained upwards and sideways on the wall of a house or up the pillars of a pergola. A creeper such as Wisteria can be pruned to form a standard and grown in the open in the form of a shrub.

Pruning after transplanting has been discussed in Chapter III. Here the top growth of a tree has been pruned back and the root has also been pruned, so that the whole tree can start growing afresh. Root pruning is a drastic method used to encourage better fruit when branch pruning has failed and to check the top wood growth of a badly pruned tree. A trench is dug around a young tree about 1 metre from its base and the roots are trimmed off cleanly. With an older tree one should trench only half a circle each successive year and also place it at a greater distance from the trunk of the tree.

One cannot generalise too much about pruning, however, as some shrubs require very little pruning or are so tidy in growth that they do not need it at all. Others, such as Magnolias, so dislike pruning that one can do more harm than good by cutting them.

It is best, therefore, to prune only when really necessary, and not to wield the clippers indiscriminately. One should study the requirements of each shrub in the descriptive lists before deciding to cut it.

When to Prune
Deciduous trees are usually pruned, like fruit trees and roses, during mid-winter when the sap is lowest.

Unfortunately, many deciduous shrubs like *Philadelphus*, the Mock-orange, flower in spring on young wood, and pruning in winter will cut away all the flowering wood. With many spring-flowering shrubs, therefore, it is best to prune in early summer, or immediately after the shrub has flowered. The branches which have just flowered will then be cut off, and new growth will spring up vigorously, ready to flower in the following spring. For the amateur gardener this has a definite advantage, for he is able to pick branches of his shrubs quite freely for the vase, knowing that he is benefiting the shrub. Weigela, cut with long stems, lasts for several days in the vase and is most decorative, so that it is a great pleasure to prune or pick it. One may inspect spring-flowering shrubs like *Forsythia* and *Philadelphus* towards the end of summer and remove old wood, so as to allow the young strong wood that will flower well to take over.

Evergeen shrubs often continue to flower throughout the year. The golden rule to observe is that one should prune immediately after flowering, particularly when there seems to be no special time for the shrub to be dormant.

Pruning should take place more than just once a year. Summer pruning is very useful and weak growths can be cut off before they grow too long so that the sap is directed into making the strong growths stronger. One should not, however, remove a large quantity of leaves at the same time. The shrub needs its leaves for healthy growth, which is the best insurance against disease. If you do summer pruning, therefore, do it over a period of weeks or even months, especially when a shrub needs only slight pruning. In the early summer, while growth is still rapid, it does not hurt to cut back those spring-flowering shrubs that need hard cutting.

Tender trees and shrubs should be pruned only when all danger from frost is over. The frost will often prune them for the gardener by cutting them back. In this case, one should merely cut off the damaged growth, improving the shape if necessary. The more old wood that can be left on a tender shrub, the less likely will it be to succumb from frost in the following winter.

How to Prune

Any cuts which are made must be sharp and clean and made with a special strong cutter. One should really wipe the cutter with a rag dipped in disinfectant in order to prevent carrying disease from one shrub to another, if one is a perfectionist.

Do not cut at any place in the stem, but always look for the joint between stem and leaf and cut just above that. There is always a little bud hidden at the point from which the leaf grows from the stem, and this will be stimulated by the cutting to grow into a new stem. As this is the case, one should also try to arrange for the new stems to grow in the required direction. In other words, if one wishes the new stem to grow outwards, one should cut above a leaf or bud that faces outwards, and if one wishes the new branch to grow to one side, one should try and cut above a leaf that points towards the required side.

Sometimes one must cut off a complete branch or stem. In this case, take no notice of leaves, but cut right back against the old wood, without leaving a stump if possible. Large branches must sometimes be sawn off. Use a special light saw and try not to damage any nearby bark by cutting into it or it will make an entry for disease. A heavy branch will often fall half-way through the sawing operation and tear a strip of bark off the trunk of the tree. This damage is unnecessary, for it can be prevented. First make a cut upwards underneath the branch and then saw down to meet it. If the weight of the branch makes it fall, the tear will go no further, and one can neaten the ragged edge of the tear when the branch is removed. After cutting a branch anything over 2 cm in diameter, it is best to paint this with tree-sealing compound in order to prevent the entry of insects or disease.

Tree Surgery

Careful pruning, as described above, which aims to prevent disease, is a form of tree surgery and this term is also applied to re-shaping neglected or old trees or repairing trees when branches have been broken off or the bark damaged.

Branches must be neatly sawn off without leaving stumps or removing too much bark and the exposed area painted over with sealing compound. Large branches which are beginning to split may be bolted together by drilling a rod through the branches and bolting it into place. Do not tie wire or chains around the branches as these will cut into the bark. Branches which rub together can be kept apart by bracing them with an iron rod. Cavities may be repaired by cleaning out decay and painting the exposed surface with a fungicide and then with tree-sealing compound. Further decay may be prevented by filling the cavity with concrete containing 2 parts of sand to 1 of cement. This must be rammed in well and finished off inside the cambium layer so that the bark will grow over the edge of the filling. These methods should only be used if the tree is an important specimen or part of a planting scheme, otherwise it is better to plant a new one.

Prevent injury to trees by treating them well. Do not use trees as a support for wire fences and do not scrape the bark with the lawn-mower. Water even mature trees in times of severe drought and destroy insect pests before they cause too much damage. Do not use too many insecticides or any weed-killers in the soil near a tree and do not allow motor oil to seep over the surface. Do not allow clinging vines to grow on all the branches of the tree as they deprive the bark of light and air, but keep them to one side and do not allow them to climb too high. Keep the soil area aerated by not paving the entire surface around a tree and do not pile soil around the trunk if one is changing the level, but build an encircling low wall to allow for air circulation (this is called a tree "well") and place a layer of loose stones over the root area before piling on the soil, so as to encourage aeration.

PESTS AND DISEASES

The best insurance against pests and diseases is healthy growth. Prevention is definitely better than cure, and if one can only be bothered to give the shrub its requirements as far as watering, feeding and position are concerned, there will seldom be any need for treating its diseases.

Shrubs are like people in that a healthy person will not catch diseases as quickly as a person who is run-down. If your shrubs are kept clean and free from weeds and tangled growth, if they are fed occasionally and watered sufficiently, and if their position has been chosen with care, there is no reason why they should ever become diseased, unless this disease spreads from another plant or the individual shrub has a tendency to get such disease. For example, citrus is inclined to get scale. When shrubs are planted with an adequate amount of compost, they will grow with such vigour that they can repair the ravages of pests as well as resist disease in the first place.

Fertile soil will stimulate growth of shrubs and trees and organic fertilizers will restore the fertility of the soil. Fertilizers derived from living material include guano, bone or fishmeal.

One very seldom sees shrubs which are attacked by pests or diseases and this is one of the reasons that makes them so easy to maintain. If a shrub is attacked by scale or by that most hideous of insects, the soft, white, woolly-bodied Australian bug, then one must certainly spray it and clean it. Simply treating it to be rid of the insect, however, is not enough. It is like treating a disease without enquiring into the causes. The Australian bug, for example, is definitely a manifestation that the shrub is unhappy. Something is wrong, and unless it is corrected, the shrub will continue to be subject to attack by the pest and to be unsightly, a nuisance to care for, and a danger to the other shrubs near it through risk of infection.

One must enquire into the likes and dislikes of a shrub that is infected in this way. A Showy Hebe that I had growing in a tub on the verandah—in fact it baked in the hot sun—was attacked by Australian bug. When it was transplanted to a partially shaded and airy spot under a tree (after being sprayed intensively) it recuperated and has been doing well ever since. It may be quite a small thing that disturbs the shrub and lays it open to attack. It may be that a sun-loving shrub is planted in the shade; one shrub may be parched for water, another may not have enough drainage. A study of the requirements of each shrub will probably give the clue to the cause of its trouble. When planting in the first place, one should insure against disease by using as much well-made compost as possible. Nevertheless, insects spread disease, as well as attack and eventually destroy shrubs if they are left undisturbed. One must, therefore, keep them down as much as possible. There are certain common pests and diseases which should be controlled either by destruction or by prevention. These are mentioned briefly below and the commercial remedies described will help the gardener to keep his shrubs reasonably clean and free from disease. Prompt treatment will prevent any serious development of disease.

Green or black aphids and all *soft-bodied sucking insects* should be sprayed with a contact spray such as nicotine sulphate and soapy water in the heat of the day, mercaptothion (Malathion) or systemic insecticides like oxydemeton methyl (Metasystox). If these insects are not removed the flowers will be spoilt and the shrub will eventually be damaged. Australian bug is not penetrated by a nicotine spray, but by mercaptothion or a mineral oil spray and other *scale insects* may be controlled in the same way.

Chewing insects, such as caterpillars should be killed by using carbaryl and beetles may be controlled, when seen in summer, with carbaryl or, in some cases, with marcaptothion.

Wood-eating termites may be repelled by working γ-B.H.C. dust into the soil.

Ordinary *ants*, which disturb ladybirds that eat aphids, may be kept away by watering chlordane into the soil, mixing it into the soil on the surface, or spraying the base of the tree.

Fungus diseases sometimes attack shrubs and are blown by the wind on to healthy plants. These are indicated by spots or blotches on the leaves and include such diseases as rust or scab, as well as many hundreds of others. One can do little more for the plant than remove or burn the affected or dead portions, but preventative measures should be used in order to keep one's shrubs free from fungus diseases. Spraying in the spring, just before the leaves open, with fixed copper sprays or some of the new organic fungicides like Zineb and Maneb, is recommended. Bordeaux misture is another universal disinfectant for fungus, and one may also spray with lime-sulphur on deciduous trees in winter. This should be done during cool weather only, as lime-sulphur has been known to burn trees if it is used in hot weather.

Powdery mildew is a disease which is caused by a fungus and often occurs in shady gardens. It is indicated by a white, mealy-like appearance on the foliage and should be subjected to a very intensive spraying campaign with sulphur dusts or sprays, started from the beginning of the rainy season. One should try to improve ventilation.

In general, shrubs are delightfully hardy and nothing seems to bother them. When they are attacked by pests or diseases they can be treated successfully with one or other of the many commercial sprays and powders that are obtainable. Always remember, however, that once the disease is difficult to destroy and if it occurs again and again, one must look deeper into the requirements of the shrub and see if there is not something one can do to improve the general care given to it by the gardener. If we give our shrubs and trees a small amount of attention, we can be sure that they will repay us a thousand-fold with years of beauty, luxuriant growth and shade even during times of drought.

CHAPTER V

LAY-OUT OF THE GARDEN

"If you want to be happy for ever, make a garden"—Old Chinese Proverb

Making a garden involves planning the garden first. Planning a garden is so much a matter of individual taste that it is impossible to advocate any fixed plan for the gardener to follow. Many books have been written on the subject of garden planning, and one can obtain ideas by reading and by visiting tastefully designed gardens everywhere.

The principles of planning a garden remain the same all over the world. Stiff, formal gardens have gone out of fashion, together with Victorian and pre-war conventions, and the modern gardener aims at more natural effects in the garden. Certain parts of the garden will always be more formal than others, such as the geometrically planned rose garden, but the approach to this should be softened, if possible, by a winding path, rustic steps or an arbour of climbing roses.

The garden should be made part of the house, and planned with the same care, so that it is always a pleasure to walk out into the garden. The lawn is basic, connects the house and garden, and should be planted right up against the house if possible. Driveways are essential, but should be planned so that at least part of the lawn grows up to the front verandah, as this adds greatly to the feeling of easy access to the garden and encourages the people of the house to wander out into the garden, instead of merely "sitting on the stoep." A paved or brick-inlaid pathway can be laid across the lawn from verandah to driveway, so that one's shoes are protected in wet weather, and this should take a winding course across the lawn, or be laid straight up against the side of the house.

The garden must now be "furnished" much in the same way as the living room of the house. No one would think of arranging vases of flowers in a room empty of furniture and be satisfied with the interior decoration. The analogy can be followed in the garden, where the lawns represent the carpet, and shrubs and trees are the essential furniture of the garden that offset the temporary and everchanging colours of the flowers. A garden that is empty of shrubs and trees is flat and empty of interest, for they alone accent the attractions of parts of the garden with height and colour and can be used with tremendous artistic effect. Naturally, this depends on the taste of the gardener and some gardens will always be more artistic than others, but in the same way as everyone furnishes their own home, so is it fun to furnish the garden with shrubs and trees.

Start by planning the planting up against the house. This helps to soften the hard lines of the building. The choicest shrubs, such as purple Magnolia or Gardenia, can be planted in the lawn near the house, and if the house is facing north, or has some warm corners made by its walls, advantage should be taken of these by placing in them shrubs which require protection from frost or wind. Brazilian Glory Bush, Hibiscus and Poinsettia are shrubs which benefit from protection in areas which have cold winters, and are often seen growing against the walls of the house. Similarly, one should not forget to take advantage of the other walls of the house. Facing east one could plant dainty Lemon-Verbena, which has an unsurpassed fragrance, as well as French or English Lavender, English Lilac, and sweet-smelling Daphne amongst others. Facing south one should take advantage of the shade in order to plant Hydrangeas, Fuchsias and hardy shrubs like Wintersweet. Rhododendrons can also be planted on the south, provided that the walls are not lime-washed. (See Chapter on Soil Conditions). West is always a difficult wall, as few shrubs enjoy the heat of the late afternoon sun, although nearly all hardy shrubs will grow there, such as Hypericum and Escallonia. Some tender shrubs will also do well facing west, provided that there is some protection from cold winds. In addition to those shrubs which have a definite preference for warmth or shade, almost any hardy shrubs can be planted against the house, depending on individual choice.

Creepers, too, should be used to advantage against the sides of the house. One should try and choose those with the most attractive flowers. The Bignonias are always popular. This includes the beautiful reddish-purple Mexican Blood-trumpet or Bignonia cherere (*Phaedranthus buccinatorius*). Wisteria is magnificent on the wall of a double-storey house and there are many others which will be listed later.

Many people are afraid to plant against the house, particularly if it is situated in a low position, for fear that the foundations will be affected by the damp. Most modern houses are damp-proofed, but it is possible to construct a narrow pathway, about one metre wide, slightly sloping away from the walls of the house towards the garden, and plant the shrubs and lawn on the edge of that. Eventually the shrubs will grow and spread over the pathway so that they still soften the lines of the house. In addition, one should dig down and provide as much drainage as possible in the form of rubble under the bed, so that the water will drain away to below the level of the foundations of the house.

Apart from the planting near the house, *it is desirable to have unbroken lawn stretching for a good distance from the house*. This gives a park-like effect and a feeling of space, such as one cannot have when the centre of the lawn is pierced with formal beds of flowers. At this point one should consider the view of the garden as it appears from the house. Concentrate flower beds at the far edge of the lawn, backed by plantings of shrubs wherever possible. This leafy background of shrubs will offset the colours of the flowers and at the same time provide colour itself, as each carefully chosen flowering shrub reveals its own beauty. Here and there a bed can be cut for flowers, but it should be on the edges of the lawn, never in the middle, bordering driveways and pathways and its position will be determined by the planning and placing of the shrubs and trees.

If one has an idea of the *uses of trees and shrubs*, one can place them to the best advantage. The idea of a "*shrubbery*" where every shrub is planted at equal distances from the others, vigorous and weak ones together, and left to struggle in dusty obscurity, is thoroughly repellent. If one could remember that it is a good thing to plant shrubs together in groups, and yet arrange them in such a way that each shrub is set to show-up like a jewel as an individual specimen of beauty, then the "shrubbery" can be attractive.

Two things are essential in order to attain this end. Firstly, one must know the approximate space that each shrub will occupy when it is fully grown, in other words, its width as well as height; and secondly, one should not plant shrubs more than two rows deep, or those at the back will be obscured. If one knows the size of the shrub, one will allow it sufficient space to grow to full size and not make the common fault of planting the shrubs so closely that they soon become a tangle which is neither beautiful nor healthy, on account of the competition for light and air. If shrubs grow large and are quick, it follows that they will be vigorous and prevent the slower-growing shrub from doing well if they are too near to it. The size of the shrub also governs which shrubs can be planted near the house.

When planting two rows of shrubs, one should place the taller shrubs at the back and the shorter ones in front, and should "stagger" the rows so that no shrub is planted directly in front of the other. One could plant three "rows" if the ones in front are extremely low. Avoid uniformity and stiffness as much as possible. It is quite a good idea to use this method on the *boundary, instead of the hedge* so frequently used. In this case, one should attempt to plant the evergreen shrubs and trees on the edge near the street and the deciduous ones facing the house, so that there are no gaps in winter when the latter lose their leaves. In all cases, see that any one very large specimen is given sufficient space so that it will not prevent the growth of the others or this shrubbery will not give the desired privacy.

Even when a formal hedge is used, it is still very effective to plant two "rows" of shrubs and trees immediately inside it, allowing them enough space so that they can grow to full size without touching each other. The ground between them need not appear barren, as this is the ideal place to grow perennials and shade-loving plants such as Agapanthus, Fox-gloves or Thalictrum as well as the smaller shade-loving shrubs such as Fuchsias. Colourful annuals or perennials can be planted to emerge into the sunshine. Edge this "glade" with an irregular, undulating line, and the lawn can continue back into the garden from the border edge.

In this way flowering shrubs and trees provide variety, interest and colour in the garden. Too often one sees the unimaginative line of Deodars on the boundary of gardens where one single specimen, offset by other contrasting foliage, would be far more effective. In the small garden, where space is limited, the gardener should try not to repeat the same shrub too often, so that there is the opportunity to plant a larger variety of the attractive flowering shrubs that are available. Do not choose only short trees and shrubs for the small garden, but tall, slim trees that do not require much space at ground level. These will add important height and variety, as well as mask the sight of telegraph poles and neighbouring roofs.

Shrubs should be used to *separate one part of the garden from the other.* One of the secrets of making a garden appear bigger is to separate it into portions, so that the whole garden cannot be taken in at a glance. Different levels also help to achieve this purpose. Plant shrubs along the top of a bank so that one cannot see the lower part of the garden until one descends into it. After descending steps, border the path with flower beds backed by shrubs, so that one has to walk around the corner to see the portion of garden behind the shrubs. Separate the orchard and vegetable garden from the rest of the garden with shrubs such as Cotoneaster. Ring a large piece of lawn with shrubs to make the children's garden, enclosing sand-pit and swing. In this way shrubs will give a "cosiness" and privacy to the garden, as well as making it look most luxuriant with all the extra leafy growth even when the shrubs are not flowering.

Instead of the conventional hedge that forms the background of the herbaceous border, *let different shrubs form the background,* and add to the colour of the border with their own flowers. Small flowering trees may be used as part of the border planting. Naturally, they should be planted at least a metre behind the rest of the perennials, or these might suffer.

Shrubs can be used as hedges of different sizes. One sees many hedges of Pittosporum in the Cape. These are apt to become a little "leggy" but have a most attractive fresh green foliage. *Abelia grandiflora* makes a pretty flowering hedge, and the bright Pyracantha berries, both red and orange, are so popular in Johannesburg as to be almost commonplace.

Within the garden itself, small shrubs can be used to make low hedges to separate parts of the garden from each other. French Lavender and Rosemary are both evergreen and have an erect and tidy habit which makes them ideal for hedges that do not need clipping. Ceratostigma makes a delightful shrubby hedge with deep blue flowers, which compensates for the fact that it is deciduous with its attractive, russet, autumn colours.

Shrubs can be used in rockeries and will soften the rocks as will nothing else. Those with a hanging nature, like trailing Lantana, are particularly valuable for draping over the rocks and giving the rockery a well-grown appearance. Cotoneaster is a graceful shrub for a large rockery and *Erythrina crista-gallii* is at home amongst the rocks, having rather a wild and grotesque appearance. Rockeries, like borders, always look better with a background of shrubs.

One should consider which shrubs are evergreen and which deciduous when planning the garden. It is pleasant to keep the evergreen shrubs near the house, so that all should not look too bare in winter, but this really applies only to low-growing evergreens, or the house will be deprived of sunlight in the winter months. If one wishes to make a good deal of "outdoor living," it is delightful to plant a big tree right on the edge of the verandah which will form a natural "umbrella" and provide shade all summer. But take care that it is a deciduous tree like Sophora that will not cut out the winter sunlight. Similarly, a large, deciduous tree will help to shade a west window from the fiery, late afternoon sun. A flowering tree like the Syringa (*Melia azedarach*) or one that has beautiful foliage like Liquidamber, both make a good choice. Evergreen trees should be planted near the boundary for privacy, or in order to cut out the view of a neighbouring building. As well as making the garden more private, this all helps to create the illusion that the garden is bigger than it really is.

The excitement of watching spring blossom or new growth breaking from bare branches, symbolising the regeneration of life and beauty, can be experienced by everyone. While collecting valuable evergreens for the garden, therefore, do not neglect the deciduous trees and shrubs that will provide contrast and change.

Shrubs should be planted in groups together. It is a great mistake to "dot" them all over the lawn. In the first place, this spoils the expanse of the lawn, and in the second, shows no idea of design or grouping. It has been proved that it is detrimental to plant shrubs in the lawn, as this deprives them of moisture and air, but from a landscape point of view it is difficult to imagine a lawn unbroken by a few specimen shrubs, and it is possible to take practical steps to overcome this difficulty (See Chapter IV). If, therefore, shrubs are to be planted or "dotted" in the lawn, they should be arranged in irregularly placed groups of four or five. Asymmetrical beds can be made to surround groups of shrubs and trees and filled with decorative swathes of perennials and ground covers. Single specimens should be used to accent a spot in the garden, such as at the side of steps, at the end of a pathway or at a bend in the drive.

Grouping does not only mean placing numbers of shrubs together. They can be grouped either because they have something in common or because they contrast with one another. One could combine shrubs that have *fragrance* as well as beauty of form. It is pleasant to have the sweet-smelling shrubs, such as Lemon-Verbena, near the house, and to combine them with a collection of herbs, which could perhaps be grown between them or as an edging. This herb garden could be placed near the back of the house.

When grouping, one should consider the *foliage effect* of the different shrubs. Certain shrubs are prized only for the colour of their foliage in the summer and others for their beautiful autumn colours. *Sambucus nigra* var. *aurea* has bright yellow leaves which make a vivid splash of colour in the garden throughout the summer, and when this is planted beside *Prunus cerasifera* var. *nigra* which has almost blackish-brown leaves, the effect is greatly enhanced.

Foliage is not only effective as far as its colour is concerned, but also for the texture effect it creates. The leaves of the Tamarisk are small and needle-like, yet the effect of the whole bush is feathery and dainty and contrasts well with the smooth, glossy green leaves of Brunfelsia or Camellia.

One should consider shrubs which *flower at the same time* and sometimes plant them side by side if their flowers blend well in order to get a concerted effect. In many Johannesburg gardens the Jacaranda Tree has been planted side by side with the Silky Oak (*Grevillea robusta*). The bright golden "heads" of flowers contrast most effectively with the mauve Jacaranda blossom. Red Flowering Quince is offset by white Bridal-wreath May which flower together at the end of winter.

Finally, *we should grow shrubs as individual specimens* simply for the beauty of their flowers or berries.

There are several points to consider when we choose shrubs. We choose each shrub as an individual specimen, having either seen, heard or read about it. Basically, it is usually the flower that attracts us to a shrub, and while the landscape effects described above can be obtained with many a leafy bush, it is really the flower which makes it exciting to acquire a new one.

On the other hand, one must remember that a shrub is a permanent part of the garden, and even when the flowers are not blooming, the garden will still look complete on account of the design and placing of the shrubs. The flowers, therefore, are the "dividends" of the bush, while each shrub has a particular year-round value that no other shrub will have. Some have beauty of shape and branch pattern; some are chosen for their foliage; others again for the lack of foliage when flowering. The Pussy Willow and the Japanese Flowering Quince flower on bare branches and owe their Japanese-like beauty to this fact. There are those whose early spring leaves and blossoms are a delight; those whose autumn foliage attracts and those which are chosen simply because they make excellent cutting material for the vase.

It is the technique of planting even the old familiar favourites that "makes" a garden. One must think hard before choosing a spot to plant a shrub, considering not only its appearance in the landscape but also whether conditions are suitable for growth. All this trouble is worth it, for one will be rewarded with having to do very little work to maintain the shrub once it is established, and it will be a joy forever.

CHAPTER VI

A SELECTION OF THE AUTHOR'S FAVOURITE SHRUBS
The nucleus of a collection

Obviously one cannot hope to plant all the shrubs and trees described in this book, as lack of space in the garden is usually the biggest drawback. In addition, personal taste will influence one person to buy a shrub that does not appeal to another. Nevertheless, there are many shrubs which have such outstanding attractions that one cannot fail to be enthusiastic over them. If one were limited, for a variety of reasons, to a minimum number of shrubs in the garden, one would strive to grow the most attractive ones. If a friend were to ask me to recommend a few shrubs, I should choose the loveliest and most conspicuous ones first, hoping that as the interest in shrubs grew, the friend would see the beauty in many other shrubs that does not necessarily make itself known at a distance. A purely arbitrary list of this nature appears below for all who would like it.

One should never try to plant all one's shrubs at the same time. The need for new additions comes gradually, as each part of the landscape is planned or developed. It is more fun to spread out one's collecting over a period, and get to know a few shrubs at a time, than to attempt to buy all the required shrubs at the same time without much forethought or attention.

Remember that the different requirements in some gardens, caused by climate or by position, will rule out certain shrubs that may be grown successfully in others. For this reason, one should look up the individual requirements of the shrubs and trees listed below, in order to check whether one will be able to place them or care for them. This list has been chosen primarily for beauty of appearance, but, keeping in mind the limitations of climate, it has been divided, for simplicity, into three parts.

The first part lists those shrubs which will grow almost anywhere in South Africa and will endure frost. There are some that will not do well in sub-tropical conditions, and these have been marked with an asterisk. The second list contains those shrubs which grow most successfully in very warm, frost-free areas, but may be grown in areas which experience frost if the gardener is willing or able to give them a warm, sunny, protected position facing north or north-west. Some are tender to frost, such as Poinsettia, but others such as Petrea and Brunfelsia, although not tender, will grow better and more rapidly if they are given the same consideration. The third list contains shrubs and trees which one cannot hope to grow in areas which experience frost, except by freak of nature, and should not even be considered by those who live in such areas. Not only do these dislike frost, but they actually require a hot, sub-tropical, humid climate in which to thrive.

All these shrubs and trees with the exception, perhaps, of one or two large trees in each list, such as Jacaranda, are suitable for small as well as for large gardens.

LIST ONE

If I could plant only **twelve flowering shrubs and trees in areas which experience frost,** this is my **first choice.** Some of these require protected positions in very cold gardens. (Pr. = needs frost-protection).

EVERGREEN AND DECIDUOUS AZALEAS (*Rhododendron* species). Red, pink, white, purple and yellow flowers in spring.

PURPLE MAGNOLIA (*Magnolia soulangeana*). Purple and white flowers in winter and early spring.★

PINK BUSH TEA-TREE (*Leptospermum scoparium* var. *nichollsii*). Pink flowers throughout winter.

LATE TAMARISK (*Tamarix pentandra*). Pink flowers in early summer.

WEEPING BOTTLEBRUXH (*Callistemon viminalis*). Red flowers in early summer.

RED COTONEASTER (*Cotoneaster pannosus* or *C. serotinus*). Red berries in autumn.†

DOUBLE-WHITE GARDENIA (*Gardenia jasminoides* var. *plena*). White flowers in mid-summer.

PRIDE-OF-INDIA (*Lagerstroemia indica*). Pink, mauve or white flowers in summer.

HYDRANGEA (*Hydrangea macrophylla*). Blue or pink flowers in mid-summer.

DOUBLE-FLOWERING PEACH (*Prunus persica* var. *flore-pleno*). Red, pink or white flowers in spring.★

CAMELLIA (*Camellia japonica*). Pink, red and white flowers in early spring.†

FUCHSIA (*Fuchsia* hybrids). Red, pink, purple and white flowers throughout summer and autumn.† Pr.

Second choise—an additional twelve shrubs

DAIS OR POMPON TREE (*Dais cotinifolia*). Mauve flowers in early summer. (Pr.)

JAPANESE FLOWERING QUINCE (*Chaenomeles lagenaria*). Red flowers in winter and early spring.★

CHINESE LANTERNS (*Abutilon hybrids*). Pink or yellow flowers throughout the year.

BRIDAL-WREATH MAY (*Spiraea prunifolia* var. *plena*). White flowers in early spring.★

FAIRY TRUMPETS (*Weigela styriaca* and hybrids). Pink and red flowers in spring.★

ST. JOHN'S WORT (*Hypericum species*). Yellow flowers in spring and summer.

ACACIA (*Acacia*, several shrubby kinds). Yellow flowers in winter and early spring.

ORANGE FIRETHORN (*Pyracantha angustifolia* or *P. lalandi*). Orange berries in autumn and winter.

GLOSSY ABELIA (*Abelia grandiflora*). White flowers throughout summer and autumn.

PINK OR RED CESTRUM (*Cestrum species*). Pink or red flowers in autumn and other times.

HEATH (*Erica* species). Many kinds, long-flowering, evergreen.

SHUTTLECOCK FLOWER (*Calliandra selloi*). Pink and white flowers at intervals in summer.

★Not for sub-tropical climates.
†This will grow, but is not happy in sub-tropical districts.

Third choice—an additional twelve shrubs and trees.

HONEY MYRTLE (*Melaleuca species*). Several.

WHITE LAUREL MAGNOLIA (*Magnolia grandiflora*). White flowers in mid-summer.

JACARANDA (*Jacaranda mimosifolia*). Blue flowers in early summer.

CORAL-TREE (*Erythrina crista-gallii*). Scarlet flowers in spring. (Pr.)

CAPE HONEYSUCKLE (*Tecomaria capensis*). Flame-coloured flowers in autumn and winter.

SCENTED YELLOW-BLOSSOM TREE (*Hymenosporum flavum*). Yellow flowers in early summer.

FLOWERING CHERRY (*Prunus serrulata*). Pink and white flowers in spring.★

FLOWERING CRAB-APPLE (*Prunus malus* & hybrids). Pink and red flowers in spring.★

SCENTED CUPS (*Rothmannia capensis*). Cream bells during summer.

DOUBLE FILE VIBURNUM (*V.tomentosum*). White flowers, spring.★

PROTEA (*P.cynaroides, P.repens* & *P.neriifolia*). Flower autumn, winter, spring.

NODDING PINCUSHION (*Leucospermum cordifolium*). Orange-pink flowers in winter and spring. (Pr.)

LIST TWO

Twenty shrubs and trees which grow best in hot, frost-free areas, but will succeed in areas which experience frost if they are given a warm, sheltered position.

CHINESE HIBISCUS (*Hibiscus rosa-sinensis*). Red, pink and yellow flowers in summer and autumn.

POINSETTIA (*Euphorbia pulcherrima*). Red, pink and cream flowers in winter.

YESTERDAY, TODAY AND TOMORROW (*Brunfelsia calycina* var. *eximia*). Purple flowers changing to white, in spring and autumn.

BRAZILIAN GLORY BUSH (*Tibouchina semidecandra*). Purple flowers from spring to autumn—almost throughout the year.

PINK JACOBINIA (*Jacobinia carnea*). Pink flowers in summer and autumn.

KAFFIRBOOM (*Erythrina lysistemon*). Scarlet flowers in early spring.

SHRIMP FLOWER (*Beloperone guttata*). Rust-coloured flowers throughout year.

FIRE-DART BUSH (*Malvaviscus penduliflorus*). Scarlet flowers throughout summer and autumn. Also pink.

YELLOW BUSH TECOMA (*Tecoma stans*). Yellow flowers in autumn.

FLAME TREE (*Brachychiton acerifolium*). Scarlet flowers in early summer.

PRIDE-OF-DE KAAP (*Bauhinia galpinii*). Brick coloured flowers in autumn.

RED-FLOWERING GUM (*Eucalyptus ficifolia*). Red flowers in summer and autumn.

QUEENSLAND LACEBARK (*Brachychiton discolor*). Pink flowers in early summer.

CRANE FLOWER (*Strelitzia reginae*). Orange and blue flowers in autumn, winter and spring.

MARMALADE BUSH (*Streptosolen jamesonii*). Orange flowers throughout spring and summer.

GOLDEN CANDLES (*Pachystachys lutea*). Rich yellow flowers throughout summer and autumn.

HONG KONG ORCHID TREE (*Bauhinia blakeana*). Rose-purple flowers, autumn.

ORCHID TREE (*Bauhinia variegata*). Pink or white flowers, spring.

★Not for sub-tropical climates.

Floss-Silk Tree (*Chorisia speciosa*). Pink flowers, late summer.
Yellow Tabebuia (*Tabebuia chrysotricha*). Yellow flowers, spring.

LIST THREE

Fifteen Shrubs and Trees which will thrive only in hot or sub-tropical areas

Frangipani (*Plumeria*). Red, white, pink and yellow flowers throughout summer and autumn.

Giant Allamanda (*Allamanda cathartica* var. *hendersonii*). Yellow flowers throughout summer.

Red Ixora (*Ixora coccinea*). Coral coloured flowers throughout spring and summer.

Peacock Flower (*Caesalpinia pulcherrima*). Red or yellow flowers in summer.

Fiery-Torch Tree (*Spathodea campanulata*). Scarlet flowers in autumn and winter.

Scarlet Grevillea (*Grevillea banksii*). Red flowers throughout the year.

Red Flag-Bush (*Mussaenda erythrophylla*). Crimson bracts in summer and autumn.

Arabian Jasmine (*Jasminum sambac*). White flowers throughout the year.

Flamboyant Tree (*Delonix regia*). Scarlet flowers in mid-summer. Also yellow.

Glory Trees (*Tibouchina granulosa*). Pink or purple flowers, late summer and autumn.

Red Powderpuff (*Calliandra haematocephala*). Red flowers in summer and autumn.

Clusia (*Clusia grandiflora*). White flowers, summer.

Colville's Glory (*Colvillea racemosa*). Orange flowers, late summer.

Cassias. Several kinds of *Cassia* species with pink or yellow flowers.

Pink Tabebuia. (*T.ipe* and *T.pentaphylla*). Pink flowers in autumn, summer, spring.

CLIMBERS

Twelve Favourite Climbers that will survive frost

Trumpet Vine (*Campsis Madame Galen*). Orange flowers in summer.

Mexican Blood-Trumpet (*Phaedranthus buccinatorius*). Crimson flowers in early summer. (Pr)

Clematis (*Clematis hybrids*). Red, white or lilac flowers in summer and autumn.

Star-Jasmine (*Trachelospermum jasminoides*). White flowers in early summer.

Wistaria (*Wisteria sinensis*). Bluish-white flowers in spring.★

Japanese Honeysuckle (*Lonicera japonica*). White and yellow flowers in summer.

White Potato Creeper (*Solanum jasminoides*). White flowers, flushed mauve, in summer.

Zimbabwe Creeper (*Podranea brycei*). Pale pink flowers throughout summer. (Pr)

Mauve Bignonia (*Clytostoma callistegioides*). Mauve flowers in summer.

Cascade Creeper (*Polygonum aubertii*). White flowers in late summer.

★Not for sub-tropical climates.

Canary Creeper (*Senecio tamoides*). Yellow flowers in autumn.
Cats-Claw Creeper (*Doxantha unguis-cati*). Yellow flowers in early summer.

Ten Favourite Climbers which need a warm, sheltered position in areas which experience frost

Bougainvillea, Mrs. Butt (*Bougainvillea spectabilis* var. *Crimson Lake*). Crimson flowers in summer.
Coral-Vine (*Antigonon leptopus*). Pink flowers in summer and autumn.
Pink Mandevilla (*Mandevilla splendens*, formerly *Dipladenia*). Pink flowers in summer and autumn.
Mauve Potato Creeper (*Solanum wendlandii*). Mauve flowers in summer and autumn.
Scarlet Honeysuckle (*Lonicera sempervirens*). Scarlet flowers in summer and autumn.
Golden Shower (*Pyrostegia ignea*). Orange flowers in summer, autumn and winter.
Purple Wreath (*Petrea volubilis*). Purple flowers, spring.
Bengal Trumpet Vine (*Thunbergia grandiflora*). Bluish-mauve flowers in autumn.
Cup-of-Gold (*Solandra nitida*). Yellow flowers in spring.
Climbing Scarlet Clerodendron (*Clerodendrum splendens*). Scarlet flowers in late summer.

Eight Climbers for hot and sub-tropical localities

Giant Trumpet Climber (*Beaumontia grandiflora*). White flowers in spring.
Combretum jacquinii and *C.farinosum*. Orange or red flower-spikes, summer.
Velvet Congea (*Congea tomentosa*). Lilac flowers, early summer.
Crimson Wax Trumpet (*Ipomoea horsfalliae*). Crimson flowers in summer, autumn and winter.
Golden Vine (*Stigmaphyllon ciliatum*). Yellow flowers in summer.
Jade Vine (*Strongylodon macrobotrys*). Jade green trusses in spring, summer, autumn.
Mysore Vine (*Thunbergia mysorensis*). Brown and gold flowers in spring, summer, autumn.
Candy Corn Vine (*Wagatea spicata*). Red and orange flowers, autumn.

SHRUBS AND TREES THAT ARE GROWN FOR THEIR ATTRACTIVE FOLIAGE

Copperleaf (*Acalypha wilkesiana*). Crimson, pink and brown foliage throughout year. Evergreen. Tender. Sub-tropical.
Purple Barberry (*Berberis thunbergii* var. *atropurpurea*). Purple foliage throughout year. Deciduous.★
Snow-Bush (*Breynia nivosa*). Green foliage with white or pink markings. Evergreen. Tender. Sub-tropical.

★Not for sub-tropical climates.

BERLANDIA FIDDLEWOOD (*Citharexylum berlandieri*). Apricot leaves in autumn and winter. Semi-evergreen.

CROTON (*Codiaeum variegatum*). Variegated foliage throughout year. Evergreen. Tender. Sub-tropical.

LOOKING GLASS PLANT (*Coprosma baurii picturata*). Green and gold shining leaves. Evergreen.

JAPANESE PERSIMMON (*Diospyros kaki*). Red-gold autumn leaves and orange fruit. Deciduous.★

ELAEAGNUS (*Elaeagnus pungens maculata*). Variegated foliage. Evergreen.

MAIDENHAIR TREE (*Gingko biloba*). Golden leaves in autumn. Deciduous.★

GOLDEN-RAIN TREE (*Koelreutaria paniculata*). Gold autumn foliage. Deciduous.

SILVER TREE (*Leucadendron argenteum*). Silvery-green leaves always. Evergreen.

AMERICAN SWEETGUM (*Liquidamber styraciflua*). Crimson autumn foliage. Deciduous.†

TARATA OR LEMONWOOD (*Pittosporum eugenoides*). Fresh green foliage and black stems. Evergreen.

BROWN-LEAVED PLUM (*Prunus cerasifera* var. *nigra*). Dark brown foliage throughout year. Deciduous.★

PIN OAK (*Quercus palustris*). Crimson and copper autumn foliage. Deciduous.†

WAX TREE (*Rhus succedanea*). Bright red foliage in autumn. Deciduous.†

GOLDEN ELDER (*Sambucus nigra* var. *aurea*). Yellow foliage. Deciduous.†

SWAMP CYPRESS (*Taxodium distichum*). Russet leaves in autumn, brown in winter.

Thirty-six Shrubs and Trees which may be cut for the Vase

AZALEA (*Rhododendron* species).

PUSSY WILLOW (*Salix caprea*).

FIRETHORN (*Pyracantha*).

POINSETTIA (*Euphorbia pulcherrima*).

CORAL-VINE (*Antigonon leptopus*).

JAPANESE BEAUTY-BERRY (*Callicarpa dichotoma*).

FRANGIPANI (*Plumeria* species).

BLOUKAPPIES (*Polygala virgata*).

DOUBLE-FLOWERING PEACH (*Prunus persica* var. *flore-pleno*).

FLOWERING CHERRY (*Prunus serrulata*).

ALMOND BLOSSOM (*Prunus communis*).

PROTEA, SUIKERBOS (*Protea* species).

FLOWERING CRAB-APPLE (*Malus floribunda*).

HEATH (*Erica* species).

PINCUSHION FLOWER (*Leucospermum* species).

CRANE FLOWER (*Strelitzia reginae*).

RED CESTRUM (*Cestrum fasciculatum*).

PURPLE MAGNOLIA (*Magnolia soulangeana*).

BLUSHING BRIDE (*Serruria florida*).

NATAL-PLUM OR AMATUNGULU (*Carissa macrocarpa*).

CAMELLIA (*Camellia japonica*).

COTONEASTER (*Cotoneaster* species).

JAPANESE FLOWERING QUINCE (*Chaenomeles lagenaria*).

GARDENIA (*Gardenia jasminoides* var. *plena*).

HYDRANGEA (*Hydrangea macrophylla*).

RED IXORA (*Ixora coccinea*).

FAIRY TRUMPETS (*Weigela*).

PRIMROSE JASMINE (*Jasminum primulinum*).

DAPHNE (*Daphne*).

GOLDEN-BELLS (*Forsythia suspensa*).

SPANISH BROOM (*Spartium junceum*).

GLOSSY ABELIA (*Abelia grandiflora*).

★Not for sub-tropical climates.

†This will grow, but is not happy in sub-tropical districts.

SUTERA OR WILD PHLOX (*Sutera grandiflora*).

LION'S EAR (*Leonotis leonurus*).

AUSTRALIAN TEA-TREE (*Leptospermum scoparium* varieties).

FUCHSIA (*Fuchsia hybrida*).

Fifteen Shrubs which are Sweet-smelling

SWEETPEA BUSH (*Podalyria calyptrata*).

LEMON-VERBENA (*Lippia citriodora*).

ORANGE BLOSSOM (*Citrus sinensis*).

YESTERDAY, TODAY AND TOMORROW (*Brunfelsia calycina* var. *eximia*).

SCENTED YELLOW-BLOSSOM TREE (*Hymenosporum flavum*).

WHITE JASMINE (*Jasminum officinale, grandiflorum* or *sambac*).

WINTERSWEET (*Chimonanthus praecox*).

SPANISH BROOM (*Spartium junceum*).

FRENCH OR ENGLISH LAVENDER (*Lavandula species*).

PORT WINE MAGNOLIA (*Michelia figo*).

JAPANESE HONEYSUCKLE (*Lonicera japonica*).

ORANGE-JASMINE (*Murraya exotica*).

DOUBLE-WHITE GARDENIA (*Gardenia jasminoides* var. *plena*).

PINK SWA (*Luculia gratissima*).

SCENTED CUPS (*Rothmannia capensis*).

Beautiful Indigenous Shrubs

DAIS OR POMPON TREE (*Dais cotinifolia*). Mauve flowers in early summer.

PRIDE-OF-DE KAAP (*Bauhinia galpinii*). Brick-coloured flowers, autumn.

SWEETPEA BUSH (*Podalyria calyptrata*). Mauve or white flowers, spring.

BLOUKAPPIES (*Polygala virgata*). Purple flowers in autumn, winter and spring.

CAPE HONEYSUCKLE (*Tecomaria capensis*). Orange flowers in autumn and winter.

CURRY BUSH (*Hypericum lanceolatum*). Yellow flowers in spring, summer and autumn.

KAFFIRBOOM (*Erythrina lysistemon*). Scarlet flowers in early spring. All species of indigenous *Erythrina*.

PLUMBAGO (*Plumbago capensis*). Pale-blue flowers in spring, summer and autumn.

MOUNTAIN-BOTTLEBRUSH (*Greyia sutherlandii*). Scarlet flowers in early spring.

BALLOON-PEA or GANSIES (*Sutherlandia frutescens*). Scarlet flowers in winter and spring.

GARDENIA, KATJIEPIERING (*Gardenia thunbergia*). White flowers in summer.

SPUR-FLOWER (*Plectranthus sp.*). Purple or pink flowers in autumn.

CRANE FLOWER (*Strelitzia reginae*). Orange and blue flowers in summer and autumn.

SUTERA or WILD PHLOX (*Sutera grandiflora*). Pale blue flowers throughout the year.

LION'S EAR (*Leonotis leonurus*). Orange flowers in autumn.

KEURBOOM (*Virgilia divaricata* and *V. oroboides*). Mauve flowers in spring and summer respectively.

NATAL-PLUM or AMATUNGULU (*Carissa macrocarpa*). White flowers in spring and red fruits in autumn.

WISTARIA-TREE (*Bolusanthus speciosus*). Blue-purple flowers in late spring.

CAPE CHESTNUT (*Calodendrum capense*). Pink flowers in spring or summer.

PROTEA or SUIKERBOS (*Protea* species). Shades of pink flowers at different times throughout year.

PINCUSHION FLOWER (*Leucospermum* species). Red or orange flowers in spring.

SILVER TREE (*Leucadendron argenteum*). Silver leaves throughout the year.

BLUSHING BRIDE (*Serruria florida*). White, shaded pink flowers in winter and early spring.

HEATH (*Erica*). Different species flower at different times throughout the year and come in every colour except true blue.

CANARY CREEPER (*Senecio tamoides*). Bright yellow flowers in autumn.

PORT ST. JOHNS CREEPER (*Podranea ricasoliana*). Pale pink flowers throughout summer.

Twenty Winter-flowering Shrubs

CHINESE LANTERNS (*Abutilon.*)

PEARL ACACIA (*Acacia podalyriaefolia*).

SHRIMP FLOWER (*Beloperone guttata*).

CAMELLIA, DOUBLE RED AND SINGLE PINK (*Camellia japonica*).

JAPANESE FLOWERING QUINCE (*Chaenomeles lagenaria*).

WINTERSWEET (*Chimonanthus praecox*).

PINK MARGUERITE (*Chrysanthemum wardii*) and other species.

CONFETTI BUSH (*Coleonema pulchrum*).

HEATH (*Erica glandulosa*) Several other species

POINSETTIA (*Euphorbia pulcherrima*).

BUSH TEA-TREE (*Leptospermum scoparium nichollsii*).

PINK SWA (*Luculia gratissima*).

PURPLE MAGNOLIA (*Magnolia soulangeana*).

BLOUKAPPIES (*Polygala virgata*).

PROTEA (*Protea neriifolia*) and several others.

YELLOW FLAX (*Reinwardtia indica*).

BRIDAL-WREATH MAY (*Spiraea prunifolia plena*).

CRANE FLOWER (*Strelitzia reginae*).

WILD PHILOX (*Sutera grandiflora*).

BALLOON-PEA (*Sutherlandia frutescens*).

CHAPTER VII

ORNAMENTAL SHRUBS FOR DIFFERENT PURPOSES
For particular positions in the garden

Unless one can remember the requirements of many shrubs offhand, it is rather difficult to pick the right shrub when confronted with a special problem in the garden. If one buys a shrub for the sake of its beauty, it is easy to look up its requirements in the descriptive lists and supply these as far as possible. Sometimes, however, one wishes to choose a shrub that will thrive in a seemingly difficult spot, such as under a tree or against a hot, west wall. It is for this reason that a few short lists have been drawn up below, which will help the gardener to choose shrubs for special positions. These lists do not cover all the shrubs in this book, as many shrubs and trees are very tolerant, and will defy all known rules, but they will act as a short summary that may be taken in at a glance, and will serve as a guide to selecting some flowering or ornamental foliage shrubs for all conditions. In all cases the choice has been made from the shrubs described in this book.

SHRUBS FOR SHADY PLACES

This list includes shrubs that will do well in full shade, partial shade or even full sun if they have plenty of moisture or sometimes humidity, as in the case of Rhododendrons and Hydrangeas. All these shrubs are, however, adapted to growing in the shade, where the soil does not dry out quickly and their flowering does not seem to be affected. They will grow under the shade of trees in well-prepared, good soil, and should be well watered in order to prevent the trees from depriving them of moisture. They may also be planted on the south wall of the house.

Shrubs which will tolerate Full Shade

SPINDLE-TREE (*Euonymus japonicus*). Red berries.
HOLLY MAHONIA (*Mahonia aquifolium*). Yellow flowers.
ST. JOHN'S WORT (*Hypericum calycinum*). Yellow flowers.
GLOSSY ABELIA (*Abelia grandiflora*). White flowers.
HYDRANGEA (*Hydrangea macrophylla*). Blue or pink flowers.
FUCHSIA (*Fuchsia species*). White, red and purple flowers.
CREEPING COTONEASTER (*Cotoneaster horizontalis*). Red berries.
EVERGREEN AZALEA (*Rhododendron simsii*). White, red, pink, purple flowers.
RHODODENDRON (*Rhododendron* hybrids). All colours.
JAPANESE AZALEA (*Rhododendron japonicum*). Orange, salmon, rose flowers.
CHINESE AZALEA (*Rhododendron molle*). Golden-yellow flowers.
CESTRUM (*Cestrum* species). Red, pink, purple, yellow flowers.
SNOWBERRY (*Symphoricarpos albus*). White berries.
INDIAN-CURRANT (*Symphoricarpos orbiculatus*). Purplish-red berries.
MACKAYA (*Mackaya bella*). Pale lilac flowers.
MISTY-PLUME BUSH (*Iboza riparia*). Mauve or purple flowers.
GLOBE FLOWER (*Kerria japonica* var. *flore-pleno*). Yellow flowers.

JAPANESE FLOWERING QUINCE (*Chaenomeles lagenaria*). Red flowers.†
SNOW-BUSH (*Breynia nivosa*). Green and white foliage.★
ARABIAN JASMINE (*Jasminum sambac*). White flowers.★
PRIMROSE JASMINE (*Jasminum primulinum*). Yellow flowers.
STAR-JASMINE (*Trachelospermum jasminoides*). White flowers.
RANGOON CREEPER (*Quisqualis indica*). Red flowers.★
CRIMSON WAX TRUMPET (*Ipomoea horsfalliae*). Red flowers.★
CASCADE CREEPER (*Polygonum aubertii*). White flowers.
SNOWBALL BUSH (*Viburnum opulus* var. *sterile*). White flowers.†

Shrubs which will grow in Partial Shade

Most of these are suitable for positions facing east

CHINESE LANTERNS (*Abutilon hybridum*). Pink, orange and yellow flowers.
CAMELLIA (*Camellia japonica*). Red, pink or white flowers.†
DAPHNE (*Daphne odora*). Pink and white flowers.†
FAIRY TRUMPETS (*Weigela florida* and hybrids). Red, pink or white flowers.†
BRIDAL WREATH (*Deutzia* species). White flowers.
ESCALLONIA (*Escallonia macrantha*). Pink flowers.
GOLDEN-BELLS (*Forsythia*). Yellow flowers.†
ENGLISH HOLLY (*Ilex aquifolium*). Red berries.†
PURPLE MAGNOLIA (*Magnolia soulangeana*). Mauve and white flowers.†
PORT WINE MAGNOLIA (*Michelia figo*). Wine flowers.
MOCK-ORANGE (*Philadelphus coronarius*). White flowers.
SPUR-FLOWER (*Plectranthus ecklonii*). Purple flowers.
PLUMBAGO (*Plumbago capensis*). Pale-blue flowers.
CANARY CREEPER (*Senecio tamoides*). Yellow flowers.
REEVES MAY (*Spiraea cantoniensis*). White flowers.†
SHOWY HEBE (*Hebe speciosa*). Purple and red flowers.†
EVERGREEN CREEPING COTONEASTER (*Cotoneaster microphyllus*). Red berries.
LEMON-VERBENA (*Lippia citriodora*). Bluish white flowers.†

SHRUBS FOR DRY CONDITIONS

These shrubs will resist heat, drought and neglect. They are useful when no watering can be given them once the plant is well established. Many of them are suitable for west-facing positions which have fierce afternoon sun, and for semi-arid localities.

WATTLE TREES (*Acacia species*). Yellow flowers.
BUTTERFLY BUSH (*Buddleia davidii*). Mauve flowers.
BARBERRY (*Berberis species*). Autumn foliage.
AUTUMN CASSIA (*Cassia corymbosa*). Yellow flowers.
PEANUT-BUTTER CASSIA (*Cassia didymobotrya*). Yellow flowers.
BOTTLEBRUSH (*Callistemon species*). Red flowers.
SPANISH BROOM (*Spartium junceum*). Yellow flowers.
JAPANESE FLOWERING QUINCE (*Chaenomeles lagenaria*). Red flowers.

★Only for sub-tropical or frost-free conditions.
†Not happy in sub-tropical conditions.

TARTAN BUSH (*Cuphea micropetala*). Orange flowers.
PRIDE-OF-MADEIRA (*Echium fastuosum*). Blue flowers.
SPINDLE TREE (*Euonymus japonicus*). Red berries.
ESCALLONIA (*Escallonia macrantha*). Pink flowers.
CHERRY-PIE (*Lantana* hybrids and varieties). Red, orange, yellow and white flowers.
AUSTRALIAN TEA-TREE (*Leptospermum scoparium*). Red, pink, or white flowers.
TEA-MYRTLE (*Melaleuca nesophila*). Mauve flowers.
OLEANDER (*Nerium oleander*). Pink, white or red flowers.
BROWN-LEAVED PLUM (*Prunus cerasifera* var. *atropurpurea*). Brown leaves.
DOUBLE-FLOWERING PEACH (*Prunus persica* var. *flore-pleno*). Red, pink or white.
POMEGRANATE (*Punica granatum*). Orange flowers.
CASTOR OIL (*Ricinus communis*). Red burrs.
FALSE-ACACIA (*Robinia pseudacacia*). White flowers.
ROSE-ACACIA (*Robinia hispida*). Mauve flowers
TREE-POPPY (*Romneya coulteri*). White flowers.
BIRD-FLOWER (*Crotolaria agatiflora*). Greenish-yellow flowers.
CESTRUM (*Cestrum* species). Red, pink, purple and yellow flowers.
BLUE TUBE FLOWERS (*Jochroma tubulosum*). Royal blue flowers.
PRIMROSE JASMINE (*Jasminum primulinum*). Yellow flowers.
TRAILING LANTANA (*Lantana montevidensis*). Mauve flowers.
JAPANESE HONEYSUCKLE (*Lonicera japonica*). Yellow flowers.
ZIMBABWE CREEPER (*Podranea brycei*). Pink flowers.
PLUMBAGO (*Plumbago capensis*). Pale-blue flowers.
SUMAC (*Rhus* species). Autumn foliage.
CANARY CREEPER (*Senecio tamoides*). Yellow flowers.
WHITE POTATO CREEPER (*Solanum jasminoides*). White and blue flowers.
CAPE HONEYSUCKLE (*Tecomaria capensis*). Red flowers.
PURPLE BOUGAINVILLEA (*Bougainvillea glabra*). Purple flowers.
GOLDEN SHOWER (*Pyrostegia ignea*). Orange flowers.
CATS-CLAW CREEPER (*Doxantha unguis-cati*). Yellow flowers.

SHRUBS AND TREES FOR GARDENS IN COLD AREAS

The following selection of ornamental shrubs and trees will grow in places which experience about minus 10 degrees Celsius. Many other shrubs which are slightly sensitive to frost may also be grown in sheltered positions in cold gardens, but are too numerous to list here. These are noted in the individual descriptions under Chapter VIII.

ABELIA (*Abelia grandiflora*). White flowers.
MAPLE TREES (*Acer* species). Autumn foliage.
BARBERRY BUSHES (*Berberis* species). Ornamental foliage.
BUTTERFLY BUSH (*Buddleia davidii*). Lilac flowers.
BOTTLEBRUSH (*Callistemon* species). Red flowers.
CAMELLIA (*Camellia japonica*). Red, pink or white flowers.
CATALPA (*Catalpa bignonioides*). White, spotted flowers.
CERATOSTIGMA (*Ceratostigma wilmottianum*). Blue flowers.
JAPANESE FLOWERING QUINCE (*Chaenomeles lagenaria*). Red or white flowers.
WINTERSWEET (*Chimonanthus praecox*). Yellow flowers.

LOOKING-GLASS PLANT (*Coprosma baurii*). Glossy leaves.
COTONEASTER (*Cotoneaster species*). Red or orange berries.
LAVALLE HAWTHORN (*Crataegus lavallei*). Red berries.
WASHINGTON THORN (*Crataegus phaenopyrum*). Red berries.
MEXICAN HAWTHORN (*Crataegus stipulacea*). Large orange berries.
CIGARETTE FLOWER (*Cuphea platycentra*). Scarlet flowers.
TARTAN BUSH (*Cuphea micropetala*). Orange flowers.
QUINCE (*Cydonia oblonga*). Pale pink flowers.
DAPHNE (*Daphne odora*). Pink or white flowers.
BRIDAL WREATH (*Deutzia species*). White flowers.
JAPANESE PERSIMMON (*Diospyros kaki*). Orange fruits.
PRICKLY CARDINAL (*Erythrina zeyheri*). Bright red flowers.
ESCALLONIA (*Escallonia macrantha*). Pink flowers.
FLORIST'S GUM (*Eucalyptus cinerea*). Grey leaves.
SPINDLE-TREE (*Euonymus japonicus*). Ornamental berries.
PEARL-BUSH (*Exochorda racemosa*). White flowers.
GOLDEN-BELLS (*Forsythia species*). Yellow flowers.
DOUBLE-WHITE GARDENIA (*Gardenia jasminoides* var. *plena*). White flowers.
SILVER BELL TREE (*Halesia carolina*) White flowers.
WITCH-HAZEL (*Hamamelis mollis*). Yellow flowers.
SHOWY HEBE (*Hebe speciosa*). Pink, red or purple flowers.
SYRIAN HIBISCUS (*Hibiscus syriacus*). White or mauve flowers.
HYDRANGEA (*Hydrangea macrophylla*). White, pink or blue flowers.
GOLD FLOWER (*Hypericum species*). Yellow flowers.
ENGLISH HOLLY (*Ilex aquifolium*). Red berries.
PRIDE-OF-INDIA (*Lagerstroemia indica*). White, pink or mauve flowers.
LANTANA (*Lantana species*). Red, yellow or mauve flowers.
LAVENDER (*Lavandula species*). Mauve flowers.
LION'S EAR (*Leonotis leonurus*). Orange flowers.
TEA-TREE (*Leptospermum species*). Pink, white or red flowers.
LEMON-VERBENA (*Lippia citriodora*). White and mauve flowers.
AMERICAN SWEETGUM (*Liquidamber styraciflua*). Autumn foliage.
TULIP TREE (*Liriodendron tulipifera*). Green flowers.
HONEYSUCKLE (*Lonicera species*). Yellow, pink or red flowers.
MAGNOLIA (*Magnolia species*). White or purple flowers.
HOLLY MAHONIA (*Mahonia aquifolium*). Yellow flowers.
FLOWERING CRAB-APPLE (*Malus floribunda*). Pink flowers.
TEA-MYRTLE (*Melaleuca nesophila*). Mauve flowers.
CHINA-BERRY (*Melia azedarach*). Mauve flowers.
PORT-WINE MAGNOLIA (*Michelia figo*). Wine-coloured flowers.
OLEANDER (*Nerium oleander*). White, pink or red flowers.
MOCK-ORANGE (*Philadelphus coronarius*). White flowers.
PITTOSPORUM (*Pittosporum species*). Ornamental foliage.
BIRD-OF-PARADISE (*Poinciana gilliesii*). Yellow and red flowers.
SILVER LACE-VINE (*Polygonum aubertii*). White flowers.
ALMOND (*Prunus communis*). Pink flowers.
BROWN-LEAVED PLUM (*Prunus cerasifera*). Brown leaves.
DOUBLE FLOWERING PEACH (*Prunus persica* var. *flore-pleno*). White, pink or red
    flowers.

Japanese Flowering Cherry (*Prunus serrulata*). Pink and white flowers.
Pomegranate (*Punica granatum*). Orange flowers, scarlet fruits.
Firethorn (*Pyracantha* species). Red or orange berries.
Pin Oak (*Quercus palustris*). Autumn foliage.
Rhododendron and Azalea (*Rhododendron* species). All colours except blue.
Wax Tree (*Rhus succedanea*). Scarlet foliage.
Rose-Acacia (*Robinia hispida*). Pinkish-mauve flowers.
False-Acacia (*Robinia pseudacacia*). White flowers.
Tree-Poppy (*Romneya coulteri*). White flowers.
Rosemary (*Rosmarinus officinalis*). Lavender flowers.
Goat or Pussy Willow (*Salix caprea*). Silky grey catkins.
Golden Elder (*Sambucus nigra* var. *aurea*). Yellow foliage.
Spanish Broom (*Spartium junceum*). Yellow flowers.
May (*Spiraea species*). White, pink or red flowers.
Balloon-Pea (*Sutherlandia frutescens*). Scarlet flowers, green pods.
Snowberry (*Symphoricarpos albus*). White berries.
Coral-Berry (*Symphoricarpos orbiculatus*). Red berries.
Lilac (*Syringa* species). Lilac, white or pink flowers.
Tamarisk (*Tamarix* species). Pink flowers.
Snowball Bush (*Viburnum opulus* var. *sterile*). White flowers.
Star-Jasmine (*Trachelospermum jasminoides*). White flowers.
Laurestinus (*Viburnum tinus* and other species). Pinkish-white flowers.
Fairy Trumpets (*Weigela* species). White, pink or red flowers.
Wistaria (*Wisteria sinensis*). White or mauve flowers.

TREES AND SHRUBS WHICH RESIST WIND AT THE COAST

The important problems which beset the gardener at the sea-coast are the strong prevailing winds and the sometimes brackish soil. On the other hand, the variations in temperature of the different seasons is less marked at the coast than it is inland, and there are no frosts to hamper growth. The chief concern of the sea-coast gardener is to provide a windbreak of sturdy trees that will thrive on the exposed portions of the garden and act as a shelter to other trees and shrubs.

Improving the soil is the second important consideration. The soil is either light and sandy or a heavy clay. Both can be improved by the constant addition of large quantities of well-made compost. Sea-weed, which has had the salt washed out of it, is a valuable addition to the compost. Clay soil which is very salty is usually treated with gypsum, but light, sandy soil must be very well drained, so that the salt will be washed out to a lower outlet when watering. Fertilizers containing potash are very useful.

The following ornamental trees and shrubs will also act as windbreaks inland. Shrubs which resist wind usually have fine or narrow leaves, and the shrubs or trees that resist salt usually have leathery leaves, but there are always exceptions.

Trees

Bailey's Wattle (*Acacia baileyana*). Yellow flowers.
Knife-Leaf Wattle (*Acacia cultriformis*). Yellow flowers.
Pearl Acacia (*Acacia podalyriaefolia*). Yellow flowers.
Golden Wattle (*Acacia pycnantha*). Yellow flowers.

SHOWY TREE BOTTLEBRUSH (*Callistemon speciosus*). Red flowers.
WEEPING BOTTLEBRUSH (*Callistemon viminalis*). Red flowers.
JUDAS TREE (*Cercis siliquastrum*). Pink flowers.†
COAST KAFFIRBOOM (*Erythrina caffra*). Scarlet flowers.★
RED-FLOWERING GUM (*Eucalyptus ficifolia*). Red flowers.
SILKY OAK (*Grevillea robusta*). Golden flowers.
PYRAMID TREE (*Lagunaria pattersonii*). Pink flowers.
AMERICAN SWEETGUM (*Liquidamber styraciflua*). Autumn foliage.
TEA-MYRTLE (*Melaleuca nesophila and others*). Mauve flowers.
SOUTH AFRICAN SYRINGA (*Melia azedarach*). Lilac flowers.
NEW ZEALAND CHRISTMAS TREE (*Metrosideros excelsa*). Red flowers.
ROYAL PAULOWNIA (*Paulownia tomentosa*). Mauve flowers.
FRANGIPANI (*Plumeria species*). Red, yellow or white flowers.★
BROWN-LEAVED PLUM (*Prunus cerasifera* var. *atropurpurea*). Brown leaves.†
DOUBLE-FLOWERING PEACH (*Prunus persica* var. *flore-pleno*). Red and white flowers.†
PIN OAK (*Quercus palustris*). Autumn foliage.
SHINING SUMAC (*Rhus copallina*). Autumn foliage.
SMOOTH SUMAC (*Rhus glabra*). Autumn foliage.
GOLDEN ELDER (*Sambucus nigra* var. *aurea*). Yellow foliage.
TABEBUIA (*Tabebuia pallida*). Mauve flowers.★
SPRING-FLOWERING TAMARISK (*Tamarix parviflora*). Pink flowers.
LATE TAMARISK (*Tamarix pentandra*). Pink flowers.

Shrubs

CHINESE LANTERNS (*Abutilon hybridum*). Pink, yellow, orange flowers.
COPPERLEAF (*Acalypha wilkesiana*). Red and brown variegated leaves.★
BARBERRY (*Berberis species*). Ornamental foliage.†
NATAL-PLUM (*Carissa macrocarpa*). White flowers, red fruits.★
JAPANESE FLOWERING QUINCE (*Chaenomeles lagenaria*). Red flowers.†
ROCK-ROSE (*Cistus species*). Pink or white flowers.†
CROTON (*Codiaeum variegatum*). Variegated foliage.★
COTONEASTER (*Cotoneaster species*). Red or orange berries.
SPANISH BROOM (*Spartium junceum*). Yellow flowers.
BRIDAL WREATH (*Deutzia gracilis*). White flowers.
PRIDE-OF-MADEIRA (*Echium fastuosum*). Blue flowers.
ELAEAGNUS (*Elaeagnus pungens*). Red berries, variegated foliage.
HEATH (*Erica species*). All colours.
ESCALLONIA (*Escallonia macrantha*). Pink flowers.
SPINDLE-TREE (*Euonymus japonicus*). Red berries.
DOUBLE-WHITE GARDENIA (*Gardenia jasminoides* var. *plena*). White flowers.
HIBISCUS (*Hibiscus species*). Red, white, mauve, and pink flowers.
HYDRANGEA (*Hydrangea macrophylla*). Blue or pink flowers.
ENGLISH HOLLY (*Ilex aquifolium*). Red berries.
RED IXORA (*Ixora coccinea*). Red flowers.

★For sub-tropical frost-free conditions only.
†Not for sub-tropical conditions.

CHERRY-PIE (*Lantana camara* and varieties). Red, yellow flowers.
LION'S EAR (*Leonotis leonurus*). Orange flowers.
AUSTRALIAN TEA-TREE (*Leptospermum scoparium* vars). Red, pink or white flowers.
HOLLY MAHONIA (*Mahonia aquifolium*). Yellow flowers.
OLEANDER (*Nerium oleander*). Pink or white flowers.
SNOW-BUSH (*Breynia nivosa*). Green and white foliage.★
TARATA or LEMONWOOD (*Pittosporum eugenoides*). Fresh green foliage. Several.
BLOUKAPPIES or POLYGALA (*Polygala virgata*). Purple flowers.
PROTEA (*Protea* species). Pink flowers.
FIRETHORN (*Pyracantha* species). Orange or red berries.
YEDDO & INDIAN HAWTHORN (*Raphiolepis* species). White or pink flowers.
CORAL-BELL BUSH (*Russelia* species). Red flowers.★
SNOWBERRY (*Symphoricarpos albus*). White berries.
CORAL-BERRY or INDIAN-CURRANT (*Symphoricarpos orbiculatus*). Reddish-purple berries.
SHOWY HEBE (*Hebe speciosa*). Red or purple flowers.†

SHRUBS WHICH MAY BE USED FOR HEDGES

Low-growing Hedges

Some of these may be clipped down to about 45 cm from the ground, in the form of a box hedge, but may also be grown up to one metre in height. Some may be grown as unclipped hedges of about one metre, as they have a neat, yet rounded habit of growth, and this is labour-saving as well as softer looking.

Shrubs which should be clipped into shape:

TRAILING LANTANA (*Lantana montevidensis*). Deciduous.
JAPANESE FLOWERING QUINCE (*Chaenomeles lagenaria*). Deciduous.†
EVERGREEN CREEPING COTONEASTER (*Cotoneaster microphyllus*). Evergreen.
BARBERRY (*Berberis species*). Deciduous.†
SPINDLE-TREE (*Euonymus japonicus*). Evergreen.
ESCALLONIA (*Escallonia macrantha*). Evergreen.
BRIDAL WREATH (*Deutzia gracilis*). Deciduous.
CHRIST-THORN (*Euphorbid milii* var. *splendens*). Deciduous.★
ST. JOHN'S WORT (*Hypericum sinense*). Evergreen.
TARATA or LEMONWOOD (*Pittosporum eugenoides*). Evergreen.
SERISSA (*Serissa foetida*). Evergreen.
GIANT FIRE-DART (*Malvaviscus penduliflorus*). Evergreen.

Shrubs which may be used untrimmed:

FRENCH LAVENDER (*Lavandula dentata*). Evergreen.
CERATOSTIGMA (*Ceratostigma wilmottianum*). Deciduous.
ROSEMARY (*Rosmarinus officinalis*). Evergreen.
SHOWY HEBE (*Hebe speciosa*). Evergreen.
RED MAY (*Spiraea bumalda* var. *Anthony Waterer*). Deciduous.

★Not for sub-tropical or frost free conditions.
†Not happy in sub-tropical conditions.

Large Hedges—from two to three metres or more

Evergreen hedges for privacy on the boundary:

FIRETHORN (*Pyracantha*). Red or orange berries.
TARATA or LEMONWOOD (*Pittosporum eugenoides*). Fresh green foliage.
SINGLE CAMELLIA (*Camellia japonica*). Red flowers.†
GLOSSY ABELIA (*Abelia grandiflora*). White flowers.
KNIFE-LEAF WATTLE (*Acacia cultriformis*). Yellow flowers.
BRUSH-CHERRY (*Eugenia myrtifolia*). Red fruits.
BOUGAINVILLEA (*Bougainvillea* in variety). Purple, red, orange and pink.★
FORGET-ME-NOT TREE (*Duranta repens*). Blue flowers and yellow berries.
OLEANDER (*Nerium oleander*). Red, pink or white flowers.
TEA TREE (*Leptospermum* species). Red, pink or white flowers.
PHOTINIA (*Photinia* species). Glossy leaves.
AUSTRALIAN CHRISTMAS BUSH (*Ceratopetalum gummiferum*). Red flowers.
COFFEE (*Coffea arabica*). White flowers, red berries.★
LOOKING GLASS PLANT (*Coprosma baurii*). Glossy leaves.
YESTERDAY, TODAY AND TOMORROW (*Brunfelsia calycina* var. *eximia*). Purple and
    white flowers.★
CHINESE HIBISCUS (*Hibiscus rosa-sinensis*). Red, pink and yellow flowers.★
NATAL-PLUM, AMATUNGULU (*Carissa macrocarpa*). Red fruits and white flowers.★

Large Deciduous or Semi-Evergreen hedges
  These are useful within the garden for separating one portion from another.
They may or may not be clipped.

RED COTONEASTER (*Cotoneaster pannosus*). Red berries.
SYRIAN HIBISCUS (*Hibiscus syriacus*). Mauve or white flowers.
MOCK-ORANGE (*Philadelphus coronarius*). White flowers.
REEVES MAY (*Spiraea cantoniensis*). White flowers.†
TAMARISK (*Tamarix species*). Pink flowers.
GOLDEN-BELLS (*Forsythia*). Yellow flowers.†
QUINCE (*Cydonia oblonga*). White blossom.†
POMEGRANATE (*Punica granatum*). Orange or red flowers. Red fruits.

SHRUBS WHICH SUIT THE ROCKERY

PRIDE-OF-DE KAAP (*Bauhinia galpinii*). Brick-coloured flowers.
SHRIMP FLOWER (*Beloperone guttata*). Rust-coloured or lime flowers.
WISTARIA-TREE (*Bolusanthus speciosus*). Blue flowers.
CERATOSTIGMA (*Cerastostigma wilmottianum*). Blue flowers.
CREEPING COTONEASTER (*Cotoneaster horizontalis*). Red berries.
EVERGREEN CREEPING COTONEASTER (*Cotoneaster microphyllus*). Red berries.
TARTAN BUSH (*Cuphea micropetala*). Orange flowers.
CIGARETTE FLOWER (*Cuphea platycentra*). Red flowers.
PRIDE-OF-MADEIRA (*Echium fastuosum*). Blue flowers.
CORAL-TREE (*Erythrina crista-gallii*). Red flowers.

  ★Use as a hedge in sub-tropical or hot district only.
  †Not for sub-tropical conditions.

HEATH (*Erica* species). All colours.

MOUNTAIN-BOTTLEBRUSH (*Greyia sutherlandii*). Red flowers.

ST. JOHN'S WORT (*Hypericum* species). Yellow flowers.

YELLOW LANTANA (*Lantana camara Drap D'or*). Yellow flowers.

TRAILING LANTANA (*Lantana montevidensis*). Mauve flowers.

LION'S EAR (*Leonotis leonurus*). Orange flowers.

SILVER TREE (*Leucadendron argenteum*). Silver leaves.

PINCUSHION FLOWER (*Leucospermum* species). Red or orange flowers.

FIRE-DART BUSH (*Malvaviscus mollis*). Red flowers.

SPUR-FLOWER (*Plectranthus ecklonii*). Purple flowers.

SWEETPEA BUSH (*Podalyria calyptrata*). Mauve or white flowers.

BLOUKAPPIES OR POLYGALA (*Polygala virgata*). Purple flowers.

SUIKERBOS OR PROTEA (*Protea* species). Pink flowers.

YELLOW FLAX (*Reinwardtia indica*). Yellow flowers.

MAHOGANY CASTORBEAN (*Ricinus communis* var. *purpureus*). Purple foliage.

BLUSHING BRIDE (*Serruria florida*). White, flushed pink flowers.

CRANE FLOWER (*Strelitzia reginae*). Orange and blue flowers.

SUTERA OR WILD PHLOX (*Sutera grandiflora*). Pale blue flowers.

BALLOON-PEA (*Sutherlandia frutescens*). Red flowers.

TAMARISK (*Tamarix* species). Pink flowers.

CAPE HONEYSUCKLE (*Tecomaria capensis*). Red flowers.

EVERGREEN SHRUBS FOR LARGE POTS OR TUBS

CHINESE LANTERNS (*Abutilon* hybrids). Yellow, orange, pink flowers.

ARDISIA (*Ardisia crispa*). Red berries.

SHRIMP FLOWER (*Beloperone guttata*). Rusty flowers.

SNOWBUSH (*Breynia nivosa*). White-speckled leaves.

BOUVARDIA (*Bouvardia*). Pink, red or white flowers.

YESTERDAY, TODAY AND TOMORROW (*Brunfelsia calycina macrantha*). Purple flowers.

FALSE-CYPRESS (*Chamaecyparis*). Green or golden foliage.

CURLY PINK ROCK-ROSE (*Cistus crispus*). Pink flowers.

SWEET ORANGE (*Citrus sinensis*). White flowers, orange fruit.

CONFETTI BUSH (*Coleonema pulchrum*). Pink flowers.

DAPHNE (*Daphne odora*). White or pink flowers.

HEATH (*Erica* species). All colours, except blue.

FUCHSIA (*Fuchsia hybrida*). Pink, red, purple, white flowers.

HYDRANGEA (*Hydrangea macrophylla*). Pink or blue flowers.

PROSTRATE JUNIPER (*Juniperus chinensis pfitzeriana*). Green or yellow-tipped foliage.

PURPLE LANTANA (*Lantana montevidensis*). Purple flowers.

FRENCH LAVENDER (*Lavandula dentata*). Lavender flowers.

GOLDEN PRIVET (*Ligustrum ovalifolium variegatum*). Gold-margined leaves.

MACKAYA (*Mackaya bella*). Pale mauve flowers.

FIRE-DART BUSH (*Malvaviscus mollis*). Red flowers.

CARNIVAL BUSH (*Ochna atropurpurea*). Yellow flowers, red sepals.

GOLDEN CANDLES (*Pachystachys lutea*). Golden flower-spikes.

PENTAS (*Pentas* species). Mauve or red flowers.

Spur Flower (*Plectranthus* species). Mauve, purple, pink flowers.
Evergreen Azalea (*Rhododendron simsii*). Pink, white, mauve flowers.
Rosemary (*Rosmarinus officinalis*). Pale blue flowers.
Lavender-Cotton (*Santolina chamaecyparissus*). Grey foliage, yellow flowers.
Serissa (*Serissa foetida*). White flowers.
Crane Flower (*Strelitzia reginae*). Orange flowers.
Marmalade Bush (*Streptosolen jamesonii*). Orange flowers.
Rice-Paper Plant (*Tetrapanax papyriferum*). Large dramatic leaves.
Oriental Arbor-Vitae (*Thuya orientalis*). Compact green or gold foliage.

EVERGREENS FOR PRIVACY

In choosing trees and shrubs to create privacy on the borders of the garden, in place of, or in addition to, a wall or hedge, so as to obliterate the sight of telegraph poles, other people's houses or distant buildings, it is important to choose evergreens with dense foliage. They should grow fairly easily and be reasonably long-lived. It is better to plant a slow-grower with a long life than a tree that grows quickly only to die 10 years later, unless one needs quick cover while slow-growing trees become mature.

All the following may be grown in cold-winter areas, provided that their special requirements are noted, except where the letter T in parenthesis denotes that they are tender and suitable only for sub-tropical districts.

Acacia—several species—Wattle
Acalypha wilkesiana (T)—Copperleaf
Arbutus unedo—Strawberry Tree
Banksia ericifolia
Bauhinia blakeana—Hong Kong Orchid Tree
Brachychiton acerifolium—Flame Tree
Brachychiton populneum—Kurrajong
Burchellia—Wild Pomegranate—slow
Callistemon speciosus—Tree Bottlebrush (and others)
Camellia japonica, single
Carissa macrocarpa (T)—Natal Plum
Cassia alata (T)
Cassia multijuga (T)
Castanospermum australe (T) —Moreton-Bay Chestnut
Ceratopetalum gummiferum—Australian Christmas Bush
Cestrum aurantiacum—Yellow Cestrum
Cestrum purpureum—Purple Cestrum
Chamaecyparis—several
Clusia grandiflora (T)
Coffea arabica (T)—Coffee
Coprosma baurii—Looking-Glass Plant
Cotoneaster serotinus—Late Cotoneaster
Dodonea viscosa—Sand-Olive
Duranta repens—Forget-Me-Not Tree
Elaeagnus pungens—slow
Escallonia macrantha
Eucalyptus—several

Eugenia myrtifolia—BRUSH-CHERRY
Euonymus—SPINDLE-TREE—slow
Feijoa—PINEAPPLE GUAVA
Ficus benjamina (T)
Grevillea—several kinds
Heimia salicifolia
Hoheria—NEW ZEALAND LACEBARK
Hymenosporum flavum—tall, slender, useful for screening poles
Ilex aquifolium—HOLLY—slow
Jochroma (T)—BLUE TUBE FLOWERS
Juniperus—JUNIPERS, several
Lagunaria—PYRAMID TREE
Ligustrum ovalifolium variegatum—GOLDEN PRIVET
Melaleuca—HONEY MYRTLE, several
Metrosideros—NEW ZEALAND CHRISTMAS TREE
Millettia (T)—UMZIMBITI
Myoporum—NGAIO
Myrtus communis—MYRTLE
Nerium oleander—OLEANDER
Photinia davidsoniae—PHOTINIA, slow
Pittosporum—several
Podocarpus—YELLOW-WOOD—several, slow
Prunus laurocerasus—CHERRY LAUREL
Pyracantha—FIRETHORN
Rothmannia capensis—SCENTED CUPS
Schotia brachypetala (T)—BOERBOON—slow
Sparmannia (T)—AFRICAN HOLLYHOCK
Tecoma stans (T)—YELLOW BUSH TECOMA
Thevetia (T)—YELLOW OLEANDER
Tibouchina granulosa (T)—GLORY TREE
Virgilia—KEURBOOM—short-lived

CHAPTER VIII

INDIVIDUAL DESCRIPTION OF SHRUBS, TREES AND CLIMBERS
In alphabetical order

Abelia
(Caprifoliaceae)

Abelia grandiflora (*A floribunda* of Sim)

GLOSSY ABELIA

This is an evergreen hybrid shrub that grows to a height of almost 2 metres and spreads to the same width. It has small, glossy dark-green leaves which cover the bush closely, so that it is luxuriant in winter. It bears clusters of tiny, white trumpet flowers, about 1,5 cm long, produced profusely throughout summer and autumn. When the flowers drop off they leave pinkish sepals on the bush which remain throughout winter. These, in combination with the leaves, which turn bronze in winter, give the whole bush a pinkish-brown colour.

Glossy Abelia makes a pretty specimen shrub or can be clipped to make an attractive hedge. It is hardy to frost and extremely easy to grow. It prefers an open sunny position although it will grow anywhere. It is quite fast-growing and attains full size in about 4 years. Although its flowers are not conspicuous, it is a dependable little shrub which should be in every garden. It is excellent when used as part of a background planting. Cuttings strike easily (Illustrated Plate 1).

Abelia floribunda from Mexico, is evergreen and has rose-red flowers during summer.

Abelia schumanii from China, is an evergreen of about 2 metres, but loses its leaves where winters are severe. It has larger rosy flowers.

There are several hybrid Abelias that are grown more for their flowers than for their usefulness in the landscape.

Abutilon
(Malvaceae)

Abutilon hybrids

ABUTILON, CHINESE LANTERNS

Abutilon hybrids are extremely pretty shrubs growing to about 2 metres in height and spread, flowering throughout the spring, summer, autumn and particularly in winter. The flowers are bell-like and hang down gracefully and profusely. They come in a number of clear colours ranging from pink to orange, pure yellow and white. There is also a veined orange. The leaves of these hybrids are broad and green with a furry back.

Although sub-tropical by nature, Chinese Lanterns can stand a certain amount of frost. They are evergreen but may lose some leaves during cold winters. They prefer a position which is sheltered from the wind or they may become sparse and ragged. These shrubs will do well in the shade but prefer full sunlight and are otherwise easy and rapid growers. Cuttings strike easily and grow rapidly under humid conditions and in rich soil. The shrub will flower in poorer soil and with less water, but will not be as showy under these conditions. It can be grown as a tub-plant (Illustrated Plate 1).

Abutilon megapotamicum is a trailing species with small drooping flowers, having a dark red calyx and yellow petals. It needs a trellis or may droop over a low wall. It makes an attractive standard and may be grafted successfully on top of a straight stem of Yellow Abutilon. (Illustrated Plate 1)

Abutilon striatum is a natural species from Mexico with green and yellow variegated leaves and veined orange flowers. Several hybrids have been developed, including one with green and gold blotched leaves. (Illustrated Plate 1)

Acacia (Leguminosae)

Acacia

WATTLE

There are hundreds of wattle trees which are found in different parts of the world, but only a few are considered suitable for the garden. The well-known Silver and Black Wattles, also known popularly as Mimosa Trees, are not recommended, for they are extremely difficult to eradicate once they have taken hold. *A. cyanophylla*, the Port Jackson Wattle, crowds out the native vegetation at the Cape. The flowers of the Wattle Trees are basically the same. They are minute and clustered together to form tiny, golden, fluffy balls arranged in sprays. The leaves vary in size and shape.

The Wattles have deep tap roots and should be planted out when small. They grow rapidly, so that they should not be bought more than 1 metre high. The seed is very hard-coated and should be soaked in water which has been brought to boiling point and then allowed to cool, and left in this water for several days if necessary. Germination often takes place in nature after veldfires have cracked open the seeds. The Wattle Trees can endure heat, drought and poor soil, but do best when they have good deep soil and sufficient moisture. They are hardy except to very severe frost, which may affect them particularly when they are young. They do not require pruning, but slight pruning may be done, if necessary, after the flowering period.

Acacia baileyana

COOTAMUNDRA OR BAILEY'S WATTLE

This tree from New South Wales grows to a height of about 8 metres. It is recommended for a large garden as it spreads and requires space. It is evergreen, hardy and drought-resisting. It is fast-growing, reaching a height of 4 metres in 3 years. It may be pruned after flowering.

The foliage is particularly attractive, being a soft bluish-grey colour. Each leaf is about 3 cm long and divided and sub-divided into tiny leaflets. It is valuable as it flowers in winter and early spring and produces masses of lemon-coloured balls of flowers in sprays. Branches can be picked for the vase, and the foliage itself is so attractive that it can be picked for decoration even when the tree is not in flower.

Acacia elata see *A. terminalis*.

Acacia cultriformis

KNIFE-LEAF WATTLE

This large Australian shrub of 2–4 metres has grey foliage like the Pearl Acacia, but the leaves are pointed and triangular. It has sprays of bright yellow flowers in spring. It may be used as a clipped hedge. (Illustrated Plate 2)

Acacia galpinii
APIESDORING

A deciduous, rounded shade tree of 26 metres, this has spikes of creamy flowers in summer. A drought-resistant thorn tree from the warmer parts of the Transvaal and Botswana, it needs deep, well-drained soil. It will stand some frost.

Acacia giraffae
CAMELTHORN

A deciduous thorn tree of 12 metres with globose flowers, this has an umbrella shape, spreading about 16 metres across. Frost-hardy and drought-resistant, it is useful in dry areas with sandy or lime soil. It comes from the Transvaal, Orange Free State and northern Cape.

Acacia karroo
SWEET-THORN, SOETDORING

A deciduous tree of 7 metres, this has finely divided foliage and small scented flowers along the branches in mid-summer. The long, white, paired thorns are a feature during winter. This drought-resistant tree from southern and tropical Africa will grow in all parts of the country except where frosts are severe.

Acacia linearis (A. linifolia)
FLAX WATTLE

A tall evergreen Australian shrub, growing to 5 metres, this has open spreading branches with a feathery appearance, being closely covered with 4 cm-long, needle-like leaves. It has loose sprays of pale lemon flower balls at the ends of the branches in early spring. It does well at the coast and will grace the winter garden.

Acacia longifolia
SYDNEY GOLDEN WATTLE

A fast-growing, evergreen, Australian tree of 6 metres, this has spectacular bright gold, finger-like flower-spikes springing from between the simple, narrow leaves in early spring. It thrives both inland and at the coast (Illustrated Plate 2).

Acacia nigrescens (A. pallens)
KNOB-THORN, KNOPPIESDORING

A deciduous bushveld tree of 10 metres, this has creamy catkins of flowers in spring before the leaves. These have rounded leaflets. Small hooked thorns grow on the branches and on the pointed "knobs" on the trunk. This drought-resistant tree is suited to warm areas and may be seen in the Kruger National Park.

Acacia pendula
WEEPING MYALL, BOREE

Weeping branches and narrow leaves, up to 8 cm long, make this 8-metre, evergreen, Australian tree desirable in the landscape. Small clusters of flowers appear along the branches in spring. It is drought-resistant and likes warm conditions.

Acacia podalyriaefolia

This Australian small tree is particularly recommended for smaller gardens as it grows to a height of about 4 metres. It flowers profusely in mid-winter. The flowerballs are very bright yellow and borne in large cascades, as much as 25 cm long.

The evergreen foliage is distinctive, for it is a soft, pearly-grey colour. Each curved leaf is about 5 cm long and oval in shape, with a single vein down the centre. The tips end in tiny points. A fine, hairy down covers the leaves and stems and adds to the shrub's soft appearance. The leaves are borne closely along the thin, dainty branches and the whole tree has a graceful, arching habit of growth.

This shrub grows rapidly and endures the cold climates of South Africa. It should not be confused with *Acacia cultriformis*, the Knife-leaf Wattle, which is a similar shrub with grey foliage, but the leaves are pointed and triangular. (Illustrated Plate 2)

Acacia pycnantha

GOLDEN WATTLE

A small tree with large deep yellow balls of flowers in spring and early summer, this is recommended for its attraction and use as a sand-binder on coastal soil. It is tender to frost while young. The leaves are broad and curved. It comes from Victoria, North South Wales and South Australia.

Acacia spectabilis

MUDGEE WATTLE

An Australian evergreen shrub growing to 3 metres, this has compound feathery leaves and is spectacular in spring with its showy 12-cm sprays of golden flowers.

Acacia subulata

AWL-LEAF WATTLE

This small, dainty tree of 3 metres has long thin leaves like *Parkinsonia*. The small sprays of yellow flowers appear almost continuously. This is a hardy and drought-resistant tree.

Acacia terminalis (A. elata)

CEDAR WATTLE

This large, spreading tree comes from New South Wales. It grows up to 20 metres in height, reaching a height of 7 metres in 4 years. This is a long-lived, evergreen tree that is tender to frost when young. Protect it with grass (see Chapter I) for the first 2 or 3 winters in areas where frost is experienced. It is worth taking a little extra trouble over it, for it forms a magnificent tree that bears clusters of large, fluffy yellow balls in early summer.

Each large, compound leaf is about 25 cm long and divided into 15-cm leaflets, each one divided again into 3-cm, dark-green, smooth, narrow leaflets. The whole effect is graceful and spreading. The tree has a tendency to form 2 main stems, and after a number of years one of these may break away in a high wind. Try to train a single main stem while the tree is young and it will thicken and become sturdy in a short time.

Acacia vestita

A hardy, semi-evergreen shrub of 3 metres, this has pointed, hairy leaves, about 2 cm long, on weeping branches. It has long sprays of flowers in spring and early summer.

Acacia xanthophloea

FEVER TREE

This tall, deciduous tree is beautiful in its natural surroundings in northern Zululand, N. Transvaal and Mozambique, with its curious pale green trunk. The yellow flowers appear in summer. This is an interesting tree for gardens in warm places and may be grown in sheltered places on the highveld. It like damp soil.

Acalypha
(Euphorbiaceae)

Acalypha wilkesiana (A. tricolor)

COPPERLEAF

The *Acalypha* (pronounced with the accent on the second syllable) species form a highly decorative group of shrubs that come from India and the Fiji Islands. They will thrive in the frost-free lowveld and in semi-tropical districts. They can stand the wind on the sea-coast very well, and this is surprising since the large leaves look so delicate and papery.

Acalypha wilkesiana is prized for its ornamental foliage and grows into a large rounded shrub about 2–3 metres high, which spreads as wide again. There are many colour varieties. The most attractive of the Copperleaves in *A. wilkesiana* var. *macafeana*, which has large, heart-shaped, smooth leaves about 15 cm in diameter, almost rose-pink in colour and blotched with darker shades of crimson and brown. The leaves overlap one another so that none of the stems can be seen. *A. wilkesiana* var. *marginata* has an oval, copper-coloured leaf edged with cream or pink. Several colourful hybrids have been developed from these varieties. (Illustrated Plate 1).

Both varieties make luxuriant rounded hedges where conditions are favourable. They can be grown as hot-house plants elsewhere. Cuttings strike easily in moist, warm places.

Acanthus
(Acanthaceae)

Acanthus pubescens

PRICKLY ACANTHUS

A striking evergreen shrub that grows to 3 metres in warm districts, such as the Northern Transvaal, this has foot-long, prickly leaves, like giant holly-leaves, overlapping on the upright, cane-like stems. The dense flower-spikes stand up at the tops of the stems and are a deep rosy-mauve, blooming from July until the end of September. This shrub is suited to the wilder corners of a large garden and forms a good background to a mixed border. It suckers and may be increased by division or by seed. It may be cut back after flowering if desired.

A. pubescens will grow in ordinary soil and needs protection from frost in cold areas, which may be given by the overhanging braches of a tree. This species grows wild in central and tropical Africa. (Illustrated Plate 2).

Acer
(Aceraceae)

Acer

MAPLE

The Maple Trees, of which there are many, come from North America,

Europe and Asia, and include some garden hybrids. Maple sugar is derived from the Sugar Maple (*Acer saccharum*) but the Maples are valued in the garden mainly for their autumn foliage. This is more colourful when the days are hot, with cold nights. They are deciduous, strong growers and thrive in ordinary garden soil They are propagated by seed, although the rarer species may be budded in summer and reproduced by layers or cuttings in the spring.

Acer buergerianum   (*Acer trifidum*)

TRIDENT OR CHINESE MAPLE

This is a small, hardy, rounded tree from China, growing about 5 to 7 metres in height. It is fairly slow-growing and should be trained with a standard. The small leaves have 3 points and turn bright red in autumn. Oxford Road, Johannesburg, is lined with these Maples, where they are growing in an open, sunny position.

Acer negundo

BOX-ELDER MAPLE

This is a medium-fast-growing shade or landscape tree from North America, growing to a height of about 10 metres with a well-rounded shape. It is different from ordinary Maples in that it has compound leaves, each consisting of 3 to 5 large, oval leaflets with toothed edges. They are a pretty, fresh green and are among the first to fall in the autumn, turning yellow as they fall. Silky, green tassels of tiny flowers appear very early in spring before the leaves, giving the tree a distinctive appearance. This tree will grow in a number of varying conditions and is very hardy and sturdy. It is, perhaps, over-rated for ornamental purposes, and the varieties with variegated leaves are probably more attractive.

Acer negundo var. *argenteum* is a smaller tree with silver markings on the leaves and *Acer negundo* var. *aureum* is similar, but with gold markings.

Acer palmatum

JAPANESE MAPLE

There are many varieties of these small trees, growing about 4 to 5 metres in height, which could really be regarded as shrubs. Their leaves vary in shape and colour. *Acer palmatum* var. *sanguineum* has 5-pointed leaves which are a blood-red colour from spring to autumn. They are a much lighter red when the sun shines through them and are most distinctive. These trees have the most attractive foliage of all the Maples, but must be given suitable conditions. Japanese Maples like cool, mountain conditions and are best planted facing east in the garden, so that they receive only the early morning sun. Hailstorms mark the leaves badly, and they dislike hot winds. Among the numerous garden varieties raised there is the *semptemlobum* group, with 7 lobes to the leaves; the *dissectum* group, with 7 to 11 deeply cut lobes; *aureum* with yellow leaves changing to gold; *ornatum*, bronzy-red; *lutescens*, butter-yellow; *rosea-marginatum*, rosy-edged and *nigrum*, dark purple. (Illustrated Plate 2)

Acokanthera
(*Apocynaceae*)

Acokanthera spectabilis

POISON BUSH

An evergreen shrub which grows to 3 metres, with fragrant, small, white, starry flowers in spring, this has poisonous, plum-like fruits which were used by the Bushmen for tipping their arrows. It may be pruned after flowering to prevent the fruits from developing. *Acokanthera* needs shelter from frost and will grow in full sun or semi-shade. It needs good soil and regular watering, being drought-resistant in winter, and may be used as a tub-plant. This South African shrub is grown from cuttings.

Adenium
(Apocynaceae)

Adenium

IMPALA LILY, SABIE STAR

Dwarf, succulent shrubs, these have showy, starry flowers in pink, white or white edged with pinkish-cerise. The stems are short, smooth and thick, capable of storing water, so that the plants will endure great heat and drought, especially when dormant during winter. They dislike frost and are often grown in dry, sunny glass-houses in full sun where they have shelter from frost in winter. They rot during heavy summer rains if drainage is not exceptionally good. There is a large underground root that stores moisture. Seed germinates easily, but growth is extremely slow.

There are several species and the most attractive is the tropical African *Adenium obesum*. It has clusters of 5-pointed flowers which are white edged with pink. The gorgeous variety *multiflorum*, known as Impala Lily or Sabie Star, is similar, but the flowers are more pointed and edged on the crinkled margins with deeper cerise or red. This grows wild in the northern part of South Africa and Mozambique and it has been observed that the more south one travels in Africa, the deeper the colour form appears in the wild. The flowers appear on bare stems in late winter or early spring, followed by waxy green leaves. The plant forms a thicket, reaching a height of 1,5 metres in hot areas with dry winters and light summer rains. It may be grown in a large pot on a patio. (Illustrated plate 3).

Adenium boehmianum, from S.W. Africa, has plain pink flowers, which are sometimes white and pink. It has been cultivated in a dry greenhouse in a cool area with high rainfall. It grows in limestone in nature and its poisonous sap is used by Bushmen to tip their arrows for killing game.

Adenium swazicum is another pink or purple-flowered species that flowers in mid-summer and grows wild in Swaziland.

Adenocalymma
(Bignoniaceae)

Adenocalymma comosum

ADENOCALYMMA

A large evergreen Brazilian climber with bright yellow, flattish trumpet flowers, each about 10 cm long, this has shining, oval leaves, each about the same length as the flowers. They are grouped in threes, with the third leaf sometimes taking the form of a tendril. Prominent glands on the leaves and flowers are a diagnostic feature. Variety *nitidum* has velvety flowers.

There are more than 50 species of *Adenocalymma* from Brazil, several of which have yellow flowers. *A. comosum* needs a sub-tropical climate and grows successfully in Durban. Propagation is by cuttings.

Aesculus
(Hippocastanaceae)

Aesculus hippocastanum

HORSE-CHESTNUT

A large deciduous tree in Europe, this is slow-growing and may be treated as a shrub in the garden. It flowers when about 2 metres in height, bearing stately spires of white flowers in late spring. *A. carnea* is a hybrid with pink flowers. The foliage of the horse-chestnut is ornamental, with 5 to 7 leaflets springing from the end of the stalk. Horse-chestnuts need deep moist soil for good results and prefer places with cold winters. They grow from seed or "conkers".

Agonis
(Myrtaceae)

Agonis flexuosa

WILLOW–MYRTLE

A small Australian evergreen tree of 12 metres, this has graceful stems with drooping, willow-like foliage and small white blossoms during summer. It should be pruned after flowering. It is sensitive to frost and best recommended for mild districts. It needs moisture while young but becomes drought-resistant when mature. Propagation is from seed. A variegated shrubby form with cream and pink markings is known, but is not easily obtainable.

Agonis juniperina has very short, narrow leaves and globose flower-heads, also growing to 12 metres.

Akebia
(Lardizabalaceae)

Akebia quinata

FIVE–LEAF AKEBIA

A vigorous evergreen climber that becomes deciduous where winters are severe, this has small, fragrant purple flowers and purplish edible fruits containing numerous black seeds embedded in white pulp. The small leaflets are arranged in fives, springing from a central point.

This interesting plant is useful for gardens with cool, moist winters, as it grows more easily in the northern hemisphere than in the southern and it is difficult to raise from seed. It grows wild in China, Japan and Korea.

Alberta
(Rubiaceae)

Alberta magna

ALBERTA

This small, South African tree comes from Natal and Pondoland, and grows to a height of 4–5 metres. It has bunches of 3 cm, scarlet, tubular flowers at the end of winter and in spring. A curious feature is that 2 of the tiny bracts at the base of the flower become enlarged until they are about 3 cm in length and about 5 mm in width. They have a papery appearance and are a glowing, deep scarlet. The bracts are even more showy than the flowers and remain on the tree almost throughout summer. They last well if picked. Ultimately, they turn brown and are scattered by the wind, acting as wings which carry the seed. The leaves are about 12 cm in length and about 4 cm across. They have a thick, waxy texture and are a shining, deep, olive-green.

This tree is very slow-growing and is more frequently seen as a shrub in cultivation. There is a magnificent group to be seen at Kirstenbosch. Alberta has a neat and formal appearance, growing erect and trimly from the base, so that it is suitable for planting near the house. For best appearance, the branches should be allowed to grow from the base, or removed to allow only a very short standard.

Alberta thrives in a warm, frost-free climate and will stand only very slight frost. It enjoys moisture and humidity and should be well watered in the garden. It thrives all along the coast from Natal to the Cape, and may be grown inland in warm, frost-free areas. It is rarely grown in private gardens, but is well worth trying (Illustrated Plate 3).

Albizia
(Leguminosae)

Albizia julibrissin

A deciduous Asian tree of about 10 metres, this has an attractive spreading shape with the finely divided, fern-like leaves arranged in flat layers. Showy clusters of flowers appear at the ends of the branches in early summer. Each flower consists of a 4-cm-wide puff of silky stamens, each about 2 cm long, which are pink, shading to white near the base. Variety *rosea* has smaller, brighter pink flowers. This hardy and drought-resistant tree will grow in ordinary light soil and may be raised from seed sown in spring. *Albizia* belongs to the *Acacia* family, but has no thorns (Illustrated Plate 3).

There are several Albizias from the warmer parts of Natal and the Transvaal, mainly with white flowers, some of which are attractive flat-topped trees. *A. adianthifolia* (*A. fastigiata*) from Natal, Pondoland, the Transvaal and Tropical Africa, is a deciduous flat-topped tree of 10 to 13 metres with globular cream flowers and rusty coloured foliage. *A tanganyicensis*, the Paper-Bark Tree, from the Northern Transvaal, has creamy flowers in November.

Allamanda
(Apocynaceae)

Allamanda cathartica

This is the common *Allamanda* which comes from Brazil and is an evergreen climber or rambling shrub. There are many varieties with different sized flowers. They look best on a sloping bank or overhanging a garden wall. They flower very freely for a long period in the summer and have flowers of various sizes. They are most attractive and showy, but will not stand frost. They do well in hot, moist areas, particularly on the sea-coast. They like good rich soil and should be kept fairly dry in winter. They reproduce from seed or from cuttings. Their sticky sap is said to be poisonous.

Allamanda cathartica var. *hendersonii* has the largest flowers of the yellow-flowered varieties. They are trumpet-shaped and very open at the mouth, measuring about 10 cm across. Their colour is a pure, bright yellow and the texture of the petals is waxy and almost translucent. The leathery leaves are dark green and rough-backed, 7 cm long, narrow and grouped all along the stems (Illustrated Plate 3).

Allamanda violacea has pretty, mauve-pink flowers which have the same trumpet shape but are half the size. The leaves are a brighter green but also smaller and rougher in texture. It blooms in early summer and comes from Brazil.

Alstonia
(Apocynaceae)

Alstonia scholaris

An evergreen shrub of nearly 3 metres, this bears clusters of 5 to 7 white flowers during summer. Each flower has a narrow tube opening into 5 pointed, slightly twisted petals. The ribbed, smooth leaves have prominent veins. This shrub belongs to the same family as Frangipani and has a milky juice. The bark has medicinal properties and yields caoutchouc or raw rubber. It comes from India, where it is called Pali-mari. There are many other species in the tropics of the Old World.

This grows easily in the open at the coast both at the Cape and in Natal, requiring protection from frost on the highveld. It grows from cuttings.

Amherstia
(Leguminosae)

Amherstia nobilis

This rounded tropical evergreen tree from Burma is said to be the most striking tree in the world and it is certainly most spectacular when its gorgeous chandelier of bloom, fully a metre in length, hangs from the branches in early summer. The coral-scarlet, stalked flowers resemble orchids arranged in a long, graceful raceme and have a waxy texture. The large dark green leaves are divided into broad leaflets. The tree grows to 10 or 15 metres and requires a hot, humid climate in order to thrive. There is only one species, which may be grown from seed or cuttings, but it does not set seed easily and is difficult to propagate, so that it remains an inspiring challenge to the sub-tropical gardener. It has been grown occasionally on the sub-tropical east coast of Natal and blooms magnificently in Rio, Brazil. (Illustrated Plate 4).

Amorpha
(Leguminosae)

Amorpha fruticosa

A deciduous shrub of 3 to 5 metres, from the southern states of America, this has 15-cm spikes of dark purple flowers, sometimes varying to blue or white, in midsummer. The soft leaves are divided into numerous 4 cm-long leaflets. It needs sunshine, light soil, moisture in summer and is hardy to average frost. Propagation is by seed, cuttings or layers.

Antigonon
(Polygonaceae)

Antigonon leptopus

This delightful, Mexican creeper has sprays of numerous, tiny, lantern-shaped, cerise flowers borne on delicate stems which stand away from the foliage. The effect is extremely dainty and yet bright pink and conspicuous. There is also a white-flowered variety, not to be confused with *Polygonum*. The leaves are soft textured and heart-shaped. The main stems are thin and dainty. The plant is tender and deciduous and flowers all through summer and autumn. It does particularly well in Durban and all warm, frost-free areas, but it will flower in Johannesburg after a mild winter. If one can protect it for a few years, it will not die back altogether as a result of frost. One should try to give it a warm, sunny wall in order to prevent loss, and stack grass around the base during winter in cold areas.

Antigonon grows with medium rapidity, but does not grow very big. It is useful for covering a medium-sized wall or fence. It should be planted in well-drained soil mixed with compost and given abundant water in summer but dry conditions in winter. *Antigonon* makes excellent cut material for the vase. It does not need pruning, but if it must be trimmed then this should be done in the spring when all danger of frost is over (Illustrated plate 4).

Antigonon guatamalense, Guatamala Coral-Vine, is even more floriferous, with larger pink flowers and broader leaves. It comes from Guatamala and needs sub-tropical conditions. (Illustrated Plate 4)

Aphelandra
(Acanthaceae)

Aphelandra squarrosa

A bushy soft-wooded shrub that grows to about 2 metres, this has decorative large green leaves veined with white. The flower-spikes are yellow with densely overlapping orange bracts and stand above the foliage. The variety *leopoldii* has yellow flowers in red bracts and var. *louisae* has golden bracts. All come from Brazil. This species is similar to *Sanchezia* in its variegated foliage.

This shrub is useful in that it grows in shade under trees, but needs good soil and adequate moisture. It does best in warm, frost-free areas and can be grown as a pot plant in cold climates. It may be pruned back after flowering.

A. sinclairiana is a large soft shrub to 3 metres, bearing numerous spikes of overlapping coral-pink bracts in clusters at the ends of the branches. The leaves are plain green. This shrub comes from Central America. There are several other Aphelandras, notably the small *A. tetragona* with narrow, scarlet flowers.

Arbutus
(Ericaceae)

Arbutus unedo
STRAWBERRY TREE

A slow-growing evergreen tree of 10 metres, this is better treated as a shrub. The dark green foliage is neat and the tiny, urn-shaped, white flowers fairly insignificant, but it has curious, strawberry-like, edible fruits in autumn and winter. It comes from Southern Europe and Ireland.

This shrub needs regular watering, but will resist drought when mature. It is wind-resistant at the coast. It belongs to the Erica family, but tolerates alkaline soil. Propagated by cuttings or seed. (Illustrated Plate 4).

Ardisia
(Myrsinaceae)

Ardisia crispa (*A. crenata*)
ARDISIA

Generally grown as a pot plant, this small stiff evergreen shrublet of about 60 cm may be grown out-of-doors under trees in mild areas. It has clusters of bright red berries and glossy, serrated, tapering leaves. It needs shade and moisture and is grown from seed in spring or cuttings of half-ripe wood.

Aristolochia
(Aristolochiaceae)

Aristolochia elegans
DUTCHMAN'S PIPE

Curious, pipe-shaped, reddish-purple flowers, streaked with white and yellow, as well as the basket-like seedpods, make this vigorous evergreen climber interesting. It has heart-shaped leaves. It does best in warm, frost-free areas, coming as it does from Brazil. *A. durior* from north-east America is hardier, but has smaller flowers. Both grow from seed.

Aristolochia grandiflora has giant, mottled purple and cream flowers, up to 25 cm wide, and climbs to 3 metres. There are several forms from Central America. *Aristolochia gigantea* is similar. (Illustrated Plate 5).

Aucuba
(Cornaceae)

Aucuba japonica
AUCUBA

An Asian evergreen shrub, this grows from 2 to 4 metres and is hardy in southern Africa. It is grown for its shining ornamental foliage, although the female plants also bear clusters of scarlet berries. Berries only appear if the female is grown close to a male plant. Plants grown in glass-houses must be hand-fertilized. The chief virtue of this shrub is that it will grow in very shady situations and, in fact, will be scorched by hot sun. It may be grown indoors as a pot plant or in a tub on a shady verandah. It needs good soil, regular watering and will grow from cuttings.

The large leaves are oval, tapering, coarsely toothed above the middle and grow up to 18 cm in length. There are several varieties, the most popular being *variegata*, the Gold-Dust Bush, which has leaves splashed with gold. Variety *dentata* has smaller, toothed leaves.

Azalea—See under *Rhododendron*

Banksia (Proteaceae)

Banksia

BANKSIA

These are striking Australian members of the Protea family with long Bottle-brush-like flower spikes in red or yellow. All species are interesting and may be found in specialist nurseries. They grow fairly easily from seed. Banksias need full sun, warm conditions and well-drained, acid soil, but tolerate average garden soil. Although drought-resistant, they should be watered regularly through winter.

Banksia ericifolia

HEATH BANKSIA

A large evergreen shrub that grows to 4 metres, this has distinctive needle-like leaves like Heath. It has beautiful burnt-orange flower-spikes that grow to 30 cm in length. This is said to be the finest Banksia for the garden and is the best-known. (Illustrated Plate 5).

Banksia baxteri. This interesting evergreen grows to 2 metres or more and has long leaves to 20 cm that are deeply divided into broad triangular sections. The globular head of yellow flowers is about the size of an orange and appears in mid-summer. (Illustrated Plate 5).

Banksia coccinea, SCARLET BANKSIA, has short "cobs" of scarlet flowers during spring and early summer. The leaves are broad and short with spiny edges and the bush grows to about 3 metres.

Banksia grandis, BULL BANKSIA, grows into an evergreen tree of 10 metres with extremely long leaves to 20 cm that are deeply divided to the mid-rib. The cylindrical head of yellow flowers is almost as long as the leaves. The flowers attract nectar-seeking birds like Sugarbirds at the S.W. Cape.

Banksia speciosa. The sculptural quality of the huge silvery cones of flowers, fully 18 cm long and 12 cm wide, and the spirals of narrow serrated leaves of this species are its chief attraction. It makes a large bush of about 2 metres, which forms an interesting accent. The flowers open to a creamy yellow and bloom in spring or early summer. (Illustrated Plate 5).

Barleria (Acanthaceae)

Barleria obtusa

BARLERIA, BUSH-VIOLET

A soft, spreading, evergreen shrub of about 1 metre, this has clusters of bluish-mauve, 2–3 cm wide, five-petalled flowers in autumn and winter. It has small oval leaves. This plant will grow in full sun or semi-shade and needs a position protected from frost in cold areas. It is drought-resistant in winter, but needs moisture in summer. It grows wild in the eastern Cape, Natal and the Transvaal, and may be propagated by seed or cuttings. Several other species have white, bluish or red flowers.

Bauhinia (Leguminosae)

Bauhinia

This is a large family of about 300 species of trees, shrubs and climbers, with origins as far afield as India, Australia, Brazil and South Africa. Some are ornamental and some are useful for their timber. The common name is derived from the shape of the winged leaves, which are 2-lobed and are supposed to resemble the footprint of a camel when laid flat. Most of them have pretty flowers and grow easily from seed.

Bauhinia blakeana

HONG KONG ORCHID TREE

Probably the most magnificent of all the Orchid Trees, this is an evergreen bushy tree growing to a height of about 5 metres in hot frost-free areas. The branches are laden with large 5-petalled flowers, spreading up to 15 cm across, which are a rich deep rose-purple colour, veined with a paler shade. They appear in masses from autumn throughout winter into early spring and frequently bloom again in early summer in the summer-rainfall area. The 2-winged leaves are larger than those of *B. variegata* and form a dense background to the flowers. Although it does best in frost-free areas, it grows surprisingly well in sheltered gardens in Johannesburg, where winters may be very cold. It needs full sunshine and good, well-drained soil.

This tree was first discovered in 1908 growing wild in Hong Kong, where it is used as the city's floral emblem. As it does not set seed, it is thought to be a sterile natural hybrid and must be propagated by cuttings or air-layers. (Illustrated Plate 6).

Bauhinia corniculata (B. candicans of Sim.)

WHITE CAMELSFOOT

This Brazilian tree grows rapidly to a height of about 6 metres. It has a most distinctive shape, as the stem leans over at an angle, in jagged steps, while the top of the tree is broad and flattened. This gives it an artistic and somewhat wild appearance, which, in addition to the fact that it sends up suckers, makes it suitable for a roomy corner in a large garden. It could be quite a feature of the landscape on a large, natural rockery. The flowers are white, with thin, curving petals, and are poised like showy butterflies on the pretty green foliage during the latter half of summer, opening in the afternoon. The White Camelsfoot thrives at the coast, particularly in Natal, where it is common. It also grows inland, and can stand frost, provided that this is not excessive. It is usually evergreen, but may also become deciduous, according to the climate. It is also drought-resistant. Propagation is made by transplanting the suckers found near the parent tree, which otherwise grows easily and rapidly. It should not be confused with *B. variegata* var. *candida*. (Illustrated Plate 6).

B. macrantha is another white-flowered large shrub with slender petals and small leaves which grows wild in the northern Transvaal and Rhodesia.

Bauhinia galpinii

This spreading shrub will grow to cover a large area of about 7 metres square, but can be kept in check if necessary. It comes from the eastern Transvaal, particularly from the de Kaap valley near Barberton.

It is covered with groups of showy, brick-red flowers resembling nasturtiums. The leaves are characteristic. This shrub is particularly recommended for a large, natural rockery, where it can drape, unchecked, over the rocks. It can also be grown in a corner of a garden against a hedge where it will lean most effectively. It is seen at its best in March and April. *Bauhinia galpinii* can be grown very easily from seed or from cuttings. It prefers warmth, although it can stand light frosts, and thrives in a sun-baked position (Illustrated Plate 6).

Bauhinia glauca (B. corymbosa, B. scandens)

PINK CLIMBING BAUHINIA

This woody climber has small pink flowers, about 3 cm across, which may also be white, veined pink, with bright red stamens. It comes from South China and is fairly hardy.

Bauhinia hookeri

HOOKER'S BAUHINIA

A large tree from Queensland, this has white flowers edged with crimson, about 5 cm wide. This does best in warm, frost-free districts.

Bauhinia variegata

ORCHID TREE, PINK CAMELSFOOT

This beautiful *Bauhinia* comes from India, where it is called Ebony Wood and its bark used for tanning. It is fairly hardy and easy to grow, so that it should have a place in every large garden. It is used successfully as a small street tree in Pretoria and can be pruned with a standard so as to form a shade tree for a small garden. Otherwise, it forms a rounded bush about 4 metres in height and spreads to the same width. It becomes a much larger bushy tree in hot places.

The flowers are so closely borne along the stems that the whole bush appears to be a rich pink. They are large, about 7 cm across, and shaped like an open trumpet with one half cut off. The long stamens curve out gracefully from the base. The 5 broad petals are a rich, mauvish-pink and the top petal is marked with a dark, purplish-red patch of colour. The flowers appear in spring, usually without the leaves, depending on the weather, making this one of the showiest of spring-flowering shrubs. It endures dry and cold climates with a reasonable amount of frost, where it is deciduous, and also grows enormous in moist, hot areas where it remains evergreen. Late autumn and winter rains cause the leaves to remain on the bush for a longer period. It requires no pruning, although long sprays may be picked for the vase where they will last a day or two.

Bauhinia variegata grows easily and rapidly from seed, reaching a height of 1 metre in 2 years and frequently begins to flower at that stage. The seed should either be planted where it is intended to be grown, or the seedling transplanted when 5 to 8 cm high, as it quickly forms a long tap root which cannot be handled once it has grown too long. Larger specimens can be bought in tins and from nurseries and transplanted, but it is best to buy the smallest and youngest specimens as these form the most natural-shaped bushes (Illustrated Plate 6).

There is a pure white-flowered variety of this species (*B. variegata* var. *candida*) which has a similar habit of growth and similarly shaped flowers and leaves. It should not be confused with *B. corniculata*. (Illustrated Plate 6).

The Pink Camelsfoot is sometimes incorrectly called *Bauhinia purpurea*, which is a different tree, having flowers with narrower, darker petals and more deeply divided and pointed leaves. It is not as showy as *B. variegata*.

Beaumontia (*Apocynaceae*)

Beaumontia grandiflora

GIANT TRUMPET CLIMBER

This strong, evergreen climber comes from the East Indies. In early spring it is festooned with clusters of huge, white, fleshy, funnel-shaped trumpet flowers which are 8–10 cm long and about 8 cm across at the mouth. It is a most spectacular sight to see these enormous flowers in full bloom. The dark green leaves are large, oval and about 12 cm long. The branches are very woody and heavy, and need a strong support such as a wall, or the weight of the vine may cause the support to collapse. It needs an area of fully 7 square metres in which to spread and also requires adequate root-room.

This climber is tender to frost and thrives in sub-tropical areas. It is considered to be one of Durban's most showy climbers. It can also be grown inland in a very warm position and will stand frosts if the day temperature is hot enough and if it is grown in a sheltered position. There are some magnificent specimens to be seen in Pretoria—facing north in the gardens at Government House and facing west at the side of the Union Buildings. This vigorous climber should be planted in good, strong soil containing compost. It needs full sun for flowering and likes sun on the base of its woody stem. For this reason the lower leaves and branches should be removed if necessary. Severe pruning should take place after flowering, in order to grow new flowering shoots for the following season. Propagation is by cuttings. (Illustrated Plate 5).

Beloperone (*Acanthaceae*)

Beloperone guttata

SHRIMP FLOWER

This attractive shrub comes from Mexico and flowers practically the whole year round where conditions are favourable.

The bracts of the flowers are pinkish-rust in colour, flushed occasionally with mustard. There are some lighter and deeper variations in colour, while one distinctive cultivar has lime-yellow flowers, known as "Yellow Queen". They overlap, forming an arched tube concealing the flowers, all except one which protrudes from the end. It is white, spotted with purple. The whole thing looks remarkably like a cooked shrimp. The leaves are a pretty, green colour, oval and soft-textured.

The shrub is low-growing, about 1 metre high, and rounded in proportion. It does best in warm, frost-free areas, either dry or humid, but should be well-watered. It can be grown in areas with cold winters, but should be given a warm, sunny corner so that there is some protection from frost. It can also be grown as a pot-plant. It can be reproduced by seed or from cuttings. *Beloperone* should not be confused with *Pachystachys*. (Illustrated Plate 7).

Berberis
Berberis
(Berberidaceae)

BARBERRY

The Barberries make up a group of attractive shrubs which come from the northern hemisphere and contain many hybrids. Many have brilliant red foliage in autumn and bear thick clusters of yellow flowers followed by red or black berries. They are very easy to grow and not particular about soil. As a rule they like a sunny position but will endure semi-shade. They do best in the cooler districts and can be propagated by seed, layers or cuttings.

They are divided into two sections. The true *Berberis* has simple leaves and sharp thorns along its stems. It may be either deciduous or evergreen. The *Mahonia* is generally evergreen, has compound leaves and no thorns, and is now regarded as a separate genus. It is described separately under that name.

Berberis thunbergii var. atropurpurea

PURPLE JAPANESE BARBERRY

This attractive deciduous shrub comes from Japan and has the most distinctive foliage. The leaves—as well as the stems—are always a deep shade of purple. They are perfectly smooth, rounded and small—about 2–3 cm long. There are groups of sharp purple spines at intervals up the stems. The Purple Barberry has pale yellow flowers and sparse red berries. It should be grown in full sun and will stand severe frost. This is a valuable landscape shrub of about 2 metres but should not be planted too close to a path-way as it is so prickly.

A hybrid with rosy, variegated foliage is called "Rose Glow".

B. thunbergii, the original Japanese Barberry, has green summer foliage which turns brilliant scarlet in autumn and shining red fruits. It also needs full sun and likes cold winters.

Berberis julianae

WINTERGREEN BARBERRY

This attractive shrub from China is almost evergreen, losing its leaves for a short period. The leaves are narrow and oval, about 8 cm long, and a shining, fresh green. They have prickly edges. In the autumn they turn brilliant scarlet and are most decorative. The stems have groups of sharp spines and the flowers are bright yellow. This shrub grows to a height of about 2 metres and there is also a dwarf form. It is hardy and easy to grow, liking a sunny position, especially the early morning sun (Illustrated Plate 7).

Berberis stenophylla

ROSEMARY BARBERRY

A very hardy hybrid, evergreen, 2 metre shrub, this has golden yellow flowers along the arching, spiny branches in late spring, and dark green, narrow leaves. It likes good soil and moisture, but is fairly drought-resistant. It likes a cold winter and is suitable for a south wall. It may be grown with afternoon shade in hot climates.

Berzelia
(Bruniaceae)
Berzelia lanuginosa

KOLKOL

An erect, evergreen shrub with feathery, needle-like foliage, this has clusters of creamy, pea-sized flower "balls" during spring and early summer. It is native to

76

the South Western Cape, where it may be seen in the mountains with high rainfall. *Berzelia* likes very moist soil, and is suited to the waterside, but will grow in any well-watered position. Give it a sheltered position in areas with cold winters. It grows from seed.

Bignonia (Bignoniaceae)

Bignonia capreolata

ORANGE BIGNONIA OR CROSS-VINE

This beautiful hardy climber comes from the southern States of America. It is naturally evergreen but loses its leaves in districts which have cold winters. It bears large drooping bunches of spectacular orange or terra-cotta coloured trumpets about 8 cm long, which are about 6 cm wide at the mouth during summer. The foliage is made up of large, shiny, green leaves which are divided into numerous small leaflets.

This vigorous, woody climber grows rapidly and should be given plenty of space in which to spread. It has tendrils with tiny discs that cling to a wall so that it needs no further support. It can be pruned back severely in the spring in order to keep it within bounds. The main stems, as well as the side shoots, can be shortened considerably, if desired. The old wood at the base should be exposed to the sun for best results. It is propagated by cuttings or by seed.

Other climbers which belong to the Bignonia family, but which have been separated into different genera, and under which names they will be found, are as follows:
Campsis radicans (*Bignonia radicans*) TRUMPET VINE;
Clytostoma callistegioides (*Bignonia speciosa*) MAUVE BIGNONIA OR ARGENTINE TRUMPET VINE;
Doxantha unguis-cati (*Bignonia tweediana*) CATS-CLAW CREEPER;
Pandorea pandorana (*Bignonia australis*) WONGA-VINE;
Phaedranthus buccinatorius (*Bignonia cherere*) MEXICAN BLOOD-TRUMPET;
Pyrostegia ignea (*Bignonia venusta*) GOLDEN SHOWER, FLAME VINE.

Bixa (Bixaceae)

Bixa orellana

BIXA, LIPSTICK-TREE

This is an interesting shrub for a large, sub-tropical garden. It comes from South America and likes a hot, moist climate at altitudes of about 600 metres down to sea-level.

The waxy flowers resemble large, pink peach blossoms about 5 cm across, and the buds are also pink. It flowers throughout summer and autumn. The fruits appear together with the flowers and make interesting material for the vase. The fruits are dark-red, soft burrs which are borne in clusters, and contain bright red seeds, the skins of which supply the Annatto dye of commerce. The leaves are large, heart-shaped and smooth. Bixa is raised very easily from seed or cuttings and grows rapidly into a large, rounded shrub which spreads about 3 metres in diameter. It bears flowers and fruits after 2 years. It likes a good soil mixed generously with compost. It may be pruned for planting in small gardens.

A brilliant variety with crimson burrs is obtainable. (Illustrated Plate 7).

Bocconia
(Papaveraceae)

Bocconia frutescens

The large deeply-notched leaves of this shrubby plant from Mexico and tropical America make it decorative. They are about 25 cm long, bluish-green above and white-felted below, clustered along the cane-like stems that grow up to 2 or 3 metres in height. The large clusters of flowers are greenish-white. Evergreen in mild climates, this may be grown in areas with cool winters at high altitudes if placed in partial shade under large trees that will serve to protect it from frost. The soil should be light, containing compost. Propagation is by seed. This species should not be confused with the perennial Plume Poppy, formerly *Bocconia cordata*, now *Macleaya cordata*.

Bolusanthus
(Leguminosae)

Bolusanthus speciosus

WISTARIA-TREE

This deciduous tree comes from the warmer parts of the Transvaal, Swaziland and Portuguese East Africa. It grows about 5–7 metres in height and has a grey, woody trunk and gracefully arching branches. In October, it bears numerous, 15-cm sprays of bright purple, pea-shaped flowers which resemble Wistaria. The dark-green, compound leaves are divided into narrow pointed leaflets, each about 2 inches long.

This tree is tender to frost and requires a warm, sheltered position. There are some beautiful specimens to be seen in Pretoria. It is also grown at The Wilds, Johannesburg. The tree grows with medium rapidity in its native home and is slower in areas with a lower temperature. It grows best in sub-tropical conditions. It can be raised from seed but this is very slow. Other names for this tree are Elephant's Wood and Van Wyk's Hout.

Bombax
(Bombacaceae)

Bombax

COTTON TREES, SHAVING BRUSH

Bombax is the name of a genus that belongs to the Bombax family, *Bombacaceae*, which consists of numerous large trees that grow wild in the tropics, especially of America. The Baobab, *Adansonia digitata*, which is native to the warmer parts of southern Africa, belongs to this family. Several genera, like *Chorisea* and *Ceiba* do surprisingly well even in temperate areas and it would be well worth trying other spectacular trees needing a hotter, moister climate than *Chorisea*. They are best grown from seed, but may also be rooted from cuttings.

Bombax ellipticum, SHAVING BRUSH, is a tall deciduous tree with "shaving-brush" flowers, 8 cm long, consisting of rose-pink filaments, borne on bare stems in spring. These are followed in early summer by large leaves which are wine-red, later turning green. It comes from tropical America.

Bombax malabaricum, RED SILK COTTON, is a gigantic deciduous tree from India with 5-petalled waxy red flowers in spring, borne on bare wood. The fruits contain reddish floss. It may be pruned back and flowers when small. It is successful in Durban.

Boronia
(Rutaceae)

Boronia

There are about 100 numerous Australian Boronias with 4-petalled blue, red, pink or yellowish flowers, but there are not many in cultivation. They are propagated by seed or cuttings and generally need plenty of water, with well-drained, acid soil.

Boronia heterophylla, Red Boronia, is regarded as the best species. It grows to 2 metres and has cyclamen, scented flowers in spring. It enjoys warm, swampy conditions.

Boronia megastigma, Brown Boronia, grows from 60 cm to almost 2 metres and has fragrant brown flowers. There is a variety with tiny, greenish-yellow flowers, known as *lutea*. The flowering branches should be picked as a form of pruning, which is said to prolong the short life of the plants.

Bougainvillea
(Nyctaginaceae)

Bougainvillea

These vigorous and extremely showy climbers from South America come in several brilliant colours. The large coloured bracts make these climbers showy, for the flower itself is simply the yellow portion in the middle, which most people think is the stigma.

The purple Bougainvillea (*Bougainvillea glabra*) is almost too well known to need description. It climbs vigorously and a single specimen can cover a large area. Many people give it the support of an evergreen tree, so that the tree itself looks as if it is in flower. The purple Bougainvillea is hardy and prefers a warm, sunny spot. Its bracts are a deep, rich purple colour and are freely borne throughout summer and autumn. It can be pruned back at the end of winter.

The red and rust-coloured Bougainvilleas, derived from *B. spectabilis* and *B. lateritia* respectively, are more tender and really only thrive in frostless areas. If one has a warm, sunny wall, sheltered from wind, it is possible to grow these varieties in areas with light frost. There are so many named horticultural varieties, ranging from brilliant reds (Mrs. Butt or Brilliant); cherry-red (Killie Campbell); orange-red (McLean); incandescent pinkish-lilac, (Pride of Singapore) golden yellow (Lady Mary Baring) to palest hues (like dusty pink Natalia or the more hardy Gladys Hepburn) and pure white, that it is a matter of taste to make a choice when they bloom. The richly double forms, in several colours, are most suitable for hot districts.

These climbers have hooked spines and dark-green foliage which is completely hidden when the flowers are in bloom. They can be pruned to keep them in bounds. They can also be clipped into bush form or grown as hedges in warm localities, but must be trimmed continuously in order to be kept flowering and to prevent long shoots from growing out. Nip out the growing tip of flowering sprays as they come into bloom, in order to promote flowering. They can be grown as ground-covers on flat ground or on banks and may be trained as standards. If there is no space to grow Bougainvilleas, they may be grown in pots and placed in warm positions on a sunny verandah, as they may be pruned drastically to shape. The lack of nutrients in the pot will limit growth and induce flowering, for the plants do not like overfeeding or they will produce more leaves than flowers. Lead the shoots around horizontally in order to obtain thick main stems covered with a ball of blooms, then shorten these later and retain the thick main trunk.

Bougainvillea is extremely easy to grow and will thrive in any soil, but does best in sandy, well-drained soil that is not too rich. It needs full sunlight for best results. Reproduction is by cuttings or layers, and the plants begin to flower while small. New hybrids are produced by seed after cross-pollination. (Illustrated Plate 8)

Bouvardia (Rubiaceae)

Bouvardia

BOUVARDIA

Small, evergreen shrubs, growing to about 1 metre in height, these have showy, tufted heads of red, pink or white flowers. Each long-tubed flower opens into 4 tiny starry petals. Some are scented. They bloom in summer and autumn. The leaves are generally oval in shape.

These plants are suited to the greenhouse, but may be grown out of doors provided that they are given a sheltered position in places with cold winters. They will grow in the sun or semi-shade and like a rich soil with plenty of moisture. They come originally from Mexico and Central America, but most of the plants available are garden hybrids. They are propagated by cuttings. (Illustrated Plate 9).

Brachychiton (Sterculiaceae)

Brachychiton acerifolium (Sterculia acerifolia)

FLAME-TREE

Often included with *Sterculia* from which they differ slightly, the *Brachychiton* trees come from Australia. The Flame-Tree is almost evergreen, but usually drops its leaves before the flowering period in early summer, so that the bright flowers make a magnificent show on bare branches. The individual flowers are tiny, 15-mm, scarlet bells which hang in open clusters, so that the whole tree looks as if it is wreathed in delicate flames. The leaves are bright green, glossy and shaped like maple leaves. The trunk is straight and tapers from a thick base to the top. The bark looks like an elephant's hide.

The Flame-Tree does best where frost is absent and enjoys hot conditions, whether moist or dry, but will grow in places with cold winters like Johannesburg. This is a tree worth having, but one requires the patience to forget about it for several years, as it is rather slow-growing and does not flower until it is quite large. Unfortunately, even large trees do not flower regularly and sometimes miss a flowering season, but this tree is such a never-to-be-forgotten sight when it does flower, that it should be planted in every large garden where it has suitable conditions. Copious watering will make it grow more rapidly. It is grown from seed or from cuttings (Illustrated Plate 9).

Brachychiton discolor (Sterculia discolor)

QUEENSLAND LACEBARK

This large, deciduous tree loses its leaves for a short period at flowering time. It is commonly called Pink Sterculia in Natal. It thrives in hot, moist conditions, but can withstand drought and is quite common in Rhodesia where it does very well. It flowers in Johannesburg where it is all too rare. It should be given a warm, sheltered spot in a fairly large garden and is well worth waiting for, as it does not flower while young.

The flowers are large, just over 3 cm across the width, and trumpet-shaped. They look as if they have been cut out of stiff pink velvet, have a bright yellow centre, and grow in groups at the ends of the branches. This exciting tree bears its unusual flowers during early summer, usually on bare stems. The leaves are dark green, maple-shaped and have a furry texture on the back. The new growth is distinctive, for the tiny leaves grow in stiff circles at the tips of the branches and look as if they are made out of dark red velvet. The tree grows upright and tall, with a similar shaped trunk to the other species of *Brachychiton*. It is green, overlaid with a grey, lacy pattern. The Queensland Lacebark usually grows up to 10 metres, but can grow much taller in nature (Illustrated Plate 9).

Brachychiton populneum (*Sterculia diversifolia*)
KURRAJONG

This Australian tree has flowers that are similar in size and shape to those of the Flame-Tree, but they are a pale, greenish-lemon colour, dotted with reddish-brown spots. They are curious more than showy, but the tree is prized for its dark, evergreen foliage which makes it a luxuriant landscape tree in winter. The Kurrajong trees have 2 or 3 shapes of shiny foliage on the same tree and can be recognised by their typical "bole" or trunk which resembles an elephant's leg. They are slightly tender to frost and slow-growing at first, but are hardy later and grow to a height of 9–15 metres. They can be transplanted from tins when quite a good size, but not from the open ground.

Breynia (*Euphorbiaceae*)   *Breynia nivosa* (*Phyllanthus nivosus*)
SNOW–BUSH

This evergreen shrub comes from the South Sea Islands and makes a rounded bush of about 2 metres in height. It is grown for its ornamental foliage and has deep-green, rounded leaves which are from 4 to 5 cm long. The upper leaves appear to be sprinkled with white markings and the topmost leaves and tips of the branches are pure white, so that the bush looks as if it has been showered with snow.

This shrub is very tender and is grown in semi-tropical climates where it is used as a pleasing, rounded hedge. There is a well-grown hedge in the Durban Botanical Gardens. It stands up well to the wind at the sea-side and is easily grown, but must be given a shady or semi-shaded position. Drought-resistant in humid surroundings, it should be well-watered in warm areas of low elevation away from the sea. It is slow-growing and can also be grown as a pot-plant. Propagation is by cuttings or from seed. There are also varieties mottled with pink or with red. (Illustrated Plate 9).

Brownea (*Leguminosae*)   *Brownea grandiceps*
ROSE OF VENEZUELA

A tender deciduous tree from Caracas which grows to 20 metres, this is admired for its rounded clusters of large red flowers, likened to *Rhododendron*, at the tips of the branches in summer. The compound leaves, in 12 pairs, are reddish when new, becoming green after a few days. This tree does well in a sub-tropical climate with a dry winter and blooms successfully in Durban. Propagation is by seed. Several other species from Central America would make good garden subjects, but seed is difficult to obtain.

Brunfelsia (Solanaceae)

Brunfelsia calycina var. eximia

This tender, evergreen shrub comes from Brazil and is well worth a place in every garden. In spring it is completely covered with flat, 2-inch purple flowers, each with 5 rounded petals. The next day these change to a light mauve colour and the next day to pure white. This interesting habit gives this shrub its common name. New buds open continuously so that the shrub bears all 3 colours at the same time. In addition, the flowers are very strongly and sweetly-scented like Jasmine, so that this shrub is delightful when placed near the house. Flowers reappear in autumn, though not so profusely. The leaves are dark green, smooth, pointed and half-folded over down the centre to reveal a lighter green on the reverse side. The young leaves are bronze-coloured.

Yesterday, Today and Tomorrow is a rounded shrub growing to about 2 metres in height. In Durban it grows much larger and is often used for hedges. It stands clipping very well and is often trimmed into a perfectly rounded bush. It likes moisture and should be well-watered. It is fairly slow-growing, but begins to flower when only about 35 cm high. Tender to severe frost, it prefers a warm, sunny spot in cold areas and will grow in semi-shade. It is best propagated by cuttings (Illustrated Plate 10).

Brunsfelsia calycina var. *macrantha* is a smaller shrub from Peru that has larger purple flowers, with a white eye, and larger leaves. It was formerly called *B. grandiflora*. (Illustrated Plate 10).

Brunfelsia americana (Lady-of-the-Night) has creamy flowers fading to yellow and fragrant at night. (Illustrated Plate 10).

Buddleia (Loganiaceae)

Buddleia davidii (B. variabilis)

BUTTERFLY-BUSH

This shrub, growing to about 2 metres in height and spread, comes from China. In early summer, butterflies are attracted by the pungent scent of its flowers, thus giving it its common name. The lilac-coloured flowers are tiny and borne in closely-packed, tapering sprays about 20 cm long. The best flowers come first and these may be removed to increase the size of the following flowers. They make good cut flowers. The flowering spikes are borne at the ends of long, arching branches and have a delightful, old-fashioned air about them. Unfortunately, they are short-lived, lasting only a few weeks. The leaves are silvery green and soft textured.

Buddleia likes an open, sunny position and will grow in any soil, but prefers well-drained, good garden soil. It is deciduous and hardy, liking cool winters. It is apt to become very ragged in appearance with poor flowers if it is not pruned severely every winter. Cut off all side growths leaving 8 or 9 bare main stems and shorten these to about 60 cm from the ground, increasing the height gradually with the years. The new branches will spring up strongly, growing several feet very rapidly and flowering shortly afterwards. It can be increased by cuttings (Illustrated Plate 10).

B. alternifolia is deciduous and has small clusters of lilac flowers all along the arching stems and between the alternately placed leaves.

Buddleia globosa, semi-deciduous, has rounded heads of orange flowers.

B. madagascariensis, a large rounded bush, has bright yellow flower-spikes in winter.

B. salvifolia, Sage-Wood, is a semi-deciduous, indigenous species with creamy or pale lilac, tobacco-scented flowers in winter. (Illustrated Plate 10).

Burchellia (Rubiaceae)

Burchellia bubalina (B. capensis)

WILD POMEGRANATE, WILDEGRANAAT, BUFFELSHOORN

A South African evergreen shrub of 3 metres, this has clusters of bright, tubular, coral flowers during summer, and large glossy leaves. It flowers when quite small. It requires shelter from frost in places with cold winters and will thrive in full shade if protected by the overhanging branches of a tree. It does best with rich loamy soil and moisture and grows from cuttings or seed. (Illustrated Plate 9).

Butea (Leguminosae)

Butea frondosa

FLAME-OF-THE-FOREST, DHAK TREE

A slow-growing medium-sized tree from East India and Burma, this has spectacular clusters of crimson-scarlet pea flowers, about 5 cm long, on bare branches in early spring, similar to *Erythrina*. The leaflets are hard and arranged in threes. This is an excellent subject for sub-tropical gardens, but seeds are difficult to obtain. It is said to grow 60 cm a year and to take 8 years to bloom.

Butea superba is an enormous climber from India, with clusters of upstanding orange-scarlet flowers in early summer. It will clamber over large trees. (Illustrated Plate 10).

Caesalpinia (Leguminosae)

Caesalpinia

Some species that were formerly classed under *Poinciana* are now *Caesalpinia*, while *Poinciana regia* is now *Delonix regia*. This is a large group of trees and shrubs, some of which are extremely decorative and widely grown throughout the world. They belong to the Legume family and grow easily from seed.

Caesalpinia ferrea

LEOPARD TREE, BRAZILIAN IRONWOOD

This tall erect tree has peeling white bark that gives the trunk a mottled appearance. It bears its yellow pendant flowers at the end of the branches in late summer, following *C. peltophoroides*. The fine ferny foliage casts light shade.

Caesalpinia gilliesii (Poinciana gilliesii)

BIRD-OF-PARADISE

Probably the most commonly grown because it is the hardiest, this large well-known Argentinian shrub grows to about 2 or 3 metres in height. The flowers are very freely produced for a long period in early summer and again in late summer, often brightening the garden when few other shrubs are in bloom.

Each flower has yellow, spoon-shaped, overlapping petals and brilliant crimson, silky stamens that grow to about 12 cm, curving outwards in a conspicuous fashion. The dainty compound leaves are fern-like, being divided and sub-divided into tiny leaflets. Bird-of-Paradise is evergreen in warm areas and deciduous during cold winters.

This shrub grows very easily. It likes a sunny position in a warm, dry, sandy soil and requires practically no watering once it is established. Although it thrives in poor soil, it will flower more profusely if the soil is enriched with manure and compost. It requires no pruning, but can be trained with a standard if desired, and will form a well-rounded head. This shrub will grow in warm climates near the sea or in warm dry areas. It will also stand frost and cold winters with a temperature as low as 7°C. It grows easily and rapidly from seed, which should be soaked in warm water before planting. (Illustrated Plate 11).

Caesalpinia peltophoroides

SIBIPIRUNA

A tall-stemmed, flat-crowned tree that grows to 12 metres in height, this is covered with bright golden-yellow flowers in early summer. Each thick upright spike of pea-shaped flowers is about 15 cm long and they emerge above the pale green foliage, making this a very showy tree. It loses its leaves in dry areas, but is semi-evergreen in tropical places. Although it grows wild in Brazil it occurs at higher altitudes and does well wherever the Jacaranda flourishes. It is drought-resistant during winter and likes well-drained sandy soil. It grows from seed. (Illustrated Plate 11).

Caesalpinia pulcherrima (*Poinciana pulcherrima*).

PEACOCK FLOWER

This shrub is also known as Barbados Pride and as Dwarf Flamboyant. The Peacock Flower is a large, rounded, tropical shrub that grows to about 3 metres in height. It is very free-flowering and large heads of flowers appear on the ends of every branch and side-branch for a long period in summer. The flowers are a bright orange-scarlet marked with yellow, and the petals are broad and crinkled in texture. The flowers have protruding red stamens which are not as distinctive as those of Bird-of-Paradise. There is also variety with rich golden-yellow flowers and a rosy-pink form. The evergreen, dainty compound leaves are finely divided and sub-divided.

Peacock Flowers are easy to grow and have the same cultural requirements as Bird-of-Paradise. They are tender to frost, however, and will grow only in warm, sub-tropical areas. They like sea-air and will thrive in humid coastal situations. (Illustrated Plate 11).

Calliandra (Leguminosae) *Calliandra*

SHUTTLECOCK FLOWER, POWDERPUFF TREE

There are many *Calliandras* which are all spectacular in flower, generally blooming during the latter part of summer. The flowers are grouped in tightly packed heads and are inconspicuous in themselves, but have numerous delicate filaments which combine to form a glistening puff. This resembles a shuttlecock in some cases and is completely globular in others. The stamens are generally rose or red and the lower half is often white. Calliandras are called Angel's Hair in Mexico.

Calliandras like a warm, sunny situation in well-drained loamy soil, and do well in warm gardens, but are not especially tender to frost. They thrive in sub-tropical and coastal areas, where they remain evergreen. They grow from seed, but do not always set seed easily, and may be grown from layers or cuttings over bottom heat. There has been some confusion in the past in distinguishing between the different species of *Calliandra*, but they may be identified chiefly by their leaves (See below). They should not be confused with *Albizia julibrissin*. There are over 100 species of *Calliandra*, both trees and shrubs, which come mainly from tropical America.

Calliandra guildingii. This small, evergreen shrub from Brazil is very similar to *C. selloi* in size and flower colour. It is distinguished by its leaves which have few oval, 15-mm long leaflets, slightly assymetrical in shape.

Calliandra haematocephala (*C. inequilatera*)

RED POWDERPUFF TREE

This is a spectacular large evergreen spreading shrub or tree of about 3 metres with red globular flowerheads, which blooms in late summer and autumn, flowering when young. It has leaves divided into 2 branchlets, each carrying large, oval, oblique leaflets up to 4 cm long, which distinguish it clearly from *C. tweedii*. Thought to come from South America, its true origin is unknown. (Illustrated Plate 11).

Calliandra selloi (= *C. brevipes*).

SHUTTLECOCK FLOWER

A showy Brazilian shrub which grows to about 2 metres, suitable for the small garden, this has showy globular heads of powderpuff flowers in summer, opening at intervals, especially after rain. The 4-cm-long filaments are half white and half bright mauvish-pink or rose. The colour of the flowers may vary, but this species is distinguished by its tiny leaves, which are only about 3–4 cm long and divided into numerous tiny narrow leaflets. The leaves are joined together in pairs where they spring from the main woody stems. *C. selloi* is evergreen in warm climates and is used as a hedge plant in Petropolis, Brazil. It is not very tender and may be grown successfully on the highveld. (Illustrated Plate 11).

Calliandra surinamensis

Roughly resembling the flowers of *C. selloi*, this has white stamens with bright pink tips, but is a variable species. The distinguishing feature is in the foliage, for the small leaflets are grouped along the entire length of the branches in pairs, springing from the same point in the shape of a "V". This species seeds itself freely and comes true from seed. It forms a large spreading bush which can become immense in a sub-tropical climate, and will grow in full sun or partial shade near lofty trees. It comes from Guiana, South America. (Illustrated Plate 11).

Calliandra tweedii (*Inga pulcherrima*) is similar to *C. haematocephala*, but its flowers are darker in colour—almost purplish-red according to some records—and the leaves are a little smaller.

Callicarpa (Verbenaceae)

Callicarpa dichotoma (C. purpurea)

JAPANESE BEAUTY-BERRY

This low-growing, deciduous shrub, nearly 2 metres in height, comes from Japan. It has inconspicuous pink flowers, but is prized for its clusters of glossy, violet berries that look like tiny beads. These are ringed in clusters all the way up the stems and appear in autumn with very little or no foliage. The stems last very well in the vase and always excite comment. There is also a white-berried variety *alba*.

This shrub grows best in warm, frost-free localities, but can stand slight frosts. If it is cut back by a severe frost, new shoots will grow up vigorously in the spring. It prefers an open, sunny position and should be planted in soil of a neutral or acid reaction which is mixed generously with compost. Pruning, in the form of cutting out old growths, may be done while the plant is dormant in the winter. It is propagated by seed, cuttings or layers. (Illustrated Plate 12).

Callicarpa americana, from the U.S.A. has deep violet, larger berries and much broader leaves.

Callistemon (Myrtaceae)

Callistemon

BOTTLEBRUSH

There are about 18 species of Bottlebrush which make a distinctive group of Australian shrubs and trees. They all have flower-spikes made up of tiny flowers clustered around the stem, with 3-cm long, stiff stamens protruding all around, so that the whole spike resembles a bottle-brush. This varies from 8 to 15 cm in length. The flowers and stamens are usually coloured different shades of scarlet and crimson and are extremely showy. There is also pale yellow species (*C. salignus*).

The Bottlebrushes are easy to grow, are hardy to average frost and can resist drought and unfavourable conditions. They are not particular about soil, but need plenty of sunshine. Every 3 or 4 years the growth may be pruned in order to increase the number of blooms. They grow from seed or from cuttings of ripened wood.

Callistemon citrinus

An evergreen small tree, usually seen as a shrub of 2.3 metres, this has brilliant crimson bottlebrushes, tipped with gold, in October. The form *splendens* is even more spectacular. The leaves are narrow and flat.

Callistemon lilacinus (C.violaceus)

PURPLE BOTTLEBRUSH

A rounded evergreen shrub which may grow to 3 metres, this has violet-purple bottlebrushes and pointed, narrow leaves up to 10 cm in length. A variety has reddish-purple flowers.

Callistemon speciosus

SHOWY TREE BOTTLEBRUSH

This small tree comes from Western Australia and grows about 2 to 5 metres high. The 15 cm, deep crimson spikes of flowers stand up stiffly. The leaves are dark green, very narrow and long—up to 8 or 10 cm.

The decorative, woody seedpods persist on the tree and become quite prominent as the tree matures. The Tree Bottlebrush is slower-growing than the Weeping Bottlebrush, but is a hardy decorative evergreen for the landscape. (Illustrated Plate 12).

Callistemon viminalis

WEEPING BOTTLEBRUSH

The long arching branches of the Weeping Bottlebrush droop to the ground. It is an extremely graceful, small tree that grows from 3 to 7 metres high. The flowers are vermilion in colour and hang down profusely in early summer. The leaves are narrow, tough and bright green. The young growth is soft and pink. This evergreen Bottlebrush likes a warm, sunny position. The stem should be staked until it is strong enough to form a standard for the curving branches. (Illustrated Plate 12).

Calodendrum (Rutaceae)

Calodendrum capense (Calodendron capense)

CAPE CHESTNUT OR WILD CHESTNUT

The botanical name of this tree is derived from the Greek meaning "beautiful tree of the Cape." This is a large forest tree, conspicuous when flowering, that is found growing in the Cape, in Natal and in the Northern Transvaal. In the forests it grows up to 20 metres in height, but in the open it is much lower and more branched and symmetrical in shape. It flowers in early or mid-summer. The flowers are grouped in large showy clusters at the ends of the branches. Each has 5 oblong, narrow, wavy petals, about 5 cm long, that are a pale rosy-pink, shading to dark red near the base. The leaves are broad and oval in shape, up to 15 cm long and 8 cm wide. They have slightly ruffled edges and many parallel veins like a chestnut leaf.

This tree is usually evergreen but may be deciduous in cold climates. It is tender to severe frost and grows best in warm, frost-free areas, where it is suitable for a very large garden. It needs a good rich soil and lots of water. It grows quite rapidly in suitable conditions and begins to flower when about 5 years old. It may be grown from seed. (Illustrated Plate 12).

Calothamnus (Myrtaceae)

Calothamnus

NET-BUSH

These are Australian evergreen shrubs, growing to about 2 metres, which all have interesting scarlet flowers with claw-like stamens in spring. They are hardy, drought-resistant and cultivated like Bottlebrush (Callistemon). Propagation is by seed or cuttings. C. quadrifidus, to 2 metres, has needle-like foliage. (Illustrated Plate 12). C. villosus is smaller and has soft, hairy, pine-like leaves and rich red flowers.

Calycanthus (Calycanthaceae)

Calycanthus floridus

CAROLINA ALLSPICE

A 3-metre, deciduous, American shrub, this has fragrant apple-scented, 5 cm flowers which are dark reddish-brown. The 12-cm, oval leaves are pale and downy beneath, but this is a variable character. It is hardy and prefers rich, well-drained soil. Propagation is by seed and by separating suckers. *Calycanthus praecox* is now *Chimonanthus praecox*. (Illustrated Plate 12).

Camellia (*Theaceae*)   *Camellia japonica*

Camellias are evergreen shrubs that originally came from the East. There are many varieties available today that include both single and double flowers. Their beauty lies in their delicate waxy texture and in the fact that they are large—from 8 to 10 cm across—and have glorious clear colours. The single flowers are white, pink or red and have a single row of petals, with a prominent centre of bright yellow stamens. The double varieties have generously overlapped petals arranged in slightly varying ways. They include a pure sparkling white, a popular rose-pink, bright red and a very dark crimson. There are also varieties with pink and white on the same flower, but these are not as lovely as the plain shades, although this is simply a matter of individual taste. All the flowers are produced most profusely at the end of winter and in early spring, making excellent cut-flowers. The leaves of the Camellia are decorative in themselves and form a perfect foil for the flowers. They are oval in shape, dark green and glossy.

Camellias are slow-growing, but will grow more rapidly with careful treatment. Position of planting is important and this is still a debatable problem. The modern tendency is to plant Camellias right out in the open sun, where the bushes, if properly watered and cared for, do very well. Nevertheless, in areas which experience cold winters, the flowers are browned and spoilt by the early morning sun (see Chapter I). It will be noticed that the only perfect flowers are those that grow on the south or shady side of the shrub or deep in the centre of the bush where they are shaded by the leaves. In order to get the best results, therefore, it is advisable to plant the Camellia where it will receive shade in the early morning and either full or filtered sunshine during the rest of the day. Camellias may also be grown in full shade, as on a south wall, but they do grow more rapidly and luxuriantly if they receive some sunlight during the day. They should also be planted near some windbreak, as the delicate petals may be bruised by strong winds.

Camellias like a good rich soil well-mixed with compost. They dislike lime and may be treated with tea-leaves (see Chapter II). They dislike sub-tropical as well as dry conditions. They enjoy a winter rainfall and do well at the Cape. In dry areas they should be watered in winter, and, in fact, enjoy good watering always. They should be mulched with a thick acid mulch of leaves in order to prevent the roots from drying out. The flower buds often drop off if the plant does not receive sufficient water.

The single varieties grow more rapidly than the double, and form large rounded bushes about 5 metres in height. These make beautiful, if somewhat expensive hedges, in which case they should be planted at a distance of about 2 metres apart. The double varieties grow into neat, erect bushes which fill out with age and vary from 2–5 metres in height. The stems and branches are woody. Short cuttings may be taken and given a warm place in which to grow. They are very slow, however, and take a number of years before they reach the size at which one can buy them from the nurseryman. Camellias do not need pruning, but long growths may be shortened in the spring. (Illustrated Plate 13).

Campsis
(Bignoniaceae)

Campsis radicans (Bignonia radicans)

TRUMPET VINE

A hardy, deciduous, vigorous climber from North America, that clings to walls by means of aerial roots, this has large orange trumpet flowers during summer. There are several varying colour forms. The toothed leaflets have no tendrils. *C. chinensis* from China is similar. *Campsis* Madame Galen is a very showy hybrid between the two. Propagation is by cuttings. (Illustrated Plate 7).

Cantua
(Polemoniaceae)

Cantua buxifolia

FLOWER-OF-THE-INCAS

A slender, evergreen weeping shrub from the Andes, this grows from 1–2 metres in height. It is covered with spectacular, pendulous flowers in spring. Several colour forms occur in Peru, varying from deep crimson to scarlet, but only the bi-coloured form is seen in southern Africa. Each flower measures 8 cm in length and has a salmon-yellow tube flaring out into cerise, rounded petals. The graceful stems are covered with tiny leaves. *C. buxifolia* like a light, loamy or sandy soil with plenty of moisture and a sheltered position in places with cold dry winters. Propagation is by cuttings and division of the root (Illustrated Plate 13).

Carissa
(Apocynaceae)

Carissa macrocarpa (C. grandiflora)

NATAL-PLUM OR AMATUNGULU

This spiny, evergreen shrub comes from Natal and Zululand. It grows to a height of 2 to 3 metres and is frequently grown as a hedge. The fragrant flowers are large, waxy, white and 5-petalled, resembling Jasmine, and measure over 3 cm across. They are followed by large, round, tomato-coloured, plum-like fruits, about 4 cm in diameter. These are edible and may be made into jelly. They ripen irregularly. The leaves are dark green, oval and glossy. The stems have long thorns which are nearly 3 cm in length. The Indian flower-sellers in Natal stick extra fruits on to the thorns, and the sprays are sold for indoor decoration, lasting very well in the vase.

The Natal-Plum is tender to frost and likes a hot, sub-tropical climate. It enjoys a summer rainfall and moist soil, It will also grow in warm, dry areas without severe frosts if it is well watered. It can be pruned into shape and may be grown as a low, clipped hedge. It is fairly slow growing except in very hot climates, and is propagated by means of seed or layers. Low-growing or prostrate hybrids have been developed in America and used as groundcovers.

Caryopteris
(Verbenaceae)

Caryopteris incana

BLUE SPIREA, BLUEBEARD

A small deciduous shrub, from 60 cm to 1 metre in height, this has greyish foliage and clusters of soft blue flowers in late summer. It needs shelter from severe frost and should be pruned back at the end of winter. It will grow from cuttings.

Cassia
(Leguminosae)

Cassia

CASSIA, SHOWER TREE, CANDLE TREE

There are a great many Cassias, including both trees and shrubs, found mostly in tropical and sub-tropical parts of the world. Some are called Senna, having long, flat seed–pods. Some species are grown for their medicinal value and others make decorative specimens for the garden.

Most Cassias have yellow flowers, but there are several exciting pink-flowered species which are generally tender and need hot, sub-tropical conditions. It is frequently difficult to distinguish between the various species. (See Plate 14).

Cassia abbreviata var. granitica
LONG–TAIL CASSIA, CANDLE TREE, KERSBOOM

This small deciduous tree of about 5 metres has showy yellow flowers during October, together with the bright green pinnate leaves. These are followed by long cylindrical pods, up to 75 cm. This drought-resistant tree comes from the warmer parts of Southern Africa and does best in places with mild dry winters.

Cassia alata
CANDLESTICK SENNA, GOLDEN CHAIN TREE

An evergreen shrub that grows to 3 metres, this has erect spikes of golden yellow flowers at the ends of the branches in late summer. It may be recognised by its very large leaves that are divided into numerous large broad leaflets, growing to 6 cm in length, and by its angled pods that grow to about 12 cm in length. This species grows wild in tropical America. (Illustrated Plate 14).

Cassia artemisioides
SILVER CASSIA

A bushy evergreen Australian shrub of 2 metres, with narrow, feathery, silvery foliage, this bears masses of small yellow buttercup flowers in spring. It should be pruned after flowering. The Silver Cassia requires well-drained soil and a sunny position (Illustrated Plate 14).

Cassia corymbosa (C. floribunda)
AUTUMN CASSIA

This delightful, autumn-flowering shrub brightens the garden considerably at a time when it is needed. It comes from South America. It grows up to 2 or 3 metres in height and spread, and produces a large number of canes at the base, which arch gracefully, bearing thick clusters of rich, golden-yellow, 3-cm-wide buttercup flowers at the ends. The stamens curve out from the flower and have long brown anthers. The bright green compound leaves are 8 cm long, and divided into 3-cm, oval leaflets, which fold together at night. This shrub is tender to frost but will grow up again in the spring. It likes a warm, sunny position. It may be propagated by cuttings. This is a more desirable species than the Wild Senna from Mexico (C. laevigata), with its numerous pods that seed so freely that they become a nuisance in gardens.

Cassia didymobotrya
PEANUT–BUTTER CASSIA

This striking tropical African shrub grows to about 4 metres in height in Durban, but smaller in Johannesburg and spreads at least to the equivalent of its height.

The buttercup-shaped, canary yellow flowers are freely borne during most of the year in erect 15-cm spikes. The wide bracts are a dark nigger brown and form a conspicuous part of the spike, for the flowers open from the bottom and the closed buds at the top are covered with the dark, brown bracts, which fall off as the flowers open. The flowers and buds have a strong smell of peanut-butter. The bush grows easily and rapidly from seed, attaining a height of 2 metres in 2 years. The compound leaves are up to 30 cm long and divided into numerous, dark-green leaflets about 4 cm long and oval in shape.

This Cassia is evergreen in frost-free localities and semi-deciduous in cold-winter areas. It is tender to frost which will cut it back, but it will grow up again in the spring, particularly if it is protected for the first winter. It should be planted in a warm, sunny position where it has room to spread. It will endure poor soil. It can be cut back, but is best left unpruned. Unfortunately, it is a short-lived plant (Illustrated Plate 14).

Cassia fistula
GOLDEN SHOWER, PUDDING-PIPE TREE

This small semi-deciduous tree comes from the drier parts of India and Ceylon. It is suited to hot, semi-dry conditions, but will also do well in hot, moist areas up to 600 metres above sea-level. It is most attractive in Durban in December, January and February.

The bright yellow, butter-cup flowers are clustered on long sprays about 30 cm long which hang downwards from the tree. They usually appear before the leaves. This tree is also called Indian-Laburnum, as the sprays hang down like Laburnum. The leaves are large, compound and green, with oval, pointed leaflets. The tree is grown from seed. The back seed-pods are very long, almost 60 cm, and hang down like cylindrical pipes, giving the tree its common name. (Illustrated Plate 14).

Cassia javanica
PINK CASSIA, PINK SHOWER

This tree comes from Java and Sumatra and grows into quite a large, spreading tree about 8 metres in height. It bears large clusters of pink flowers here and there amongst the foliage in January and February, tailing off in March, and is an effective landscape tree. Pink Cassia prefers semi-tropical conditions but is half-hardy and will stand slight frost. It is reproduced from seed contained in long, cylindrical pods to 60 cm in length.

Cassia nodosa, Jointwood, is similar, with bright pink flowers in dense racemes. Some believe that this is a form of *C. javanica*. Others distinguish between the two, stating that *C. nodosa* flowers before the leaves and comes from tropical central and South America. It seems to bloom in early summer and the blossoms appear at the same time as the foliage in northern Brazil. Some of the flowers are whitish at the centre, but this is a variable character on both kinds. (Illustrated Plate 14).

Cassia grandis is another gorgeous pink-flowered tree, from Brazil, which grows very tall and forms a broad crown of pale pink, very effective in the tropical landscape. There are several other pink-flowered species.

Cassia multijuga

A large rounded bush or small tree to 6 or 7 metres, this is covered with large plumes of bright yellow flowers in late summer. They stand erect above the evergreen foliage which consists of long leaves with up to 40 pairs of narrow leaflets, each about 8 cm long. It has flattened pods about 15 cm in length. This species comes from South America and the West Indies and thrives in the coastal area of Natal. (Illustrated Plate 14).

Other yellow-flowered Cassias to be recommended, which are obtainable, are:
Cassia carnaval, a fairly hardy tree from Argentina,
Cassia candolleana (C.bicapsularis), a variable rambling shrub or tree from the sub-tropics,
Cassia speciosa, a broad, medium-sized tree from Brazil (Illustrated Plate 14),
Cassia splendida, a small tree from Brazil.

Castanospermum (Leguminosae)

Castanospermum australe

A spreading, evergreen, Australian tree of 20 metres, this has bunches of fleshy orange pea flowers in summer, sometimes varying to yellow and red. The long, dark green leaves are divided into large, 12-cm leaflets, and there are chestnut-like pods. This tree is suited to warm, frost-free localities and does well at the coast from the Cape to Natal as well as in the low-veld. It can be grown in sheltered gardens in Johannesburg. It needs good soil with adequate moisture and is grown from seed. (Illustrated Plate 13).

Catalpa (Bignoniaceae)

Catalpa bignonioides

This large, spreading American tree grows rapidly to a height of about 13 metres. It has large, 20 cm, upstanding sprays of trumpet flowers in early summer, which resemble Jacaranda blossoms upside-down, but are whitish in colour and spotted with brown or purple inside. It has very large, rough, heart-shaped leaves which are greyish green and drop off very early in autumn. They cast a light shade. The branches are thick and satiny brown, speckled with grey. They are wide-spread and should be given at least 7 metres in which to spread in a large garden. Catalpa should not be confused with Paulownia tomentosa.

The trunk should be allowed to branch at about 1 metre from the ground, for if it is grown with a high standard, a strong wind may break off the head of the tree. It may be pruned back in the winter in order to keep it within bounds or improve its shape. It likes a moist soil, especially in spring, and should be well watered in the garden. Drought will retard its growth. It is hardy to frost and will also grow in hot climates provided that it has sufficient moisture. Propagation is by seed, cuttings or layers. There is a smaller garden variety with golden leaves that likes cool situations (C. bignonioides var. aurea).

Ceanothus (Rhamnaceae)

Ceanothus, Gloire de Versailles

The chief attraction of this quick-growing, semi-deciduous shrub is that it has blue flowers. These are arranged in feathery spikes at the ends of the branches in spring and early summer. It is a hybrid that grows up to about 2 metres in height.

This shrub is hardy to the cold weather experienced in South Africa and does not like sub-tropical conditions. It grows easily in ordinary garden soil, enjoying a sunny or semi-shady position which is not too dry. It may be grown from seed or from cuttings. There are numerous species of *Ceanothus*, mainly North American, and many garden hybrids. They may be evergreen or deciduous. They usually have blue flowers, but some have pink or white flowers.

Ceanothus dentatus from California grows to almost 2 metres and has small rounded clusters of deep blue flowers in early summer and small oval wrinkled leaves which are evergreen. (Illustrated Plate 13).

Ceanothus gloriosus from California is prostrate and spreading, with dark blue flowers and shining toothed leaves. Variety *exaltus* grows upright to 4 metres.

Cecropia (Moraceae)

Cecropia palmata

SNAKEWOOD TREE

Tall silvery trees that gleam above the green forests of Brazil and central America, the *Cecropia* trees are equally beautiful when young, with their immense palmate-lobed leaves at the ends of the branches. They have an attractive umbrella shape and the dense crimson spikes of flowers in summer are curious rather than showy. Male and female occur on different trees.

These trees make decorative accents in a sub-tropical garden, where they thrive. They may be grown in dry inland areas with mild winters, needing protection from frost and plenty of water during summer. Propagation is by seed or cuttings. (Illustrated Plate 15).

Ceiba (Bombacaceae)

Ceiba leianthera

THORNY KAPOK

This large tree from Brazil may be grown if only for the beautiful thorns on its spreading stems. It makes a fascinating plant for a large container on a patio. It has creamy flowers and the typical palmate leaves of other members of the *Bombax* family, like *Ceiba pentandra*, the tropical African Kapok Tree and the tropical *C. casearia*, which is a source of fibre.

Centaurea (Compositae)

Centaurea cineraria (C. candidissima)

DUSTY MILLER

A soft, shrubby perennial of 1 metre, this is useful for the sunny rockery or mixed border, but needs to be replaced from time to time. It has many branches bearing rosettes of oblong whitish leaves, finely and deeply cut along the edges and may be recognised by its tufted heads of mauve or purple flowers in early summer, resembling the cornflower. Detached stems will form new plants. Several others are perennials rather than shrubs.

Centradenia (Melastomacea)

Centradenia

WONDER-OF-PERU

There are 4 species of *Centradenia* which originate from Mexico and Central America. They are related to *Tibouchina* and their small orchid-pink flowers are like miniatures of this genus. There are several colours, varying from pale pink to deep orchid pink and purple. The deeply-veined leaves are somewhat hairy and some species have reddish tones beneath. The bushes grow to about 1 metre in height, sending out long canes in summer. The two best species are *C. floribunda* and *C. grandiflora*, the latter being recognised by its 4-angled stems. (Illustrated Plate 13).

Centradenias need shelter from frost in cold places and will grow in the semi-shade of overhanging branches, but do best in sunny positions with plenty of water in summer and rich soil. They bloom in autumn. Propagation is by cuttings or division of the root.

Ceratopetalum (Cunoniaceae)

Ceratopetalum gummiferum

AUSTRALIAN CHRISTMAS BUSH

A cylindrical evergreen tree from New South Wales, this grows erect to about 10 metres, but can be pruned as a bush of 2 metres. The small white starry flowers appear in early summer, but the creamy bracts enlarge and turn pinkish-red in mid-summer, being freely produced in showy clusters. The narrow leaflets have toothed edges. It should not be confused with the New Zealand Christmas Tree, *Metrosideros excelsa*.

This attractive tree grows easily in good, well-drained soil, but requires regular watering, especially in spring and early summer. It does well at the coast or inland, and will grow in sheltered gardens in Johannesburg, being reasonably hardy to frost. It grows from seed or cuttings of half-ripe wood (Illustrated Plate 15).

Ceratostigma (Plumbaginaceae)

Ceratostigma wilmottianum

CERATOSTIGMA

Ceratostigma is a delightful, low-growing sub-shrub from China growing to about 60 cm in height and spread, and should have a place in every garden. It is useful for flanking steps or for making a low dividing hedge.

The flowers are small and similar to those of the Plumbago, to which the shrub is related. They are a striking, deep, rich blue and are borne very profusely, appearing every few days throughout spring and summer, so that they make an eye-catching blue splash in the garden. The leaves are small, narrow and green, and are covered with tiny, prickly hairs, which also cover the thin, woody, reddish stems. In the autumn, brown pompons of bracts are left on the bush, which are quite decorative throughout winter. The shrub is deciduous and the leaves turn red before they fall.

Ceratostigma grows very easily, liking a warm, sunny position. It is hardy to frost and prefers a neutral or acid soil. It seeds itself to freely that there are always small plants around it that can be given to one's friends. The bracts can be cut away if liked and, in fact, the whole shrub can be cut back like a perennial, but be careful not to spoil its compact, rounded shape. (Illustrated Plate 15).
C. plumbaginoides is a similar, creeping perennial or groundcover.

Cercis (Leguminosae)

Cercis siliquastrum

JUDAS TREE

The Judas Tree comes from South Europe and is really a large tree up to 12 metres in height, but usually grows in a bushy shape not larger than 6 metres in cultivation. It is deciduous and bears clusters of tiny, mauvish-pink flowers all along the leafless stems and branches in the spring. Although the flowers are only about 15 mm in length, they are so numerous that the whole tree seems to be wreathed in pink. Each flower is pea-shaped with turned-back upper petals like the wings of a butterfly. They are followed by brown seedpods. The foliage is very neat and attractive. Each leaf is heart-shaped and round, about 9 cm across. It is smooth and a pretty, soft green colour. The branches of this tree are lovely for picking and may be soaked in water to open the buds prematurely indoors ("forced").

The Judas Tree is tender to frost and should be protected while young. It likes a sheltered position in full sunlight, and well-drained soil, well-mixed with compost. It enjoys plenty of water but will resist a certain amount of drought. No pruning is required except to improve the shape, and this should be done in summer after flowering. The tree sometimes develops an unsightly fungus disease called Coral Spot, in which case any dead branches should be cut off and burned and one should spray with a fungicide before the buds open. The tree is inclined to develop a bushy form with many branching stems but may be trained to grow a main stem. It should be transplanted while young. It grows from seed and will flower when about 4 or 5 years old. (Illustrated Plate 15).

Cercis canadensis, Red-bud, has similar flowers and distinctive heart-shaped leaves that turn yellow in autumn. It comes from the U.S.A. and is very hardy.

Cercis chinensis, a hardy species from China and Japan, has rosy-purple flowers in spring and roundish leaves that end in a point.

Cestrum
Cestrum (Solanaceae)

Tropical American shrubs which are very useful and easy to grow, these come in several colours and forms. They all have clusters of tubular flowers at the ends of delicate twigs. Cestrums grow rapidly in ordinary light soil. They are half-hardy, but usually come on again if they are frosted in winter. They prefer full sun, but will also grow in semi-shade and benefit from the shelter of overhanging tree branches. They can be pruned back severely in spring or trimmed when necessary. They grow from seed or cuttings, but are most easily propagated by division of the roots in autumn, winter or spring.

The shrub often erroneously called Blue Cestrum is described under the name *Jochroma*.

Cestrum aurantiacum, Yellow Cestrum, is a semi-evergreen shrub of 2–3 metres, which flowers in summer and autumn. The short sprays of orange-yellow flowers are fragrant at night. They are followed by white berries. The smooth oval leaves have a pungent smell. (Illustrated Plate 15).

Cestrum diurnum, Day-Jessamine, is similar in appearance to Red Cestrum, but has fragrant, pale yellow flowers in a dense head. It is a graceful evergreen shrub. (Illustrated Plate 15).

Cestrum fasciculatum, Red Cestrum, semi-evergreen, is the most attractive and popular species, with vivid carmine flowers borne at the ends of the graceful branches. There are several colour varieties and one hybrid called *C. newellii*, with bright crimson blooms. The chief flowering time is late autumn, but this shrub also blooms in summer and winter. The small dark green leaves are rough textured. It grows to 3 metres in height and spreads over the same width with graceful, arching branches. (Illustrated Plate 15).

Cestrum nocturnum is a very large shrub that grows to 4 metres, with loose, open spikes of pale, greenish-yellow flowers that are fragrant at night. It is tender and comes from the West Indies.

Cestrum purpureum (*C. elegans*) Purple Cestrum, is a large, evergreen spreading bush of 3–4 metres, which is suitable as a screen in a large garden. The 2-toned dull purple flowers are not as showy as the other species. The narrow shiny leaves have a pungent smell.

Cestrum roseum, Pink Cestrum, is desirable in any garden with its clusters of pink flowers followed by satiny pink berries. There is also a salmon pink form which is more common.

Chaenomeles (Rosaceae)

Chaenomeles lagenaria

JAPANESE FLOWERING QUINCE

This deciduous Japanese shrub, previously known as *Cydonia japonica*, grows to about 2 metres. It bears its beautiful flowers on bare stems in mid-winter and early spring. The flowers are large, waxy, single blossoms growing right against the twiggy, interlacing branches. If the branches are picked in bud, they will all open in the vase, and the red flowers will fade to pink and then to white if they are kept in water for 2 weeks or more. They are delightful for picking and make typically Japanese flower arrangements. The leaves are dark-green, shiny and oval. The most popular colour is a rich rose-red, but there are various shades of crimson available, as well as pink, pure white, and there are a few double forms. The variety *moerloosei*, known as Apple Blossom, has white flowers flushed with pink.

This shrub likes a sunny position, but is adapted to growing in partial or full shade. It should have a soil well-mixed with compost. It is hardy to frost and likes cool winters, but is not suited to sub-tropical conditions. It will survive dry conditions and may be pruned into a low hedge. It is slow-growing and most easily propagated by division of the root (Illustrated Plate 16).

Chaenomeles japonica (Previously known as *Cydonia maulei*) is a dwarf variety from Japan which has orange-scarlet flowers and spiny branches. It is pruned to form a low cushion between rocks in Japan.

Chamaecyparis (Cupressaceae)

Chamaecyparis

FALSE-CYPRESS

Large evergreen trees of the Cypress family, these have branches in flattened sprays, covered with tiny green leaves, that have a soft and graceful appearance. The foliage is dense to ground level. These trees have rounded cones. All require good deep soil with plenty of moisture. They are hardy to frost and do best in cool, moist areas, but will also grow in warm places with sufficient moisture.

Numerous types exist in the northern hemisphere, where they are valued as hardy evergreens. Although they may be grown from seed, the best forms are reproduced by cuttings. Specialist growers are now cultivating these in South Africa, so that one may select them according to taste.

Chamaecyparis lawsoniana, Lawson's Cypress, is an evergreen tree of 8 metres with many varieties. Variety *lutea*, the Golden Cypress, grows from 3 to 7 metres and has green leaves with golden tips at all times. It needs ful sunshine to keep its colour. Variety *glauca* has steel-blue foliage, but is rare here. (Illustrated Plate 16).

Chamaecyparis pisifera, from Japan, is a similar tree to *C. lawsoniana*, with more drooping foliage. Variety *aurea* has golden-yellow young growth and var. *argentea* has whitish tips to the branches. Var. *filifera* is a bush with several forms, some very dwarf, including *filifera aurea*, which has golden branchlets. (Illustrated Plate 16).

Chamaelaucium (*Myrtaceae*)

Chamaelaucium uncinatum

GERALDTON WAXFLOWER

A slender evergreen of about 2 metres, this has sprays of Tea-Tree-like flowers in early spring. Several colour forms include white, red and pink. The foliage is soft and needle-like. This Australian shrub needs sun and excellent drainage, dying if over-watered. Prune after flowering. It grows from cuttings or seed. (Illustrated Plate 16).

Chilopsis (*Bignoniaceae*)

Chilopsis linearis

FLOWERING WILLOW

A deciduous small tree of 7 metres, this has bignonia-like, lilac flowers about 5 cm in length, and long, very narrow leaves. It is drought-resistant, reasonably hardy and grows with medium rapidity. It comes from dry areas in Texas, California and Mexico and grows from seed.

Chimonanthus (*Calycanthaceae*)

Chimonanthus praecox (*C. fragrans*)

WINTERSWEET

Useful for its hardiness, this deciduous 3-metre shrub can be grown on a cold south wall or in semi-shade. It has sweetly-scented, pale yellow flowers on bare stems in mid-winter. It needs regular watering and grows from seed.

Chionanthus (*Oleaceae*)

Chionanthus

FRINGE-TREE

Deciduous hardy shrubs, these have 10-cm clusters of interesting fringed white, narrow-petalled flowers at the ends of the branches. They bloom in early summer together with the fresh green leaves and may be grown from seed, which is dark blue.

C. retusa, from Japan, grows to 3 metres and *C. virginica*, from North America, has longer, narrow leaves and can be three times as tall, but both grow slowly and require cold winters with rich soil and plenty of moisture in summer in order to thrive. (Illustrated Plate 16).

Chorisia
(Bombacaceae)

Chorisia speciosa

A tall, deciduous tree with spreading branches, which forms a symmetrical pyramid, this comes from South America and can be recognised by the rose-like thorns which usually appear on the trunk, which is green while young. The clusters of large starry flowers, about 15 cm in diameter, have 5 slim petals, speckled at the base, which may be rose-pink, mauve, white or yellowish. The leaves are distinctive, consisting of 7 long tapering leaflets radiating from the end of a long stalk. The silky floss on the seeds has been used for stuffing pillows.

This is a beautiful specimen tree for a large garden and should be allowed to spread its branches to the ground. It will grow in high-veld gardens if it is planted against the shelter of other trees, and will grow up again if frosted. It thrives in hot, mild districts and needs plenty of moisture in summer. It is grown from seed and belongs to the *Bombax* family. *Chorisia* should not be confused with the pink or white-flowered Kapok-Tree of commerce, *Ceiba pentandra*, from Tropical Africa. (Illustrated Plate 17).

Chorizema
(Leguminosae)

Chorizema cordatum

Small and evergreen, this Australian shrub grows to a height of about 1–2 metres and makes a pretty plant in the rockery. It has showy, small flowers with unusual, bright colouring. They appear in sprays in very early spring and continue to flower for a long period into the summer. Each tiny flower is shaped like a flat-faced sweetpea. The upper petals are orange, marked with bright yellow at the base, and the lower petals are Fuchsia-red. The leaves are small, rounded and edged with tiny spines.

This shrub will stand light frost and should have some protection from early morning sun in cold-winter areas. It will grow in full sun or in semi-shade. Good soil well-mixed with compost should be provided. It can be grown from cuttings and blooms when very small. It may also be grown as a pot or tub-plant. (Illustrated Plate 16).

There are several attractive species of *Chorizema* which are all worth growing.

Chrysanthemum
(Compositae)

Chrysanthemum

The bushy forms of *Chrysanthemum* are extremely useful in the garden and may be used in the mixed border or in the rockery. Many flower during winter and some are everblooming. They may be cut back severely in spring. All grow easily and rapidly from cuttings taken in spring and are hardy and easy to grow, adapted to most conditions both inland and at the coast. They come from the Canary Islands.

Chrysanthemum anethifolium. White Daisy-Bush. A widely-spreading bush, this has very finely cut, bluish-green foliage and masses of white daisies for most of the year, especially in winter and spring.

Chrysanthemum frutescens. Yellow Daisy-Bush. A bushy plant of 1 metre with fleshy green leaves, coarsely divided, this has lemon yellow daisy flowers, up-standing on single stalks, flowering chiefly in mid-winter. There is also a white form. (Illustrated Plate 17).

Chrysanthemum ptarmicaeflorum. Lace-leaf. A tall plant of almost 2 metres, this has very fern-like, lacy, silvery-grey foliage and white daisy flowers. It is not easy to propagate by cuttings.

Chrysanthemum wardii. Pink Marguerite. This 1-metre shrub has large, rose-pink daisy flowers, chiefly in mid-winter, and light green, divided foliage.

Cienfuegosia (Malvaceae)

Cienfuegosia sturtii (Gossypium sturtii)

STURT'S DESERT ROSE

A small, rounded evergreen Australian shrub that grows to about 1 metre, this flowers all through spring, summer and autumn in favourable conditions. The flowers are borne singly and resemble Syrian Hibiscus, being about 7 cm long and a clear, pinkish-lavender, blotched with purplish-maroon in the throat. The bluish-green leaves are oval, about 5 cm long and reminiscent of *Eucalyptus*.

This is a desert-type plant that is easy to grow in light, well-drained soil and a sunny position, but it dislikes "wet feet". Propagation is by seed or cuttings. (Illustrated Plate 16).

Cistus (Cistaceae)

Cistus

ROCK-ROSE

There are about 20 species of *Cistus* which all come from the Mediterranean region, from which many hybrids are now available. The shrubs are evergreen and vary from dwarf specimens of 30 cm in height to those of 2 metres in height. The flowers are like delicate single roses and appear in early summer, each one lasting for a single day, but new buds open each day. They come in lovely shades of pink and white, and some are marked with patches of colour in the centre. The leaves are usually narrow and dark green, rough, sticky and aromatic. Labdanum, which is used in perfumery, is obtained from the leaves of some of the species.

The Rock-Roses make delightful shrubs for the rockery, but are not popularly grown in South Africa. They have special requirements which do not fit in very well with the greater part of our climate. They like a warm, sunny position and can stand only a very slight frost. In areas where frost is experienced they should be given protection in the winter or be planted in a sheltered position. They like sea air and will grow at the coast in the Cape where the climate is ideally suited to them. It is most important that they have a well-drained, light soil, for they will not survive if their roots are water-logged. They like lime in the soil. They dislike pruning. If the shape must be improved, this can be lightly done after flowering in the summer. Pinch back young plants to encourage bushy growth. Transplanting must be done very carefully, and preferably while the plants are young. They are grown easily from cuttings taken in autumn and protected over winter.

Cistus crispus

CURLY PINK ROCK-ROSE

This is a dwarf shrub of about 60 cm in height that is delightful for the rockery. It is covered with 8-cm rose-pink flowers, for a long period in summer. It has dark, rough, waxy, oblong leaves. Variety *Sunset* grows to 30 cm and has smaller rosy flowers almost throughout the year.

Cistus ladaniferus

This is an upright shrub which grows to a height of almost 2 metres. It has aromatic, rough, sticky leaves and fragile white flowers, about 8 cm across, which look like poppies. There is also a variety (*C. ladaniferus* var. *maculatus*) which has chocolate coloured patches at the base of the petals.

C. purpureus is a hybrid with rosy 8 cm flowers with dark red blotches at the centre. It forms a rounded bush and flowers freely in spring. It is also called "Brilliancy" (Illustrated Plate 17).

C. villosus is a 1-metre, rounded shrub with 6-cm purple or rose flowers. The grey-green leaves are wavy. It is fire-resistant. (Illustrated Plate 17).

Citharexylum
(*Verbenaceae*)

Citharexylum berlandieri

BERLANDIA FIDDLEWOOD

The large oval leaves of this tree, up to 10 cm long, turn a beautiful apricot colour during autumn and winter, remaining spectacular for many weeks. They drop off at the end of winter, just before the new foliage emerges. Small spikes of creamy flowers appear during summer. This tree generally grows to 5 metres, but may grow to 13 metres in hot climates. It thrives in places with mild winters, such as Salisbury and Durban, but will grow elsewhere if it is sheltered from frost, especially when young. The Fiddlewoods come from Tropical America and are grown from seed. There are several other species which colour in autumn.

Citrus
(*Rutaceae*)

Citrus sinensis

SWEET ORANGE

The Sweet Orange comes from sub-tropical Asia and is grown commercially for its fruit, but also makes a delightful, evergreen, ornamental tree for the garden. The Navel Orange is a form of the Sweet Orange. It should not be confused with the sour or Seville Orange (*Citrus aurantium*) which is used for making marmalade.

The golden fruit hangs on the tree for months during the winter, providing a bright splash of colour. The Orange blossom, which comes out several times a year, has a magnificent fragrance which scents the whole garden, especially towards evening. The white, waxy, curled-back blossoms are conspicuous against the smooth, green foliage, and one spray in a mixed vase will perfume the whole room. It is small wonder that the Orange Tree was a feature of old Spanish gardens many hundreds of years ago.

Orange Trees do best in warm areas, but they will also do well in Johannesburg if they are covered during their first 3 or 4 winters (see Chapter I). They are slow-growing at first and reach a height of about 1 metre in 4 years. They generally bear their first fruit in their sixth year, and they bear this abundantly, so that the little trees are quite laden with the fruit.

The secret of growing Orange Trees well and fairly quickly, is to give them an abundance of water. Irrigation plays an important part in the growing of Oranges commercially, and gardeners should apply the same methods to their Oranges, watering them copiously. The reward will be constant fresh green growth and masses of oranges and orange-blossom. If often helps to spray the trees with the hosepipe in order to prevent any dusty look on the leaves. Orange Trees do not need pruning, but can be clipped or thinned out. They are often attacked by black aphis which can be controlled quite easily. Named varieties should be bought from nurserymen, for they are grafted on to common stock.

Other members of the citrus family which can be grown as ornamental trees in the garden are the Lemon, Lime, Grapefruit, Kumquat and Naartjie, which require similar treatment to the Orange. The Lemon is hardiest and the Lime does best in hot frost-free areas. Citrus, especially Kumquat, Calamondin Tangelo and Lemon, make attractive pot plants, but must be well watered and fed, especially when in flower, or the fruit will drop off.

Clematis (Ranunculaceae)

Clematis jackmannii

CLEMATIS

A garden hybrid, this has large, violet-purple flowers measuring up to 12 cm across. Each has 4 to 6 petal-like, tapering sepals with a puff of stamens at the centre. There are numerous hybrids from this type with similarly large, white, red or lilac flowers. They are all hardy, deciduous vines which flower in summer and autumn on new wood, and require hard pruning back in August, almost to within a foot of the ground.

The soil should be loamy, alkaline, moist, yet well-drained. Clematis likes an open, sunny position, but should be shaded at the root by annuals or perennials. It will grow in partial shade and is not suited to sub-tropical climates. Clematis vines should be allowed to ramble freely over a rustic arch, a stump or another shrub, rather than be neatly tied against a wall. Propagation is by grafting or by cuttings of half-ripe wood in autumn. (Illustrated Plate 17).

Clematis montana has smaller flowers, about 6 cm across, which make a sheet of white in early summer. The leaves are divided into 3 leaflets. There are several varieties with lilac or white flowers. *C. montana* var. *rubens* has rosy red flowers. This vigorous, deciduous climber blooms on the previous year's wood and its main stems should not be pruned back. Weak, thin or dead wood should be removed after flowering.

Clematis brachiata, Traveller's Joy, is a deciduous, indigenous, rambling shrub with masses of small, creamy flowers followed by fluffy seedheads. It should be kept dry in winter.

Clerodendrum (Verbeniaceae)

Clerodendrum (Clerodendron)

GLORY BOWER, CLERODENDRON

This is a group of tender, evergreen shrubs, trees and climbers from China, Japan and Tropical Africa. The colours of the flowers range from scarlet to dark reddish purple, blue and white. Some are reproduced from seed and some from cuttings. Some are especially valuable as they will grow in shade.

Clerodendrum bungei (C. foetidum)

LILAC GLORY BOWER

A slender evergreen Chinese shrub growing to 2 metres, this has rosy-lilac heads of flowers about 15 cm across. The large, coarsely toothed leaves are reddish underneath and are pungent when handled. This plant seeds itself freely in gardens. It grows easily in the shade in highveld gardens, but will tolerate sunshine. (Illustrated Plate 18).

Clerodendrum speciosissimum (*Clerodendron fallax*)
SCARLET GLORY BOWER

A low-growing shrub of about 1 metre in height, having the appearance of a herbaceous plant, this has large, soft, heart-shaped green leaves and striking clusters of flowers which stand up above the leaves in large spikes. Each dainty flower is a vivid scarlet, and has protruding stamens, making one think of butterflies. The flowers are followed by black berries that remain on the spike together with the new flowers opening at the top. This shrub is grown in the open sun in semi-tropical areas, but needs protection against a warm north wall in cold areas. It is very tender to frost.

Clerodendrum splendens
CLIMBING SCARLET CLERODENDRON

A spectacular twining shrub from tropical Africa, with 10-cm clusters of bright scarlet flowers and large, wrinkled, shiny leaves, this is suitable for a low fence in sub-tropical areas, where it will grow in shade or sun. (Illustrated Plate 18).

Clerodendrum thompsoniae
THOMPSON'S GLORY BOWER

A climbing evergreen shrub from West Africa, this has showy crimson flowers with a large white calyx, reminiscent of "Bleeding Heart". The leaves are large and oval. There is a variety with larger flowers (*Balfourii*) and one with variegated leaves (*variegatum*). It does well in the shade and is a favourite greenhouse plant in cold climates. A hybrid called *C. speciosum* has a pinkish calyx and a rosy-violet corona. (Illustrated Plate 18).

Clerodendrum trichotomum
HARDY GLORY BOWER, DRUNKARD'S NOSE

A small, Japanese, deciduous tree of about 3 metres, this is noteworthy because it is a hardy species. It has fragrant, spidery white flowers in late summer, followed by small blue berries changing to black, which cling to a red calyx, like *Ochna*. The oval leaves are 12 cm long in young plants. The variety *fargesii*, with blue berries and red calyces, is now regarded as a separate species from China, *C. fargesii*.

Clerodendrum ugandense (*Clerodendron ugandense*)
BLUE CLERODENDRON OR OXFORD AND CAMBRIDGE BUSH

This distinctive shrub with blue flowers comes from Uganda and grows from 1–2 metres in height. It is tender to frost and should have a warm, sunny spot against a north wall in cold areas. It will do well in Johannesburg. Blue Clerodendron grows rapidly and its stems radiate from the base forming a rounded shape. It bears its distinctive, 3-cm, blue flowers in February. Each flower has 4 sky-blue petals and 1 long, dark-blue scooped-out petal. The flower is cut-off and the long stamens curve out from the base. These flowers also look like butterflies and are followed by black berries. The leaves are oval, about 8 cm long, smooth-surfaced and have serrated edges (Illustrated Plate 18).

Clethra
(Clethraceae)

Clethra arborea

LILY-OF-THE-VALLEY TREE

A small evergreen tree of 4 metres, from Madeira, this has sprays of fragrant white flowers, like Lily-of-the-Valley, during summer and 10 cm oval leaves, shining above. It dislikes warm or cold dry areas and needs a moist, cool, frost-free climate such as at the Cape coast or in the mountains. It is allied to the Erica family and needs similar treatment. It may be grown from seed, cuttings under glass or layers.

Clianthus
(Leguminosae)

Clianthus

DESERT-PEA, GLORY-PEA

Spreading evergreen sub-shrubs, these have showy red pea-flowers, reminiscent of *Crotolaria*, which are suited to dry areas, for they are not easy to grow or keep in cultivation in areas of high rainfall. They grow quickly in the right conditions and should be successful in Karoo areas. New plants should be grown from seed every 2 or 3 years.

Clianthus formosus (*C. speciosus, C. dampieri*), the Sturt Desert-Pea, is a low perennial, spreading over several feet, with upstanding spikes of vivid scarlet flowers marked with a black patch. The soft, greyish leaves are divided into small leaflets. This plant is best grown on a dry, well-drained bank or in sandy soil in a tub. Seed should be soaked in boiling water and sown in its permanent situation. It comes from the arid parts of Australia.

C. puniceus. This is a 2-metre, spreading shrub from New Zealand, that is easier to grow than *C. formosus*, but is also not long-lived in the garden. It has bunches of large crimson flowers and there is a white variety. The leaves are dark green and divided. It is best suited to a well-drained rockery. Seed may be grown in pots and transplanted when a few inches high, coming into flower in the second season.

Clitoria
(Leguminosae)

Clitoria ternata

BUTTERFLY PEA VINE, BLUE PEA

A slender twining plant from tropical Asia, this is suitable for growing on a low fence or for scrambling down a rocky bank. The bright blue, flattened pea flowers are about 5 cm long and half as wide, with a raised crest down the centre. There is white form and a rich double blue. They are used as a dye in the east. The leaves are divided into 5 or 7 leaflets.

The plants grow easily in warm frost-free areas with dry winters and may be grown in greenhouses in pots where winters are severe. Propagation is by seed or cuttings. (Illustrated Plate 18).

Clusia
(Guttiferae)

Clusia grandiflora

ONION-OF-THE-FOREST

A magnificent evergreen rounded tree that grows to 10 metres, this comes from the Amazon. The gorgeous camellia-like flowers open from rounded buds, which give it their common name in Brazil. They bloom in early summer, opening about 10 cm across, and consist of white, waxy petals, flushed pink at the centre, where there is a disc of numerous stamens and a glistening yellow spot which attracts pollinating insects. The fascinating and decorative seedpod splits open like a sunburst and dries into a curly brown bowl. The flowers are in groups near the branch tips, facing downwards, and half-concealed by the dense foliage. Each large leaf is leathery, oval and narrower at the base.

C. grandiflora needs a humid, sub-tropical climate in order to flower profusely and will resist salt spray and coastal wind. It does well on the Natal coast. It is said to be epiphytic, seeding itself in other forest trees before growing down into the soil, but may be propagated normally from seed, as well as from cuttings. (Illustrate Plate 19).

Clusia hilariana has smaller flowers about 6 cm across which are deep rose and shiny, with a smooth, knob-like centre. This is an evergreen tree from Minas Gerais, Brazil. (Illustrated Plate 19).

Clytostoma (Bignoniaceae)

Clytostoma callistegioides
(Bignonia speciosa)

ARGENTINE TRUMPET VINE
OR MAUVE BIGNONIA

This evergreen, Argentinian climber flowers in early summer. It has flattened trumpet flowers about 6 cm long, which are creamy at the base and flushed with lilac at the mouth. The inside and lips are streaked with lines of deep purple. The bright-green, shiny leaflets are oval, pointed, and have wavy edges. The young foliage is bronze-coloured.

This climber may become sparse during cold winters and lose its leaves, but survives average frosts. It thrives in warm, moist places where it grows more luxuriantly. The soil should be good and moist. It requires sunlight in order to flower well, but will also grow where it has the sun for part of the day, preferably in the afternoon. It climbs by means of tendrils and will cling to rough surfaces. It makes a good ground cover for a sloping bank or can be planted to hang over a terraced wall. It grows from cuttings. (Illustrated Plate 18).

Cobaea (Polemoniaceae)

Cobaea scandens

PURPLE-BELL CLIMBER

This large, vigorous climber comes from Mexico and is evergreen. Fast-growing, it will climb from 3 to 7 metres in a season, clinging by means of tendrils. The flowers resemble Canterbury Bells. They are about 6 cm in length and a pale green colour at first, changing to pale mauve and then to deep purple. If the flowers fall off, the fleshy, saucer-shaped calyx remains on the vine, pale-green and decorative. A long green fruit, shaped like a small cucumber, appears at the end of summer, for this climber flowers continuously from spring until the end of summer. The compound leaves have large, oval leaflets which are deep-green, smooth and rubbery in texture. Purple-Bell Climber is tender to frost but can be cut back and treated as a perennial. It grows so easily and quickly from seed that it could even be treated as an annual.

Codiaeum (Euphorbiaceae)

Codiaeum variegatum varieties and hybrids

CROTON

These shrubs come from the West Indies. They have inconspicuous flowers but are prized for their attractive foliage which has a large variety of shapes and colours and can be cut for the vase. The leaves are thick and leathery in texture and simple in outline. The colours vary from a single bush in bright yellow to one containing a large mixture of autumn colours. One of the most attractive has 15 cm long, flat, oval leaves coloured with blotches of red, yellow, brown and green. Another has long, narrow, curled leaves in a deep mahogany colour with green stripes.

These evergreen shrubs are suited to tropical or semi-tropical conditions with no frost, where they make excellent hedges or specimen shrubs. They stand windy conditions and will grow in any good soil. They grow best when they receive sufficient watering and have better colourings if they grow in full sun. They can be reproduced by cuttings. (Illustrated Plate 19).

Coffea (Rubiaceae) — *Coffea arabica*

COFFEE

The commercially important coffee bush, which originated in Abyssinia and Angola, makes an attractive evergreen hedge or background shrub for warm areas with mild winters, as in the lowveld and at the east coast. It grows to 5 metres and has glossy foliage with clusters of white, starry, fragrant flowers at intervals in spring and summer, followed by showy crimson berries. Both often appear at the same time. It will grow in light shade or full sun and likes plenty of water, particularly during summer. It is best propagated by ripe cuttings, but may be grown from seed.

Coleonema (Rutaceae) — *Coleonema pulchrum*

CONFETTI BUSH

A neat, winter-flowering, evergreen shrub of about 1,5 metres, this has tiny heath-like leaves and small, pink, confetti-like flowers which appear on the bush for 6 months from April to September. It flowers when very small and deeper colour forms may be selected. *Coleonema* needs a sunny position and will grow in ordinary soil. It needs moisture during winter and will endure summer drought at the coast. It is hardy and needs full sun, but may be given semi-shade. It grows easily from seed. *C. album* is a larger bush with white flowers (Illustrated Plate 19).

Colquhounia (Labiatae) — *Colquhounia mollis*

COLQUHOUNIA

An evergreen soft-wooded shrub from the Himalayas, this grows to 3 metres. It has long thick clusters of orange tubular flowers at the tips of the stems in late summer. The large soft tapering leaves are rough-textured and similar to *Buddleia* in appearance, grouped in opposite pairs and about 15 cm long.

This shrub grows easily from cuttings and will tolerate partial shade near trees which will serve to protect it from frost. There are two other species which are similar. (Illustrated Plate 19).

Colvillea (Leguminosae) — *Colvillea racemosa*

COLVILLE'S GLORY

A spectacular deciduous tree from Madagascar, this has long thick clusters of burnt orange flowers in autumn. The clusters grow to about 15 cm in length and hang from the top of the tree, being composed of numerous orange buds opening into winged red flowers with protruding yellow stamens. The ferny leaves resemble those of *Delonix regia*, but are much longer and it has a more cylindrical seedpod. The tree forms a broad crown and grows to a height of about 15 metres.

This is a sub-tropical tree that is frost-tender. Specimens may be seen in Durban, but it will also grow in warm places like the north of Pretoria. Propagation is by seed. (Illustrated Plate 22).

Combretum (Combretaceae)

Combretum

COMBRETUM

Several Combretums with red flowers make showy climbers for large gardens, notably *C. coccineum* from Madagascar, with one-sided cushions of scarlet flowers in summer and *C. farinosum* from Mexico, with long spikes of red flowers in summer. *C. jacquinii*, from Brazil, is a large rambling shrub with spectacular orange and yellow flower-spikes in summer. (Illustrated Plate 19).

Numerous *Combreturm* trees with 4-angled fruits grow wild in South Africa and make interesting specimens in large gardens with mild, dry winters. *C. zeyheri* has the largest fruits. These dry out and persist on the branches which are bare in winter.

Combretum microphyllum

BURNING BUSH

Spectacular in bloom, this bushy, deciduous climber is suitable for hot climates with mild dry winters and summer rainfall. The tiny flowers, with protruding red stamens, are grouped in thick mats along the whip-like branches, from mid-July until October. The rounded leaves are large near the base and tiny near the ends of the branches. This plant is suitable for overhanging a hot bank or for growing over a pergola. It is propagated by division of the root and by sowing fresh seed in early summer. It grows wild in the warmer parts of the Transvaal and in Tropical Africa.

Congea (Verbenaceae)

Congea tomentosa

VELVET CONGEA

A huge deciduous rambling shrub that will climb as high as a double-storey house, this forms a billowing mass of velvety pink when its bracts turn colour in early summer, lasting for several weeks. The tiny white flowers are insignificant as the colour lies in the bracts. These may be powdery mauve or a pinkish-lilac, creating an elegant and pretty spectacle. The sprays may be dried for flower decoration. The leaves are oval and up to 15 cm long, falling in winter. *C. tomentosa* is propagated by seed or stem cuttings. It comes from India, Burma and China and is the most wide-spread species in cultivation. (Illustrated Plate 20).

Conifers —See under *Chamaecyparis, Cryptomeria, Cupressus, Juniperus, Thuya*.

Coprosma (Rubiaceae)

Coprosma baurii

TAUPATA, LOOKING–GLASS PLANT

A hardy evergreen New Zealand shrub of 2 to 3 metres, this is grown for its compact, glossy foliage. The rounded leaves are a shining dark green. A variegated form has leaves with creamy-yellow edges. Variety *picturata* is blotched with yellow. Both have orange-yellow berries on female plants.

Coprosmas grow rapidly, are drought-resistant and resist wind at the sea. They may be used for hedges and will grow in sun or semi-shade. Increase by cuttings or seed. (Illustrated Plate 20).

Cordia (*Boraginaceae*)

Cordia dodecandra

SERICOTE

A tall branching tree with clusters of brilliant orange, tubular, frilled flowers in autumn on almost bare stems, this has edible fruits. The large leaves have a sandpapery texture and are used for cleaning pots in Yucatan, where the tree grows wild, in company with *Tecoma stans*. *C. dodecandra* enjoys a dry, frost-free climate, preferring the sub-tropics. There are numerous other Cordias, mainly with white flowers.

Cordia sebestena

GEIGER TREE

This is an evergreen shrub of about 3 metres, from the West Indies, with large, rough-textured leaves to 25 cm long and clusters of bright orange-scarlet, bell-shaped flowers, each about 2 cm wide. These bloom in spring, summer and autumn. This attractive shrub withstands sea air and is suited to the sub-tropical coast. The small white fruits are edible and propagation is by seed. (Illustrated Plate 20).

Cordyline (*Liliaceae*)

Cordyline australis

PALM LILY

A palm-like evergreen tree with a slim trunk from 5 to 12 metres, topped with narrow leaves, this is useful for creating an upright accent in the garden with a somewhat tropical flavour. The large sprays of creamy flowers that emerge during mid-summer, after several years of slow growth, are not important as the tree is grown mainly for its architectural value. There is a variety with bronze foliage, as well as one with reddish-ribbed leaves.

This hardy plant from New Zealand is related to *Dracaena*. It is also known as Giant Dracaena and as Cabbage Tree. It is grown from seed.

Two other species are grown mainly in greenhouses and propagated from stem cuttings, namely *C. stricta* from the warmer parts of Australia, which grows to 2 metres, and the tender *C. terminalis* from Asia. One attractive variety of the latter is var. *marginata*, with red-edged leaves, frequently called *Dracaena marginata*.

Cornus (*Cornaceae*)

Cornus

DOGWOOD

These small hardy trees have attractive "flowers" composed of 4 bracts. They need cool, moist conditions with acid soil and partial shade. Several have tinted autumn foliage and may be grown from seed.

Cornus florida. Dogwood. This deciduous, North American tree is the most spectacular in bloom, enlivening the woods with its blossom-like white flowers in spring. They are up to 10 cm in diameter and there is a form with pink flowers, which must be reproduced from cuttings and grafted for best results. Cultivars include deep pink, double-flowered and 'xanthocarpa'—with yellow fruit instead of the usual red. *Cornus florida* is a dainty tree growing from 3 to 5 metres, with orange-scarlet autumn leaves that are about 10 cm in length. (Illustrated Plate 20).

Cornus alba sibirica is a deciduous shrub of about 3 metres with tiny cream flowers, but is notable for its bare red stems in winter. It comes from Siberia and China.

Cornus capitata. Evergreen Dogwood, comes from China and grows to 4 metres. It has 10-cm creamy flowers in early summer, followed by dull red, strawberry-like, edible fruits. The greyish, oval leaves droop slightly. Though hardy, it will only flower successfully in a position which is sheltered from frost, so that it needs morning shade and moist soil.

Cornus kousa. This Chinese deciduous tree, of about 4 metres, has creamy flowers and pinkish strawberry fruits similar to the Evergreen Dogwood, but has darker green leaves.

Corokia (Cornaceae)

Corokia cotoneaster

COROKIA

An evergreen shrub from New Zealand, that grows to 2 metres or more, this is valued for its drought and salt-spray resistant qualities. It has small silvery-grey leaves and dark interlacing twiggy stems, with tiny yellow starry flowers in summer, followed by tiny red fruits. It will grow in open sun at the coast, preferring partial shade inland, where it is hardy to frost. It is propagated by seed.

Correa (Rutaceae)

Correa

AUSTRALIAN FUCHSIA

Small Australian evergreen shrubs of about 1 metre, these have interesting tubular flowers hanging downwards like Fuchsias, in white, red or green, with oval glossy leaves. They like well-drained, sandy soil and some stand up to salt spray at the coast. Some grow in semi-shade. They are grown from cuttings, which strike easily in autumn, and from seed.

Cotinus (Anacardiaceae)

Cotinus coggygria (*Rhus cotinus*)

SMOKE-BUSH

This hardy European shrub, of 3 to 5 metres, is distinctive in summer with its feathery grey plumes of flowers. The round leaves turn yellow before falling. It likes rich soil and moisture. The purple-leaved variety *purpureus* is striking and even more attractive. Propagate by seed or layers.

Cotoneaster (Rosaceae)

Cotoneaster

COTONEASTER

Cotoneaster (pronounced with 5 syllables) species come from different parts of Asia and Europe and are delightful shrubs which should have a place in every garden. The ending '*er*' is usually treated as female, but not in this case, so that it is correct to use the ending '*us*' for the different species.

The best garden species have red or orange berries and their branches are excellent for picking, especially as they have no thorns. Several, like *C. horizontalis* and *C. microphyllus*, are low-growing and useful for covering banks and rocks, while most of the others grow into large shrubs.

Cotoneasters grow very easily and do well in any soil, preferably with adequate moisture. They thrive in full sun but will also grow in semi-shade as on a cold south wall, for they are hardy to cold. They will grow, but are not particularly happy in sub-tropical regions. Propagation is by ripe seed, layers or cuttings.

Cotoneaster adpressus. Similar to *C. horizontalis*, this deciduous, prostate, spreading species grows to 30 cm in height. It has red berries and the small leaves turn red before they fall.

Cotoneaster conspicuus. An evergreen shrub which is similar to *C. microphyllus*, this is either erect, growing to 2 metres, or low and spreading. The variety *decorus* forms a low dense mat. This has brilliant red berries during winter and small shiny leaves.

Cotoneaster franchettii, Orange Cotoneaster. This is similar to *C. pannosus*, but only reaches 2 to 3 metres and is fairly slow-growing. The orange berries are flushed with red and are sparser than those of *C. pannosus*, but are attractive in the vase. The branches arch gracefully and have small oval leaves backed with silvery felt. This shrub needs good soil and moisture.

Cotoneaster frigidus. This large deciduous shrub will grow into a small tree if it is untrimmed. It has large oval leaves, from 8–12 cm long, dull green above and woolly beneath. Clusters of crimson berries persist into winter. There is a weeping variety *pendulus*.

Cotoneaster henryana

This evergreen bushy shrub grows almost into a small tree of 4 metres and can be pruned into a tree-like shape. The shoots are downy and the large narrow-oval leaves measure up to about 8 cm in length, said to be the largest leaves of the evergreen species. They are dark green above and greyish-woolly beneath. The large bunches of longish crimson fruits appear in late autumn and are about 1 cm in length. This Chinese shrub is hardy and grows quickly in sun or partial shade.

Cotoneaster horizontalis
CREEPING COTONEASTER

This deciduous, low-growing shrub, about 1 metre in height, has spreading branches, many-branched like a fish-bone. It has tiny, rounded, smooth green leaves and bright red berries. It will creep, fan-like, against a wall or may be used to overhang rocks or a low garden wall, tolerating poor soil. (Illustrated Plate 21).

Cotoneaster microphyllus
EVERGREEN CREEPING COTONEASTER

A low-growing, evergreen shrub that arches to 1 metre in height, this has woody, fish-bone branches that make an excellent rock cover. It forms roots where it touches the ground and may be severed to form new plants. The tiny, oblong, dark green leaves are shiny above, hairy beneath and deeply lined down the middle. The bright cerise, pea-sized berries are covered with a fine bloom. Variety *thymifolius* is more dwarf, with smaller, narrower leaves.

C. bullatus is similar, but with a more dwarf congested habit. *C. dammeri* is prostrate and similar, with coral berries.

Cotoneaster pannosus

RED COTONEASTER

The most commonly grown species, this large spreading bush of 4 metres in height and width is best grown as a single specimen. It is extremely graceful as its long, slender branches arch and droop, weighted with berries. These hang in small clusters along the stem, like tiny red apples, 8 mm long, which start to redden in March and persist into winter. The 3-cm long oval leaves are a shiny dark green above and thickly felted beneath.

This species is not recommended as a hedge for privacy as it becomes sparse in winter. It can be cut back severely in spring and large specimens may be transplanted. It grows rapidly, reaching a height of 2 metres in 2 years, responding to sunshine, a well-drained soil and regular watering.

Cotoneaster salicifolius. A graceful evergreen Chinese shrub of 5 metres, this has slender, pointed, wrinkled leaves, from 4–8 cm long, and bunches of bright red berries. The stems branch in flattened sprays and there are several forms of varying heights, including a prostrate variety. The specific name means "leaf like a willow".

Cotoneaster serotinus (*C. glaucophyllus serotinus*)

LATE COTONEASTER

One of the best of the large evergreen Chinese species, this has very large bunches of oval scarlet berries in late autumn, produced profusely along the stems and persisting into winter. The leaves are broadly oval, up to 8 cm long, shiny above and smooth below, when mature. Some turn red in winter. It grows very rapidly to a height of 3 metres and does not resent pruning or picking. It will grow in poor soil or semi-shade and is extremely hardy. It withstands heat and drought. (Illustrated Plate 21).

C. wardii. An evergreen shrub of 2 to 3 metres, from Tibet, this has large, oval, shining leaves, felted with white beneath that may become orange in autumn. It has large clusters of orange-red berries in late autumn.

Couroupita (Lecythidaceae)

Couroupita guianensis

CANNON-BALL TREE

A huge evergreen tree from the Amazon basin, that needs a humid tropical climate, this is a curiosity because of its huge round fruits and exquisite flowers, about 10 cm across. They resemble a large sea-anemone with deep salmon and cream waxy petals and a fringed centre. They hang in enormous clusters near the base of the trunk, facing downwards. This tree is too large for the average garden and is more suitable for a large estate or botanical garden. It is rare in cultivation and a challenge to the grower. Cross-pollination is necessary in order to set seed in cultivation. It grows at the Fairchild Tropical Garden, Miami. (Illustrated Plate 20).

Crassula (Crassulaceae)

Crassula portulacea
PINK JOY, JADE PLANT

A succulent shrub from the south-eastern Cape, this forms a rounded bush of 2 metres or more. It is covered with small rosettes of pale pink starry flowers from late autumn to late winter, persisting for weeks on the bush and in the vase. The smooth green, waxy leaves are rounded and taper towards the thick, fleshy stems.

C. portulacea is popular in the U.S.A. as a pot plant suitable for growing indoors, where it is called Jade Plant, as its form resembles the artificial flowers fashioned from jade in China.

This is a drought-resistant plant which prefers partial shade and it is valuable for growing under trees, especially in areas with cold winters, as the tree branches protect the blooms from frost damage. Plenty of light is necessary for successful flowering, however, and the plants may be grown in open sunshine in areas with mild winters. The soil should be light and well-drained. Propagation is from seed or from large cuttings inserted directly into the ground, which flower while small.

Crassula arborescens is similar, but has white flowers.

Crataegus (Rosaceae)

Crataegus lavallei
LAVALLE HAWTHORN

This is one of many Hawthorns, the best-known being the English Hawthorn (C. oxycantha). Ripe seeds of the Hawthorn take 2 years to germinate when sown and kept in a cool place, and must first be separated from the fruit by soaking in water. Rare sorts such as the Lavalle Hawthorn must be grafted on to C. oxycantha, and as this is so slow at first, they are quite expensive to buy.

The Lavalle Hawthorn is a particularly striking hybrid. It grows slowly into a small deciduous tree about 4 metres in height. It has bunches of white flowers in the spring which are very effective, followed by fruit which turns bright red in autumn, hanging on to the branches after the leaves have fallen. The oval fruit is large—about 2 cm long—and the skin is shiny and bright scarlet when ripe. The tough, dark-green leaves are shiny on the top surface, oval and pointed with serrated edges. There are 5 cm-long thorns on the stems.

This Hawthorn prefers a sunny, open position and is hardy to frost. It likes moisture and a rich, light soil which is neutral or very slightly acid (pH 6.5). One must watch for growths of the stock growing up from the bottom and rub them off with the fingers, or they will spoil the tree. (Illustrated Plate 21).

Crataegus phaenopyrum
WASHINGTON THORN

A slender deciduous tree that grows to about 5 metres, reaching 10 metres in its native woods in N. America, this has bunches of shining scarlet berries in autumn, each about 3 cm across. The small triangular toothed leaves have 3 to 5 lobes and turn orange and scarlet before falling. A very hardy tree for cold gardens, this should be watered during summer. It grows easily from seed and may send up suckers which can be detached. (Illustrated Plate 21).

Crataegus stipulacea (C. pubescens, C. mexicana)

MEXICAN HAWTHORN

A useful, hardy, semi-evergreen tree of 6 metres, this has profuse, large, showy, golden berries in late autumn. It grows rapidly and has few thorns. The leaves are downy beneath. (Illustrated Plate 21).

Red Mexican Hawthorn is a hybrid with large red berries and smooth leaves.

Crotolaria
(Leguminosae)

Crotolaria agatiflora

BIRD-FLOWER

This evergreen shrub comes from East Africa and there are many species which come from South Africa, Australia and India. It has long, 30 cm spikes of greenish-yellow flowers with blackish-purple tips. Each flower is well over 3 cm long and shaped like a bird's beak. The leaves are divided into 3 smooth, oval, soft-green leaflets. The Bird-Flower grows to about 2–3 metres in height. It is suitable for the wilder portions of the garden and will grow with very little attention, enduring both drought and neglect. It likes sunshine and flowers profusely during the second half of summer.

It will grow almost anywhere in South Africa, and is often seen as a rounded, unclipped hedge. It does not like frost and will be cut back in cold winters, but grows up rapidly again in the spring. It grows from seed soaked in warm water and from cuttings. (Illustrated Plate 21).

Cryptomeria
(Taxodiaceae)

Cryptomeria japonica

JAPANESE CEDAR, SUGI

There are numerous varieties of this hardy, slow-growing member of the Pine family that are of especial interest to growers of conifers. Some are compact and others graceful, while some have shoots variegated with white or yellow. Variety *elegans* has bronze foliage in autumn and winter. They do well in areas of high rainfall, disliking wind and hot, dry weather. The soil should be good, deep and acid.

This species comes from Japan where it grows into a tall forest tree, to 50 metres in height, with a huge trunk. It has a light, fragrant wood that is used for many purposes, including lacquerware. The short, pointed leaves, from 1 to 2 cm in length, are soft when young and stiff when old. They cover the spreading drooping branches with a soft green curtain. The tree withstands severe pruning and is used for hedges in Japan, as well as for Bonsai. It may be grown from seed, while the varieties are propagated by cuttings.

Cryptostegia
(Asclepiadaceae)

Cryptostegia grandiflora

CRYPTOSTEGIA OR RUBBER VINE

The rambling, evergreen shrub from Tropical Africa grows to about 2 metres in height and spreads to a width of about 4 metres. The pale mauve flowers are shallow trumpets about 5 cm across. They have 5, over-lapping, pointed petals flushed with darker mauve along the edges and throat. There are clusters of pointed buds at the tips of the long, thick, brown branches, and only a few open at a time. The leaves are dark-green, smooth and shining. They are arched, half-folded down the middle and have pointed tips.

Cryptostegia flowers for a long period in summer, and enjoys sub-tropical conditions. It is easy to grow in warm areas and requires very little attention, but is tender to frost. It is suitable for the wilder corners of the garden, and can be grown against a low fence. It can be pruned back and will continue to flower freely. It can be increased by cuttings.

Cuphea
(Lythraceae)

Cuphea platycentra (*C. ignea*)

CIGARETTE FLOWER OR CIGAR FLOWER

This small, evergreen shrublet, about 45 to 60 cm in height, has small oval, pointed dark-green leaves. They make an excellent background for the narrow, bright scarlet, tube-like flowers with dark purple and white tips that look like lighted cigarette-ends. The flowers are scattered among the branchlets all through the spring, summer and autumn, and continue throughout winter in frost-free areas. This shrub comes from Mexico and grows in warm, sunny positions inland and on the coast. It is cut back by frost in winter, but comes on again in the spring. It is easy to grow and not particular about soil, even growing under trees. It is increased by cuttings or by division. (Illustrated Plate 22).

Cuphea micropetala (*C. jorullensis*)

TARTAN BUSH

The Tartan Bush, also called Large Cigar Flower, comes from Mexico and grows up to 10 cm in height. Its sticky, tube-like flowers are just over 3 cm in length. They are a brilliant vermilion at the base, flushed with yellow near the mouth and tipped with tiny green spots, which, incidentally, are really the petals. These flowers are clustered up the red stems and in between the dark green leaves, so that the whole effect is variegated and colourful, like a Tartan. The tapering leaves are up to 10 cm in length and turn bronze in autumn.

This shrub is showy from mid-summer until late autumn, flowering into winter in frost-free areas, where it is evergreen. It will be cut back by frost, but grows up rapidly in the spring. In cold-winter areas it should be given a warm, sunny spot and will do well against a west wall. It can be increased by cuttings and is so easily increased by division that it could almost be treated as a perennial.

Cupressus
(Cupressaceae)

Cupressus sempervirens var. stricta

PENCIL CYPRESS, ITALIAN CYPRESS

This conifer forms a tall, slim dark green column made famous in the Italian landscape, where it grows from 10 to 20 metres. It endures dry and hot conditions, but grows best when it is watered regularly throughout the year and has deep, good soil. It dislikes the tropics. Slim trees should be grown from cuttings of good stock, otherwise they may become loose and untidy. The species is broader than the variety. Used chiefly as accents in the landscape, they are also useful for privacy in the small garden when planted in irregular groups on the boundary.

Many other Cypresses are grown in gardens, including *C. macrocarpa*, the Monterey Cypress, which is generally thought of as unattractive because it has been so overplanted and neglected in the past.

Cydonia
(Rosaceae)

Cydonia oblonga (*C. vulgaris*)

QUINCE

The common Quince is usually grown for its edible fruit, from which quince-jelly is made, since it is rather astringent when eaten raw. It should, however, be grown for its exquisite spring blossom. The buds are furled like an umbrella and are a delicate pink, opening slowly into white blossoms. They open a few at a time and make dainty floral arrangements.

The Quince comes from Persia and is a deciduous, large shrub of about 2–3 metres. It has numerous canes springing from the base which arch gracefully. The leaves are green, rounded and felted with white underneath. It is often grown as a hedge, but makes a better single specimen. It can be increased by division of the root. Slow-growing, it needs a rich, moist soil for best results. Sometimes troubled by Quince borer.

The Japanese Flowering Quinces are no longer called *Cydonia*, but have been given their own name of *Chaenomeles*, and will be found under that name.

Cyphomandra (Solanaceae)

Cyphomandra betacea

TREE–TOMATO

A Brazilian tree-like shrub of about 2 metres, this has large, soft, shaggy-looking leaves, but it is grown for its ornamental orange-red fruit that is freely produced in autumn. Egg-sized, it has a smooth skin and flavour combining Guava and Cape Gooseberry. It can be cut into fresh fruit salads, stewed or made into jam. It is short-lived, but bears fruit in 18 months from seed. Frost-sensitive, it must be given a sheltered, sunny nook in places with cold winters. (Illustrated Plate 22).

Cytisus (Leguminosae)

Cytisus

BROOM

Evergreen shrubs with yellow or white flowers, there are numerous species and hybrids which are all attractive, but not easily differentiated. They generally have leaves divided into 3 leaflets, but sometimes the branches are almost leafless. *Cytisus* differs in small botanical details from *Genista* and should not be confused with the Spanish Broom, *Spartium junceum*.

C. *canariensis*, Canary Broom, is known to florists as *Genista*. It grows to 2 metres, and has tiny fragrant yellow flowers in spring, arranged in clusters along the twiggy branches and between the leaves. These are divided into small leaflets of about 1 cm in length. Prune after flowering.

C. *scoparius*, Scotch Broom, has yellow flowers with several varieties and hybrids. Var. *andreanus* has showy yellow and mahogany flowers.

Dais (Thymelaeaceae)

Dais cotinifolia

DAIS OR KANNABAST, POMPON TREE

The name Dais is pronounced as 2 separate syllables. This delightful, South African, small tree grows wild in the eastern Cape, Natal and the northern Transvaal.

The massed flowers are effective in early summer. Each small ball of flowers is about 4 cm across and coloured a pale, lilac pink. The individual flowers are waxy and smooth. The fresh neat leaf is smooth and a soft, bluish-green colour. The bush usually forms a rounded shape, but grows tall and lanky at the beginning, filling up with age. It grows rapidly, reaching a height of 4 metres in 4 years, and begins to flower when only a metre in height. *Dais* is semi-evergreen during warm winters and deciduous during cold winters. It is not affected by average frost. It also likes heat and can be grown quite successfully against a west wall. A warm, sunny position is best. It requires no pruning. Propagation is by underground suckers or by seed (Illustrated Plate 22).

Dalbergia (Leguminosae)

Dalbergia sissoo

SISSOO

A spreading, deciduous, Indian tree of about 20 metres, this has sprays of creamy pea flowers in early summer, followed by 10 cm pods. The leaves are divided into 5 leaflets. This tree is tender to severe frost and is best grown in mild districts. It grows from seed or cuttings.

Dalechampia (Euphorbiaceae)

Dalechampia roezliana

DALECHAMPIA

A small Mexican shrub growing to about 1 metre in height, this has pretty rose-coloured bracts, each about 6 cm long and toothed along the edges, arranged in winged pairs at the tips of the stems. The true flowers at the centre are yellow. *Var. alba* has white bracts. The coarsely-toothed tapering leaves grow to about 15 cm.

This much-branched erect shrub is tender to frost and must be grown in a sheltered position in cold areas. It is cultivated in greenhouses, but will grow out-of-doors in warm sub-tropical places. It tolerates shade, provided that there is ample light. The soil should be light, loamy and well-drained, with plenty of moisture in summer. Propagation is by cuttings.

Daphne (Thymelaeaceae)

Daphne odora (D. indica)

DAPHNE

Low-growing and evergreen, Daphne comes from China and Japan and grows to a height of about 1 metre. The tiny flowers are clustered in a posy at the tips of the smooth, woody branches, and are backed by the dark green, smooth and waxy leaves. These grow up to about 7 cm in length and taper at both ends. The flowers appear during winter and in early spring, and have a penetrating, sweet and spicy fragrance. Each small flower is about 2 cm long, opening into 4, pointed, waxy petals which seem to glisten with silvery dust. There are a few colour varieties. *D. odora* var. *alba* has pure white flowers. *D. odora* var. *rubra* has wine-red or purplish-pink, stained on the outside, with the inside white. *D. odora* var. *variegata* has leaves edged with yellow and pink flowers. They all last well in the vase.

Daphne is slow-growing and needs special requirements, but the lover of small, sweetly scented flowers should cultivate it patiently. It likes a well-drained soil generously mixed with compost and should not be water-logged. It likes partial shade, particularly in a position facing east so that it is shielded from the hot afternoon sun and from wind, and will even grow in full shade under trees. Daphne does not thrive in sub-tropical conditions and is hardy to frost. It requires lime-free or acid soil and the roots should be kept cool with a mulch of compost or leaves such as pine-needles. Propagation is by cuttings, taken in autumn and planted out in spring, or by seed, which is extremely slow. Layers should be allowed to take root in several inches of compost in spring and left for a year before transplanting. This shrub may also be grown in a tub. It does not require pruning.

Daphe cneorum is another evergreen species which has sweetly-scented pink flowers. It is much shorter and has smaller leaves, growing up to an inch in length, while the branches are hairy. This shrub likes lime. There are several other species of Daphne, some of which are deciduous, but they all have strongly perfumed flowers.

Datura *Datura candida var. plena* (formerly known as
(*Solanaceae*)
D. cornigera = Brugmansia knightii)

MOONFLOWER, ANGEL'S TRUMPET

This semi-tropical shrub from Mexico grows to a height of 2 to 3 metres. It has large, double, fleshy, white trumpet flowers which are 15–20 cm long. They are strongly scented at night. They are borne in profusion throughout the summer, and hang down gracefully all over the bush. Heavy rain spoils them, but fresh flowers appear every few days. The leaves are large, greyish-green and velvety, and the shrub has a soft appearance. The sap is poisonous and the leaves must not be eaten.

The Moonflower is evergreen in areas which have no frost. It may be partially cut back by frost, but grows up quickly again in the spring. In the high-veld it should be given a warm, sheltered position avoiding the morning sun. It will grow in full sunlight or semi-shade. There are also single flowered species, but the double flower is the most attractive for the garden. It can be reproduced by cuttings (Illustrated Plate 23).

There are several other species of Angel's Trumpet which are grown in gardens. *Datura arborea*, from Peru, grows to 3 metres and has single flowers with 5 long points and a musky odour. *D. suaveolens* from tropical America is similar, but has short pointed lobes. It has white single or double flowers and grows to 5 metres.

Datura mollis, Pink Moonflower, from Equador, has single, wide-open salmon-pink and orange flowers which are most decorative. It forms a bush of about 2 metres and is tender to frost. (Illustrated Plate 23).

Datura chlorantha, Yellow Moonflower, is a yellow-flowered plant of unknown origin.

Davidia *Davidia involucrata*
(*Nyssaceae*)

DOVE TREE

A tall, deciduous Chinese tree, this blooms while young. Large white bracts hang down from the globular flowers in spring, like the wings of a dove. It likes cool, moist conditions and is grown from large ribbed seed, cuttings or layers, but propagation is not easy.

Delonix *Delonix regia* (*Poinciana regia*)
(*Leguminosae*)

FLAMBOYANT TREE, ROYAL POINCIANA

This large deciduous tree comes from Madagascar and grows up to about 15 metres in height. It has a spreading, flat-topped habit that is particularly noticeable in young trees. It is cultivated in many tropical lands where it is probably the most conspicuous of flowering trees, since it is a mass of scarlet flame in mid-summer. On closer inspection it may be seen that the individual flowers are borne in loose sprays and each measures about 8 cm across. The petals are gracefully curved and are broad at the tip, tapering to a thin claw at the centre. Some of the upper petals are striped with yellow. Several colour variations occur on different trees, varying from deep scarlet to vermilion and orange-scarlet, while there are also golden and pale yellow forms, one with red-tipped petals.

The leaves of the Flamboyant are huge—up to 60 cm in length—and feathery-looking, for they are finely divided and sub-divided into tiny, oval leaflets. They have a very neat appearance and are a beautiful, bright, fresh green. Long, flat, brown seedpods appear in the autumn, measuring from 30 to 60 cm in length, and are quite a feature of the tree.

The Flamboyant is, unfortunately, very tender to the slightest frost, and may only be grown in hot, frost-free climates. It is particularly suited to the humid conditions near the sea, such as are found on the coastal strip of Natal. It can also be grown in hot, dry districts inland, provided that it is planted in deep, rich soil and watered well while young. It is often most spectacular in drier districts where the foliage is sparser at flowering time. The Flamboyant Tree grows rapidly and makes an excellent shade tree. It is easily grown in the right climate and likes an open, sunny position in any good garden soil. It does not require pruning, which usually spoils its graceful, symmetrical shape, although this may be done if necessary. It should be given plenty of space, for it spreads as much as 10 metres or more. It can be grown very easily from seed, which may require soaking in hot water. (Illustrated Plate 23).

Delonix adansonioides, from Madagascar, has pale yellow flowers and a very thick trunk.

Delonix elata, from Arabia, has white flowers, becoming cream with maturity.

Deutzia (*Saxifragaceae*) *Deutzia*

BRIDAL WREATH

Deutzias come from China and Japan and there are numerous hybrids available. They are deciduous shrubs, upright in growth and from 2–3 metres in height. They are among the showiest of white, spring-flowering shrubs and flower profusely in sprays. Each flower has 5, spreading petals springing from a disc and looks very like a fruit blossom. There are both single and double forms. *Deutzias* are very easy to grow and hardy to frost. They prefer regular moisture but withstand drought and heat and will grow almost anywhere. They like well-drained soil. Do not prune except for very occasional thinning out of old wood after flowering, although the shrub will stand trimming. Propagation is best and quickest by cuttings, although it may also be grown from seed.

Deutzia gracilis grows to about 1 metre in height and has bright-green, oval, pointed leaves with serrated edges. The hybrid *D. lemoinei* is very hardy and a more vigorous grower. *D. scabra* (*D. crenata*) has both single and double flowers which may be slightly tinged with pink. Both the shrub and the leaves are larger.

Diervilla —See *Weigela*

Dichorisandra
(Commelinaceae)

Dichorisandra thyrsiflora

This is an interesting tropical shrubby perennial from Brazil. It has bamboo-like stalks which grow about 2 metres in height, each one bearing the erect flower spikes. The leaves are bamboo-like, about 25 cm long and narrow in proportion. The rich, blue flower-spikes are about 25 cm in length and 10 cm thick. They consist of clusters of small purple bells opening into fleshy, royal-blue, 3-petalled flowers showing a waxy, yellow centre. These petals are white at the base and 3 white waxy sepals show between them from the back. Round green seedpods follow the flowers. There is also a pale, periwinkle-blue-flowered variety, and these both look very effective when grown together in clumps under the shade of trees, flowering at the end of summer and in autumn.

This shade-loving plant is tender to frost and may be planted under trees in sub-tropical districts. It may be grown as a pot plant in colder areas. It requires lots of water in the growing season, but dies down in winter and should not be watered much. Once established, it will flower regularly. It is best grown from cuttings (Illustrated Plate 24).

Diospyros
(Ebenaceae)

Diospyros kaki

There are many varieties of the Japanese Persimmon, ranging from trees that are 4 metres in height down to dwarf trees that grow no larger than 2 metres in height. They are usually grafted and the foliage, as well as the fruits, vary a great deal. The leaves are always large, deep green and shining and have beautiful red-gold autumn colouring before they fall. The flowers are unimportant, but the fruit is very decorative and can be eaten. It is about 9 cm in diameter and varies from a tomato-shape to an oval, pointed shape. The skin is firm like a mango's and orange coloured, darkening to deep red when very ripe and becoming soft like a ripe tomato. The flesh is very astringent on the tongue if the fruit is eaten before it is fully ripe, and it is then very rich, soft and sweet.

New Japanese named hybrids have been developed which have large, firm, sweet fruits, similar to apples in texture. These must be grown from cuttings from mature wood in spring, with bottom heat. Sweet named varieties include Edo, Matsumoto, Fuyu and Jiro. Some are more astringent and resist colder weather better than the sweeter kinds. The astringency is caused by tannin in the fruit and Japanese growers reduce this in several ways, thus sweetening the fruit. Alcohol may be sprayed on the skins before packing the fruit or it may be stored for a week in CO gas, tightly packed. It may also be kept for two days in hot water, about 40°C.

The different varieties of the Japanese Persimmon have different rates of growth. One will grow several feet in a season so that it is nearly full size, and another will grow quite slowly. They all bear fruit in the 3rd year of growth, however. They do not need much attention and will tolerate most soils except very wet ones. They like moisture but should be planted in well-drained, rich soil generously mixed with compost. The tree likes warmth, but is hardy to our average frosts. No pruning is needed, except for the thinning out of trees that bear an over-abundance of fruit. Pruning of hybrid Persimmons, however, is necessary in order to ensure regular fruiting, as flowers are formed on branches of the previous year's growth. Branches which have borne fruit in the previous year seldom bear plump fruiting buds in the following year. Cut above a node immediately below the fruit-bearing branches when harvesting. The non-fruiting areas below the cut will then bear fruit in the following year.

Persimmon Trees are difficult to transplant as they have long tap-roots. If they must be moved then this may be done in winter, lifting as much of the root as possible and severely pruning back the top of the tree (Illustrated Plate 24).

Diospyros virginiana is the American Persimmon. It is a small-sized tree of about 7 metres in cultivation, and bears much smaller fruits than the improved Japanese varieties, varying from 2 cm to 5 cm long. Seedlings are used as under-stock for grafting or budding Oriental varieties.

Dipladenia —See *Mandevilla*

Distictis
(Bignoniaceae)

Distictis riversii

DISTICTIS

Similar in growth and appearance of leaf and flower to the Mexican Blood-Trumpet (*Phaedranthus*), this has showy purple flowers during summer. Cultivate in the same way as *Phaedranthus*. It grows from cuttings, but this is not easy. (Illustrated Plate 24).

Dodonea
(Sapindaceae)

Dodonea viscosa

SAND–OLIVE, HOPBUSH

A small, hardy, evergreen tree of 7 metres, this has long, sticky, narrow leaves and clusters of greenish or russet papery seedpods. There is a purple-leaved form from New Zealand, called *D. viscosa purpurea*, which comes true from seed. *Dodonea viscosa* is native to all countries of the southern hemisphere. It is useful as a drought-resistant, quick-growing evergreen which forms a dense screen and may be used as a hedge.

Dombeya
(Sterculiaceae)

Dombeya burgessiae

WEDDING FLOWER, PINK AND WHITE DOMBEYA

A bushy evergreen shrub of 3 metres, this has large clusters of white or pale pink blossoms in late summer, which turn brown as they age and make long-lasting dried flowers. The flowers of *D. burgessiae*, which is native to South Africa, in Natal and the Transvaal, are streaked with deep pink at the base of the petals. The clear pink form, previously known as *D. calantha* or *D. rosea*, has never been seen in the wild and is believed to have been developed from *D. burgessiae*. It hybridises easily and hybrids are being developed in America, being selected for compact form and deep colour, with some facing upwards like Peonies. The broad, toothed leaves are soft and hairy.

Dombeya will grow in full sun or light shade in ordinary well-drained soil, but needs protection from the morning sun in areas with cold winters. Propagation is easiest by cuttings. Several other species are cultivated. (Illustrated Plate 25).

Dombeya tiliacea (D. dregeana, D. natalensis) has white flowers.

Dombeya rotundifolia, Wild Pear, is a small S. African tree with clusters of white flowers, like pear blossom, on dark bare branches in spring. It grows easily from seed, is drought-resistant and needs a warm situation.

Dombeya macrantha, from the highlands of Madagascar, grows to 3 metres. It has drooping cream bells, flushed salmon, about 4 cm long, and very large furry leaves, up to 20 cm in length. (Illustrated Plate 25).

Dombeya pulchra is similar to *D. burgessiae* in every respect, but for the leaves, which are densely hairy beneath.

Doxantha (*Bignoniaceae*)

Doxantha unguis-cati (*Bignonia tweediana*)

CATS–CLAW CREEPER

This dainty evergreen, Argentine creeper owes its name to the fact that it has tiny tendrils, divided into three parts that curve over with sharp points at the ends, resembling the claws of a cat. It flowers in early summer and has bright, clear-yellow trumpet flowers. These are about 6 cm long and slightly flattened. The long, trailing stems have pairs of small, dark-green leaflets all along their length. The young growth is pink.

This creeper climbs best on a wire support or trellis and makes a light tracery rather than a thick screen. It grows fairly rapidly, depending on the climate. It likes a warm, sheltered position in areas which have cold winters, and is quite hardy to the average frosts experienced on the high-veld. It requires full sunlight in order to flower freely and should be well-watered. It would make a good ground cover on an embankment and is suitable for hanging over a garden wall. Propagation is by cuttings, but it roots freely and new plants may be detached and replanted. (Illustrated Plate 24).

Duranta (*Verbenaceae*)

Duranta repens (*D. plumieri*)

FORGET–ME–NOT TREE

This large, evergreen shrub or small tree from South America varies from 2 to 5 metres in height, according to the climate. The flowers are tiny and resemble a Forget-Me-Not, but they are borne so profusely in graceful, trailing sprays that they colour the whole bush pale-blue at periods during spring and summer, flowering almost continuously. These flowers are followed by bunches of golden berries like tiny gooseberries, intermingling decoratively with the flowers at the end of summer and being quite showy on their own during autumn and winter.

The Forget-Me-Not Tree can be grown very easily inland or at the coast, except in extremely cold and dry areas. It likes a warm, moist climate and does particularly well in Natal, where it grows extravagantly. It should be given a sunny position and watered well. It is not particular about soil, but should be planted with a generous mixture of compost. This shrub will stand severe pruning and is quite attractive when grown with a short standard which supports the drooping branches. It makes a good hedge, but should also be grown as a single specimen and makes an excellent background. There is also a white-flowered variety which is similar. Both can be increased by seed or by cuttings.

Echium
(Boraginaceae)

Echium fastuosum

This low-growing, compact shrub, growing to about 1 metre in height, comes from Madeira. It has thick, branching stems, becoming woody with age, with thick rosettes of long greyish-green leaves at the ends. Each leaf is about 12 cm long, narrow, pointed, deeply lined by the veins and covered with stiff hairs. From the centre of these leaves, the tall erect spikes of sky-blue flowers grow up in early spring.

These cylindrical spikes of flowers have a thick core and are from 20 to 25 cm long. Tiny, sky-blue flowers are clustered thickly around the spikes, so that the total effect is very blue. Pride-of-Madeira likes warm climates and is tender to frost. It can be grown in Johannesburg, where it will flower beautifully after a mild winter, but unless it is grown in a warm, sunny sheltered position, preferably facing west, a severe frost will spoil the flower spikes just as they are forming. It does well in Pretoria and is one of the features of the garden at Government House in the spring. It is propagated by seeds, cuttings and layers. There is also a deeper colour variety which is frequently seen at the Cape (Illustrated Plate 25).

Elaeagnus
(Elaeagnaceae)

Elaeagnus angustifolia

RUSSIAN OLIVE

A deciduous small tree, growing to 5 metres, this has willow-like, silvery leaves in a billowing mass in spring and summer. There are small, fragrant, yellow flowers and tiny thorns on the tree, but it is grown mainly for the foliage. This species is hardy and native to Southern Europe and Asia.
fruits. It is commonly called SILVERBERRY and grows wild in the Central U.S.A.

E. argentea is another deciduous hardy shrub with silvery leaves and silvery fruits. It is commonly called SILVERBERRY and grows wild in the Central U.S.A. U.S.A.

Elaeagnus pungens

JAPANESE ELAEAGNUS

A spreading evergreen shrub of 2 to 4 metres, this is hardy and useful as a hedge or background plant. The variegated forms are more frequently grown for ornament. Var. *maculata* has oval leaves with a central yellow patch; var. *aurea* has leaves margined with yellow and there are several other forms. The small white flowers are sometimes followed by dark red berries. Prune back long growths. *Elaeagnus* is both wind and drought-resistant and fairly quick growing. Propagate by seed or cuttings.

Embothrium
(Proteaceae)

Embothrium coccineum

FIRE TREE

A hardy evergreen tree that comes from Chile, this will grow to 10 metres or more. It has brilliant clusters of tubular orange-scarlet flowers along the branches in early spring, each about 3 cm in length. The dark green glossy leaves are narrowly oval. A form with much narrower leaves is said to grow more easily than the species. It needs good, deep acid soil and plenty of moisture, especially in winter. Propagation is by seed.

Embothrium wickhami is a Queensland species that is more tender, with flat-topped, Waratah-like, brilliant red flowers in spring. It is known as the Tree Waratah or Red Silky-Oak in Australia. The variety *pinnatum* has narrow leaflets that give it a ferny effect. (Illustrated Plate 25).

Eranthemum
(Acanthaceae)

Eranthemum nervosum (E. pulchellum)

ERANTHEMUM

A soft evergreen shrub of about a metre, this has pretty clear blue flowers at the tips of the branches in spring and large, oval, veined leaves. It needs protection from frost. It will grow in full sun or semi-shade, and may be grown in a glass house. Give it rich light soil and adequate moisture. This shrub comes from India and may be increased by cuttings. There is a form with bright yellow leaves called "Eldorado".

Erica
(Ericaceae)

Erica

HEATH

The Heaths of the Cape Peninsula have long been enjoyed by South Africans as cut flowers. They are extremely attractive and showy in the garden. Some flower in winter, others in spring and some bloom at intervals throughout the year. The flowers are so thickly clustered that they make a sheet of colour. They vary in size and shape from tiny bells, which are 5 mm or less in size, to long waxy tubes, nearly closed at the mouth in some cases, and up to 4 cm long. The translucent colours include crimson, purple, vermilion, cyclamen, pink, bright yellow, greenish yellow and papery white. Many of the tubes are tipped with other colours, such as red edged with green and white edged with scarlet. The leaves are small and narrow—some almost needle-like.

There are about 600 species of Heath which are indigenous to South Africa, the majority varying from short bushes, 60 cm in height, to tall, compact shrubs about 2 metres in height, so that one cannot generalize too much about them, but they do have certain requirements in common. Heaths have a reputation of being rather temperamental to grow and this has probably discouraged the average gardener from trying them. They do require special attention until they are established, as well as special requirements, but these are quite easy to provide, and with a little extra care, Heaths could become quite a feature of the garden.

The Heaths which are native to the Cape are accustomed to good, well-drained soil containing leaf-mould. They like moisture and have a heavy winter rainfall plus occasional rain in summer and moisture from clouds on the mountains, but the excess moisture is always drained away. Good drainage will solve the problem of heavy summer rainfall. The secret of growing them is to provide a sunny, well-drained position and to keep the roots constantly moist, but never water-logged. They should be grown in a group together so that the soil can be especially prepared for them, and are excellent for the rockery. Dig down and provide drainage under the bed in the form of rubble, if necessary, and fill the hole with a half-and-half mixture of good soil and compost, which will retain moisture and yet aid drainage. Avoid lime, manure or a clay soil. One could raise a bed above the level of its surroundings in order to avoid water-logging. Some species make good container plants. Small stones scattered over the surface of the soil act as a mulch and help to keep the roots moist and cool. It has been proved that Heath is one of those shrubs that need a mycorrhizal association (see Chapter II). Even if the small plants grow, they might never progress without the special fungus which stimulates their growth. If possible, therefore, take a little soil from the spot in which Heaths are thriving and add it to your soil when planting. Compost itself stimulates the activity of the soil fungi, so that it is an essential.

Heaths may be purchased in tins and may be planted out when they are about 15 to 30 cm in height. They should be planted in autumn at the Cape, but are best planted in spring in the summer rainfall areas, when all danger of frost has passed. Do not allow the soil in the tins to dry out before planting and take care not to damage the roots, cutting down 3 sides of the tin and removing the ball of soil intact. If liked, only the bottom of the tin can be cut off and the whole tin planted. Do not plant them deeper than they were in the tin and keep the soil moist, especially while they are young. The use of plastic bags in raising seedlings makes transplanting easier, but drainage must be checked carefully.

Some species stand frost better than others. *E. glandulosa*, the Sticky-leaved Heath, is particularly hardy, while *E. patersonia*, the Mealie Heath, is tender and needs a protected position. In places with cold winters, it is best to give the Heaths a sunny position sheltered from frost, but most of them withstand a few degrees of frost when mature.

Cut the flowers freely for the vase as they do not drop off when they fade. Prune back the long branches after flowering in order to keep the bush tidy, some requiring more severe pruning than others.

Heaths may be propagated by seed or cuttings. Both methods are very slow and the amateur is advised to purchase plants. Seed is obtainable from Kirstenbosch and may be sown in March or August. It takes about 6 weeks to germinate. The use of boiled, minced moss as a growing medium has been found to give good results. The seedlings are very tiny, but have long, hair-like roots which are about 4 times as long as the portion above ground. As soon as they are big enough to handle (a little less than 2 cm in height) they should be pricked out carefully so that the soil is disturbed as little as possible. They may be transplanted into individual tins or clay pots so that the soil may be tipped out in one piece, without disturbing the long roots, when they are transferred to their permanent position. The pots should be stood in water each day so that they can absorb it from the bottom and the tins should be watered carefully. Shade the plants at first, gradually accustoming them to the sun after several months and plant them out when 10 cm high. They may then be shaded, with two bricks placed flat on the ground at right angles to each other, so as to shield the plant from the hot midday and afternoon sun until they grow above the height of the bricks. They will then be well-established and need very little attention beyond correct watering. Heaths may also be grown by cuttings taken from the tips of young shoots near the base of the plant and kept in a constantly moist, shaded place. Grow these in individual tins and pinch out the tips to encourage bushiness. This method is not easy, unless mist spray cultivation is used.

These fascinating plants may be studied in full detail in *South African Wild Flowers for the Garden*, by the author, or *Ericas in Southern Africa*, by Baker and Oliver. The following selection of attractive species, most of which are easy to grow, will act as a guide to gardeners:
(*T*—*tender*; *H*—*hardy*; *Win.*—*flowering in winter*; *spr.*—*spring*; *sum.*—*summer*; *aut.*—*autumn*).

E. baccans. Berry Heath (2 m). Deep pink bells in win. and spr. T.

E. bauera. Bridal Heath (1 m). White tubes. Pink and bicolor vars. All year, especially spr. H.

E. blandfordia. Blandford's Heath (1 m). Short yellow tubes, spr. sum.

E. blenna. Lantern Heath (1 m). Puffed orange tubes. Var *grandiflora* is larger form. Spr. Not easy to grow. T.

E. cerinthoides. Red Hairy Erica (1 m). Scarlet hairy tubes. Win. spr. early sum. H.

E. chamissonis. Grahamstown Heath (60 cm). Feathery, pinkish-mauve bells. Mainly spr. H.

E. decora. (60 cm). Deep rose bells. Mid to late summer.

E. densifolia. Knysna Heath (1 m). Red tubes tipped greenish yell. Spr. sum. aut. H.

E. diaphana. Translucent Heath (1 m). Pinkish-mauve tubes, tipped white. Win. spr. T.

E. dichrus. (1 m). Red tubes tipped green. Mainly sum. Similar to *E. versicolor.*

E. filipendula var. major. (60 cm). White, pale green, mauve or yellow tubes. Sum. aut.

E. glandulosa. Sticky-Leaved Heath (2 m). Rose-salmon tubes. All year esp. aut. H.

E. glauca. Cup and Saucer Heath. (1 m). Crimson and purple. Sum.

E. glauca var. elegans. Petticoat Heath. (1 m). Pale pink. Summer.

E. grandiflora. Orange Heath. (1 m, spreading). Orange tubes. Sum. aut.

E. lateralis. Globe Heath. (1 m). Small pink bells. Mid-summer. H.

E. mammosa. Red Signal Heath (1,5 m). Scarlet tubes. Also pink, cream, purple, green forms. H.

E. mauretanica. (*E. viridipurpurea*). Purple Heath. (1 m). Tiny bells. Spr. H.

E. patersonia. Mealie Heath. (60 cm). Yellow tubes. Win. T.

E. perspicua. Prince of Wales Heath. (1 m). Rose tubes, tipped white. Win. spr. T.

E. pillansii (60 cm). Scarlet tubes. Sum. Moisture-loving, not easy to grow.

E. pinea. Yellow Summer Heath. (1 m). Yellow tubes. Also white var. Sum.

E. pulchella. (60 cm). Tiny bright purple bells. Sum. Aut.

E. quadrangularis. Pink Shower Heath. (45 cm) Tiny pink bells. Sum. H.

E. regia. Royal or Elim Heath. (1 m). Crimson sticky tubes. Mainly spring. T.

E. regia var. *variegata.* (60 cm) White, tipped with red shades.

E. retorta. (45 cm). Sticky rose tubes. Sum. Rare, moisture-loving and not easy.

E. speciosa. (1 m) Shiny deep pink tubes. Sum.

E. taxifolia. Double Pink Heath. (60 cm). Small deep pink "jars". Spr. sum. aut. T.

E. vestita. Wide-Mouthed Heath. (1 m) Crimson tubes, also rose, white, yellow. Thin, trembling leaves. Win. Spr. H.

E. walkeria. Walker's Heath. (60 cm). Delicate pink tubes with 4 lobes. Spr. H. (Illustrated Plate 26).

Ervatamia (*Apocynaceae*)

Ervatamia divaricata

(*Tabernaemontana coronaria*)

INDIAN ROSEBAY, CRAPE JASMINE

This evergreen shrub from the East Indies grows to about 2 metres and is covered with clusters of scented white flowers towards the end of summer. Each flower has five somewhat ruffled lobes and is about 5 cm across. There is a double form, called var. *plena*, that is also known as Butterfly Gardenia. The glossy oval leaves are about 10 cm in length or longer.

This is a shrub for sub-tropical gardens where it needs a sunny position and good well-drained or sandy soil. It should be watered regularly in warm places inland. Propagation is by cuttings.

Erythrina (Leguminosae)

Erythrina

This group of sub-tropical trees and shrubs has its origins in South Africa as well as the West Indies, Brazil and Australia. They are deciduous and do best in warm, frost-free areas. The conspicuous flowers usually come before the leaves and their rather angular habit of growth makes them suitable for the large rockery. They can be transplanted during winter when quite a good size. The seeds are hardskinned and should be soaked in water for several days until the skin splits before planting, after which they grow easily and rapidly. Pieces of roots may send up shoots. Some grow from cuttings.

Erythrina acanthocarpa

TAMBOOKIE THORN

This small, prickly, South African shrub, about 1 metre in height, is well suited to the rockery. In the spring it has broad 15-cm spikes of spectacular flowers on bare stems. Each flower is shaped like a 5-cm long, closed, curved tube, coloured brilliant crimson and tipped with greenish-yellow. The leaves are bright green and prickly and the stems have thorns like those on rose-bushes. The root is very large.

The Tambookie Thorn is hardy to frost, but is best planted in a warm, sunny situation. This shrub was originally found near Queenstown in the Cape, and likes an alkaline, well-drained soil. It flowers in the fourth year from seed. (Illustrated Plate 27).

Erythrina caffra

COAST KAFFIRBOOM, LUCKY BEAN TREE

This large, broad deciduous tree, that grows to about 16 metres, flowers in winter and spring on the coastal belt of South Africa, where it is native from the eastern Cape through Natal to Zululand. It has been kept distinct from the very similar E. lysistemon by virtue of botanical differences, chiefly in the flowers, that may be recognised even by the layman. The flower-spikes are broader than those of E. lysistemon, with individual flowers that curve back to reveal whiskery stamens. The colours range from deep scarlet to burnt orange, pink or cream. This is a tender tree, suitable for large, frost-free gardens, but may be pruned severely to keep it within bounds. It blooms while small. (Illustrated Plate 27).

Erythrina coralloides

MEXICAN CORAL-TREE

Erythrina coralloides, from Mexico, has distinctive flattened heads of tubular scarlet flowers at the tips of the branches in winter and early spring. (Illustrated Plate 27).

Erythrina crista-gallii

This Coral-Tree is deciduous, comes from Brazil and grows into a bushy, angular shrub of about 3 metres. The magnificently showy spikes of flowers appear in the spring with the leaves and a few appear intermittently throughout summer. The individual flowers are a deep, glowing red and are pea-shaped with a large, broad lower lip. They are clustered on long spikes and hang down gracefully.

This is one of the hardiest of the Coral-Trees and will endure frost once it has developed a stem of old wood after 2 or 3 years. The new growth usually dies back to the old wood in winter, but long shoots grow out again in the spring, bearing the conspicuous flowers. At the end of winter, the dead wood should be cut back to the thick trunk, the height of which varies according to the climate. As the tree grows older, the branches will also develop thick wood, and should be left to do so. The thick branches of the Coral-Tree grow out at awkward angles, and can be pruned into shape, but this tree looks best in a large rockery or roomy corner of the garden. It grows rapidly once it is established, and develops thick, pithy roots. It grows easily from seed. (Illustrated Plate 27).

Erythrina falcata has similar scarlet flowers, but the tree is much larger. It grows wild in the Andes, Peru.

Erythrina humeana (E. humei)

This shrub has similarly shaped coral flowers to those of the tree Kaffirboom, *Erythrina lysistemon*, but the spikes are not so thickly clustered with flowers. It blooms in mid-summer and varies from 2 to 4 metres in height, depending on the climate. The stems and branches are smooth and greyish-white with prickles on them. The leaves are large and arranged in 3's, forming a triangle. This shrub may be treated in the same way in the garden as *Erythrina lysistemon*. It is found on the slopes of the Drakensberg in Natal, near Grahamstown in the Cape and in the eastern Transvaal. (Illustrated Plate 27).

Erythrina lysistemon

This is the true Kaffirboom that one sees growing wild in South Africa from the eastern Cape, through Natal to the warmer parts of the Transvaal. It was formerly known as *Erythrina caffra*, but this name is now given to a similar species, the Coast Kaffirboom, which occurs wild only along the eastern coastline. *E. lysistemon* is a deciduous, medium-sized tree which flowers during winter and early spring in frost-free districts and has bright scarlet flowers that are striking and effective. The individual flowers are tube-shaped, curved and about 5 cm long. They are clustered at the ends of the bare, grey, thorny branches in such a way that they resemble a cockscomb. The heads are more compact than those of *E. caffra* and the tree itself seems more compact. Natural hybrids occur where the two species grow near one another. Although the normal colour of the flowers is bright scarlet, there are occasional pink or cream forms, but no orange hues.

E. lysistemon is not as tender as the Coast Kaffirboom, *E. caffra*. If placed in a warm, sunny spot and covered for the first few winters of its life, it may be grown in frost areas, but will not flower regularly each year unless the winter has been mild. The Kaffirboom needs a dry winter in order to flower really well. Large cuttings of this tree strike easily and it can be raised from seed. It requires no pruning (Illustrated Plate 27).

Erythrina zeyheri
PRICKLY CARDINAL OR UNDERGROUND KAFFIRBOOM

This is an indigenous Kaffirboom with a large, underground stem. The thick stalks which appear in spring are about 45 cm high and crested with the bright red flower-spikes similar in shape to the true Kaffirboom. It is hardy and can be grown in cold districts. It is found in the central Transvaal, Lesotho, eastern O.F.S. and the midlands of Natal. It grows easily and rapidly from seed and has large, prickly-backed leaves. It is suitable for the rockery and disappears completely in winter.

Escallonia
(Saxifragaceae)

Escallonia
ESCALLONIA

Escallonia comes originally from South America and hybridists have produced many named varieties that are hardier and more desirable for the garden. They are adaptable and very useful shrubs with red, pink or white flowers that are nearly all evergreen and will thrive under most conditions. They are hardy to the average frosts inland and can resist windy conditions on the sea-coast. They are not particular about soil but do need sufficient water in their early stages. Later, some can withstand drought. They are useful for hedges or specimen shrubs as well as for background planting.

Escallonia macrantha is an evergreen shrub which has deep, rich pink flowers. These are tiny, 2-cm trumpets borne in short sprays on the ends of the many branching stems. Although they are never so showy that they cover the bush, there are always a few flowers throughout the summer months, and they are particularly profuse in autumn. The leaves cluster neatly all along the arching branches. Each oval leaf grows about 3 cm long, is dark green, glossy, speckled with brown underneath and has serrated edges. The stems are covered with tiny, reddish-brown hairs. This species is one of the hardiest to frost and grows fairly quickly to a height of about 2–3 metres and is rounded in proportion. It does not require pruning, but can be cut back severely to keep it within bounds. Branches root easily to form new plants (Illustrated Plate 26).

E. langleyensis is a slender, semi-evergreen hybrid with gracefully arched branches and more showy sprays of rosy flowers in early summer. The hybrid "Apple Blossom" has clusters of pretty pink and white flowers. (Illustrated Plate 26)

Eucalyptus
(Myrtaceae)

Eucalyptus
GUM TREES, MALLEES

A huge Australian group of over 500 species, these are difficult to distinguish from one another, but all bear curious lidded buds which open to reveal a fluff of stamens that are colourful in the most ornamental garden species. Some species are grown only for their foliage.

These are most valuable drought-resistant trees that generally grow quickly and easily. Some of the larger kinds such as the Blue Gum (*E. globulus*) are too large for ordinary gardens, but valued for their timber. Some are tender to frost and may be grown as pot plants under shelter. They all grow easily from fine powdery seed, which should be sown in early spring. Colour varieties are seldom true to the parent and cannot be guaranteed by nurseries, but grafting is not practised commercially.

The smaller flowering gums are called Mallees and are suitable for small gardens, generally growing from 2 to 5 metres in height, with yellow or red flowers. These are becoming increasingly available from specialist growers.

Eucalyptus caesia

GUNGUNNU

This small tree grows to 8 metres and is especially recommended as it starts flowering in winter and continues into spring. It is hardy to frost and drought and may be grown in place of *E. ficifolia* in cold inland districts. The rich-pink flowers, about 2,5 cm wide, hang down in large bunches and the buds, as well as the stems, are "frosted" with white. The colour comes true from seed. The leaves are green and oval-pointed, becoming narrow as the tree matures. This species has attractive "peeling" bark.

Eucalyptus cinerea

FLORIST'S GUM, SILVER DOLLAR GUM

This slender evergreen tree comes from Australia and grows to a height of about 7 metres. It is grown for its silvery foliage and decorative, ashen-grey appearance. The foliage is covered with a distinctive mealy-white bloom. The trunk of the tree is smooth and the bark does not peel off in strips like that of other Eucalypts. The leaves are very pretty and easily recognised. They are oval or heart-shaped and have no stalks. They are attached in pairs around the main stem and each pair is at right-angles to the one below it, so that the effect is that of tier upon tier of leaves. These leaves are similar in shape to the "juvenile" foliage which is found on many Gum trees, but whereas the others give way eventually to the ordinary, tapering blue-gum leaves, the foliage on this tree remains the same when the tree has reached maturity. The branches are often used by florists in mixed bouquets, as the leaves are so decorative. This tree grows easily and rapidly, like many other Eucalypts. It is hardy to frost and likes a moist soil. It is propagated by seed. (Illustrated Plate 28)

Eucalyptus ficifolia

RED–FLOWERING GUM

This magnificent Australian tree is most striking. It has a similar appearance to the ordinary Eucalyptus tree, but bears brilliant red flowers which consist mainly of a mass of waxy stamens. The flowers appear in clusters outside the foliage at intervals throughout mid-summer, starting as early as November and carrying on until April or longer. The scarlet flowers are the most showy, but there is also a rosy pink, a salmon and a creamy white which are attractive. An attractive feature of the "head" of bloom is the flower-bud which opens with a little lid to release the stamens folded underneath it.

Unless the tree has already flowered, it is almost impossible to tell what colour the flowers will be on the tree you buy, and this, of course, is a definite disadvantage for the gardener. There is no satisfactory method of taking cuttings, so that the trees must be reproduced from seed. Only seed which comes from native trees in Australia is fairly true to colour, and as these trees only come from a small part of Western Australia, there are not so very many seeds available. Seed from other red-flowering gums in cultivation is seldom true in colour to its parent. Nevertheless, variations are also attractive and are worth having, except that one does require the space to keep trying. The seed-pod is hard and the size of a small plum. It must be picked before it will ripen.

The Red-Flowering Gum is not detrimental to gardens, as it has a very deep root system and plants or lawn may be grown right up to it. It grows up to about 7 to 10 metres, but is not as fast growing as the ordinary Gum tree. It does particularly well at the coast and does not like severe frosts. If one can protect it, at any rate for the first few years of its life, it will grow to a large size even in Johannesburg, and cold winters will not affect it (Illustrated Plate 28).

An alternative for cold districts is *E. leucoxylon* var. *rosea*, with rose-coloured flowers, but the colour does not always come true from seed. It grows to about 8 metres.

Eucalyptus kruseana
KRUSE MALLEE

A shrub of only 3 metres, this has tiers of very dainty tiny silvery-grey leaves, almost rounded and wrinkled. They are about 2 cm broad, but vary in size. This shrub has yellow and white flowers in autumn and winter, and blooms when very young, even when growing in pots. It is an attractive foliage plant. (Illustrated Plate 28)

Eucalyptus macrocarpa
ROSE OF THE WEST

A large ornamental shrub growing to 5 metres, this has huge flowers measuring up to 12 cm across, consisting of a mass of pink or red stamens tipped with white. They appear at intervals during spring and the first half of summer, followed by a woody seedpod that is almost as broad as the flower. The large soft oval leaves clasp the stems neatly in tiers and are covered with silvery-white bloom which reflects the light as they move in the breeze. This species needs very well-drained sandy soil and comes from Western Australia.

Eucalyptus nicholii
WILLOW PEPPERMINT

A tall quick-growing tree, this is valued for floristry as the narrow leaves are covered with pinkish-purple bloom in spring and the thin stems are red. The small flowers are white. A drought-resistant tree, this will grow in dry, poor soil.

Eucalyptus perriniana
SNOW GUM, SPINNING GUM

A quick-growing hardy tree that reaches a height of about 6 metres, this has interesting cicular silvery-grey leaves like discs, pierced by the slim stems, creating a spiralled effect. If these change shape and become longer with maturity, prune off the unwanted branches so as to regenerate the disc-like young leaves. The flowers are white and bloom in late summer.

Eucalyptus preissiana

A large shrub or small tree that grows to about 5 metres, this has large bright yellow flowers in spring and early summer. They are followed by large bell-like pods. The leaves are large and broad, tapering to the tips. This easy-to-grow bush has a loose habit, but the flowers make it extremely decorative. It is also known as the Stirling Range Mallee. (Illustrated Plate 28)

Eucalyptus rhodantha is similar to *E. macrocarpa* but forms a more compact shorter bush, with squat blue-grey leaves in pairs. It also has large rose flowers, but these are smaller than those of *E. macrocarpa* and bloom mainly in the second half of summer.

Eucalyptus tetraptera

FOUR-WING MALLEE

A spreading shrub that grows to 3 metres, this is noteworthy because of its large red pods, 8 cm in length, that are 4-angled and droop downwards so that the pink flowers hang down like a fringe. They bloom in early summer. The shiny leaves are thick and very long, up to 25 cm.

Eucalyptus torquata

CORAL GUM

Considered one of the best ornamental Gums for the average garden, this grows quickly to form a shapely tree of about 6 metres. It bears bunches of coral red flowers, each 2,5 cm across, during spring and summer. The small buds, like pixie-caps, are attractive when the lid lifts half off to reveal silky furled stamens before they burst open into a fluff of coral-red filaments topped with yellow stamens. The stalked leaves are slender and pointed, growing to 8 cm in length. This tree is frost-tender when young and should be protected during the first winter. (Illustrated Plate 28)

Eugenia (Myrtaceae)

Eugenia myrtifolia (E. australis)

BRUSH-CHERRY

This Australian, evergreen tree grows to a height of about 7 metres in cultivation, although it can grow up to 16 metres in the rain-forests of its native home.

The Brush-Cherry is one of the prettiest of evergreen trees being fresh-looking throughout the year. Its shape and foliage are exceptionally beautiful. It has a central trunk from which the leafy branches droop in cascades to the ground. This tree should be allowed to grow to the ground without removing the lower branches. The Brush-Cherry does not take advantage of its freedom, however, but grows upwards in quite a compact, cylindrical fashion. The young leaves are a delicate, brownish-pink while the older, fresh green leaves are narrow, smooth and satiny. In early summer the tree is covered with white flowers made up of feathery stamens, and in late summer these become oval, purplish-red fruits about 2 cm long. Additional flowers appear at the same time as the ornamental fruit, which hangs down most gracefully. It has a tart flavour, but can be made into jam.

The Brush-Cherry requires moisture, especially when young, and appreciates a summer rainfall. Although it endures light frosts, a severe frost may cut back the tender young growth and even kill the tree altogether. In warmer districts this tree can be used as a high, ornamental hedge. It prefers a warm, sunny position. It grows quite rapidly when conditions are suitable, although it is a little slow at first. It can be grown from seed and should be transplanted when small, although fairly large specimens can be transplanted from tins (Illustrated Plate 28).

Eugenia jambos
ROSE–APPLE

This is a tropical Asian tree with big yellowish, edible fruits, 5 cm in diameter, and very long leaves. It is suitable only for hot, frost-free areas.

Eugenia uniflora
PITANGA, SURINAM–CHERRY

This small evergreen tree from Brazil has distinctively fluted, crimson edible fruits in autumn. They are translucent, rounded and about 2 cm in diameter. The flowers are white and fluffy and the glossy oval leaves about 5 cm in length. Pitanga thrives in warm areas and will resist salt spray at the coast, but may also be grown on the highveld in sheltered gardens. It withstands clipping to form a hedge.

Euonymus (Celastraceae)

Euonymus japonicus
SPINDLE–TREE

There are several Spindle-Trees, both evergreen and deciduous.

This evergreen shrub of about 3 metres comes from Japan. It has inconspicuous flowers but bears masses of attractive, rose-coloured berries in winter, which split open to reveal bright orange seeds which resemble lucky-beans. It has dark green, rounded, waxy, shining leaves. This slow-growing shrub is useful as a background or windbreak and can be clipped into a hedge. It will thrive in most conditions including those at the sea-side. It is extremely hardy to frost and can be grown successfully against a cold, south-facing wall. It can be clipped in the summer and long growths can be checked as required. It is propagated by 10 cm cuttings taken in autumn and given gentle bottom heat (Illustrated Plate 30).

The following variegated forms are obtainable:
E. jap. albo-marginatus has white-bordered leaves.
E. jap. aureo-marginatus has gold-edged leaves.
E. jap. aureo-variegatus has leaves blotched with yellow.

Euonymus radicans, Winter Creeper. This is an evergreen shrub which may be creeping or bushy, with several varieties. The close-creeping form variegatus (including "Silver Queen") has white-edged leaves and is used as a slow-growing ground-cover under trees. It will also creep on walls.

Euonymus alatus, Winged Spindle-Tree, may be recognised by the corky "wings" on its branches. It has orange berries and attractive red autumn foliage. This hardy deciduous shrub grows to 2 or 3 metres and comes from China and Japan. It likes a cool, moist climate.

Eupatorium
(Compositae)

Eupatorium sordidum (E. ianthinum)

A showy Mexican evergreen, this shrub grows to about 2 metres, bearing large heads of violet Ageratum-like flowers in spring and early summer. It likes semi-shade and shelter from frost. Propagate by cuttings in spring. (Illustrated Plate 30).

Euphorbia
(Euphorbiaceae)

Euphorbia

SPURGE

This large group of plants has many decorative garden species with colourful bracts, while some succulent types are valued for their distinctive sculptural forms. They have a milky sap which is an irritant. They are generally drought-resistant and do best in hot climates with mild winters, needing protection from frost. Cuttings strike easily and some species grow freely from seed. The Poinsettia (E. pulcherrima) is the best-known garden species. E. lathyrus, the Mole-Plant or Caper Spurge, is a biennial with blue-grey overlapping leaves that is said to keep away Moles.

Euphorbia cotinifolia

BRONZE EUPHORBIA

This species from Tropical America is a decorative foliage plant for sub-tropical areas. It has oval, purple-bronze leaves that are similar in shape to those of Cotinus and it forms a bushy, leafy plant growing to a height of about 2 metres. It seeds itself freely. (Illustrated Plate 29).

Euphorbia fulgens (E. jacquiniflora)

SCARLET PLUME

This slender, weeping shrub from Mexico grows to about a metre and has thornless, slender stems with showy sprays of tiny, red, button-like flowers at the tips in spring. The leaves are long and narrow. This is suitable for a pot on the verandah or for a hot sunny position overhanging rocks. Give it a warm sheltered position against a wall in places with cold winters. It grows easily from cuttings.

Euphorbia leucocephala

WHITE LACE EUPHORBIA

This large shrub or small tree from Guatamala grows to 2 or 3 metres and forms a lacy cloud of tiny white flowers in autumn. It makes an extremely pretty spectacle in a warm climate, needing well-drained, good soil. It may be grown in a large container, but does not like to be pot-bound. The slender, narrow leaves are a fresh green. It grows easily from seed. (Illustrated Plate 29).

Euphorbia milii var. splendens

CHRIST-THORN

This curious, low-growing spiny shrub comes from Madagascar and grows from 30 cm to 1 metre in height. The flowers are borne in regular groups of 8 and their colour is provided by brilliant, rosy-scarlet, rounded bracts that look like flat buttons almost 2 cm across. They appear nearly all the year, but are most profuse in early spring. There are long thorns on the thick, silvery-brown, angular branches. The leaves are small, oval and green. They are numerous on the new growth but the old stems are almost leafless. There is a form with long, very large leaves.

Christ-Thorn is tender, but will survive slight frost if it is protected in a warm, sunny corner. It likes warm, well-drained soil and is suitable for the rockery where it will hang down and drape over the rocks. In Natal it is frequently grown as a low-clipped hedge. It can be grown in a pot in cold areas. Cuttings strike easily in spring. It likes a slightly acid soil (pH 6). (Illustrated Plate 28).

Euphorbia pulcherrima (*Poinsettia pulcherrima*)
POINSETTIA

This spectacular, tropical American shrub is freely grown in southern Africa and in warm climates throughout the world. It grows to about 3 metres in height and 2 metres in width. It is deciduous inland, but remains evergreen at the coast. It will not stand severe frosts, but gardeners in cold-winter areas plant them in warm, sheltered corners made by the walls of the house, where they are very showy, but are not as magnificent as those grown in warm districts. The Poinsettia quickly develops a short trunk made of hard, blond pithy wood, and even when the frost cuts back the young wood, this will continue to send up annual shoots. The leaves are broad, green and dense.

The brilliant effect is produced by numerous, large scarlet bracts borne at the tips of the branches which look like petals, the real flowers being the tiny yellow circles in the centre. There are both single and double Poinsettias and the double variety has additional clusters of bracts in the centre. They are the size of a small dinner plate when at their best and have the most intense red colour. There are also pale pink and creamy-yellow varieties.

A fully double, almost spherical form, called *Ecke's Flaming Sphere*, has its flowers at the ends of arching branches. It grows slowly to form a bush of about 2 metres and does best in hot, frost-free areas. (Illustrated Plate 29). Dwarf hybrids are grown in pots for florist decoration, notably scarlet *Paul Ecke*, which has broad bracts. When planted in the garden, it makes a compact shrub of about 1 metre, but grows taller in sub-tropical places. (Illustrated Plate 29).

Unfortunately, the vivid bracts are just developing when early frosts often cut them back in cold areas. In Durban and Pietermaritzburg, where they are outstanding, the bracts remain attractive on the bush for the whole winter and until they are pruned back at the beginning of spring. This pruning keeps the bush from growing too large and encourages long arching stems to grow out from a short thick trunk. It also gives the shrub a period of rest. Poinsettias make good cut flowers, and if the ends of the stems are burnt or plunged into boiling water the flowers will last in the vase. Cuttings root easily and pieces of root will send up new plants in summer (Illustrated Plate 29).

Exochorda (*Rosaceae*)

Exochorda racemosa (*E. grandiflora*)
PEARL–BUSH

A deciduous shrub from China that grows to about 3 metres, this requires about 2 metres in which to spread. It has showy, white flowers in spring. The sprays of buds resemble pearls and these open into 3 cm, 5-petalled, snow-white flowers, with a cluster of delicate stamens in the centre. The sprays make good cut-flowers. The branches are slender and graceful and have bright-green, oval leaves with serrated edges. All the named varieties are worth growing.

These shrubs are hardy to frost and do not like sub-tropical conditions. They may be planted in a sunny or semi-shady position in light, well-drained soil. Propagation is by seed, cuttings or layers, but is slow. Sizeable specimens of 1,5 metres can be bought quite easily and inexpensively. Pruning is unnecessary, but faded flowers should be removed, and this means that the flowers can be freely picked for the vase. Pruning must be done immediately after the flowering.

Fabiana (Solanaceae) — *Fabiana imbricata*

CHILE-HEATH

A slender evergreen shrub of 2 metres, with waving branches covered with tiny leaves, this has tubular, white, heath-like flowers in early summer. It is hardy and grows from cuttings. It belongs to the Potato family, despite the common name. (Illustrated Plate 31).

Fabiana violacea is similar, with mauve to lilac flowers.

Feijoa (Myrtaceae) — *Feijoa sellowiana*

PINEAPPLE GUAVA

A Brazilian evergreen shrub growing up to 5 metres, this has dark green, oblong leaves backed with silvery-grey. The flowers bloom in early summer and measure about 4 cm across. They have 4 pink, cupped petals and a central tuft of crimson stamens. The green, oblong fruits ripen in autumn and fall when mature. They should be stored and allowed to soften before eating raw or made into jam.

Feijoa is suitable for sub-tropical climates, but prefers a cool, moist climate. It is, nevertheless, an adaptable shrub, enduring dry, cold winters on the highveld and a fair amount of drought. It will grow in ordinary good garden soil, in the open sun or in partial shade. Pruning is not necessary and propagation is by seed or cuttings of young wood (Illustrated Plate 31).

Felicia (Compositae) — *Felicia filifolia* (*Diplopappus filifolius*)

WILD ASTER

A low evergreen South African shrub that grows to 1 metre, this becomes a sheet of small mauve yellow-centred daisies in spring, blooming for about a month. They are about 2 cm wide and vary from light to dark mauve. The needle-shaped leaves cover the twiggy stems and bear witness to the plant's drought-resistant qualities. It is fairly hardy, but needs protection from frost in very cold areas. It is adapted to rainfall at any time of the year and long periods of drought. The soil should be light and well-drained. This shrub is useful for growing on sloping soil or rockeries. Propagation is by seed sown in autumn or spring.

Fernandoa (Bignoniaceae) — *Fernandoa magnifica*

FERNANDO'S TREE

A slender tree from East Africa, this has clusters of large wide-open trumpet flowers which are orange flushed with yellow at the throat in early summer. Although it grows wild at the sub-tropical coast, it can be grown at high altitudes if given protection from frost. It grows in ordinary, well-drained garden soil with moisture in summer, but is drought-resistant in winter. It is propagated by seed.

Ficus *Ficus*
(Moraceae)

ORNAMENTAL FIG

Although the *Ficus* trees do not have attractive flowers, some have beautiful fruits and foliage. Most of them are huge evergreen trees from the warmer parts of the world, yet the Rubber Tree, *F. elastica*, is grown as an indoor pot plant and others like *F. pandurata*, the Fiddleleaf Fig, make decorative house plants. *F. carica* is the edible fig of commerce. *F. pumila* is the creeping Fig that clings to walls, covering them with small oval leaves.

Numerous large Fig trees are grown in warm gardens, many of them well-known. These include *F. macrophylla*, the Moreton Bay Fig; *F. benghalensis*, the Banyan; *F. religiosa*, the Pepul Tree of the Hindus, under which Buddha is said to have meditated. This is the only Fig Tree with a long "tail" to the heart-shaped leaf. *Ficus pretoriae*, the Wonderboom, is a huge tree north of Pretoria that has been proclaimed a national monument.

Ficus benjamina is a lovely tree from Asia for sub-tropical gardens, with its slender drooping branches covered with glossy, pointed leaves. It has cherry-like red fruits in autumn in warm areas.

Forsythia *Forsythia*
(Oleaceae)

GOLDEN-BELLS

There are numerous species of Golden-Bells which come from different parts of China, Japan and Europe and include a number of hybrids. They grow approximately 2 to 3 metres in height and are deciduous, flowering profusely in early spring before the leaves appear. The flowers are clustered close to the long stems and grow almost completely along their length. Each flower is almost 2 cm long and has 4 oblong petals, curving outwards like a snow-drop. They are a clear, golden yellow and very dainty. The branches may be picked for the vase, and are often picked while in bud, opening indoors. Forsythias are more showy in countries which have cold winters and where the transition from winter to spring is more sudden than it is in most parts of South Africa.

Golden-Bells are generally easy to grow and have strong constitutions. They are hardy to frost and like full sunshine or partial shade, but do not enjoy sub-tropical conditions. They are not particular about soil, but this should be well-drained and reasonably good, but they do need water. They may be planted near trees, but in this case, should be well mulched in order to conserve moisture. They make good plants for a south wall. Pruning should take place as the flowers die in order to check rambling growth. Worn-out wood can also be removed after flowering, but not too drastically. Propagation is easiest by cuttings, although the plants will also grow from seed.

Forsythia intermedia. This tall, 10-feet hybrid shrub has more showy flowers than *F. suspensa*. They are thickly and more uniformly produced. There are many varieties of which *spectabilis* is considered the best (Illustrated Plate 31).

Forsythia suspensa has whip-like branches, with flowers produced intermittently in spring, summer and autumn, together with the leaves. This was the species most commonly cultivated in the past.

Fuchsia (Onagraceae)

Fuchsia hybrida (F. speciosa)

The original Fuchsia species came from tropical America and many hundreds of hybrids were developed from these, dating from early in the nineteenth century. The Fuchsia reached the height of its popularity in mid-Victorian times and to-day there is a newly-awakened interest in these old-fashioned, picturesque plants, for a "Fuchsia Society" was formed in England in 1938, which is occupied with the rediscovery of the known hybrids.

Fuchsias are the most graceful and elegant of small evergreen shrubs, varying from 60 cm to 90 cm in height. The flowers droop down in sprays from the branches and have often been compared to the dress of a ballet dancer. The coloured, waxy calyx curves back to show differently coloured petals below, which are either single or double in type. They come in different combinations of white and red, pink and purple, and flower freely throughout spring, summer and autumn. The fresh green leaves are small, oval and waxy.

These shrubs are often grown in tubs, hanging baskets or pots on the verandah, as well as in greenhouses. They grow very successfully out-of-doors, however, and will stand the average frosts experienced in South Africa. Although their parents come originally from tropical lands, the hybrids are not really happy in sub-tropical conditions. They will grow in the sun, but prefer partial or complete shade and are most valuable for growing under the shade of trees. Fuchsias are very easy to grow once they are established and can be transplanted while quite large, either in autumn or in spring. They should be given a great deal of water in summer but fairly dry conditions in winter. They are heavy feeders and should be planted in rich soil and given a mulch of compost and well-rotted manure during the year. They should have some shelter from wind.

Fuchsias are often grown on slopes or in rockeries as they have a pendent habit of growth. If one can train and stake the main stem straight upwards, the remaining branchlets will cascade down to the ground, and one can plant the Fuchsia on level ground. Cuttings of young wood strike easily at any time of the year and grow rapidly in favourable conditions. There are many named hybrids available, which are delightful when grouped together in a shady corner of the garden. There are several species that vary in character (Illustrated Plate 30). *Fuchsia magellanica* var. *gracilis* has very slender, smaller, dainty flowers that droop down in great profusion. *Fuchsia procumbens* is the Trailing Fuchsia. *F. fulgens* has tubular, cerise-red flowers. (Illustrated Plate 30).

Galphimia (Malpighiaceae)

Galphimia glauca (Thryallis glauca)

An evergreen bush from Mexico and tropical America that grows to a height of nearly 2 metres, this has neat foliage composed of simple glossy oval leaves growing to about 5 cm in length. The long clusters of small bright yellow starry flowers stand above the foliage and are prolific throughout summer. This is a useful shrub for sub-tropical districts where it may be used as a hedge. It will grow in cold areas on the highveld if given the protection of a wall. It is grown from cuttings or seed. (Illustrated Plate 31).

Gardenia (Rubiaceae)

Gardenia jasminoides var. plena (G. florida)

DOUBLE-WHITE GARDENIA

This is an excellent evergreen shrub which comes from China and Japan and should be grown in every garden. It makes a neat, compact bush of about 1–2 metres, with large, glossy, oval, deep-green leaves. The heavily-scented flowers are so numerous in midsummer that new buds open each day over quite a long period and can be picked freely for low bowls or corsages. They are an expensive florist's flower as the petals bruise very easily when touched. Each flower is about 5 to 8 cm across and has a double row of milk-white, waxy, slightly-curled petals. The shrub is slow-growing, but begins to flower when only 35 cm in height, and a small bush of 60 cm will provide dozens of blooms (Illustrated Plate 31).

Gardenias are very easy to grow but require an acid soil (pH 6) generously mixed with compost, and respond well to the tea-leaf treatment (see Chapter II). The surface of the soil should be mulched with compost and the shrub should be watered copiously, particularly while small. It should be planted in an open, sunny or partially shaded position, and is quite hardy to our average frosts. It does not require pruning, except for the removal of dead flowers. Gardenias transplant easily while they are small. The plant may be reproduced by cuttings, but this is very slow. G. jasminoides var. fortuniana (var. fortunei) has larger, but single flowers. One indigenous species, Gardenia thunbergia, Wilde Katjiepiering, is a larger shrub with fragrant, long-tubed, single flowers and can be grown for interest in a large garden. (Illustrated Plate 31).

Genista (Leguminosae)

Genista monosperma var. pendula

WHITE WEEPING BROOM

A tall broom with weeping branches covered with fragrant white pea-flowers in spring, this is almost leafless. This decorative shrub comes from Spain and North Africa and will resist drought, particularly in summer. It grows from seed.

Several other Genistas have yellow pea-flowers and are much confused with Cytisus and Spartium.

Ginkgo (Ginkgoaceae)

Ginkgo biloba

MAIDENHAIR TREE

A tall, narrow, deciduous tree from China, this grows slowly to 30 metres. It is thought to be the most ancient of plants that date back to fossil times. Its beautiful, fan-shaped leaves, resembling those of maidenhair fern, turn rich gold in autumn. The olive-shaped 'nuts' are edible, but should be boiled. Ginkgo needs plenty of moisture and good, well-drained loamy soil. It requires a cold winter and dislikes the sub-tropics. Male and female trees must be grown together in order to produce seed. Propagation is by seed, cuttings, layers and by grafting horticultural forms. (Illustrated Plate 32).

Gliricidia
(Leguminosae)

Gliricidia sepium (G. maculata)

A dainty deciduous tree that is laden with clusters of sweetly-scented pale pink pea flowers, each about 2 cm long, that appear before the foliage in spring and early summer, this grows from 5 to 9 metres in height. The leaves are about 25 cm long and divided into paired leaflets. The tree casts a light shade and is popularly used in Mexico to shade cocoa and coffee plantations. It is native to central tropical America.

Although the flowers are edible, the seeds, bark and leaves are said to be poisonous to rodents and mixed in powder form with bait as a rat poison, but the tree is not poisonous to cattle. This tender tree is suited to warm, frost-free districts and grows easily from seed or from large cuttings inserted directly into the soil.

Gompholobium
(Leguminosae)

Gompholobium

AUSTRALIAN PEA

Several species of these Australian evergreen shrubs have yellow or red pea-flowers. G. latifolium is cultivated in this country and has inch-wide, yellow flowers, in spring and early summer. It grows to 2 metres and has leaves divided into three 5-cm leaflets. It requires well-drained soil and a sunny situation. It is drought-resistant and will grow near the coast. Propagation is by seed.

Grevillea
(Proteaceae)

Grevillea

Grevillea is a large Australian genus containing about 200 species, many of which have very different flowers and foliage. They belong to the Protea family, but grow more easily than most members of this large group. They have pin-cushion-like flowers with "curly" styles and come in shades of red, yellow and white. Selected hybrids and varieties are continuously being added to the large range available at specialist nurseries and should be chosen in flower if possible, as they are often confusingly alike. Some are densely evergreen and useful for creating privacy.

The majority are drought-resistant, but need water during winter and spring if grown in the summer-rainfall area. They are soil-tolerant, preferring slightly acid conditions such as are found in most garden soils. Drainage is important and they do best in light soil containing compost. Propagation is by seed, but selected hybrids are grown from cuttings.

Grevillea banksii

SCARLET GREVILLEA

The Scarlet Grevillea is a small tree or large shrub, growing to a height of over 3 metres. It is evergreen and its leaves are divided into long, dark-green fern-like leaflets. It bears striking, rosy-scarlet flowers nearly all the year in moist, warm, frost-free areas, and during summer in areas with light frosts. Severe frost will kill it. Protection from morning sun near a wall will enable one to grow it in cold gardens. The flowers are thickly clustered in a spike resembling a Bottle-brush, but are waxy in texture and the stigmas form "loops" all around them before uncurling. Scarlet Grevillea is grown from seed and begins to flower when very small. It requires a deep, composted soil and lots of moisture (Illustrated Plate 32).

Grevillea banksii var. *alba* is a white-flowered variety. It was formerly thought to be the species, with variety *fosteri* as the red form, but the latter variety is no longer recognised.

Grevillea caleyi is a similar red-flowered shrub, smaller in size, with a shorter flowering period.

Grevillea barkleyana
TOOTH-BRUSH GREVILLEA

A large spreading evergreen bush which grows to 2 metres in height and spread, this has broad long leaves that resemble those of a Gum tree. The one-sided "tooth-brush" flower-spike is a pretty rose pink. This is one of several "tooth-brush" Grevilleas from Australia. (Illustrated Plate 32).

Grevillea biternata

A delightfully graceful shrub, this starts growth as a groundcover, spreading its dainty, needle-like foliage closely over the soil. It then sends up long slender stems that grow to about 2 metres, billowing in all directions when laden with clouds of creamy small flowerheads in spring.

This is a noteworthy shrub for a large rockery or sloping bank and would lean effectively alongside a flight of garden steps. (Illustrated Plate 32).

Grevillea juniperina
JUNIPER GREVILLEA

Very similar to the Rosemary Grevillea, this has sharp-pointed needle-leaves about 2 cm in length. The red flowers are silky-hairy and the bush grows from 1 to 2 metres in height. Var. *rubra* is more spreading and longer in flower. (Illustrated Plate 32).

Grevillea lanigera
WOOLLY GREVILLEA

Similar to the Rosemary Grevillea, this is a slightly smaller bush with woolly stems and lighter, blunted needle leaves. It has lighter reddish-pink flowers. Some forms have red and yellow flowers.

Grevillea lavandulacea
LAVENDER GREVILLEA

A short spreading bush that scarcely reaches 1 metre, this has greyish needle leaves to about 3 cm in length, resembling the colour of lavender. It is covered with red flowers in spring and there are several forms available, notably Black Range.

Grevillea robusta
SILKY OAK

This large, evergreen tree comes from New South Wales and grows to a height of 16 to 32 metres. It has ornamental foliage, for its long, 25-cm compound leaves are divided into dark-green, irregularly-shaped leaflets, with a fern-like and feathery appearance. On the underside they are covered with fine silky, silvery hairs. This tree is often called Silver Oak as well as Silky Oak.

In early summer, the tree bears large showy "cushions" of massed golden-orange flowers on the branches, which can be seen from a long distance and last for about 2 months. The Silky Oak looks particularly effective if it is planted alongside a Jacaranda Tree which bears its soft, blue flowers at the same time.

The Silky Oak grows rapidly and makes an effective windbreak. It reaches a height of about 5 metres in 4 years. It is a coastal tree but does well inland and endures frost except when it is very young. It likes moisture and deep, good, lime-free soil, although it is drought-resistant when it grows older. It grows from seed which must be planted when fresh. It can be trimmed but this usually spoils its natural pyramidal shape.

It should be planted where its almost continuously falling leaves will not be a nuisance.

Grevillea rosmarinifolia

ROSEMARY GREVILLEA

A spreading evergreen, which grows to 2 metres, this has distinctive, rosemary-like foliage and red flowers in early summer. This is one of the most commonly grown Grevilleas and extremely useful as a dense evergreen. It forms a larger bush than either *G. lanigera* or *G. juniperina* which resemble it, but has darker, coarser prickly leaves. There are two variations, one with greyish, softer foliage, called Vectis, and one with massed flowers at the ends of the branches, known as Jenkins.

Grewia
(*Tiliaceae*)

Grewia occidentalis

FOUR CORNERS, KRUISBESSIE

A slender, evergreen tree of over 3 metres, this has elm-like leaves and 3-cm, pinkish-mauve, starry flowers in mid-summer. It needs shelter from the east in cold climates, but will withstand some frost. It grows easily in ordinary soil in sun or semi-shade and is drought-resistant in winter and spring. It may be grown from fresh seed, which is arranged in clusters of four.

Greyia
(*Melianthaceae*)

Greyia sutherlandii

MOUNTAIN-BOTTLEBRUSH, BAAKHOUT

This semi-deciduous shrub is most suitable for the rockery, for it comes from the mountain slopes of South Africa, particularly in Natal. It is sparse and tall —almost a small tree in its native surroundings—and has thick reddish stems carrying bright scarlet flowers, with protruding stamens, massed in a 12-cm spike, like a Bottlebrush. It is showy and distinctive, flowering freely during the end of winter and early spring, and has large, round leaves. It is accustomed to dry, well-drained conditions, really only enjoying moisture during summer. It grows from seed, and cuttings can be taken from any new shoots that are sent up. Beautiful specimens can be seen at The Wilds, Johannesburg. It needs shelter from the east in cold areas (Illustrated Plate 32).

Greyia radlkoferi, Transvaal Baakhout, is similar, but has smaller flower-heads and leaves felted beneath with white. It forms a rounded bush to 5 metres.

Greyia flanagani is similar, but may be recognised by its shorter, fewer flower-spikes and smooth, light green leaves.

Halesia
(Styracaceae)

Halesia carolina (= H. tetraptera)

SNOWDROP-TREE, SILVER-BELL

A dainty deciduous tree of about 7 to 13 metres, this bears myriads of small white bell-flowers in late spring. The large oval leaves turn yellow in autumn. This tree comes from central North America and is hardy, preferring moist, rich, acid soil. It is grown from seed, layers or cuttings.

Hamamelis
(Hamamelidaceae)

Hamamelis mollis

WITCH-HAZEL

Especially useful in cold climates, this hardy Chinese shrub can be planted on a south wall in semi-shade, with good soil and moisture. It bears its delicate flowers on bare branches in mid-winter. These are bright yellow with thin petals. It grows slowly, ultimately becoming a small tree. Propagation is by layers, as seed takes 2 years to germinate.

Hardenbergia
(Leguminosae)

Hardenbergia comptoniana

LILAC-VINE

This showy evergreen vine rivals the Petrea for a short period in September, when it is covered with small sprays of purple pea-flowers, each marked with 2 pale green spots. There is a pink-flowered variety. The leaves are divided into long narrow leaflets. It is suitable for growing over a wall. *H. monophylla* has similar purple flowers with pink and white-flowered varieties, but is more shrubby and has oval leaves. It may be grown over a tree stump. Both species endure hot, very dry conditions and grow from seed. (Illustrated Plate 34). Several other species are hardy.

Hebe
(Scrophulariaceae)

Hebe speciosa *(Veronica speciosa)*

SHOWY HEBE (VERONICA)

The evergreen, shrubby kinds of *Veronica*, which come mostly from New Zealand, now belong to the genus *Hebe*, and should be referred to by that name, as distinct from the perennial *Veronica*. There are many species and hybrids of these lovable, small shrubs, some growing up to nearly 2 metres in height, but this species grows to a height of about 1 metre. It has large numbers of 10 -cm, richly coloured spikes of tiny flowers. The most common colour is a deep purple, but there is also a beautiful crimson. There are some hybrids with white or pink flowers. There are always a few spikes of flowers throughout the year, but winter and spring are the most showy periods, when they flower incessantly. The foliage is attractive, for the leaves are dark green, oval, smooth and waxy, with a mauve vein running into them from the purple stems of the new growth. They grow symmetrically up the stems and the whole bush has an extremely clean, trim look.

Showy Hebe is hardy to average frosts, but is not very happy in sub-tropical climates, preferring the cooler districts. It thrives at the coast and likes moisture in summer. It will grow in an airy, open, sunny position and likes partial shade, especially from the hot afternoon sun. It may be used as a low, untrimmed hedge as it is so neat. It is propagated by seed or by cuttings taken in autumn, and flowers in the following season. (Illustrated Plate 34).

H. andersoni is a hybrid between *H. speciosa* and *H. salicifolia* with soft lavender blue flowers. The form *variegata* has attractive white-edged leaves and grows up to 1,5 metres. It does best in partial shade in hot areas. *H. franciscana variegata* has very small, variegated leaves.

Hedera
Hedera
(Araliaceae)

IVY

Evergreen climbers which are almost too well-known for description, these do best in rich, moist soil, but are most adaptable and easy to grow, thriving in cold, sunless places and clinging by means of aerial roots. They are useful for covering walls in shady places or may be grown as groundcovers on slopes or under trees. They should not be allowed to grow on trees and smother foliage or the tree will die through being robbed of light. Although Ivies are shade-tolerant, the variegated kinds must have sufficient light or sunshine if they are to retain their colouring.

Slow-growing at first, they will cover large areas and bear fruit only when they have stopped climbing. Cuttings taken from plants at this stage will grow into bushy "tree" forms. Ivies may be grown as ornamental pot plants and shaped in many ways, some being trained to cover wire structures. They may be cut back severely at the end of winter in order to keep them under control. Propagation is easiest by severing rooted pieces of stem, but cuttings will grow roots in water.

Hedera canariensis

CANARY ISLANDS IVY

This evergreen climber from the Canary Islands and N. Africa has large leathery leaves from 10 to 20 cm wide, which are heart-shaped at the base and have 3 to 5 lobes. The variety with cream variegations is most popularly grown, retaining its colouring best in bright light. It is hardy in the southern hemisphere, needing shelter only in very cold areas.

Hedera helix

ENGLISH IVY, COMMON IVY

This hardy European climber has numerous forms, which are variously named in nurseries and gardens, so that collectors are recommended to select them personally. The normal species has leathery dark green leaves up to 10 cm long, which may be broadly oval or triangular, with 3 to 5 lobes. It has bunches of small, round black fruits.

The most attractive forms include those with broad, ruffled leaves; miniatures with pointed leaves which remain smaller when confined to a pot; small-leaved kinds with gold centres, creamy centres or margins and one which develops rose-pink edges in autumn. A hybrid with *Fatsia japonica* is called *Fatshedera lizei*, which makes a hardy evergreen shrub for shady places or for indoor culture in pots.

Heimia
(Lythraceae)

Heimia salicifolia

A Mexican evergreen shrub of about 3 metres, this has narrow leaves and small rosette-like yellow flowers appearing singly along the branches. Being compact, it is useful as a screen.

Heliotropium
(Boraginaceae)

Heliotropium peruvianum

HELIOTROPE, CHERRY-PIE

A soft, old-fashioned, evergreen shrub of 1–2 metres, this has flat heads of purple, strongly scented flowers. The original species from Peru varies in colour from pale lilac to violet and is the parent of many horticultural forms. The plants flower from spring to autumn. Heliotrope may be grown in the open sun in frost-free places or in partial shade in cold-winter areas. It makes a good tub-plant for a verandah. Prune it back at the end of winter. It is grown from seed or cuttings. (Illustrated Plate 34).

Hibbertia
(Dilleniaceae)

Hibbertia volubilis

SNAKE VINE

An evergreen Australian climber with bright yellow flowers in summer, like 5-cm single roses, this is suited to growing on a low fence or to covering a bank or rocky outcrop. It needs well-drained soil and full sun. Propagation is by seed, cuttings or layers.

Hibiscus
(Malvaceae)

Hibiscus

HIBISCUS

The genus Hibiscus is extremely large, containing about 400 species of different kinds. All the shrubs may be propagated quite easily by cuttings. The following are examples of the most attractive for garden use.

Hibiscus rosa-sinensis

CHINESE HIBISCUS

Chinese Hibiscus is a large, neat evergreen shrub of about 4 metres with dark, shiny green leaves. It is tender to frost and grows best in sub-tropical conditions. It is often used as a most attractive hedge in warm areas. It can be grown in areas which have cold winters provided that it is given the protection of a warm wall. It can be pruned quite severely after the winter and before new growth commences, and may be trimmed almost at any time. It is used as a hedge in hot districts.

This Hibiscus has the most showy and profusely-borne flowers imaginable. Each flower lasts for 1 or 2 days, but there are so many buds on the tree that the effect of the blooms is almost continual. There are single and double-flowered forms, all of which are 12–15 cm across and of a rich, clear colour. The most common, because it is the hardiest, is the single, scarlet-flowered Hibiscus which is covered with vivid blooms most of the summer. Among the single flowers are a lemon-yellow with a red base and an apricot colour. The double forms are very frilly and rich looking and 2 attractive colours are a deep rosy-cerise and a very pale shell-pink. They are variously named in the trade (Illustrated Plate 33).

Canary Island, pale pink with a deep rose throat, is borer-resistant at the South Coast. *Pink Butterfly*, a hybrid from Hawaii, has been trained to make an attractive weeping standard, almost 2 metres in height, and used as an ornamental in Durban. The stem is severed at the top of the trunk and the pendulous branches droop down, laden with pretty pink flowers in summer and autumn. The branches may be pruned to shape or drawn down with stones as weights, if necessary. (Illustrated Plate 33).

Hibiscus mutabilis

TREE–HOLLYHOCK

This semi-deciduous shrub comes from China and is cultivated in sub-tropical regions. It is half-hardy, which means that it will endure some frost but not severe frosts. It can be grown in the Transvaal if it is given the protection of a warm sunny corner, and even if it is cut back a little, will come up again and flower in late summer.

Like all other Hibiscus shrubs, the Tree-Hollyhock flowers freely, and the conspicuous 8-cm flowers, resembling Hollyhocks, are poised all over the bush. There are several varieties with both single or double flowers in white and rose-pink. One of the attractive features of the single, white-flowered variety is the fact that the buds, resembling the buds of a Hollyhock, appear continuously with the flowers and are coloured a pretty rose-pink. The buds are large, about 3 cm across, and the effect of both pink and white on the tree is very arresting. Some flowers open white and change to pink during the day, darkening in the evening. The double flowers are known as *H. mutabilis* var. *flore-pleno*.

The bush or small tree, for it grows about 3 metres in height and spreads to the same width, is suitable for the wilder corners of the garden. The leaves are broad and greyish-green and the young wood is thick and soft-green. Cuttings strike easily and it can be grown from seed. It is herbaceous in appearance and grows fairly quickly (Illustrated Plate 33).

Hibiscus schizopetalus

FAIRY HIBISCUS

This shrub comes from tropical Africa and grows into a large, rounded bush about 3 metres in height with small, waxy green leaves. The flowers are bright red and very dainty against the dark foliage. They hang downwards from delicate stalks and their petals are curled back and deeply fringed. The long stamen-columns hang down below the flowers and add to the feeling of daintiness. The Fairy Hibiscus thrives in semi-tropical districts and stands up to the wind on the sea-coast. Improved hybrids have been developed in Hawaii. (Illustrated Plate 33).

Hibiscus syriacus

SYRIAN HIBISCUS

This deciduous Hibiscus, also known as the Rose-of-Sharon or Althea, comes from Eastern Asia. It can be grown very easily as a hedge or as a single specimen. It is hardy to frost and requires no protection. It has a tall, fairly narrow habit of growth, about 3 metres in height and over a metre in diameter. The flowers are about a quarter the size of the Chinese Hibiscus flowers and are borne closely along the main stems and branches in summer. There are also single and double forms which are obtainable in white or mauve. The single mauve flower has a deep-red base and powdery white stamens. It has light-green leaves, similar in shape but not in size or texture to the Chinese Hibiscus. Although not as attractive as the Chinese Hibiscus, this is an extremely useful and pretty shrub for areas with cold winters. (Illustrated Plate 33).

Hoheria *(Malvaceae)*

Hoheria populnea

NEW ZEALAND LACEBARK OR OTAGO RIBBONWOOD

An evergreen small tree of about 7 metres, this comes from New Zealand and has clusters of 3-cm, starry white flowers in autumn. It belongs to the Mallow family and has large, oval, toothed leaves. It likes moisture and a cool situation. It is quick-growing, reasonably hardy to frost and may be grown from seed or cuttings. There is a variety with silvery leaf markings and one with purple-backed leaves.

Holmskioldia *(Verbenaceae)*

Holmskioldia sanguinea

RED CHINESE-HAT PLANT

The Red Chinese-Hat plant comes from the sub-tropical Himalayas and grows into a large, rounded bush about 3 metres in height. The long, slender branches grow straight upwards bearing the small flowers between the leaves and at the tips of the branches in autumn and early winter. Each flower has a terra-cotta coloured, rounded calyx like a small Chinese hat, 2 cm across, and the tube-like scarlet flower droops down from the centre of it. The leaves are olive-green, oval and pointed, and grow up to 6 cm long.

This shrub is evergreen and does best in warm, frost-free areas, but will survive light frosts, particularly if it is protected with grass over the first few winters. It should be grown in a warm, north-facing corner for best results in cold-winter areas, where it is usually deciduous. Long growths can be pruned back in the spring. It can be grown from seed or from cuttings. (Illustrated Plate 34).

Holmskioldia speciosa, is the mauve Chinese-Hat Plant, which comes from Komatipoort in the Transvaal and is tender to frost. The round calyx is a dull, pale mauve and the small protruding flower is purple, making an interesting combination. The flowers are borne in large clusters during summer and the shrub grows rapidly to a height of about 4 metres, with a narrow, compact habit of growth. The small, 3-cm leaves grow all along the slender stalks and are broad and tapering, with serrated edges. There is also a dull-gold variety known as the Apricot Holmskioldia.

Holmskioldia lutescens, from Barbados, has rich yellow flowers.

Hovea *(Leguminosae)*

Hovea chorizemifolia

HOLLY-LEAF, HOVEA

A small Australian evergreen shrub of 30 to 60 cm, this has prickly, holly-like leaves and clusters of tiny purplish-blue pea-flowers in early winter. Shelter from frost and do not overwater. It grows from seed.

Hovenia *(Rhamnaceae)*

Hovenia dulcis

JAPANESE RAISIN TREE

Curious rather than beautiful, this deciduous tree grows to 10 metres and has sweet red pulpy fruits containing seeds that develop after the inconspicuous greenish-white flowers have bloomed. They are reminiscent of raisins. The branches radiate gracefully from the central trunk and the light foliage consists of oval, tapering leaves up to about 9 cm long.

This tree is cultivated in Japan, but grows wild in China and the Himalayas. It is hardy and easy to grow, requiring well-drained soil and moisture in summer. Propagation is by seed.

Hoya
(Asclepiadaceae)

Hoya carnosa

WAX PLANT

Delightful pink posies, 5 cm across, of waxy starry flowers, appear annually on the old stems of this slender, evergreen climber from South China. It needs protection from frost and well-drained soil which should be fairly dry in winter. It may be grown in the full sun out-of-doors in mild areas, or in a pot on a shady verandah or even indoors in cold areas, but must be given a support on which to twine. It grows easily from cuttings. There is a variety with variegated leaves.

Hydrangea
(Saxifragaceae)

Hydrangea macrophylla (H. hortensis)

HYDRANGEA

Hydrangeas are probably the most popular shrubs in South Africa, where they are also called Christmas Flowers, and grow in most parts of the country. They come from Asia and grow into well-rounded bushes up to 2 metres in height. They have showy flowers during summer and are at their best in mid-summer. The leaves are large, fleshy and shining.

The flat sterile flowers are grouped in large heads up to 30 cm across and come in beautiful, clear and often blended shades of pink, white, red and blue. Choose good colours when the plants are in bloom at the nursery. There are several varieties worth growing, apart from numerous named hybrids. The variety mariesii has a flat corymb of small flowers encircled by showy sterile flowers, like a posy. One has ornamental green and white variegated leaves.

In soil which is slightly acid (pH 6) Hydrangeas will produce pink flowers, but in very acid soils (pH 4.5) the flowers will turn blue. The colours can be intensified or even changed artificially. They will change to pink shades if watered with a weak solution of lime water once in three weeks, and to blue if watered with aluminium sulphate in a weak solution of a tablespoon to a bucket of water. Pieces of iron and tin in the soil will help to keep the blue colour. Chemical preparations can be mixed with the soil to intensify blue colours. It is best to grow the same colours together in one spot or the water will run from one to the other and change the colours. The flowers often become russet with age and some change to pale green in the autumn. They are great favourites for the vase, but will last longer if their hard, woody stems are pounded at the ends so as to assist quick water absorption. The heads can be freshened by immersing them in a bath of cold water overnight.

Hydrangeas are evergreen in warm areas and deciduous in areas with cold winters. They like plenty of moisture in the summer and revel in the humidity at the coast. They are magnificent in the Cape Peninsula. They prefer partial shade, particularly inland, where they do well on south-facing walls, but will flower in the open sun at the coast. Hydrangeas must be watered copiously and the soil should not be allowed to dry out in summer. On hot, dry days the foliage should be sprayed with water. The plants like a good, rich porous soil which should be mulched with compost or very well-rotted manure at least once a season. Artificial fertilizer may be given before flowering.

Pruning is essential, or the flowers will become very small and space should be cleared for new growth. At the end of autumn or in mid-winter, the main stalks should be cut down to about 60 cm from the ground, just above a leaf-bud. Very old, worn-out wood can be cut out at the base. Insignificant twigs should be cut away, leaving strong main stalks growing from the base. Heavy frost will cut back Hydrangeas that have not been pruned, and the dead stalks must be removed. They are hardy, however, and will send up new growth in the spring. It is best to give them the protection of tree branches in cold areas to prevent recurrent frost damage.

Pruning may be done in several different ways according to one's needs. Very heavy pruning in mid-winter will result in late summer or autumn flowers. Light summer pruning, which means removing spent flowers with a 20-cm length of stem in late summer (January or February) followed by a second light trimming in July, will result in a massed display in mid-summer. In all cases, however, gnarled old wood should be sawn off at the base in winter and weak twigs removed.

Hydrangeas should be replaced after about 15 years. They may be increased by cuttings or by suckers separated from the root. They flower when very small and make good tub-plants. (Illustrated Plate 35).

Hydrangea quercifolia. A hardy, North American, 2-metre shrub with long sprays of white flowers, turning purple, this has interesting oak-like large leaves that turn mahogany before dropping in winter. (Illustrated Plate 35).

H. petiolaris. A tall, self-clinging climber from Japan, this has white flowers in open clusters, but is slow and needs a cool position.

H. paniculata. A hardy, tree-like, deciduous species which grows to about 3 metres, this has 35-cm, pyramidal heads of white flowers in summer. It needs cool, moist conditions and must be pruned at the end of winter. It is sometimes called the Peegee Hydrangea, after the initials of the form *H. paniculata grandiflora.* Variety *praecox* flowers 6 weeks earlier. (Illustrated Plate 35).

H. serrata. A deciduous shrub of almost 2 metres from Japan, this has pretty, 8 cm, flat flower-heads in blue, soft pink or white, with a few small sterile flowers, during summer. The leaves are smaller, thinner and duller than those of *H. macrophylla.* There are several varieties, of which var. *acuminata* has slender, longer leaves and usually blue flowers and var. *rosalba* has pink and white sterile flowers.

Hymenosporum (*Pittosporaceae*)

Hymenosporum flavum

SCENTED YELLOW-BLOSSOM TREE

This delightful evergreen tree comes from Queensland and New South Wales and grows to a height of about 8 metres. It flowers profusely in early summer and is very showy and bright for about two months. The individual flowers are borne in sprays and are creamy-yellow at first, about 3 cm across, and have gracefully turned-back petals. They deepen with age to chrome yellow and are strongly and sweetly scented.

The foliage is pleasant, with dark shining green leaves, 10 to 12 cm long and tapering to a point. The seed-pods open in the shape of spread wings. The tree forms a narrow pyramid, and the branches hang down gracefully. They are very woody and brittle and the tree should be firmly staked or sheltered from strong, prevailing winds. Alternatively, it can be grown as a large bush without a standard. This tree has a medium rate of growth—about 2–3 metres in 4 years, and flowers properly when it is 3 or 4 years old. It is hardy to average frost, and likes warm climates, but does not like drought. It should be planted in deep, well-drained soil and watered well. Propagation is by seed. (Illustrated Plate 34).

Hypericum (Hypericaceae)

Hypericum

ST. JOHN'S WORT, OR GOLD FLOWER

There are many species and garden hybrids of these shrubs which come originally from many parts of the world. As they are sometimes given the name of Rose-of-Sharon (see Syrian Hibiscus, which also has this name) one should make sure that one is buying the right shrub. Perhaps the best common name for this genus is Gold Flower.

These shrubs vary in size from spreading plants of 30 cm in height (*H. calycinum*) to rounded bushes about 2 metres in height. The flowers are all golden, cup-shaped and filled with a mass of delicate stamens. They make a bright show on the bush in summer and at intervals throughout the autumn. There is one species (*H. patulum* var. *forrestii*) growing to a height of about 1,5 metres, that has smooth, narrow, pale-green leaves and is deciduous for a very short period, but its leaves turn beautiful russet colours before they fall, particularly during rainy spells. There are also many evergreen species, including *Hypericum sinense*, which has larger blooms, and flowers for a very long period. (Illustrated Plate 34).

The imported species of Gold Flower have no scent, but one South African species has a strong, curry smell. This is the Curry Bush (*H. lanceolatum*, formerly *H. leucoptychodes*). Often, while walking in The Wilds at Johannesburg, the scent leads one unmistakably to the bush. The curry odour is wafted into the air by glands in the leaves, but when one tries to smell parts of the plant in order to locate the scent, it seems to disappear mysteriously, only to drift back as soon as one moves away. The leaves of this plant are very small, narrow and neatly arranged along the twiggy stems. The bush becomes large and straggly—about 3 metres in height and 3 metres in diameter—but may be pruned back in order to keep it within bounds. Its size, together with its strong smell, would make this shrub more suitable for a large garden than a small one.

The Gold Flowers are extemely hardy and very easy to grow. They enjoy full sun but will also grow in partial shade. *H. calycinum* will grow in full shade under trees. These shrubs may be grown almost anywhere as they are not particular about soil. They may be severely pruned at the end of winter, and old wood may be thinned out from time to time if necessary. Propagation is by seed, cuttings or division of the root.

H. moserianum is a semi-deciduous hybrid with russet leaves and the form *tricolor* has variegated green, white and pink leaves.

Hypericum "Rowallane's seedling" is a hybrid with extra large flowers.

Iboza
(Labiatae)

Iboza riparia

IBOZA, MISTY PLUME BUSH, GINGER BUSH

A delightful evergreen shrub for mild districts, this may be grown in cold climates in a sheltered position, and is especially valuable as it will grow in partial or full shade. The feathery tasselled plumes of flowers appear in autumn and mid-winter, making a cloud of lilac on the bush. They last in the vase. There are several colour forms ranging from palest lilac to deep purple. The aromatic leaves have a scent of ginger.

Iboza grows rapidly to 15 cm in light loamy soil with moisture in summer and dryness in winter. Trim back after flowering. It grows easily from cuttings. It is native to South Africa, Rhodesia and tropical Africa (Illustrated Plate 36).

Idesia
(Flacourtiaceae)

Idesia polycarpa

IDESIA

This hardy, deciduous tree from China and Japan has decorative grape-like bunches of scarlet berries in autumn, remaining after the heart-shaped leaves have fallen. It grows fairly slowly from 8–13 metres in height and makes an excellent street tree in climates with cold winters. Propagation is by seed.

Ilex
(Aquifoliaceae)

Ilex aquifolium

ENGLISH HOLLY

A evergreen tree, growing up to 10 or 13 metres, this is so slow-growing that it is seldom seen as large, and may be pruned severely to keep it down to size. It is called English Holly as it is such a favourite in England, but it really comes from central Europe and Asia. The flowers are insignificant, but the shiny, pea-sized scarlet berries, which appear in winter, are very attractive. They are used traditionally for Christmas decoration in the northern hemisphere. The distinctive leaves are a dark, glossy green, oval in shape and up to 8 cm in length. The edges are scooped out and tipped with sharp spines.

English Holly dislikes sub-tropical conditions. It may be grown successfully in areas with cold winters, as it enjoys frost. Holly should be planted in rich, very acid, well-drained soil. It may be grown in the open or in partly shaded positions, preferring a situation facing east rather than west. It grows well under trees if the soil is good and well mixed with compost. It should be well watered all through the year. A watch should be kept for scale on the branches, and the affected parts sprayed immediately. Transplanting should be done only when plants are young. They may be moved in winter or in spring, but nearly all the leaves should be stripped off in order to ensure success. The bush may be cut back if it is on the large side. Holly is not usually pruned as it is so slow-growing, but long growths may be shortened during summer.

Many garden forms of Holly are cultivated in Europe and America. Some have gold or silver variegated leaves and others have weeping branches. There are well over 200 species, both evergreen or deciduous. The females bear the berries and these are most profuse when both male and female are grown together. Increase by cutting is very slow. Many varieties are budded or grafted. (Illustrated Plate 36).

Ilex cornuta

This is a slow-growing evergreen shrub of 3 metres, with 5 long points on the oblong glossy leaves, and scarlet berries in late summer. It grows more successfully in warm districts than the English Holly. Sometimes the leaves have fewer or no spines.

Ilex verticillata

WINTERBERRY, BLACK-ALDER.

A deciduous spreading shrub to 3 metres, this has clusters of bright red berries scattered gaily over the whole bush from late summer. The small oval leaves are deeply veined and slightly toothed. This hardy, North American shrub grows easily on the highveld and may be propagated by seed. Male and female bushes should be grown together. *Var. chrysocarpa* has yellow berries. (Illustrated Plate 36).

Ipomoea (Convolvulaceae)

Ipomoea arborescens

TREE-CONVOLVULUS

This comes from Mexico and grows into a graceful woody tree about 5–7 metres in height. It is covered in late autumn with 5-cm white flowers, like the annual Morning Glory, and has velvety twigs and foliage. It grows well in sub-tropical Natal, but will also flourish in warm, dry areas without frost. It grows from seed. (Illustrated Plate 36).

Ipomoea horsfalliae var. briggsii

CRIMSON WAX TRUMPET

This beautiful climber comes from the West Indies. Huge clusters of fat, shiny buds open a few at a time and go on for months throughout summer, autumn and into winter. Each flower is a dark red, waxy, wide-open trumpet about 5 cm across with powdery, white stamens. The dark-green, shiny leaves which have ruffled edges, spring from a central point at the ends of the branches, forming a rounded fan. This climber is quick-growing, evergreen and easy to grow, but is liable to attack by hairy caterpillars which must be collected and destroyed or sprayed with insecticides. It does well at the sea-coast and in sub-tropical conditions, but will not survive frost. It can be increased by cuttings or by seed.

Ipomoea tuberosa

WOOD-ROSE

A vigorous tropical climber with ornamental, deeply-cut foliage, this will cover a large wall, but will only flower in mild or sub-tropical climates. It is tender to frost. The yellow trumpets appear in autumn and the sepals and ovary expand and become woody to form the "petals" and "heart" of the Wood-Rose. When mature, they should be hung in a dry airy place to cure before being used in dried flower arrangements. The Wood-Rose grows easily from seed.

Isopogon
(Proteaceae)

Isopogon cuneatus

Curious Australian members of the Protea family, the Isopogons have their flowers clustered into a rounded brush springing from a ball-like cone. These appear near the ends of the branches in spring. They grow from seed, preferring sandy, well-drained, acid soil with water during winter.

There are about 30 species of which some are dwarf and others grow to 1 or 2 metres. The best species with rose-coloured flowerheads include *I. dubius* (*I. roseus*) and *I. latifolius*. *I. cuneatus* has purple flowers. *I. anethifolius* has yellow flowers and fern-like needle leaves, like *Serruria*.

Itea
(Saxifragaceae)

Itea virginica

A deciduous, hardy shrub, this is useful for cold gardens where it will grow both in sun and shade. It grows to 3 metres and has upright spikes of white fragrant flowers during summer. The narrow, toothed leaves are 10 cm long and turn red in autumn. Sweet Spire comes from North America and is propagated by seed, cuttings or division.

Ixora
(Rubiaceae)

Ixora coccinea

Ixora coccinea comes from India and Ceylon and there are numerous species, including both shrubs and small trees. They are all evergreen and have showy flowers varying in colour from white to salmon, orange, yellow, rose-pink and red.

Red Ixora grows into a 2 metre, compact shrub, bearing 10 cm clusters of coral-coloured flowers. Each flower has a thin, wire-like tube opening into a small, five petalled-rosette, about 1 cm across. From the front of the cluster, only the small flat faces of the flowers can be seen, creating a vivid mass about 8 cm across. They make good cut flowers and flower from spring until the end of summer. The branches are woody and blackish-brown, with a rough bark. The olive-green leaves are bunched along the stems and are oval, smooth and leathery in texture.

Ixora grows in sub-tropical or low-veld conditions, and will not survive frosts. It is not particular about soil and grows easily, if a little slowly, but needs to be well-watered. In cold areas, it may be grown as a pot plant. It can be propagated by cuttings in spring but this is very slow. (Illustrated Plate 36).

Ixora lutea is similar to *I. coccinea* and is said to be of garden origin. It has yellow flowers in looser heads than the best hybrid forms of *I. coccinea*. (Illustrated Plate 36).

Ixora macrothyrsa, the Giant Ixora from Sumatra, has very large, broad leaves and much larger heads of deep red to crimson flowers than those of *I. coccinea*. (Illustrated Plate 36).

Jacaranda (Bignoniaceae)

Jacaranda

There are numerous species of *Jacaranda* from South America and the West Indies, but only one is popularly in cultivation. Several others have been introduced into American horticulture without great success. The tall, palm-like *J. copaia* is said to have violet flowers in pendulous sprays, 1 to 3 metres long, at the ends of the branches. It comes from the eastern forests of Peru at altitudes of about 600 m. Articles made from Jacaranda wood are freely obtainable in Brazil. The name Jacaranda is commonly used in Brazil for other woods that are not related, such as that of *Dalbergia*.

Jacaranda acutifolia. English botanists regard this species, from the eastern mountains of Peru, as different from the well-known tree that is cultivated in gardens under the name of *J. mimosifolia*. A specimen at the Paris Herbarium, with fewer pinnae on the leaves, straighter flowers and smaller seed-pods, is the foundation for separating *J. acutifolia* from *J. mimosifolia*. The Peruvian taxonomist, Dr. Ramon Ferreyra, states, however, that *J. acutifolia* is the correct name for the tree that is cultivated so freely in all temperate and sub-tropical countries. It was also regarded thus in Flora Brasiliensis. As the name puzzle is beyond the layman, the name *J. mimosifolia* will be used until such time as fresh specimens are gathered from the wild in Peru and further botanical investigations undertaken.

Jacaranda mimosifolia (*J. ovalifolia*)

This large, rounded tree from Brazil, grows up to 13 metres or more in height and requires as much space in which to spread. It is deciduous inland but almost evergreen at the sub-tropical coast. It flowers in early summer and the trees are usually seen at their best during October and in November. The flowers are a unique, deep mauvish-blue, which has come to be known as Jacaranda blue. They are short, puffed trumpets, about 4 cm long, and borne in large clusters all over the tree. The tree is seen at its best in areas where it is deciduous, and the flowers appear on leafless branches making the Jacaranda an intense mass of colour and one of the showiest of flowering trees. The flowers fall easily and there is always an attractive mauve carpet beneath the tree during flowering time. Rain spoils the delicate blossoms temporarily. The compound leaves are very large, up to 35 cm in length, and divided and sub-divided into tiny leaflets, so that the foliage is dainty and fern-like. There is a rare white-flowered form, which is reproduced from cuttings.

Jacarandas are easy to grow. They are tender to frost while young, but as large specimens can be transplanted from the open ground quite easily in winter, this need not affect the average gardener. They like warmth and can resist a certain amount of drought.

The distinctive seed-pods are mussel-shaped and open to release the winged seeds. The tree grows easily from seed or cuttings. It begins to flower when about 4 years old and 2 metres in height. Jacarandas grow with medium rapidity in cool areas, but very rapidly at the sub-tropical coast where they are usually grown to save time and then distributed to different parts of South Africa. Pretoria has become world-famous for its Jacarandas which line nearly every street and make a blue haze over the city, attracting many visitors. The trees are also impressive in Johannesburg, Durban and many other places.

The weight of the foliage makes the lower branches droop to the ground and these branches may be sawn off. Jacarandas should not be planted where they will interfere with overhead wires as they lose their graceful appearance when they are ruthlessly cut back, although this severe pruning (or pollarding) does not affect them otherwise. They look best when grown as a single specimen tree in the garden and are given ample room to spread naturally. The colour of the Jacaranda blossom contrasts well with the golden flowers of the Silky Oak (*Grevillea robusta*) which appear at the same time *J. mimosifolia* grows wild in N.W. Argentina, N. Brazil and eastern Peru. (Illustrated Plate 37).

Jacobinia (*Acanthaceae*)

Jacobinia carnea (*Justicia carnea*)

PINK JACOBINIA

Showy heads of deep pink, hooded flowers in summer, make this evergreen Brazilian shrub attractive. It grows to about a metre, but should be cut back after flowering or at the end of winter. Although tender, it may be grown in semi-shade under a tree or in a sheltered patio. Propagate by cuttings (Illustrated Plate 36).

Jacobinia floribunda (*Libonia pauciflora*) Red Jacobinia, has drooping tubular red flowers tipped with yellow in winter. It grows to 60 cm and is evergreen. It needs protection from frost and will grow in semi-shade.

Jacobinia umbrossa, Yellow Jacobinia, has striking bright yellow flower-heads, up to 20 cm in length, and large, broad leaves. It grows to 2 metres in sub-tropical places and flourishes in partial shade. It is native to tropical America. (Illustrated Plate 36).

Jacquemontia (*Convolvulaceae*)

Jacquemontia pentantha (*J. violacea*)

MINIATURE MORNING GLORY

A small delicate vine to 2 metres, with an open lacy habit of growth, this has tiny morning-glory flowers nearly 3 cm across. They are bright blue with white centres. New blooms open each day almost throughout the year. The small leaves are heart-shaped.

This plant needs a warm sunny position in well-drained soil. It grows easily, but will die down during cold winters. It needs a trellis or grille on which to twine or may be allowed to overhang a wall or rocks. It comes from Central America and the southern U.S.A. Propagation is by seed.

Jasminum (*Oleaceae*)

Jasminum

JASMINE

There are about 200 species of Jasmine, native to the warm areas of Europe, Asia and Africa. They are easy to grow and prized for the intensely sweet perfume of their waxy flowers. Jasmines are reproduced by cuttings or layers.

Jasminum officinale

The White Jasmine (not to be confused with the Star-Jasmine, *Trachelospermum jasminoides*) comes from Persia and is an evergreen, rambling shrub that requires the support of a low fence. The fragrant flowers have narrow tubes opening into 5, star-shaped petals. Clusters of flowers appear at the ends of the branches in summer. The leaves are made up of 5 or 7 leaflets, such as are found on roses, but are smooth, dark-green and glossy. This shrub is hardy to our average frosts and may be reproduced by cuttings. It can stand semi-shade as well as full sun. It may be pruned or thinned after flowering.

Jasminum grandiflorum or ROYAL JASMINE, is similar, but has larger white flowers and is the Jasmine cultivated in Europe for the manufacture of perfume.

Jasminum sambac is called ARABIAN JASMINE but comes from India. It is a large, semi-climbing shrub with long, slender, arching branches which are flanked by dark-green, rounded and slightly heart-shaped leaves. Clusters of starry white flowers, a little over 3 cm across, are very strongly and sweetly scented. They are usually double and have up to 8 or 9 narrow petals. Arabian Jasmine is tender to frost and does very well in sub-tropical climates, where it flowers almost perpetually, and does well in the shade.

Jasminum multipartitum, MANY-PETALLED JASMINE, is a beautiful spreading shrub from the eastern Cape and Natal, with white waxy flowers, about 5 cm wide, similar to those of *J. sambac*, with 8 to 12 pointed petals. The glossy leaves are oval and pointed and it has black berries. (Illustrated Plate 37).

Jasminum humile var. revolutum

YELLOW BUSH JASMINE

This shrub comes from Tropical Asia and grows into a rounded bush about 3 metres in height. It has bright yellow flowers which are similar in shape to those of the White Jasmine, but have more oblong petals, and measure nearly 3 cm across. It is faintly perfumed. This shrub flowers profusely in early summer and blossoms fall freely to the ground making a circular, bright yellow carpet. The branches are green and very twiggy, bearing clusters of flowers at the end of each twig. The bush is evergreen and hardy but becomes sparse during cold winters. The thick green leaves have 3 to 5 oval leaflets.

Jasminum polyanthum

CHINESE JASMINE

A delightful, dainty Chinese climber, this has become deservedly popular. It bears 10 cm clusters of sweetly-scented white flowers, rosy outside, in spring, and has dark-green, dainty leaves of 7 leaflets. It remains evergreen in mild situations and turns brown during severe frost, but comes on again in spring. It may be grown in all parts of southern Africa and multiplies easily by division of the root. (Illustrated Pate 37).

Jasminum primulinum

This deciduous, semi-climbing shrub needs the support of a low fence. It has long, spreading, whip-like branches and leaves made up of 3 leaflets arranged like a triangle. The flowers are large, over 3 cm across and a clear, primrose yellow. The petals are rounded and the flowers are often double. They are borne very profusely all along the stems in spring, looking very showy for about 2 months. They make good cut-flowers but have no perfume. The shrub is quite hardy to frost and easy to grow. It may be pruned after flowering. (Illustrated Plate 37).

Jasminum stephanense

PINK JASMINE

This hybrid, evergreen shrub has clusters of fragrant, pink flowers, and is the best of the pink-flowered Jasmines. It flowers in spring and summer and is very vigorous.

Jatropha (Euphorbiaceae)

Jatropha

CORAL-PLANT

There are several species of *Jatropha* from tropical America which make decorative garden plants. They are tender to frost, but may be grown as pot-plants in places with cold winters. They belong to the Euphorbia family and their milky sap as said to be poisonous. They grow easily from cuttings of slightly dried young branches and seed themselves in warm climates.

Jatropha hastata

PEREGRINA

This leafy evergreen shrub grows to almost 2 metres, bearing clusters of cup-shaped red flowers at the tips of the branches. It comes from Mexico and Cuba. (Illustrated Plate 38).

Jatropha multifida

CORAL-PLANT

Common in sub-tropical gardens, this is a large evergreen shrub that grows from 2 to 4 metres in height. It has curious, waxy scarlet flowers that are shaped like a bunch of coral at the tips of the stems in summer. They stand above the large, glossy ornamental leaves that are deeply divided into a number of narrow, pointed lobes with their points forming a circle. This plant grows slowly and should be planted in light, sandy soil in a large, sub-tropical garden where it needs very little attention. (Illustrated Plate 38).

Jatropha podagrica

PANAMA CABBAGE, GUATAMALA RHUBARB, TARTOGO

A striking plant with a swollen trunk that grows to over a metre in height, this has coral-like red flowers on long stalks above the distinctive foliage. Each broad, bluish-green waxy leaf is deeply indented, forming 3 to 5 lobes. This species makes a decorative pot-plant against a hot, sunny wall in areas with cool winters, but may be grown in an open position in hot climates with mild winters. It comes from tropical America. (Ilustrated Plate 38).

Jochroma *Jochroma tubulosum* (also *Iochroma*)
(*Solanaceae*)

This large, evergreen, South American shrub grows up to about 3 metres in height and spreads over 2 metres across. The flowers hang in thick, graceful clusters at the ends of the branches. Each flower is a rich, shiny royal-blue or violet colour and is formed in the shape of a narrow tube about 4 cm long, which is curved outwards at the mouth. These are freely produced throughout summer, autumn and into winter. The young stems and leaves have a velvety texture, while the older branches are thick and woody. The stalked leaves are bright green, oval and pointed, and covered with white, woolly hairs underneath. The whole shrub grows in rather a wild, soft-wooded fashion, and is best suited to the less formal part of the garden.

The Blue Tube Flower is easy to grow but is tender to severe frost. It should be grown in a north-facing position amongst other shrubs in cold areas. It may lose its leaves in very cold weather. If it is cut down by frost, it will grow up again vigorously in the spring. This is a very fast-growing shrub that is not particular about soil requirements. It flowers best in a sunny position, but will also grow in partial shade. It enjoys plenty of water during the summer months, but is able to withstand drought once it is well-established. It may be pruned back in early spring in order to keep it within bounds. This shrub grows very easily and rapidly from cuttings or from a division of the root. It is popularly, but mistakenly, called Blue Cestrum. As I and J are interchangeable in Latin, it is considered more convenient to use the initial letter J for the generic name of this shrub. (Illustrated Plate 38).

Juniperus *Juniperus*
(*Cypressaceae*)

Junipers, which belong to the Cypress family, are hardy, slow-growing evergreen trees and shrubs which are valued particularly in the Northern Hemisphere where they are native. They are not so useful in the Southern Hemisphere, where there are so many flowering evergreens to enliven the winter garden. Some of the prostrate or smaller species are decorative in the landscape and suited to rockeries and banks. Junipers have small leaves like Conifers, but may be distinguished from Conifers in that they bear berries, not cones.

Junipers need good soil containing compost and regular watering. Browning of foliage indicates lack of moisture. They do best in cool mountain areas. Comparatively few are obtainable in this country, chiefly those that grow from seed, but specialist growers are increasing the variety available.

Juniperus chinensis is normally a tall tree, but there are numerous varieties. The variety *pfitzeriana* is prostrate, with greyish-green branches, and there is a yellow-tipped form called *pfitzeriana aurea*, previously called var. *japonica aurea*. (Illustrated Plate 38).

Juniperus horizontalis, Prostrate or Creeping Juniper, is a low shrub with prostrate branches that spread widely and cover the ground about 3 metres or more across. There are several varieties among which var. *douglasii* has bluish-green foliage that turns purplish-bronze in autumn and var. *variegata* is variegated with cream. (Illustrated Plate 38).

Kalmia
(Ericaceae)

Kalmia latifolia

CALICO-BUSH

A 2-metre, evergreen, spring-flowering shrub from eastern North America, this is suited to cool conditions with plenty of moisture and needs a peaty acid soil. It is not easy to grow, needing mulching and treatment similar to *Rhododendron*. It has clusters of cup-shaped pink flowers, each 3 cm across, with red-tipped stamens lining the cup. The oval leaves are glossy and leathery. It can be grown from seed, but it is best to purchase large specimens if available.

Kennedya
(Leguminosae)

Kennedya rubicunda

CORAL-PEA

A drought-resistant, evergreen Australian climber with large red pea-flowers similar to *Clianthus*, this flowers in early summer. It needs very well-drained soil and a warm situation. Grows from seed. *K. nigricans* has black and yellow flowers. *K. prostrata* is a prostate species with red flowers.

Kerria
(Rosaceae)

Kerria japonica var. flore-pleno

GLOBE-FLOWER

This deciduous, hardy shrub comes from China and grows from 1 to 2 metres in height. It forms a thicket of thin green stems with short side twigs, which should be given room to spread. In early spring these stems are thickly festooned with bright-yellow pompons of flowers, which are very showy and unusual. There are also single forms of the flowers which are not so effective. The leaves are oval, toothed and deeply veined. They are a fresh green colour and turn yellow in autumn before they fall, leaving the pale green stems bare throughout winter.

The Globe-Flower looks best against a background of a hedge or wall. Partial shade from this background or from the overhanging branches of a tree will also prevent the golden flowers from bleaching, although the shrub can also be grown in full sunlight. A severe frost might burn the tips of the stems but the shrub will not otherwise be affected by frost. It will do well on a west-facing wall. It should be planted in good, well-drained soil and is most easily reproduced by division of the root. The old wood may be completely cut out in winter. (Illustrated Plate 39).

Kigelia
(Bignoniaceae)

Kigelia pinnata

SAUSAGE TREE

A spreading, semi-evergreen African tree of 10 metres, this is noted for its 45-cm sausage-like, woody fruits. The large, reddish-purple flowers have an elongated lower lip and bloom in spring, dropping quickly. This tree is suited to mild, sub-tropical climates and is fairly drought-resistant, but needs summer rain. It grows from seed.

Koelreuteria
(Sapindaceae)

Koelreuteria paniculata

GOLDEN-RAIN TREE

Valued for its showy heads of deep yellow flowers in summer and gold autumn foliage, this small, hardy, deciduous tree from China and Japan grows to about 7 metres, but grows slowly if it is neglected. It needs sunshine, especially in the morning, good soil and adequate moisture during summer. It withstands drought when mature and prefers a dry winter. It is grown from seed.

Kolkwitzia
(Caprifoliaceae)

Kolkwitzia amabilis

A deciduous, hardy, Chinese shrub of 2–3 metres, this has pink flowers which resemble *Abelia*, to which it is related. The mature bush is covered with sprays of blooms in early summer. Do not prune as it flowers on old wood. It grows from cuttings. (Illustrated Plate 38).

Kunzea
(Myrtaceae)

Kunzea

There are about 20 of these Australian shrubs which are reminiscent of Callistemon and Melaleuca, to which they are related. They are easy to grow, being hardy and drought-resistant. Although not particular about soil, they need good drainage.

Kunzea baxteri grows almost to 2 metres, with an open habit. The crimson bottlebrush flowers have stamens in tufts and the leaves are short and needle-shaped. (Illustrated Plate 38).

Kunzea parvifolia. A low shrub of about 1 metre, this is covered with small globular heads of reddish-purple flowers in spring.

Kunzea sericea grows to 2 metres or more, forming a graceful rounded bush that is covered with deep red short bottle-brush flowers in spring. The short grey leaves are silky.

Others include *Kunzea ambigua* with white flowers; *K. capitata*, with small heads of pink flowers; *K. pomifera*, a prostrate shrub with pale yellow flowers and edible blue berries and *K. recurva* with globular rosy-lilac heads and tiny curved leaves.

Laburnum
(Leguminosae)

Laburnum

These spectacular, small, hardy, deciduous trees of about 5 metres, which brighten the spring in cold European countries with their long, drooping sprays of brilliant yellow pea-flowers, need a cold moist climate in order to flower successfully. They could be given a cold south wall and need good soil and plenty of moisture. The Common Laburnum (*L. anagyroides*) grows easily from seed and has shorter flowering sprays than the hybrid *L. watereri*, (*L. vossii*), which is grown from hardwood cuttings.

Lafoensia
(Lythraceae)

Lafoensia glyptocarpa

An evergreen tree with solitary yellow crinkled flowers resembling *Lagerstroemia*, this is easy to grow in warm areas, but needs protection from frost and wind. It blooms in mid-summer and has shining simple leaves.

It is used as an ornamental shade tree in Brazil, where it is native. Propagation is by seed. There are several other species with white or yellow flowers from Argentina or tropical America.

Lagerstroemia (Lythraceae)

Lagerstroemia indica

PRIDE-OF-INDIA

This extremely showy, large deciduous shrub or small tree grows to a height of about 5 metres and is rounded in proportion. It can be kept much smaller by pruning and is one of the most popular shrubs in South Africa. It is believed to have come originally from China, but is so extensively cultivated in India that it is associated only with that land. It is also known as Indian-Lilac or Crepe-Myrtle.

In midsummer the tree is a mass of bloom, which lasts for several weeks. The flowers are borne in large, upright sprays or plumes, about 30 cm long, which have a feathery, dainty effect. Each individual flower is from 3 to 4 cm across and has a papery, delicate texture. The petals are crinkled and have extremely ruffled edges like crepe paper. The colour of these flowers is, naturally, a deep, rosy pink, but there are also mauve and white varieties. The different colours appear at different times. The mauve varieties usually flower earlier and lose their leaves earlier. The tree is almost evergreen at the coast, but deciduous in areas which have frost. The leaves are thick, oval and deep-green, about 5 cm long, and turn the most beautiful russet colours in autumn before they fall, especially when there are autumn rains, with cold nights and warm days.

This tree is extremely easy to grow. It is hardy to frost and can be grown all over the country. It grows very well at the sea-coast as well as inland. It is not particular about soil requirements, but will benefit from deep, good soil and likes moisture in spring. Pride-of-India can be raised from seed and has flowers in the first year.

The colours are not always true to the parent plant so that it is best to take cuttings which strike easily. Pruning is optional. If the trees are left unpruned, they will form large, rounded bushes and the flower sprays will be smaller, but extremely numerous and showy, covering the complete bush with its bloom. Severe pruning produces larger sprays with larger flowers borne at the ends of long, vigorous shoots. This pruning has no effect on the tree which, in fact, seems to enjoy it, and does help to keep it within bounds in a small garden or in areas where growth is extremely rapid, such as in Natal. Severe pruning means cutting back all main stems to a distance of 1–2 metres from the ground in winter. Naturally one could also train the tree with a small standard or short trunk. One sometimes sees these trees used as a hedge, but this is not successful in areas where they are deciduous. (Illustrated Plate 39).

Lagerstroemia speciosa (L. flos-reginae)

QUEEN CREPE-MYRTLE, PRIDE-OF-INDIA

This is a larger tree in every way, and comes from India. The magnificent plume of flowers is 40 cm long and 25 cm across. The flowers come in a number of shades of pink, red and mauve, and some change colour during the day. The oval, smooth and shiny leaf is about 12 cm long. This tree is treated and pruned in the same way as *L. indica*. Unfortunately, it does not like frost and is suited only to sub-tropical and low-veld conditions. It forms a beautiful street tree in the right climate and has red autumn foliage. (Illustrated Plate 39).

Lagunaria (Malvaceae)

Lagunaria pattersonii

PYRAMID TREE

A symmetrical upright tree with rough, grey-green leaves, this has pink bell-shaped flowers during late summer. The seed-pods contain fine splintery seeds. This is a drought-resistant evergreen tree from Australia, which grows fairly slowly to about 8 to 10 metres. It resists salt spray and wind at the coast. (Illustrated Plate 39).

Lambertia (Proteaceae)

Lambertia formosa

MOUNTAIN DEVIL, HONEY-FLOWER

A small evergreen shrub from Australia that grows to 2 metres, this has cup-shaped flowers about 5 cm long that are a translucent crimson. The curious woody pod is thought to resemble the head of a beast. The narrow leaves have rolled edges and this makes a neat bush in the garden. It needs acid soil and regular watering. It belongs to the Protea family and is grown from seed. (Illustrated Plate 40).

Lantana (Verbenaceae)

Lantana

LANTANA, CHERRY PIE

Lantana camara, an evergreen shrub from tropical America, has been declared a noxious weed in Natal and in the warmer parts of the country, where it has become an agricultural weed that is prickly and difficult to eradicate. Although the orange and red-flowered *L. camara* (best called Wild Lantana) and its mauvy-pink colour form need not be cultivated, it is a pity to condemn the named hybrids which do not seed freely. *L. montevidensis*, the purple Lantana, is harmless and has not been condemned by the authorities, so that it should be planted without restraint.

Lantana Drap D'Or, Yellow Lantana, is a compact, low-growing shrub that spreads over an area of 4 metres and is very good on a sloping lawn. It has rich yellow, verbena-like flowers that are particularly profuse in autumn. It should be pruned in spring to cut out old wood and is propagated by cuttings. Lantanas lend themselves to shaping and are often used to form standards. They may be used as small, rounded standards in containers for a patio. (Illustrated Plate 39).

Lantana "Snowflake" is a similar white-flowered hybrid and there is a red hybrid.

Lantana montevidensis (*L. sellowiana*), Purple Lantana, is a trailing, ever-flowering shrub from South America that is so useful that it should have a place in every garden. Low-growing, it is ideal for overhanging rocks, garden-walls, tubs or window-boxes. The bright, pink-purple flowers bloom almost through-out the year, going off during winter in cold places, where the shrub is deciduous. It remains evergreen and blooms perpetually in mild areas. The small, rough leaves are dark green. Purple Lantana grows quickly and flowers when young. It is drought-resistant and not particular about soil, but needs sunshine. It should be trimmed in spring and may be used as a low, clipped box-hedge. It multiplies by division of the root and grows from cuttings. (Illustrated Plate 39).

Lapageria (Liliaceae)

Lapageria rosea

RED CHILE-BELLS

An evergreen, shade-loving climber of the Lily family, this has 10 cm, rose-red, bell-like flowers during summer. It is the national flower of Chile. It requires rich, well-drained soil, with full shade, so that it can be grown in a tub on the verandah or in a cool greenhouse. It may be grown from seed, cuttings or layers.

Lavandula (Labiatae)

Lavandula dentata

FRENCH LAVENDER

This evergreen, low-growing shrub comes from the Mediterranean region. It grows into a neat, compact bush of about 1 metre. The attractive foliage points upwards, hugging the stems. Each soft green leaf is about 3 to 5 cm long and very narrow, but is toothed along both edges, giving it a dainty appearance. The flowers are borne in upright spikes that grow at the top of slender stalks above the foliage and look like tiny ears of corn. They are deep purple and borne in profusion during spring, summer and autumn. The flowers, as well as the leaves, are fragrant when crushed and are used for satchets.

French Lavender makes an attractive, neat, unclipped hedge in the garden. Individual specimens are effective flanking steps or pathways, or in the rockery. The shrub requires a dry, well-drained, light soil containing lime and does not like a moist or rich soil. A mulch of well-rotted manure or compost may, however, be added in the autumn. Add lime from time to time. Give it full sunlight and plenty of air. It is hardy to our average frosts. Cuttings of the young growth taken in spring or autumn grow easily, but should be shaded at first. The bushes do not require pruning, but this may be done in late spring. Dead flowerstalks should be removed during summer.

Lavandula officinalis (L. vera, L. spica)

TRUE LAVENDER

This not nearly such an attractive shrub, but is grown for the superior fragrance of its flowers. This is the True Lavender from which Oil of Lavender is distilled and used in perfumery. It is also called English Lavender by gardeners, for Old English Lavender water is made from it. This shrub also comes from the Mediterranean, but grows only 30 to 60 cm in height. It has narrow, fleshy, grey leaves that roll back at the edges. The twiggy flower stalks stand well up above the foliage and the lavender flowers are carried in little whorls at their tips during summer. They should be removed after flowering. This shrub should be cultivated in the same way as French Lavender.

Leea (Vitaceae)

Leea coccinea

LEEA

A neat evergreen Burmese shrub growing to 2 metres, this has dainty foliage consisting of rounded tapering dark green leaflets with ruffled margins. The clusters of scarlet flowers resemble *Ixora* and they are followed by red berries.

This shrub will grow in deep shade against a wall or indoors, making a decorative greenhouse plant as it blooms while small. It is tender and must be given protection from frost. The soil should be light and rich, containing compost. Leea needs plenty of moisture and humidity in summer with dryness in winter. Propagation is by seed or cuttings. (Illustrated Plate 40).

Leonotis (Labiatae)

Leonotis leonurus

LION'S EAR OR WILD DAGGA

This is a South African shrubby perennial, about 2 metres in height, which is useful for a border or rockery. It is harmless, in spite of its common name, and grows wild in Natal, the Transvaal and the Cape. It has bright orange flowers in autumn and early winter that go on for many weeks. There is also a white-flowered form. Each flower is like a velvet, hairy tube that has been likened in texture to a lion's ear. The flowers are thickly clustered in circles at intervals up the long, straight, reedy stems that branch out freely from the base. They should be pounded at the ends in order to make them last in the vase. The rough, green leaves are soft, narrow and about 8 cm long, with serrated edges. They grow thickly at the base, and thin out towards the top of the stems.

Leonotis is very easy to grow and thrives almost anywhere. It is evergreen in warm localities and deciduous in areas with cold winters. It likes a warm, sunny position and is happiest amongst the rocks. The soil should be light, good and well-mixed with compost. The plant likes plenty of water in the summer. It is unaffected by average frosts, although a severe frost may cut it back. In any case, the long stalks should be pruned back severely at the end of winter like any perennial, and this will encourage long fresh stalks to grow up in the following summer. It is best grown from seed, but may also be propagated by division of the root (Illustrated Plate 40).

Leptospermum (Myrtaceae)

Leptospermum laevigatum

AUSTRALIAN OR SMALL-LEAVED MYRTLE

This 5-metre small tree with white flowers is useful for growing in sea-sand and withstands coastal winds. It is also called Coast Tea Tree.

Leptospermum scoparium

AUSTRALIAN TEA-TREE

This is a large Australian shrub which has white flowers. Many varieties and hybrids have been found and produced, especially in New Zealand, including dwarf and double-flowered forms.

They are all evergreen, and quite easy to grow, but must have one requirement —a lime-free or acid soil. The Tea-Trees have a false reputation for being temperamental, and this is probably because they are not given the right soil reaction (see Chapter II). Also, the roots must be very carefully handled when planting out. They should be transplanted when quite small, about 40 cm high, and may be planted together with the tin, with only the bottom of the tin cut off, if desired. They should be given soil which is well-mixed with compost. They are tender to severe frost.

The Tea-Trees may be grown in most parts of South Africa. They do very well at the coast in sandy soil and in windy localities, their tiny leaves being especially suited to these conditions. They require no pruning, but the top may be pinched out when the plant is young in order to encourage bushiness. Seed-pods should be removed, more on some varieties than on others, even if this means removing long branches, in order to encourage flowering. Sprays of flowers last well in the vase. The varieties are best reproduced from short cuttings made from the tips of the branches, and they also grow from seed. The seed-pod must be picked before it will release the seeds.

Leptospermum scoparium var. grandiflorum

LARGE PINK WEEPING TEA-TREE

This evergreen shrub comes from New South Wales and grows to a height of about 2 metres. Its branches spread out gracefully and when covered with its showy pink blossoms all along the stems, the whole bush looks as if it is laden with pale pink snow. It flowers in autumn, starting as early as February.

The flowers are about 2 cm across and come in a delicate pale pink which glistens in the sun. The leaves are dark-green and slightly broader than the usual Tea-Tree leaves which resemble tea-leaves, and they are sharply pointed and prickly. It is said that Captain Cook and his men brewed a tea from the leaves of this shrub. The bush grows with medium rapidity and flowers properly only when several years old.

Leptospermum scoparium var. nichollsii

CRIMSON BUSH TEA-TREE

This is an evergreen, winter-flowering shrub which grows to a height of about 2 metres and eventually spreads about 1 metre across. It comes from New Zealand and is so attractive that it excites admiration from all who see it. In winter and early spring it is covered with red, 5-petalled tiny flowers, about 2 cm across, which are so closely borne that they colour the whole bush. There is also a rose-pink colour form and a double-flowered form. The flowers linger for months, at a time when one needs colour most. This shrub flowers when very small and grows with medium rapidity. It reaches 2 metres in 5 years.

The Crimson Bush Tea-Tree is upright, compact and neat in growth, the leaves being about the size and shape of tea-leaves. They are dark-green in colour and sometimes turn bronze. The stems are reddish and this helps to create a bronze effect. This shrub was awarded the Royal Horticultural Society's gold medal in 1914–15 and a prize of £1,000. New hybrids keep replacing older varieties and may be chosen at the nursery in early spring, as they flower when very small. (Illustrated Plate 40).

Leschenaultia (Goodeniaceae)

Leschenaultia biloba

BLUE LESCHENAULTIA

A small evergreen Australian shrub to 1 metre in height, this is admired because of its rich blue 5-lobed, phlox-like flowers, each about 3 cm wide. They bloom in spring and early summer. The tiny heath-like leaves verify its drought-resistant character. It needs sunny, very well-drained soil with moisture in winter and shelter from frost. Propagation is by cuttings or seed. There are several other species with red, yellow or white flowers.

Leucadendron (Proteaceae)

Leucadendron argenteum

SILVER TREE

This beautiful tree that comes from the slopes of Table Mountain is famous throughout the world. It grows to a height of about 5 to 8 metres, has a symmetrical shape and is outstanding for its foliage. Each leaf is 10 to 12 cm long, narrow, pointed and covered with fine, silvery hairs that gleam in the sunshine. The leaves are pale greenish-silver in colour and clustered along the long, thick, woody branches, pointing upwards and concealing them. They are a magnificent sight rippling in the breeze.

The Silver Tree can stand a few degrees of frost and is resistant to summer drought, but must be watered in the winter. It can be grown from seed and acclimatises itself quite well in the Transvaal and Natal. It should be transplanted when quite small or from a tin. Seeds are best sown in autumn in light, sandy soil mixed with compost and planted not deeper than twice their thickness. The soil should be firmed down, well-watered and kept moist. It should be shaded in dry, sunny climates but not at the Cape. Germination is slow, taking about 3 or 4 weeks. After developing 2 or 3 leaves, the young seedlings should be planted out into individual tins and into their permanent position when about 1 year old and 30 cm in height. They should be carefully transplanted into well-drained, good soil mixed generously with compost. The tips may be pinched to encourage bushy growth. The Silver Tree is fairly slow growing, takes about 4 years to reach a height of about 2 metres and is usually treated as a shrub in cultivation. The trees often die suddenly, even on Table Mountain, for no apparent reason, but it is thought that this is a result of drought at the end of summer, which is the dry season at the Cape. The Silver Tree should have plenty of sun and air and tolerates coastal winds, but dislikes cold winds. The seeds of the Silver Tree are borne on the female tree in a cone which will open and release its seeds when dried. Seeds are obtainable from Kirstenbosch. Branches make excellent decoration for the vase, lasting for over a week in water. Silver Trees seldom live longer than about 20 years, but are worth growing as they are beautiful while young. They will grow from cuttings under mist-spray. (Illustrated Plate 41).

Leucadendron species

GOLD-TIPS

There are many other species of *Leucadendron* which are chiefly shrubs of about 2–3 metres that grow wild at the Cape. They are decorative in that their top-most leaves and flower bracts turn yellow or shades of rose in the spring, so that they may be called Gold-Tips. The bracts surround the flowers that appear at the tips of the branches in spring. The female flowers are small cones and the males a fluff of stamens.

Amongst the best yellow-flowered species are *L. discolor*, Sunshine Bush, *L. eucalyptifolium* and *L. salignum*. (Illustrated Plate 41). Rose Cockade, *L. tinctum* has showy rose-coloured bracts. Some have interesting woody seed-cases such as *L. platyspermum*, Knobkerrie Bush, and the female form of *L. rubrum*.

Leucadendrons are easy to grow in average well-drained soil and are useful evergreens for large gardens inland or for sea-coast gardens. They mix well with Proteas in the vase. For a fuller selection, see *Proteas for Pleasure*, by the author.

Leucospermum
(Proteaceae)

Leucospermum

PINCUSHION FLOWERS

Members of the Protea family, these are unique and showy evergreen shrubs of which there are about 47 species, varying from prostrate plants to large bushes. All are worth growing for interest, but the following provide magnificent, long-lasting flowers for the vase and the best spectacle in the garden. All are native to South Africa, the majority coming from the winter-rainfall area of the south-western Cape.

It is now possible to obtain plants freely for the garden and it is best to plant them out when they are about 15 cm high in their tins. *Leucospermums* are propagated by seed, but this requires patience as the seed must be fertile and germinates erratically, sometimes after being in the seed-bed for over a year. Seedlings must be transplanted into individual tins when very small. They grow from cuttings under mist-spray.

Plants grow easily with certain requirements. The soil should be light and well-drained, preferably containing well-rotted compost. Slightly sloping ground is ideal as it is well-drained and rockeries make a perfect setting. Young plants must be watered regularly at all times, but preferably not over the foliage. Established plants require watering about twice a week throughout the year, but are able to withstand drought in summer. They must have water in winter. They thrive in an open sunny situation. Pincushions will stand a few degrees of frost, but should be protected during the first winter in cold areas by placing an upturned cardboard box over the little plants at night and removing this during the day. Plants may go into the open ground at any time, but they are best planted in autumn at the Cape or in spring and summer in the summer rainfall area. They generally start flowering when they are about 3 years old. They do not need pruning as the flowers disintegrate after blooming, unlike Proteas, but long branches may be cut freely for the vase.

The most attractive garden species are *L. cordifolium*, *L. lineare*, *L. reflexum* and *L. tottum*, while a few others listed here would be of interest to collectors.

Leucospermum catherinae, Catherine's Pincushion, has large, champagne-yellow firewheels in spring, on a bush of 2 metres.

Leucospermum cordifolium (L. nutans)

NODDING PINCUSHION

This probably is the best-sized species for the average garden. It forms a low spreading bush of about 1 metre, which is attractive in the landscape. It has tough green or greyish-green leaves. The flowerhead looks like a waxy pincushion, 10 cm across, varying in colour from flame to apricot. They last for 1 month in the vase, flowering most profusely in September and October, but also from May onwards, depending on the weather (Illustrated Plate 41).

A yellow-flowered form was previously called *L. bolusii*, but this name is now given to another species with tiny white flowers. (See *Proteas for Pleasure*).

Leucospermum grandiflorum, Rainbow Pincushion, has interesting yellow tufted heads, about 10 cm across, that deepen to red with maturity. It grows to 2 metres and is fairly hardy.

Leucospermum lineare, Narrow-leaf Pincushion, has similar flowers but may be recognised by its narrow needle-like foliage.

Leucospermum prostratum, Creeping Pincushion, forms a prostrate mat covered with tiny 5-cm yellow flowerheads that deepen to apricot with maturity. Although pretty, it is not easy to grow and short-lived, so it is of chief interest to collectors.

Leucospermum reflexum

This outstandingly spectacular landscape shrub is suited to the large garden, for it spreads over an area of 4 metres and grows to the same height. The slender, neat branches spread outwards and upwards from the base and are luxuriantly clothed with small, oval leaves in a distinctive dove-grey colour. Large bushes have hundreds of blooms appearing at the tips of the branches at the same time, flowering chiefly from early September until November. Each 10 cm flower-head is shaped like a rounded pincushion in a soft scarlet-orange. The individual scarlet tubes, tipped with silver hairs, curve outwards and upwards, curling down and out as they open, so that they look like a rocket-head when nearly spent (Illustrated Plate 41).

Leucospermum tottum, Firewheel Pincushion, has a stiff, flattish, flowerhead in a combination of salmon, scarlet and yellow. It has the merit of flowering later than most Pincushions, from October into mid-summer. (Illustrated Plate 41).

Leucospermum vestitum, Notched Pincushion, is very similar to *L.cordifolium*. It has large flattened heads of flowers and the leaves have 2 to 4 deep notches at the tips. *L. glabrum* has similar notched leaves, with as many as 14 teeth at the tips, but the flowerheads are more pointed and hairy at the centre.

Leucothoë (Ericaceae)

Leucothoë catesbaei (Andromeda)

A 2-metre, evergreen shrub with spikes of tiny, white urn-shaped flowers between the leaves in spring, this comes from North America. Like *Pieris*, it belongs to the Heath family and requires moist acid soil and partial shade. It likes cool conditions but not severe frost. It is grown from seed, cuttings or underground runners and can be transplanted easily.

Leycesteria (Caprifoliaceae)

Leycesteria formosa

A deciduous shrub of about 2 metres, this has large, heart-shaped leaves growing to 18 cm in length, and drooping spikes of tiny purple flowers, each with a purple, leaf-like bract. These are followed by blackish berries. It comes from the Himalayas and prefers cool mountain conditions, but is tender to frost in places with dry cold winters, so that it should be given shelter in semi-shade under a tree in highveld gardens. It prefers sun in mild areas, but needs plenty of moisture. It bears flowers at the ends of new long basal growth in spring. Propagation is by seed or cuttings.

Ligustrum (Oleaceae)

Ligustrum ovalifolium variegatum

A useful variegated small tree of 3–4 metres, this has evergreen leaves heavily margined with gold. Any green growths must be removed immediately. It needs full sunshine in order to keep the leaf-colouring. Golden Privet is hardy, except to very severe frost, drought-resistant and quick-growing. It may be grown in a tub and clipped to keep it compact. It has a strong root-system and is not suited to a very small garden. Propagated by cuttings.

This is a better species than the golden variegated form of *L. lucidum*, the common evergreen Privet which forms a small tree and seeds itself too freely in gardens.

Lippia
(Verbenaceae)

Lippia citriodora *(Aloysia citriodora)*

LEMON-VERBENA

This large, deciduous shrub comes from South America and grows rapidly to a height of about 3 metres, with a very spreading habit. It has sprays of minute white and mauve flowers in summer which are grown not so much for their dainty appearance as for their fragrance. This is intensified when they are dried and they are often used for satchets and potpourri. The leaves are bright-green, narrow and pointed with a rough surface. They have a delightful lemon fragrance when crushed and are more strongly-scented than the flowers.

Lemon-Verbena will grow easily in any soil, including poor soil, although it does not like lime, as a rule. It will stand frost and cold as well as heat. It is inclined to grow very large in South Africa and one can prevent straggling by pinching the growing shoots in spring. It can also be pruned back at the end of winter and may be trained with single standard if desired. Cuttings of young growth strike easily.

Liquidamber
(Hamamelidaceae)

Liquidamber styraciflua

AMERICAN SWEETGUM

This large, ornamental tree from North America and Mexico grows up to 32 metres in height in its native home, but only up to about 10 or 12 metres in cultivation. It is grown mainly for the autumn colours of the leaves before they fall. The smooth leaves have 5, gracefully pointed lobes with serrated edges and seem to run the whole gamut of autumn tints. Some leaves remain green, others turn yellow, bronze and scarlet, and finally a deep, dark crimson. The total effect is beautiful. This tree grows into an erect, rather pyramidal shape. It should not be bought too tall and thin or it takes years to fill out in shape. It has a medium rate of growth, but it is best to buy a tree that is not more than about a metre in height in order to grow a shapely specimen. The trunk and branches are whitish and corky with a deeply furrowed bark. The spreading branches are covered with stiff, sturdy, short twigs bearing the buds of the following year's foliage. The name *Liquidamber* refers to the juice or resin that comes from the tree, which was used in the manufacture of chewing-gum, thus giving the tree its common name.

Liquidamber is hardy and can grow in warm climates as well as in areas with cold winters. It withstands salt air. Its main requirement is a deep, moist soil with copious watering always, but especially in spring and summer. It does not require pruning, but if it must be shaped, this should be done in winter. It should be well-pruned back if it is transplanted. It is propagated by seed, which is difficult. (Illustrated Plate 41).

Liriodendron
(Magnoliaceae)

Liriodendron tulipifera

TULIP TREE

This large, deciduous, North American tree grows up to 32 metres in height in moist, rich soil and much taller in its native surroundings. The flowers appear in spring when the tree is about 8 years old. They are not showy on the tree but make extremely interesting flowers for floating. Each flower is shaped like a Tulip but has more open, rolled-back petals and measures about 6 cm across. The petals are waxy and light-green, marked with deep orange splashes at the base inside. The foliage is very distinctive in shape. Each leaf has 2 large lobes at the base, measuring about 12 cm in breadth from tip to tip, and what appears to be a third lobe between them, is sharply cut off in a straight line half-way up. The leaves are a fresh, light-green and waxy in texture, turning yellow in autumn.

The Tulip Tree likes rich, deep, moist soil and will grow more rapidly in these conditions, as it otherwise grows slowly. It should be watered regularly throughout the year, and particularly in spring. It stands frost well. It may be transplanted at the end of winter or in early spring, but dislikes pruning. It grows from seed, many of which do not germinate, and this is difficult and slow.

Lonicera
(Caprifoliaceae)

Lonicera

HONEYSUCKLE

The Honeysuckles or Woodbines are a large group of usually climbing shrubs that are grown mainly for the fragrance of their dainty flowers.

Lonicera heckrottii

PINK OR BUSH HONEYSUCKLE

The Bush Honeysuckle is also known as *L. gigantea superba* and may be grown as a shrub of about 2–3 metres in height, or as a climber if it is given support. It is an American hybrid which is evergreen and hardy. It becomes deciduous in cold countries. Several hybrids in this group are offered in the trade. The flowers grow in clusters near the tips of the branches in spring and early summer and are about 5 cm long. They have long, thin tubes which open at the top into broad, turned-back petals, revealing protruding stamens. They are creamy inside and a pretty rosepink on the outside, particularly attractive before they open. The leaves are bluish green, from 5–8 cm in length and have a rounded, oval shape. The top pair of leaves is joined together around the stem.

This shrub will grow anywhere. It likes the sun but will grow as well in the shade. It likes average good garden soil and will stand drought once it is established. It does not need pruning, but may be trimmed freely in order to train it. This should be done after flowering. It is propagated by cuttings. It is frequently infested with black aphis which must be sprayed intensively.

Lonicera etrusca, from the Mediterranean area, is similar, with paler flowers.

Lonicera hildebrandiana

GIANT HONEYSUCKLE

Suitable for warm, frost-free areas, this evergreen Burmese climber has 15-cm oval leaves and 18 cm-long flowers in clusters, opening yellow and deepening to red. (Illustrated Plate 42).

Lonicera japonica

JAPANESE HONEYSUCKLE

This well-known vigorous climber reaches a height of about 5 metres and is more or less evergreen. The flowers are in clusters and have very thin tubes flaring out into dainty, curled-back petals with protrucing stamens. They are white at first and change to deep yellow. They are very fragrant and free-flowering in spring and summer. The smooth, fresh green leaves are nearly oblong but taper to a point and are from 5–8 cm inches long.

This is a quick-growing hardy climber that is very easy to grow, having the same requirements as the Bush Honeysuckle, but requiring support. A golden variety (*L. japonica* var. *aureo-reticulata*) has green leaves laced with yellow, and is excellent on a sunny bank. It is not grown for its flowers, which are sparse. (Illustrated Plate 42).

Lonicera nitida
BOX HONEYSUCKLE

A Chinese evergreen shrub of about 1 metre, this has tiny glossy leaves and arching branches so that it is useful on a slope. The flowers are insignificant, but it may be clipped as a low hedge. It is hardy and will grow in sun or semi-shade.

Lonicera sempervirens
SCARLET HONEYSUCKLE

This American climber is also known as the Trumpet Honeysuckle and requires support. The flowers have wider tubes that are bright orange-scarlet and are grouped in clusters that are very showy, but they are not fragrant. They appear during most of the year. The rounded, smooth leaves are joined together across the stem near the tips of the shoots. This climber is tender to severe frost and grows best in warm, frost-free areas. (Illustrated Plate 42).

Luculia (Rubiaceae) — *Luculia gratissima*
PINK SWA

A delightful evergreen shrub of 2 metres, this has loose heads of fragrant, pink, phlox-like flowers in late autumn and winter. The soft leaves are long and pointed. It needs good soil mulched with compost and must have shelter from frost. Cut it back at the end of winter. It is grown from cuttings of ripe wood. *L. gratissima* comes from Nepal and there are several other species from the Himalayas and S.W. China. (Illustrated Plate 42).

Luehea (Tiliaceae) — *Luehea divaricata*
LUEHEA

A small, semi-evergreen tree of about 7 metres, this comes from Paraguay and is related to *Sparmannia*. The showy, 5-petalled pink flowers measure about 4 cm across and have a puff of stamens, appearing while the tree is young. The 8-cm leaves are green and hairy. This tree is reasonably hardy to frost and has been grown in Pretoria. There are several species with pink or white flowers.

Mackaya (Acanthaceae) — *Mackaya bella* (*Asystasia bella*)
MACKAYA

Shade-loving, this bushy evergreen of 1–2 metres, with glossy leaves, has mauve, foxglove-like flowers, which are profuse in late spring and early summer. It turns paler in colour if grown in full sun. There is also a pure white form. It can be grown in a tub or under a tree where it will be protected from frost and does well in shade on the highveld. It needs light loamy soil with moisture, particularly in summer, but is fairly drought-resistant. This South African shrub grows easily from cuttings taken after flowering, when it may be trimmed back. (Illustrated Plate 42).

Magnolia (Magnoliaceae)

Magnolia

There are many different Magnolias which come from Japan, China and America, but they are all acknowledged to have the most regal and exciting flowers. They dislike lime and respond well to the tea-leaf treatment (see Chapter II). They prefer neutral or acid soils, with a pH as low as 4.0 in some cases. They should be mulched with compost or acid mulches. They also like a great deal of water—at least twice a week and every other day if possible. Magnolias need to be looked after when young and until they are well-established. They can be propagated by seed if it is freshly sown, but this is very slow. The best method of propagation is by cuttings or by layers, but as Magnolias are extremely slow-growing at first, the average gardener should buy as large a specimen as he is able to obtain in a tin.

Magnolias are shade-loving but do equally well in full sunlight. They are hardy to frost although a late frost might sometimes harm the flowers on a spring-flowering Magnolia, so that this should really be shielded from early morning sun. Magnolias thoroughly dislike pruning, and this should not be done unless absolutely necessary. Cuts heal badly and should be painted with tree-sealing compound.

The Port-Wine Magnolia, *Magnolia fuscata*, will be found under the name of *Michelia figo*.

Magnolia grandiflora

This large, evergreen tree comes from the southern states of North America. It grows into a large tree of about 16 metres in height (and much taller in its native home) but is so slow-growing that this might well take 40 years. Nevertheless, *Magnolia grandiflora* is well worth waiting for, and will flower while quite small—about 2 metres in height. It can be grown almost anywhere in South Africa, enjoying warm climates and warm positions in cool areas. Be generous with compost and water and growth will be more rapid. It can be transplanted up to quite a good size (2–3 metres, but even if parts of it die back, continue to water copiously and for several months before giving up hope.

The flowers measure about 20 cm across and look like waxy, white saucers on the tree. They bruise easily and should be handled with care when picked. They are unbelievably magnificent and very fragrant. They are borne in profusion in midsummer and glow against the dark green, shiny foliage. The leaves are large, waxy, and oval, rather like the leaves of a Loquat Tree in shape. They are bright green when the tree is young but darker on large trees. (Illustrated Plate 43).

Magnolia soulangeana

Several garden hybrids are called Purple Magnolias or Saucer Magnolias, and were originally produced in a nursery near Paris by one of Napoleon's ex-officers,

Etienne Soulange-Bodin. Sometimes called a Tulip Magnolia, it should not be confused with *Liriodendron*, the Tulip Tree.

Purple Magnolias are deciduous, small trees about 5 metres high which broaden with age. The tree takes many years to form, so that Purple Magnolias are usually seen as small bushes of about 3 metres in height. They start flowering when quite small—about 1 metre in height—if soil conditions are correct and they receive a great deal of water, but are generally slow-growing.

The tulip-shaped flowers have petals that are at least 9 cm long. They are white on the inside and various shades of rosy-purple on the outside, with a thick, waxy texture. There are several named colour varieties which have slightly different purple or pinkish colouring, and different flowering times. Variety *lennei* is the darkest colour form. There is also a pure white flowered hybrid. The dark stamens accentuate the exotic appearance of the flower. These spectacular flowers are produced very prolifically on bare stems during winter and earliest spring. Unfortunately, this is sometimes a windy period and the shrub should be given some protection or its flowers will be blackened and bruised by a strong wind. Also, if the flowers are picked, the petals should not be touched for fear of bruising. The leaves appear after the flowers and are very large, oval in shape and bright green. Long stems grow out quite rapidly from the base of the bush in summer, particularly during rainy weather and when the soil is acid. The shrub should be planted in compost mixed with some good garden soil, and an acid mulch added from time to time.

The Purple Magnolia can be transplanted when in full flower at the end of winter, but its roots must be handled very carefully and taken with a good ball of earth. It can be transplanted later, during rainy weather, but there is always a risk of it dying back when the leaves are on the bush, unless one is extremely careful to water almost continuously. It is not happy in sub-tropical conditions and prefers the cooler districts, where it produces golden autumn colours. (Illustrated Plate 43).

Magnolia stellata

STAR MAGNOLIA

A low, spreading Japanese shrub which ultimately grows to 5 metres, this flowers while young. The starry white flowers, about 8 cm across, bloom freely on bare branches in early spring. Variety *rosea* has flowers which are a soft pink outside. The oval leaves grow to 12 cm. Blue Grape Hyacinths planted around the shrub form an attractive foil. (Illustrated Plate 43).

Mahonia (Berberidaceae)

Mahonia aquifolium

HOLLY MAHONIA

This evergreen shrub, from western North America, was formerly included with *Berberis*, but is now regarded as a separate genus. It grows about 1,5 metres in height and bears thick clusters of yellow flowers in the spring, followed by purplish-black berries. The compound leaves have dark green leaflets, resembling holly leaves. This shrub is grown mainly for its attractive foliage that colours bronze in autumn. It is extremely easy to grow, for it will endure a variety of conditions. It will stand frost or heat and will grow as well under the shade of trees as in the open sun. It does not mind poor soil and can be grown almost anywhere. It is the state flower of Oregon, where it is called Oregon Grape. (Illustrated Plate 43).

Malus
(Rosaceae)

Malus floribunda (Pyrus pulcherrima)

This is a deciduous, large shrub or small tree introduced from Japan. In early spring it bears masses of rose-pink buds unfolding to exquisite whitish flowers. They are the loveliest of all blossoms and are very abundant and showy. They appear just before or when the leaves unfold. The leaves are oval, pointed, glossy-green and have serrated edges. Small, yellowish fruits often remain for a long time on the tree. (Illustrated Plate 44).

The Crabs make broad, round bushes. They are very easy to grow, requiring a well-drained, light soil. If they are attacked by scale, they should be sprayed in the same way as fruit trees. The Crabs may be grown from seed as well as grafted. Although fairly slow-growing, they bloom when only a few years old.

Malus aldenhamensis is a hybrid with purplish-red flowers and dark red rounded fruits. (Illustrated Plate 44).

Malus eleyi is a similar hybrid with rich red flowers and more conical, purplish-red fruits. (Illustrated Plate 44).

Malvaviscus
(Malvaceae)

Malvaviscus mollis (Pavonia coccinea)

FIRE-DART BUSH

This evergreen shrub comes from Tropical America and grows about 2–3 metres in height. It has bright red, erect flowers that stand away from the foliage and appear throughout summer and autumn. The petals are scarlet, shining and tightly furled together like a fat umbrella. They are about 4 cm in length. The column which bears the stamens protrudes for at least 3 cm and adds to the dainty appearance of the flowers. This stamen-column resembles that of the Chinese Hibiscus and the plant belongs to the same family, but is a distinct genus, and should not be referred to as a type of Hibiscus. The leaves are large, soft and heart-shaped, with a velvety texture, and measure from 12 to 20 cm in length.

The plant has a very soft, herbaceous appearance and requires a good deal of moisture, as well as good soil. It can stand a certain amount of frost but prefers warmth and grows with wild luxuriance in warm, humid climates. In areas which experience frost it should be given a sun-baked nook and it will also grow in semi-shade under trees. If it is cut down by frost it will grow up rapidly once more. It can be pruned back in the spring if desired and to encourage new growth in poor conditions. It is grown from cuttings in the spring and the spreading branches form roots easily in good soil (Illustrated Plate 44).

Malvaviscus penduliflorus

GIANT FIRE-DART

This soft shrubby plant is similar to *M. mollis*, but the flowers are double the size and hang downwards instead of standing erect. They are brilliant red and bell-like. This is a decorative plant from Mexico which may be used as an evergreen hedge in warm frost-free areas. It will grow in warm places with cool winters if given wall protection and does well in Pretoria. There is a pretty shell-pink colour variety that is propagated by cuttings. (Illustrated Plate 44).

Mandevilla (Apocynaceae)

Mandevilla (Dipladenia)

These are evergreen tropical American climbers with pink, white or mauve trumpet flowers, which are closely related to *Allamanda* and the pink ones are erroneously referred to as pink *Allamanda*. These were formerly called *Dipladenia* until placed as a synonym of *Mandevilla*.

These climbers must be given the support of a trellis as they climb by twining. They need rich, well-drained soil with plenty of water during summer and fairly dry warm conditions in winter. They are often grown in pots in greenhouses, but may be grown out-of-doors in mild climates or in a warm sheltered position. They will grow in partial shade or full sun, provided that they are not baked dry in hot weather. If grown in pots, they need fertilizing with weak liquid manure. They bloom profusely in mid-summer. Propagation is by cuttings of young shoots in spring. They have tuberous roots that are difficult to transplant.

Mandevilla splendens

The rich pink trumpet flowers of this Brazilian climber grow from 6 to 12 cm across, enlarging during the few days that they open wide, and their colour deepens with age from a pale to rich rose pink. Sometimes all variations may be seen on the climber at once, especially when it is well grown and the flowers appear in clusters. The large oval leaves are glossy and deeply marked with veins.

There are two varieties which are said to bloom more freely, var. *profusa* and var. *williamsii*. Several other pink-flowered species, such as *M. eximia*, are known in cultivation, but all have smaller flowers than the beautiful *M. splendens*. One purple-flowered species with smaller flowers is *M. atropurpurea*. It comes from Brazil. *M. bolivensis* has small white tubular flowers with a yellow throat. (Illustrated Plate 45).

Mandevilla suaveolens

A deciduous climber from tropical America, this has clusters of white, fragrant trumpet flowers in summer. The stalked, soft leaves are heart-shaped and about 9 cm long. It climbs by twining on a fence or trellis. It grows vigorously on the highveld, either in a sunny, warm position or in partial shade under the over-hanging branches of trees. It needs rich, light soil and moisture in summer, with shelter from frost, but is not as tender as *M. splendens*. It is propagated by cuttings (Illustrated Plate 45).

Manettia (Rubiaceae)

Manettia bicolor

A slender twining evergreen from Brazil, this has tubular, 3-cm-long, scarlet flowers, tipped with yellow, all along the stems. It blooms almost throughout the year. It grows easily in ordinary soil and may be grown in semi-shade in a tub on the verandah. It will grow out-of-doors if given protection from frost. It is propagated by cuttings or seed.

Manihot
(Euphorbiaceae)

Manihot utilissima var. variegata

This South American evergreen shrub is grown for its ornamental green and yellow foliage, which forms a mound of colour up to 2 or 3 metres in height. Each large green leaf has 5 to 7 segments, richly splashed with yellow down the centres. It has tuberous roots that are bitter and poisonous, but these are treated to remove toxins in order to prepare the edible Tapioca of commerce, as well as Manihot or Cassava meal. It is a plant of economic importance, together with the related Sweet Cassava, *M. dulcis*, from Brazil.

Manihot is tender and will grow out-of-doors in a humid, frost-free climate, needing full sun in order to keep its coloration. It may be grown in a pot in a greenhouse in cold winter areas. It needs well-drained soil with ample water in summer. Propagation is by cuttings of young shoots. (Illustrated Plate 45).

Markhamia
(Bignoniaceae)

Markhamia

Several of these yellow-flowered evergreen trees from tropical East Africa or Asia are known in cultivation, but not often seen in this country. They have short trumpet flowers and belong to the Bignonia family.

M. hildebrandtii, Mho, grows to 10 metres and blooms during summer. It has dark green foliage and is drought-resistant and fairly hardy. *M. platycalyx*, Nsambya, is smaller and suited to warmer districts with plenty of moisture. Both species grow from seed.

Maurandia
(Scrophulariaceae)

Maurandia barclaiana

This dainty, Mexican climber is very useful as it grows so rapidly, reaching a height of about 3 metres in a single season. It belongs to the Antirrhinum family and the flower is very much like a Snapdragon in shape, except that it has a wide-open mouth and spreading lobes. It is not quite 5 cm long and the tube and lips are stained with violet-purple, while the throat of the flower is white. There are also white and pink-flowered varieties. The flowers are produced profusely all summer and autumn. The deep-green leaves are very dainty for they are tiny, about 2 cm long, and heart-shaped or triangular. They cast a very light shade if they are used as a screen.

This is an evergreen climber in warm areas, but it dies down in areas with cool winters. It should be pruned right back to a distance of 30 cm from the ground in the winter for best results. The base becomes woody and twiggy and the pruning encourages fresh, supple growth. The plant grows very easily from seed in the spring and will bloom in the first season. It will seed itself freely in damp soil. Cuttings taken in autumn also grow easily. Maurandia likes a warm, sunny position and damp soil. The roots should not be allowed to dry out completely in the winter. The soil should be light, good and contain compost. This climber needs the support of a trellis or wire-netting, for it climbs by means of twining.

Medinilla
(Melastomaceae)

Medinilla magnifica

A beautiful tropical evergreen shrub from the Philippines, this grows about 1 metre in height and has 4-angled woody breanches and large thick leathery leaves to 30 cm in length. The magnificent 30 cm flowerhead hangs downwards from the top of the stem in late summer, remaining in bloom for several weeks. It is made up of deep pink coral-shaped flowers, with purple anthers, surrounded by large pink bracts.

Medinilla will grow in partial shade in humid sub-tropical gardens and needs rich, light well-drained soil containing loam with plenty of water in summer. It is grown as a greenhouse plant in cold climates. The plants need fertilizing during spring and summer if grown in pots and should be pruned after flowering to keep them compact. Propagation is by cuttings taken in spring. (Illustrated Plate 45).

Megaskepasma (Acanthaceae)

Megaskepasma erythrochlamys

MEGAS, RED MEG.

This soft evergreen shrub from Venezuela becomes very large in sub-tropical places, needing plenty of space in which to spread, but may be kept in check by pruning after flowering. It will grow to a height and spread of 3 metres, bearing masses of dark rose-red flowerheads at the tips of the branches. Several plants may be grown together to form a spectacular show in the autumn. Each flowerhead grows up to 20 cm in length and owes its colour to the overlapping bracts that are typical of the Acanthus family. These are arranged like a pyramid, about 15 cm wide at the base and tapering to the tip. The real flowers are tubular and white, curving outwards from between the bracts. The large leaves are simple and deeply veined, growing to about 30 cm in length.

This shrub does well in partial shade near tall trees and may be used to fill spaces in a large border. It will also grow in the open sun in humid areas, preferring the sub-tropics to dry inland places. It needs protection from frost in cold districts and plenty of moisture during summer. The soil should be light and contain humus. Propagation is by cuttings. (Illustrated Plate 45).

Melaleuca (Myrtaceae)

Melaleuca

HONEY-MYRTLE

There are over 100 species of Melaleuca, which are evergreen, Australian trees or shrubs. They have red, white, yellow or mauve flowers and are related to Callistemon, the Bottlebrush. They differ from Callistemon in having stamens in bundles opposite the tiny petals. They flower mainly in spring and early summer and usually grow quickly and easily in ordinary light soil, resisting drought and heat. Some grow in sandy soil at the coast. They are fairly frost-resistant and may be grown in cool as well as warm climates, but need a sunny position. They may be grown from cuttings or from seed, but the woody seed cases must be picked before they will open to release the fine seed.
The following are obtainable:

Melaleuca armillaris

BRACELET HONEY-MYRTLE

This bushy small tree grows to a height of 5 to 10 metres and is a useful, dense evergreen that grows quickly. The creamy bottlebrush flowers are not fluffy like those of M. linariifolia and the leaves are smaller, thin and needle-like. (Illustrated Plate 46.)

Melaleuca bracteata

This small, hardy tree grows to 8 metres and has longer leaves than those of
M. styphelioides, but they are not prickly. The bottlebrush flowers are creamy.
This is useful for creating privacy in gardens in cold areas.

Melaleuca decussata

This large evergreen shrub will grow to 4 metres and has short mauve bottlebrush flowers on the slender branches that are covered with very tiny narrow
leaves. It grows in dry places.

Melaleuca diosmifolia. A tall, rigid shrub with dense spikes of large, greenish-
yellow flowers, this has distinctive smooth, oblong leaves, barely 1 cm long,
arranged neatly along the branches.

Melaleuca elliptica

GRANITE HONEY–MYRTLE

A shrub of about 3 metres, this has thick wine-coloured gold-tipped brushes,
about 8 cm long and 3 cm wide in spring and early summer. The small grey-green
roundish leaves are dotted beneath.

Melaleuca fulgens

A spreading shrub of about 2 metres, this has scarlet bottlebrushes, about 10 cm
long, in summer. The leaves are short, slender and slightly grooved.

Melaleuca hypericifolia

The bright red Bottlebrush flowers are somewhat hidden amongst the branches
of this vigorous shrub that grows to 3 metres, but it has attractive foliage with
3-cm leaves arranged neatly along the slender stems, reminiscent of *Hypericum*.
It flowers mainly in spring (Illustrated Plate 46).

Melaleuca incana

A graceful shrub of 3 metres, this is worth growing for its weeping branches
covered with grey, soft foliage. The flowers are small yellow brushes, about
3 cm long.

Melaleuca lateritia

ROBIN REDBREAST BUSH

This 3-metre shrub has bottlebrush flowers in orange-scarlet and narrow 7-mm
leaves all along the arching, cane-like branches.

Melaleuca linariifolia

FLAX–LEAF PAPERBARK

This evergreen tree is very showy when it is covered with masses of fluffy
white flowerspikes in early summer. It is upright and narrow when young, but

spreads when mature, growing to 15 metres in height, with a rounded crown. The upright stems are closely covered with 3-cm narrow leaves. It will grow in swampy places or ordinary soil, but likes moisture. (Illustrated Plate 46).

Melaleuca nesophila
TEA–MYRTLE

A Western-Australian tree from 3 to 10 metres, this has pompon flowers that consist of a ball of mauve stamens tipped with gold. They are freely produced in spring and summer and are distinctive and dainty, if not showy. The leaves are small, oval, dark green and smooth, about 7 mm wide and 2 cm long (Illustrated Plate 46).

Melaleuca pubescens
BLACK TEA TREE

A bushy species of about 5 metres in height, this has tiny leaves which darken to bottle green with age. The flowers are tiny cream bottlebrushes. This tree will grow in sandy coastal soil.

Melaleuca squarrosa
SCENTED PAPERBARK

This shrub is recommended for damp soils and will grow to 4 metres in height. It has small cream bottlebrushes, up to 5 cm in length, and the aromatic leaves are small, broad and downy.

Melaleuca steedmannii

A small bush of about 1 metre, this is showy in spring when covered with short crimson brushes, tipped with gold. The small leaves are narrow oval. This shrub must have particularly well-drained soil.

Melaleuca styphelioides
PRICKLY PAPERBARK

A large tree that may grow to 20 metres, this is recommended for swampy, brackish soil, but will also grow in hot, dry places. It may be recognised by its small, prickly leaves and creamy bottlebrush flowers.

Melaleuca thymifolia

A dwarf spreading shrub of about 1 metre, this has stiff, narrow leaves up to 1,5 cm long and clusters of red fringed flowers. It will grow in wet or dry soil.

Melastoma
(Melastomataceae)

Melastoma malabathricum
MELASTOMA

An Indian evergreen shrub of about 3 metres, this has 5-cm purple flowers like *Tibouchina* and similar hairy leaves. It is tender and may be grown out-of-doors in warm, frostfree areas such as the east coast and low-veld, but is a greenhouse plant for cold places. It is grown from cuttings.

177

Melia
(Meliaceae)

Melia azedarach

CHINA–BERRY, S. AFRICAN SYRINGA

This large, deciduous tree comes from the Himalayan region and parts of Asia, and grows up to 10 or 30 metres in height. In South Africa it is incorrectly called Syringa, which is really the name of Lilac, but has been so-called because of the mass of sweetly-scented, lilac-coloured flowers that appear in spring. These flowers are tiny, but are thickly clustered in large, graceful sprays up to 22 cm in length. They have a heavy fragrance, particularly towards evening. The smooth, biscuit-coloured, round fruits, about 1 cm in diameter, remain through-out winter and are ornamental both on the tree and in the vase. Unfortunately, these are poisonous and should be kept away from young children who are likely to eat them. The foliage is very attractive and dainty, casting a light shade through which the sunlight filters. The compound leaves are stalked and very large, about 60 cm in length, and divided into numerous, fresh green, shiny leaflets which are oval and pointed, about 8 cm long and have notched edges. The trunk is smooth and brown, flecked with white while the tree is young, but thickens considerably and becomes hard and grey with age.

This tree grows very rapidly so that it is no advantage to plant a large specimen. A small tree will frequently outstrip a taller, possibly root-bound specimen, as well as grow into a better shape. It is grown easily, and reproduces itself freely in warm climates such as Natal, where it runs wild. It can also stand cold temperatures very well and will grow almost anywhere in South Africa. It enjoys moisture, particularly while young, but can later resist drought. The tree grows easily from seed. Sometimes white-flowered types are found, but the seedlings revert back to the mauve types. (Illustrated Plate 46).

M. azedarach var. *umbraculiformis*, the Texas Umbrella Tree, is a variety which has an umbrella shape. The branches radiate straight out from the trunk and resemble a huge umbrella. The leaflets are not quite as broad as those of the above tree. If the trees are not cross-pollinated, the seedlings will grow true to type.

Metrosideros
(Myrtaceae)

Metrosideros excelsa (M. tomentosa)

NEW ZEALAND CHRISTMAS TREE

A large, spreading, evergreen tree of 8 metres, this has dark green foliage with silvery undersides. The crimson flowers resemble those of the flowering Gum and appear during early and mid-summer. Although slow-growing, it is wind and sea-tolerant and does very well at the coast, especially at the Cape. It needs protection from frost and thrives in mild areas. It is grown from seed.

Michelia
(Magnoliaceae)

Michelia champaca

A tall open-branched evergreen tree from India, this has fragrant, yellow, 12-petalled starry flowers, 6 cm across, and very long oval leaves. It does best in warm places with mild winters.

Michelia figo (Michelia fuscata = Magnolia fuscata)

PORT–WINE MAGNOLIA

This evergreen shrub comes from China and is also called the Banana-shrub. It belongs to the Magnolia family, but differs botanically from the Magnolia

178

genus, so that it is known under the name of the genus *Michelia*. The tiny flowers
—about 5 cm long—are brownish-yellow flushed with wine and have a breath-
taking, rich scent in spring. A few will perfume a whole room, while the bush
itself scents the garden. These tiny flowers are hidden away amongst the leaves,
but are real little treasures. They can be used in a finger bowl, but, of course,
do not last very long as they bruise like other Magnolias.

The shrub grows to a height of about 2 metres and is pleasantly rounded and
neat. The leaves are a fresh green, smooth and pointed, about 4 cm wide and
8 cm long. The young growth is covered with brown hairs. The Port-Wine
Magnolia should be grown amongst other shrubs for a number of reasons.
Firstly, it shows no flowers and should be used to contrast with other foliage.
Secondly, it appreciates a little shade, and thirdly the other shrubs give it some
protection against a possible severe frost in areas which have hard winters. It
survives the average winter of the high-veld without any risk. It likes an acid
soil containing compost and a good deal of water. Cuttings should be taken in
autumn and given bottom heat under glass, but are very slow.

Millettia (Leguminosae) — *Millettia grandis*

UMZIMBITI

A tender, evergreen, South African tree which grows to 5 or 7 metres, this has
22-cm, erect sprays of Wistaria-like flowers during mid-summer. The 22-cm
leaves are divided into shiny 8-cm leaflets. Frost-sensitive, this is drought-
resistant in winter. It is suitable for coastal gardens and is grown from seed,
flowering while young. (Illustrated Plate 48).

Mimetes (Proteaceae) — *Mimetes cucullatus*

RED BOTTLEBRUSH, ROOISTOMPIE, SOLDAAT

A neat, evergreen, shrub of almost 2 metres, this becomes colourful from
spring to mid-summer when the topmost leaves turn rosy-red, shading to yellow
at the base. Branches last well in the vase.

Mimetes needs full sunshine and moisture throughout the year, especially in
winter. The soil should be well-drained, slightly acid and contain compost.
Mimetes withstands — 10 degrees Celsius inland, where it should be sheltered when
young. It withstands wind at the coast and does best in a fresh coastal atmosphere.
It is grown from seed and planted out when one year old. (Illustrated Plate 46).

Mimulus (Scrophulariaceae) — *Mimulus aurantiacus* (*Diplacus glutinosus*)

BUSH MONKEY-FLOWER

A small evergreen shrub of about 1 metre from California, this has sticky
leaves and orange flowers like open trumpets about 4 cm across. There are colour
forms with wine and crimson flowers. This is difficult to grow in the summer
rainfall area, requiring excellent drainage and moisture in winter. It will grow in
sun or shade and likes the protection of a wall. Trim after flowering. It grows from
cuttings.

Montanoa (Compositae) — *Montanoa bipinnatifida*

TREE DAISY

This Mexican shrub grows to about 2 or 3 metres, becoming rampant in warm
climates if not kept in check. The large masses of white daisies, fully 8 cm across,

which are in clusters of at least 20 at the tips of the stems, are extremely showy when in bloom in autumn. The foliage is attractive as the broad leaves are deeply cut with all the lobes pointed. It dies down during cold winters, but will shoot up again in spring. Propagation is by seed, root cuttings or stem cuttings in early spring. (Illustrated Plate 47).

Mucuna *(Leguminosae)* — *Mucuna nova-guineensis* (M. bennettii)

SCARLET JADE VINE,
NEW GUINEA CREEPER

A large woody forest climber from New Guinea, this has vivid scarlet–crimson pea flowers, each about 10 cm long, in a long pendant spray in early summer. The leaflets are large, oval and tapering. It is commonly called the Scarlet Jade Vine as it resembles the Jade Vine, *Strongylodon*, but does not flower so profusely, nor is it as easy to grow and·maintain in cultivation. It is called "Garland of Garnets" in Thailand.

This tropical climber needs a strong support like a pergola, for it needs shade at the roots and climbs upwards to flower at the top in the open sun. It needs warmth and high humidity in summer in order to flourish. It has been grown successfully in Durban. It blooms in a year and a half from seed, but the buds are inclined to drop in the first flowering. The woody seedpods are covered with prickly golden hairs that may irritate the skin.

There is some confusion about the botanical names of this plant, some believing them to be different species, but, according to the Leyden Herbarium, both names were published during 1896 within three months of one another and the older name *Mucuna nova-guineensis* (Scheffer) published in October, 1896, takes precedence over *M. bennettii* (F. Muell.) published in December of the same year. (Illustrated Plate 48).

Muehlenbeckia *(Polygonaceae)* — *Muehlenbeckia platyclados* (Homacladium platycladium)

WIRE–PLANT,
TAPEWORM BUSH

A bushy evergreen of about 1 metre, this elongates to send out semi-climbing stems that lean against tree-trunks or other supports. It has interesting flattened stems with many joints, a little over 1 cm wide. Groups of rose-red buds I like pinheads appear in autumn, followed by tiny white stalkless flowers and fleshy purple fruits, blooming best in mild districts. The plant is drought-resistant and tender, but may be given protection from frost under tree branches, for it does well in half-shade. It comes from the Solomon Islands. It may be grown as a greenhouse plant and is propagated by cuttings. (Illustrated Plate 47).

Murraya *(Rutaceae)* — *Murraya exotica*

ORANGE–JASMINE

A 2-metre evergreen shrub from the East Indies, this has clusters of sweetly scented, white, 5-petalled flowers, followed by large red berries. The glossy dark-green compound leaves make this shrub suitable for a hedge or background in mild, frostfree areas. It will grow in sun or semi-shade and is propagated by seed or cuttings.

Murraya koenigii, Curry Leaf Tree, is a 7-metre Indian tree with aromatic pinnate leaves, used to flavour curry, which is cultivated in Durban. It has small creamy flowers.

Murraya paniculata, Satin-Wood or Cosmetic Bark Tree, is a large evergreen shrub with fragrant white flowers in autumn and spring. It is similar to *M. exotica*, but has fewer-flowered clusters and is more tree-like.

Mussaenda (Rubiaceae)

Mussaenda

FLAG–BUSH

There are about 40 species of *Mussaenda* in the tropical parts of the world, but only a few are cultivated.

Mussaenda erythrophylla

RED FLAG–BUSH

This spectacular evergreen shrub has large bright crimson velvety bracts surrounding tiny creamy flowers from early summer to autumn. The bracts are up to about 15 cm long and 8 cm wide. The large velvety leaves cover the soft-wooded plant which grows to 2 metres in height, often sprawling or half-climbing. It is tender to frost, enjoying heat and humidity, but is drought-resistant in areas with mild winters. It will grow in full sun or partial shade. Propagation is by cuttings. This species comes from tropical Africa and has become a popular plant throughout the warm countries of the world. (Illustrated Plate 47).

Mussaenda frondosa

WHITE FLAG–BUSH

This evergreen shrub from India grows into a well-rounded, compact bush about 2 metres in height and almost 3 metres in width. It is a very effective landscape shrub with an interesting appearance. The flowers are small, consisting of short tubes that flare out into flat, bright-orange, velvety flowers with 5 petals that turn backwards. Each flower is only about 2 cm across, and they are clustered in small groups. From beneath each group of flowers springs a large white bract, about 8 cm long and shaped like an oval, pointed leaf, which remains after the flowers, followed by green berries, have fallen. The leaves are almost the same shape and a rich green colour. The white bracts stand out spectacularly against the foliage and hang down from thin stalks, fluttering in the breeze like so many little white flags (Illustrated Plate 47).

This shrub is very tender to frost and thrives in sub-tropical areas and in the lowveld. It does very well at the coast in Natal and may be grown as a greenhouse plant in cold areas. The White Flag-bush is grown very easily, as it is not particular about soil requirements. It can be pruned into shape in spring and grows easily from cuttings. (Illustrated Plate 47).

Mussaenda philippica var. Donna Aurora

DONNA AURORA FLAG–BUSH

This small tree of about 6 metres has spectacular ball-like clusters of soft ivory bracts, about 20 cm in diameter, at the ends of the branches. These resemble white flowers, but are sepals surrounding tiny yellow flowers. They are almost continuously in bloom in the tropics. Constant pruning to keep the bush small induces more clusters to form.

This is a variety developed in the Philippines from the original species that has only 1 bract and yellow flowers, similar to *M. frondosa*. There are several other hybrids, including a deep pink and a red. "Sirikit" has palest pink flowers edged with rosy pink and is more delicate to cultivate. All require full sun in the sub-tropics, with good, well-drained soil and dryness in winter. (Illustrated Plate 47).

Myoporum
(Myoporaceae)

Myoporum laetum
NGAIO

A New Zealand evergreen which grows rapidly to form a dense small tree of 5 to 8 metres, this has long shining leaves spotted with yellow oil-glands. The white flowers, spotted lilac, are of secondary importance. This useful tree will withstand wind at the coast and is extremely drought-resistant. It is hardy inland, but requires shelter from frost when young. It makes a dense screen.

M. insulare, commonly called Boobiyalla, has smaller, succulent leaves, white flowers and purple berries. It is also wind and drought-resistant, but will grow at the sea. It thrives on the Cape beaches. Both species grow from cuttings or seed and should be trimmed annually.

Myrtus
(Myrtaceae)

Myrtus communis
COMMON MYRTLE

A useful evergreen, Mediterranean shrub of about 3 metres, with small, dark-green, glossy, aromatic leaves, this has white flowers consisting mainly of a puff of stamens, followed by single-stalked, bluish-black berries. It is tender to severe frost, but may be grown in full shade and is drought-resistant. It is used mainly for hedges in mild or coastal areas and may be grown from seed or cuttings. There is a white-margined variety.

Nandina
(Berberidaceae)

Nandina domestica
HEAVENLY OR SACRED BAMBOO, NANDINA

Dainty fern-like foliage makes this Japanese evergreen shrub worth having apart from its white flowers and red berries. There is a variety with white berries. Nandina is not a real Bamboo, but resembles Bamboo in its delicate foliage, and grows to about 2 metres. It has reedy stems that make it suitable for waterside planting and it is a useful subject for full shade or a tub in a patio, although it will also grow in the sun. It likes moisture and good soil and is hardy to cold, often colouring bronze in winter. Straggly bushes may be cut back at the end of winter. Woody stems are always cut out at ground level in Japan. Propagation is by fresh seed, cuttings or division of the root.

Nerium
(Apocynaceae)

Nerium oleander
OLEANDER

The Oleander is a large, evergreen shrub that comes from the Mediterranean and grows to a height of 4 to 5 metres. It needs a lot of space as it spreads in proportion to its height. The flowers are about 4 cm across and resemble small roses with a waxy texture. They are generously produced all over the bush and come in various attractive colours. White and rose-pink are the more common colours, but there is also a deep red and a delicate ice-cream pink. There are both single and double forms. These all flower at different times within a week or two of one another, and continue to flower at intervals throughout summer. The leaves are greyish-green, leathery and tapering and there is a form with variegated leaves.

The Oleander is an attractive shrub, but its greatest drawback is that its sap is extremely poisonous, and it is not recommended where there are small children who may chew the leaves. Otherwise, it is particularly easy to grow and may be grown from cuttings. It is hardy to frost and can also withstand drought, so that one often sees it growing in the neglected corners of a garden. It grows very well at the coast. It rarely needs pruning, but this may be done in the spring if necessary. (Illustrated Plate 48).

Nymania (Meliaceae)

Nymania capensis

KLAPPERBOS, CHINESE LANTERNS

Inflated rosy, papery seed-pods make this evergreen shrub spectacular, for they persist for many months, following the drooping rose-red flowers, which appear in early spring. The narrow leaves assist this 2-metre South African shrub to resist drought. It must be given a very well-drained, sunny situation and not over-watered, or it will succumb during heavy summer rains. It is hardy to cold and grows slowly from seed sown in autumn. (Illustrated Plate 48).

Ochna (Ochnaceae)

Ochna atropurpurea

CARNIVAL BUSH

An evergreen shrub of 1 to 2 metres, this is colourful over a long period with its pinkish-bronze young foliage and small yellow buttercup flowers in spring, followed by scarlet sepals and green seeds which turn black and persist until mid-summer. It needs full sun and a warm sheltered position where winters are cold. It thrives at the coast. Water regularly throughout the year and give it good soil containing compost. Trim long branches when the bush is small to make it compact. *Ochna* will grow only from very fresh seed, but seeds itself in moist gardens when eaten by birds. Several other attractive South African species are not yet cultivated generally. (Illustrated Plate 48).

Odontonema (Acanthaceae)

Odontonema (Thrysacanthus)

CARDINAL'S GUARD

Soft-wooded evergreen shrubs from Brazil that resemble *Jacobinia*, these have red tubular flowers clustered at the tops of the stems, forming a pine-like cluster or thyrse. The leaves are large, oval and pointed, with a soft texture.

They need light loamy soil with good drainage and moisture during summer. Tender to frost, they may be grown in partial shade under trees or in open sun in warm, humid areas. They may be grown as pot-plants in greenhouses, needing to be pinched back. They may be pruned to keep in check and grown from cuttings.

Odontonema nitidum grows to 1,5 metres and has small red flowers, each about 2 cm long. It comes from the West Indies.

Odontonema strictum from Central America, grows to 2 metres and has long erect sprays of 3-cm crimson flowers. It is sometimes called *Justicia coccinea* or *Pachystachys coccinea*. (Illustrated Plate 49).

Orthosiphon (Labiatae)

Orthosiphon labiatus (Nautochilus)

SHELL-BUSH

An evergreen sub-shrub from South Africa, this forms a pretty rounded bush that grows to a height of over a metre and blooms for a long period from summer to autumn. The bush is covered with a mist of pinkish-mauve tapering flower-spikes, combining pale pink Salvia-like flowers, mauve calyx and bracts. The soft, heart-shaped leaves are aromatic.

This hardy plant grows easily and is drought-resistant in winter. It will grow in full sun or partial shade. It should be trimmed back at the end of winter to improve flowering and general shape. It grows easily from seed sown in spring and will flower when 6 months old.

Osmanthus (Oleaceae)

Osmanthus fragrans

SWEET OSMANTHUS

A large evergreen shrub from Asia, this has oval, shining, leathery leaves which are finely toothed. The small white flowers, 4 cm wide, are not showy but strongly scented, blooming in early summer. This was an old greenhouse plant and is not common, but will grow out-of-doors in moderate conditions, disliking extremes of heat or cold. It is propagated by cuttings.

Pachira (Bombacaceae)

Pachira aquatica

SHAVING-BRUSH TREE

A large evergreen tree from South America, this is curious because the crimson and cinnamon shaving-brush opens at night, even in the vase, and dies the next morning, with new buds opening all through summer and autumn. The flowers are huge, about 15 cm long, and form a fluff of silky reddish-brown stamens. They appear here and there amongst the dense green foliage. The leaves are long and divided into 5 or 7 large leaflets. The fruits are large and up to 20 cm long.

This is an interesting tree for large sub-tropical gardens, requiring humid, frost-free conditions and full sunshine. It is grown from seed or cuttings. (Illustrated Plate 49).

Pachystachys (Acanthaceae)

Pachystachys lutea

GOLDEN CANDLES

Striking in flower, this soft, tender evergreen shrub comes from the eastern mountains of Peru. It grows to a height of 1 to 2 metres and forms a pyramid covered with golden "candles" of flowers in early summer, persisting for several months. The colour is provided by rich yellow overlapping bracts in a thick column of about 12 cm in length, from which emerge white tubular flowers. They resemble *Beloperone* and also belong to the *Acanthus* family. The deep green leaves are long and tapering at both ends.

This shrub needs good light garden soil containing leaf-mould. It should be watered regularly during summer and drainage is important. It will grow in the open sun if it has sufficient moisture in summer, especially at the coast, but will also grow in partial shade near trees, where overhanging branches will protect it from frost-damage. It can also be used as a pot-plant indoors, as it flowers when small, but needs light or the flowers will become greenish. Propagation is by cuttings. (Illustrated Plate 49).

Paeonia (Ranunculaceae)

Paeonia suffruticosa (P. arborea)

TREE PEONY

A deciduous Chinese shrub growing to 1 or 2 metres, this has large 20-cm rose or white flowers and deeply cut leaves. *P. delavayi* is half its height, with dark crimson, 5-cm flowers. *P. lutea* grows to about 1 metre with yellow flowers, 10 cm across. *P. mlkosewitschii* is shorter, with yellow flowers, 12 cm wide.

These Tree Peonies need extremely rich, deep alkaline soil and plenty of moisture. They will grow in full sun or semi-shade near the perimeter of trees which shelter them from late frosts and from heavy wind. They thrive best in cool climates and grow fairly easily from seed which must be kept moist and shaded. It takes about a month to germinate. Magnificent hybrids, mainly Japanese and American, have been produced and named cultivars are obtainable only from specialist growers. (Illustrated Plate 49).

Pandorea (Bignoniaceae)

Pandorea pandorana (Tecoma australis)

WONGA-VINE

A hardy, evergreen climber from Australia which is covered with pale-yellow, small trumpet flowers during summer, this has shiny compound leaves. It is vigorous and drought-resistant, but grows best in good soil containing compost, with full sun. It grows from seed or cuttings.

Parkinsonia (Leguminosae)

Parkinsonia aculeata

JERUSALEM-THORN

A dainty, spreading, deciduous tree reminiscent of Tamarisk with its tiny leaves and graceful branches, this is a cloud of yellow pea-flowers when it blooms in winter or spring. The branches are pale green with 3-cm spines. It comes from tropical America and needs a warm, sunny position sheltered from frost. It grows to about 8 metres in height, but may be cut back to form a hedge in hot climates with mild winters. Extremely drought-resistant, it also resists wind at the coast. It grows from seed. (Illustrated Plate 49).

Parthenocissus (Vitaceae)

Parthenocissus quinquefolia
(Ampelopsis hederacea)

FIVE-LEAVED OR TRUE VIRGINIA CREEPER

A rampant deciduous creeper that clings to rough surfaces by means of tiny discs, this becomes a sheet of scarlet in autumn. It may be recognised by its 5 long leaflets springing from a central point. It is native to the eastern U.S.A. and is hardy to extreme cold and drought. There are several forms. Propagation is by seed, cuttings or layers.

Parthenocissus tricuspidata

SMALL–LEAVED VIRGINIA CREEPER,
BOSTON IVY, JAPANESE IVY

This well-known hardy deciduous creeper has small, three-pointed leaves, about 3 cm in length. They colour brilliant red in autumn before falling. The plant clings to rough surfaces by tiny discs and roots easily, so that a single specimen will spread to cover a double-storey building. There is a variety with larger leaves and one with purplish leaves. This species is native to China and Japan. (Illustrated Plate 50).

The twining deciduous climber known as Variegated Virginia Creeper is *Ampelopsis heterophylla* var. *amurensis*. It has variable lobed leaves, streaked with white, and decorative blue berries in shades of bright and deep blue. It is frost-hardy, may be grown in partial shade and comes from China, Japan and Korea.

Passiflora (Passifloraceae)

Passiflora (*Tacsonia*)

PASSION FLOWER

There are over 300 species in this genus, mainly evergreen climbers from the tropics of South America, where they were found and called Passion Flowers by the Spaniards, giving this a religious interpretation. Many Passion Flowers are grown for ornament. *Passiflora edulis* is commonly grown because it bears the well-known Passion Fruit or Granadilla and is one of the hardiest to frost.

Passiflora edulis

PASSION FRUIT, GRANADILLA

The strangely beautiful flower measures from 5 to 8 cm across and consists of a disc of white petals, tinged with purple, with a thick white and purple fringe near the centre. The oval fruit is egg-sized, green at first and a dull, dark purple when ripe. The pulp is fragrant, delicious and eaten fresh, together with the seeds, or taken in the form of a juice, as well as being used as a flavouring in cakes and ice-creams. The ornamental leaves make a thick screen. They are deeply divided into three segments, each tapering and with serrated edges. They grow up to 15 cm in length and are a rich, shining green, making excellent decorative material for the vase with their long, graceful stalks, or when arranged singly in the fruit dish. The Granadilla climbs by means of long tendrils that add to its ornamental appearance.

This vine likes a warm, sunny position and plenty of space in which to spread. It must have ventilation, however, so that it should be grown on a wire fence rather than against a wall. Although the Granadilla vine is hardy to frost, the young plants must be protected in their first year, and the plants should be given a warm, sheltered position in areas which experience severe frost. The plants may be cut back in the winter if desired, and should be mulched with well-rotted manure. They like a rich, light soil containing manure and compost. In spring the plants can be grown from seed which is washed and dried, but they are slow to germinate. They can also be grown from cuttings taken in autumn. The young plants grow quickly and have a few fruits in their first year and a large crop in their second. Unfortunately, the vine does not live long, lasting only about 8 years.

Passiflora mollissima, the Banana Passion Fruit, has pink flowers and an edible, yellow fruit about 8 cm long. It is a large, rampant climber.

Passiflora manicata, the Red Passion Flower, has 10 cm scarlet flowers with a central fringe of blue. It is liable to attack by caterpillars.

Passiflora violacea has rosy-lilac flowers, a purple centre and white fringe. The 3-lobed leaves grow to 8 cm in length. It is a dainty, hardy and quick-growing vine. (Illustrated Plate 50).

Paulownia (Scrophulariaceae)

Paulownia tomentosa (P. imperialis)

ROYAL PAULOWNIA

A large, deciduous tree from China, this is frequently confused with *Catalpa* as it has very large, soft leaves, often up to 25 cm across. It has large sprays of bluish-mauve flowers, however, each about 5 cm long and shaped like a foxglove. This tree grows rapidly and requires cool, moist conditions, being hardy to our average frosts. It stands up to the wind at the coast, but does not like a tropical climate. It may be grown from seed. (Illustrated Plate 50).

Pavonia (Malvaceae)

Pavonia multiflora

PAVONIA

A dainty shrub from Brazil, this grows to about 1 metre in height and blooms in mid-summer. The flowers are grouped at the ends of the branches, each about 6 cm across and composed of numerous narrow crimson petals with a purple cone of stamens at the centre. The slender leaves are about 20 cm long.

This is grown as a greenhouse plant in cold countries, but may be cultivated out of doors in warm, frost-free areas, especially where humidity is high. It prefers partial shade and needs light, well-drained soil containing plenty of compost. Propagation is by cuttings or seed. (Illustrated Plate 50).

Pedilanthus (Euphorbiaceae)

Pedilanthus tithymaloides

BIRD CACTUS, CHRISTMAS CANDLE

Finger-thick, fleshy, angular green stems give this shrubby plant an interesting form. It grows to a metre in height. The small curved leaves are waxy and pointed, deeply keeled below. The tiny flame-like red flowers bloom at the tips of the stems in early spring and persist for a long period. There are two varieties with white-edged leaves.

Cuttings grow easily and this plant makes an interesting pot plant in a hot sunny spot in areas with cold winters, growing freely out of doors in warm, frost-free places. It needs well-drained soil with dryness in winter.

Pentas (Rubiaceae)

Pentas

PENTAS

Small, soft, evergreen shrubs that grow from 1 to 2 metres, these are free-flowering and suitable for planting in groups in a rockery or in a shrub border. These shrubs from Tropical Africa have posy-like heads of flowers in mauve, shades of red, pink and white. Varying colour forms have been developed. (Illustrated Plate 50).

These plants grow easily in good moist soil and are fairly hardy. Grow them with shelter from morning sun in cold areas, but they may be grown in the open sun in mild districts. They do well at the coast. They will grow in partial shade near trees. If they become leggy, cut them back at the end of winter. They bloom from spring throughout summer and into winter if conditions are favourable. Remove faded flowers regularly. The flowers last well in the vase. The following species are in cultivation. All grow from seed or cuttings.

Pentas coccinea. An East African species with scarlet flowers, this grows to 2 metres.

Pentas parviflora, from Kenya, is similar, with scarlet flowers.

Pentas lanceolata. This 60 cm bush from Kenya and Tanganyika has 6–7 cm mauve-pink flowerheads. This is most commonly grown.

Pentas longiflora, from East Africa, has white flowers.

Pentas purpurea. A 2-metre shrub with purple flowers, this comes from Rhodesia and Tropical Africa.

Pentas schimperiana has pale rose flowers.

Two species grow wild in the Transvaal near Barberton (*P. woodii*), and in the Ngoma forests, Zululand (*P. wylei*), both with white flowers.

Pereskia (Cactaceae)

Pereskia aculeata

SPANISH GOOSEBERRY, LEMON VINE

Scarcely recognisable as a Cactus, this plant has leaves like an ordinary shrub, but the clusters of fierce spines that develop on the stems when the plant is mature reveal its connection with the Cactus family. It is shrub-like when young, but develops into a long vine bearing masses of individual white flowers like single roses, about 6 cm across. It blooms so profusely in early summer in Mexico and tropical America, where it is native, that it is thought to resemble white Bougainvillea from a distance. The leaves are thick, broad and alternate, up to 10 cm in length. The edible fruits give it its common name.

Variety *godseffiana* has rose-variegated leaves, rosy-pink at the tips of the branches, and the flowers may be greenish-yellow or pinkish. It is the most attractive and popular *Pereskia* in cultivation. Propagation is simplest by cuttings. (Illustrated Plate 51).

Pereskia grandiflora

ROSE TREE CACTUS

This large shrub from Brazil grows to 5 metres and has a fiercely spiny trunk when mature. The pink flowers, like single roses, are in clusters at the ends of the branches and the oval, fleshy leaves grow to 15 cm.

It is often grown under the name of *P. bleo*, which is a taller, rose-flowered tree from Panama and Colombia, which has black needle spines and long thin leaves.

Pernettya (Ericaceae)

Pernettya mucronata

PERNETTYA

A hardy, Ericaceous shrub, growing to 1 metre, with small pinkish flowers in spring, followed by red berries, this is a useful evergreen with its neat, prickly, regular leaves. It must have moisture and cool conditions with acid, peaty soil, otherwise it is very slow and difficult to grow. Propagation is by cuttings, suckers and seed. It comes from the mountains of Chile.

Persoonia
(Proteaceae)

Persoonia pinifolia

A cheerful evergreen shrub to 3 metres with neat pine-like foliage clothing the waving stems, this bears tapering 15 cm spikes of golden flowers in early summer. It needs full sunshine with well-drained acid soil and regular watering during winter. *P. pinifolia* is considered the most attractive of numerous species of *Persoonia* which come from Australia. It is propagated from seed. (Illustrated Plate 51).

Petrea
(Verbeneaceae)

Petrea volubilis
PURPLE WREATH

This evergreen, twining shrub from Brazil grows in bush form to about 3 metres in height or can be trained as a climber on a trellis or other support. It is undoubtedly one of the choicest and most beautiful of shrubs in the spring and excites a tremendous amount of admiration. The elegant sprays of flowers are about 16 to 20 cm long and so freely produced in spring that the whole bush appears to be a cloud of royal blue. The individual flowers are tiny, fleshy, star-shaped and a rich purple colour. They are backed by five, oblong, lilac sepals which remain after the true flowers have fallen. This gives the impression that the flowers have two colours. There is also a white-flowered variety *albiflora*. The flowers appear again in late summer, but not in such profusion. The leaves are broad and tapering and about 8 to 10 cm long. They are wavy and half bent over down the middle.

Petrea likes a warm, sub-tropical climate where it grows rapidly and is magnificent in Durban. It is equally showy in Pretoria and there are some wonderful specimens growing in the open in the gardens at Government House. It grows in Johannesburg where it is not tender to frost, but growth is very slow and flowering is sparse unless it is placed in a warm, sunny, sheltered position facing north or north and west. They make beautiful specimens near the house. They like full sun and should have a soil well mixed with compost. They like a good deal of moisture and should be well-watered throughout the year. *Petrea* is increased by cuttings, but as this is usually slow, one should buy as large a specimen in a tin as possible. Plants begin to flower when they are about 1 metre in height. (Illustrated Plate 51).

Phaedranthus
(Bignoniaceae)

Phaedranthus buccinatorius (Bignonia cherere)
MEXICAN BLOOD-TRUMPET

This is one of the loveliest of evergreen creepers, for the colour of its flowers is exciting and variable. The flowers are 10-cm, narrow trumpets that are yellow at the base and flushed with crimson at the mouth, which consists of broad, flaring petals. Some of the trumpets are completely stained with a blood-red colour. Great bunches of flowers appear from early summer for months. The oval leaves are a dull, dark green.

This climber needs a sunny spot or the warmth of a wall for best results, but will also grow in a position where it receives sun for part of the day. It will stand a certain amount of frost, but thrives best in warm conditions. It requires very little care once it is established. The soil should be good and moist, but it will also withstand a certain amount of dryness. This vine will cling to rough brick walls by means of tendrils and will cover a fairly large area. It is propagated by cuttings, but these do not strike easily. (Illustrated Plate 51).

Phaseolus
(Leguminosae)

Phaseolus caracalla

A bean-like evergreen climber with fragrant, coiled flowers, shaded purple and yellow, this blooms profusely in spring. It requires shelter from frost and is suitable for a west wall, needing the support of a trellis. It comes from India and may be grown from seed. (Illustrated Plate 52).

Philadelphus
(Saxifragaceae)

Philadelphus coronarius

MOCK–ORANGE

The Mock-Oranges are deciduous shrubs that come from Asia and parts of the U.S.A. and Mexico. They have frequently been called Syringa, but this name belongs to the Lilacs. *P. coronarius* is the species most commonly grown, but there are numerous horticultural varieties of it and many named hybrids, which are generally called the Lemoine hybrids and are all worth growing. The Mock-Orange grows up to 3 metres in height and consists of a number of canes growing up from the base, forming a rather narrow, compact bush broadening with age.

The flowers are white and look like large fruit blossoms. There are both single and double forms as well as mottled colours available. These should be chosen when in bloom. The flowers have a sweet scent similar to the fragrance of Orange blossom. The profuse flowers are borne in thick clusters in the spring. The leaves are about 6 cm long, oval and tapering in shape. They are soft-textured and a fresh, light green.

Mock-Orange is very easy to grow and thrives on any neutral soil but prefers lime (pH 7.5). The most important attention it requires is correct pruning, which should be done immediately after flowering. The wood that has borne flowers can be cut right out, leaving only the young growths. This allows vigorous new shoots to grow up and bear the flowers of the following spring. It also prevents twigginess and the dense growth that often makes this bush untidy-looking in the winter. The hybrids are propagated by cuttings or layers.

Phlomis
(Labiatae)

Phlomis fruticosa

JERUSALEM–SAGE

An evergreen sub-shrub of about 1 metre, this has white-woolly, wrinkled leaves and bright yellow legume flowers in cylindrical spikes above the foliage. It blooms in winter and spring. It should be grown in the mixed border, not as a specimen, and pruned back annually after flowering. It grows easily in gardens in full sun and is drought-resistant, yet able to withstand salt spray at the coast. *Phlomis* comes from Southern Europe and grows from seed.

Photinia
(Rosacea)

Photinia davidsoniae

PHOTINIA

Densely evergreen, this small upright tree grows fairly slowly to a height of 10 metres and is useful as a shrub for screening and a wind-break. Flat heads of white flowers, 15 cm wide, appear in spring and occasional long, toothed leaves turn red in autumn. This hardy plant comes from China. It is very similar to the Chinese *P. serrulata*. *P. villosa* is deciduous, with smaller leaves and flowers. Propagation is by seed or cuttings. (Illustrated Plate 52).

Physocalymma
(Lythraceae)

Physocalymma scaberrima
ROSEWOOD

This dainty tree grows to about 10 metres and spreads outwards gracefully. It has slender drooping branches covered with reddish-purple crinkled flowers in early summer. These are reminiscent of *Lagerstroemia* and it belongs to the same family. It grows in the eastern forests of Peru and north-western Brazil. Semi-evergreen, it enjoys protection from frost, but does not need sub-tropical conditions. Propagation is by seed. (Illustrated Plate 52).

Physocarpus
(Rosaceae)

Physocarpus opulifolius
NINE BARK

This deciduous North American shrub is hardy and grows to about 2 metres. The white flowers, tinged pink, are in clusters at the tips of the stems in early summer, resembling *Spiraea*. They bloom together with the leaves which are rounded, deeply toothed and with 3 large lobes. It has bright red seeds in autumn and attractive peeling bark.

This shrub grows easily once established, but needs regular watering in summer. It is useful in cold climates. Propagation is by seed or cuttings of half-ripened wood.

Pieris
(Ericaceae)

Pieris (*Andromeda*)
PIERIS

P. japonica is the best known of these hardy everygreen shrubs, which belong to the Heath family. It comes from Japan and grows to 3 metres. It has tapering leaves and 15-cm clusters of small, white or pink-tinged, urn-shaped flowers in spring. This shrub is difficult to grow away from a moist, cool climate, requiring damp, peaty, acid soil and partial shade. It is grown from seed, which is not easy, from layers and from cuttings, which root slowly.

Pimelea
(Thymeleaceae)

Pimelea ferruginea
PINK RICE–FLOWER

A small, evergreen, Australian shrub of about 60 cm, this has short, narrow leaves and masses of flower heads, like pink puffs, that appear in early summer. They vary from bright to pale pink or red. Trim after flowering. *Pimelea* thrives in a warm, sunny position in the rockery. Propagation is from cuttings taken in spring. (Illustrated Plate 52) *P. rosea* is similar, with a longer leaf.

Pithecellobium
(Leguminosae)

Pithecellobium (*Pithecolobium*)
MONKEY'S EAR

Similar to *Calliandra*, this large genus of tropical evergreen trees has flowers that form a puff of thread-like stamens and compound leaves. The flattened seed-pods are often spirally twisted and the common name refers to these. They are grown from seed.

P. grandiflorum is a large Australian evergreen tree which flowers while young. Long crimson stamens extend well beyond the heads of small yellow fragrant flowers. This tree is tender to frost and prefers humid, sub-tropical conditions.

P. dulce, the Manila Tamarind, which comes from Tropical America and the Philippines, has greenish-yellow balls of flowers and edible seeds.

Pithecoctenium
(Bignoniaceae)

Pithecocteneum cynanchoides

MONKEY–COMB

An evergreen vine from Mexico that climbs by tendrils, this bears clusters of tubular white Bignonia-like flowers, each 5 cm long, at the tips of the branches in spring. The leaves are oval and pointed. It has long prickly seedpods that give it its common name.

Pittosporum
(Pittosporaceae)

Pittosporum

PITTOSPORUM

Useful evergreen shrubs and trees from Africa, Australia and Asia, these are grown for their ornamental foliage. The flowers are tiny and insignificant, generally dark and hidden in the leaves, often followed by small fruits. They usually grow easily in a sunny position in ordinary neutral soil and like good drainage. The respond to good watering, but are drought-resistant. They grow in all parts of southern Africa and stand up to the wind and salt air at the coast. They are resistant to average frost, but generally come on again if they have been frosted. They need no pruning, being tidy in habit, but may be clipped. One Australian species (*P. undulatum*) commonly called Victorian Box, is frequently used as a hedge at the Cape. All species form dense, useful screens. *Pittosporum* grows from seed or cuttings.

Pittosporum crassifolium

KARO

A New Zealand shrub or tree, ultimately reaching 10 metres, this has thick oval leaves up to 8 cm long, shiny on the top surface and greyish beneath. There is a variegated form with creamy-edged leaves, which is slow-growing but attractive. The flowers are dark purple.

Pittosporum eugenoides

TARATA, LEMON–WOOD

One of the loveliest for the garden, this grows rapidly into an upright tree of 5 to 7 metres. The foliage is a light fresh green that contrasts well with the slender, clean-looking black stalks. Each 8-cm leaf, elliptical and tapering, has wavy edges. The leaves are smooth, glossy and radiate attractively in spirals, giving the effect of rosettes of leaves. They have a delicate scent of lemon when crushed. The insignificant flowers are yellowish. This species is tender to severe frost.

Pittosporum phillyraeoides

WEEPING PITTOSPORUM

A graceful small evergreen tree to 10 metres, this has pendulous branches with willow-like leaves, fragrant yellow flowers and heart-shaped yellow berries. It will thrive in warm, dry areas and comes from Australia.

Pittosporum rhombifolium

SWEET PITTOSPORUM

Pyramid-shaped, this evergreen Australian tree grows to 5 metres. It has scented white flowers and orange berries. The diamond-shaped leaves taper to a point. It needs regular watering.

Pittosporum tenuifolium (*P. nigricans*)

Sometimes called the Small-leaved Pittosporum, this New Zealand tree, which grows to 10 metres, has dark-green oval leaves up to 5 cm, which curve backwards. Useful for a background, or for cut foliage, it grows easily and rapidly. Silver-margined and purple-leaved varieties exist in Australia and New Zealand. The tiny flowers are blackish.

Pittosporum tobira

JAPANESE PITTOSPORUM

This evergreen, 3-metre shrub has 10-cm, oval leaves which are very thick and leathery, with rolled-back margins. There is also a form with white-variegated leaves. The small, greenish-white, fragrant flowers are clustered near the tips of the branches. This species is hardy and drought-resistant, both inland and at the coast.

P. viridiflorum, Bosboekenhout, is a South African species which grows to 8 metres. The smooth, deep green glossy leaves, oval and 8 cm long, resemble those of *P. eugenoides*. The small greenish-yellow flowers are followed by orange berries. It is heat and drought-resistant. (Illustrated Plate 52).

Plectranthus (Labiatae)   *Plectranthus*

SPUR-FLOWER

These are evergreen soft-wooded shrubs of the Salvia family that are valuable for growing in shade under trees, although they will grow in full sunshine in warm or moist frost-free climates. They are protected from frost damage in cold areas by overhanging tree branches or by shelter from the morning sun against a wall. They can be grown in full shade on a south wall. Some make good indoor plants. They do not require pruning, but may be cut back at the end of winter. The following South African species flower in autumn and grow easily from cuttings:

Plectranthus behrii, Pink Spur-Flower. A narrow, shrub with 15-cm spikes of pink, salvia-like flowers, this has reseda-green leaves, backed with purple.

Plectranthus ciliatus. A low species that spreads rapidly in shady places, this has decorative reseda-green leaves, backed with reddish purple, which are similar to those of *P. behrii*. The very pale pink, erect flower spikes appear in autumn.

Plectranthus ecklonii, Purple Spur-Flower. A rounded shrub of about 1 metre, which spreads as much across, this has 22-cm spikes of dainty, deep purple flowers. The oval 10-cm leaves are green and wrinkled.

Plectranthus fruticosus, Forest Spur-Flower. Wide-branching, pyramidal, 30-cm-long spikes of royal-blue flowers make this the showiest species. It blooms from mid-summer to autumn. The bush grows to almost 2 metres and has heart-shaped leaves. This plant needs full or partial shade and plenty of moisture. (Illustrated Plate 52).

Plectranthus hirsutus var. *variegatus* is a low, spreading plant with silver and green leaves, needing shade and shelter from frost.

Plectranthus saccatus. Large-Flowered Spur-Flower. This low, spreading plant can be recognised by its single large lilac flowers, 3 cm long, and tiny rough leaves. It is useful as a ground cover between other shrubs or as an edging to a shrub border. It will grow in a shady window box.

Plumbago (Plumbaginaceae)

Plumbago auriculata (P. *capensis*)

PLUMBAGO, LEADWORT

This South African, evergreen, rambling shrub, about 2 metres in height, has sky-blue flowers almost 2 cm across, with a flat, Phlox-like appearance and a thin tube at the back. This is attached to a hairy, sticky calyx. The flowers are borne profusely in clusters at the ends of the branches for a long period in summer and intermittently in spring and autumn. The leaves are smooth, delicate and light green in colour. They are small, narrow and about 4 cm long.

Plumbago grows very quickly and will spread over a large area. It looks effective tumbling down a bank. It needs the support of a low fence if it is to climb. It can be clipped and will make a good hedge in a warm area. It should be pruned back each spring if it is to be kept tidy-looking. Plumbago grows very easily and is able to resist drought and neglect. It flowers best in the sun, but may also be grown in partial shade. It is hardy to frost and loves a warm climate, and can be grown almost anywhere in South Africa. Reproduction is from cuttings and from suckers. (Illustrated Plate 54).

Plumbago zeylanica is a similar, indigenous species, but has pure white flowers.

Plumeria (Apocynaceae)

Plumeria

FRANGIPANI

There are several species of Frangipani that come from the West Indies and Mexico, varying from small 3-metre trees to large rounded trees about 10 metres in height. All the cultivated species are very fragrant and probably the most sweetly scented of tropical flowers. They are planted near temples in India and sometimes called Temple-Flowers.

The flowers appear for several months in summer and autumn and are most spectacular and beautiful. Each flower unfurls into five, over-lapping, thick, waxy petals, and measure nearly 5 cm across. They are clustered in heads at the ends of the branches and framed by a rosette of dark green leaves. The leaves are thick, leathery and huge—about 30 cm long, with an oval, tapering shape. The branches are thick and clumsy. The stems, leaves and branches all exude a milky juice when plucked. *Plumeria alba* has pure white flowers. *Plumeria rubra* (P. *acuminata*) is the Crimson Frangipani and is most showy with its crimson and gold flowers or its clear pink variety. There are many hybrids available, including a rich apricot flushed with cream and a beautiful buttercup yellow, each one lovelier than the last. *P. rubra* var. *acutifolia* has white flowers flushed at the centre with deep yellow and sometimes with rose. (Illustrated Plate 52).

Frangipani is very easily grown, but is very tender to frost and is really suited only to a sub-tropical climate at low or medium elevations. It stands the sea-breeze well and grows magnificently in Durban. It may be grown as shrub in cooler climates if it is given a hot situation in a north-west corner. It loses its leaves for a short period in winter and should not be watered much at this time. It is easily propagated by large cuttings taken in autumn.

Podalyria
(Leguminosae)

Podalyria calyptrata

SWEETPEA BUSH OR KEURTJIE

This large, rounded evergreen, South African shrub comes from Table Mountain, reaches a height of about 4 metres and spreads to 3 metres across. It flowers profusely in spring and the whole shrub is covered with wide open flowers resembling sweetpeas, but measuring about 4 cm across. They are a clear, pretty pinkish-mauve and there is also a variety with white flowers. The flowers have a very strong, sweet fragrance. They may be cut for the vase and last better if some of the leaves are cut away. The many-branched shrub is luxuriantly clothed with leaves. These are small, about 4 cm long and a roundish, oval shape. They are dark green with a faint covering of silvery hairs that glint in the sun.

This shrub is fast-growing and able to survive the average frosts experienced in Johannesburg. It requires a good, well-drained soil mixed generously with compost. It must be well-watered in the winter. It does not require pruning, but dead branches must be removed. It lives for many years in cultivation—one has flourished for 30 years in Johannesburg. (Illustrated Plate 54).

Podalyria sericea is a small Cape shrub, growing no taller than 1 metre. It has small, mauve, scented flowers in May, followed by silvery pods. The small leaves are silvery-grey. It does not grow as easily as *P. calyptrata*.

Podocarpus
(Podocarpaceae)

Podocarpus henkelii

LONG-LEAVED YELLOW-WOOD

A handsome evergreen tree that grows slowly into a tall tree, this will reach a height of about 3 metres in 9 years in the average garden, growing more quickly in mist-belt areas of high rainfall. It should be given rich, deep, well-drained soil and watered regularly throughout ·he year, although it will tolerate some drought. It is hardy to cold and may be grown in partial shade or full sun.

Although there are three other species besides this that are native to South Africa, this is the most attractive for gardens as it is decorative even when small, with its spiralled tufts of drooping narrow, curved, leathery leaves, each growing up to 15 cm in length. It makes an excellent tub-plant, but is better planted out into the garden after a few years when it becomes root-bound.

The common Yellow-wood, *P. falcatus*, has shorter, narrow, curved leaves and the Upright Yellow-wood, *P. latifolius*, has short blunt leaves. This grows slowly to a great height of about 45 metres and the giant of the Knysna Forest is thought to be hundreds of years old. *P. elongatus* is a bushier species with ornamental drooping branches and leaves, which has made it popular as a pot-plant, especially in America.

P. macrophyllus, a small tree from Japan, is said to be one of the most commonly cultivated and has spreading branches that are pruned in tiers, sometimes with variegated foliage, while *P. nagi* is a larger tree with more pendulous branches and wider, shorter leaves, from China, Japan and Taiwan. Several other species come from New Zealand and Chile.

Propagation of all the species is easy from seed, especially in moist areas, while short cuttings form roots fairly easily.

Podranea
(Bignoniaceae)

Podranea brycei

This evergreen, showy climber comes from the Zimbabwe area. It bears huge bunches of shell-pink, 5-cm, trumpet flowers at the ends of long, spreading branches throughout the summer. The leaves are large, dark green and shiny, and divided into small leaflets, so that they have a dainty appearance. This climber is easily confused with the Port St. Johns Creeper (*Podranea ricasoliana*) which grows near Port St. Johns, as there are small botanical differences between them. At a casual glance the foliage and flowers of both species are identical, but flowers of the Zimbabwe Creeper are slightly smaller than those of the Port St. Johns Creeper and have a hairy throat and a more mauve colouring. There is also a white-flowered form of the Port St. Johns Creeper which has a purple spot in the throat.

The Zimbabwe Creeper is evergreen and can withstand a certain amount of frost. It welcomes the warmth of a wall, preferably in full sunlight facing north or west. It likes rich soil and a mulch of manure from time to time. It grows quickly and sends out long, waving branches that turn woody and thicken with age. Pruning may be done in the spring if desired, in order to keep the plant within bounds. It grows easily and can be grown almost anywhere in South Africa. Propagation is by seed or by cuttings. The Port St. Johns Creeper is cultivated in the same way. (Illustrated Plate 54).

Poinciana See *Caesalpinia* and *Delonix*.

Polygala
(Polygalaceae)

Polygala virgata

This pretty, evergreen shrub is indigenous to South Africa and grows to a height of from 2 to 3 metres. It has erect, green, fleshy stems similar to those of Broom. The flowers when closed are like tiny purple sun-bonnets, heavily streaked with darker veins. When open, they reveal a fringed tuft on the lowest petal. The flowers grow in graceful, 25-cm long spikes which are showy for a long period in the year, particularly during the winter months. The leaves are narrow, green and fleshy, and up to 5 cm in length, but are very sparse on the plant. When the plant is young it has a stiff appearance, for it grows a long erect stalk of about 1 metre, with the flower-stalks radiating out at the top only. In about two or three years the bush fills out into a densely branched head which becomes a mass of flowers. Several should be planted together for effect. The dainty flowers last for several days in the vase.

Polygala is quite hardy to frost and grows very easily almost anywhere in South Africa. It should be given an open sunny position and makes an excellent shrub for the rockery. The soil should be light and well-drained, containing compost. It enjoys moisture and seeds itself easily in moist soil. If it becomes straggly, the top can be pruned hard back after flowering and it will bush out again from that point. It grows easily from seed sown in spring or in autumn.

Polygala myrtifolia is another species which has less dense flowers, but its stems are richly clothed with overlapping leaves all through the year. These are narrow with rounded tips, just over 3 cm long, and resemble the leaves of Myrtle in their tough texture, light green colour and habit of growth. The pea-shaped, rich purple flowers are in clusters at the tips of the many short branchlets. The lowest petal has an upstanding fringed crest of purple. This useful shrub grows to about 2 metres in height and spread. It flowers for most of the year, except for about 2 to 3 months in the summer. It grows wild at the Cape. (Illustrated Plate 54).

Polygonum (Polygonaceae)

Polygonum aubertii

CASCADE CREEPER OR SILVER LACE-VINE

This deciduous twining climber comes from Central Asia. It is very fast-growing and vigorous and will climb 7 metres in a season. The flowers are white, tiny and insignificant—nearly 1 cm long—but are borne in such profusion that the vine is veiled in a cloud of feathery white flowers. It has heart-shaped, pointed green leaves and long, thin, twining stalks. This vine must not be confused with white-flowered *Antigonon*.

It is extremely hardy, being well able to survive cold and frost. It may be planted facing east or south but will grow easily anywhere. If it is grown against a 3-metre fence, it will drop down on the other side, covering the area with cascades of bloom in summer and autumn. It is essentially a picturesque, rustic climber. Cut it right down to the base in winter in order to keep it within bounds. It may be propagated by cuttings or by division (Illustrated Plate 54).

P. baldschuanicum has greenish flowers with rose-coloured edges.

Potentilla (Rosacea)

Potentilla fruticosa

POTENTILLA, CINQUEFOIL

Showy when it produces masses of bright yellow flowers like small single roses in early summer, this narrow twiggy shrub grows to about 1 metre in height. It is deciduous and hardy, but likes moisture and good soil. A sunny position is best. It comes from China and there are varieties with creamy white and pale lemon flowers. It grows from seed.

Prostanthera (Labiatae)

Prostanthera

MINT-BUSH

There are more than 40 species of these evergreen, Australian shrubs, which have mint-scented foliage. They have blue, lilac, purple, pink or white flowers which bloom profusely in spring or mid-summer. They like good soil and plenty of moisture, particularly during summer. They may be trimmed after flowering and need some protection from frost. *Prostanthera* belongs to the Salvia family and grows from seed or cuttings.

P. rotundifolia grows to 2 metres, and has lilac flowers in early summer and tiny rounded leaves. There is a pink-flowered variety. *P. nivea* stands drier conditions than most species. It has snow-white or blue-tinged flowers in early summer and grows to about 3 metres.

Protea (Proteaceae)

Protea

PROTEA, SUGAR-BUSH, SUIKERBOS

The Protea is probably South Africa's most famous flower and is generally recognised as the national flower. The most attractive species which are desirable for the garden come from the Cape. They are evergreen shrubs growing about 2 to 3 metres in height and well rounded in proportion. Each flower is borne at the tip of the branch and consists of a mass of tiny flowers topped by hairy stigmas which usually come in different shades of pink, white or red. The flowers range from small heads as in *Protea lacticolor*, to those of the famous Giant Protea, *Protea cynaroides*, which are as wide as a dinner-plate. The leaves of most Proteas are long, smooth, leathery in texture and a soft green colour.

These shrubs provide magnificent blooms for the vase, which last for several weeks on the bush. The faded flowers must be removed from the shrub, which requires no further pruning. They generally bloom in early spring, but many start blooming in autumn and continue throughout winter, so that Proteas are valuable winter-flowering shrubs.

Proteas have a reputation of being unable to grow away from the Cape, but this is not true. They cannot thrive without the right treatment. Their main requirement is a very well-drained soil. A raised bed in the rockery, containing a light, good, soil, well mixed with compost, and which has a gravelly sub-soil, is ideal. They grow well on gently sloping soil. Proteas are not tender to the frost experienced in Johannesburg and there are some beautiful specimens grown at The Wilds, Johannesburg. Another important requirement is that they must be well watered in winter—as they come from a winter rainfall-area—and not as much in the summer, when they are fairly drought-resistant. A well-drained soil will solve the problem of a too heavy rainfall in the summer. On the whole, Proteas need an acid soil except for one or two like *P. obtusifolia* and *P. susannae* which grow in limestone soil in nature. Some Proteas seem to resent potash and, as it is known that much of the soil of the south-western Cape is potash-deficient, one should not fertilize them with wood-ash or fertilizers containing potash. *P. cynaroides* has been known to die after an application of wood-ash. The plants should be staked until they bush out. They like an open, sunny position.

Protea plants are now freely obtainable and may be planted out when from 15 to 45 cm in height. They may be grown from seed, obtainable from Kirstenbosch, which should be planted in March and takes anything from 5 weeks to 1 year to germinate. Only fertile seed will germinate. The seedlings should be kept in individual tins and planted out when they are 1 year old for best results. They grow fairly quickly—up to about 2 metres in 4 years—and bear numbers of flowers in the fourth or fifth year from seed. Proteas sometimes die for no apparent reason, in the same way as other members of this family, but this is thought to be caused by drought at the end of long, dry Cape summers. See also, *Proteas for Pleasure* by the author.

Protea aristata

LADISMITH PROTEA

The large flowerhead of deep pink or red bracts, filled with deep pink hairs, appears in mid-summer on a bush of 2 metres. The stems are covered with distinctive pine-like foliage. This Protea needs good soil and plenty of moisture all through the year, but is quite hardy. (Illustrated Plate 53).

Protea barbigera

GIANT WOOLLY-BEARD

A low, spreading bush of almost 2 metres, this has large, 15-cm flowers filled with soft hairs, tipped with a black "spot" at the centre. These are generally pink but there is a yellowish-cream variety. Both are undoubtedly the most beautiful of Protea flowers, but this species is not very easy to grow, frequently damping off when very young and slow to become established (Illustrated Plate 53).

Protea compacta
BOT RIVER PROTEA

This 3-metre bush grows quickly and flowers profusely throughout winter. The clear pink, cup-shaped flowers are 12 cm long and are commonly seen at florists. Unfortunately the foliage blackens after a few days in the vase. The bush requires staking while young.

Protea cynaroides
KING PROTEA

This 1–2-metre bush is suitable for quite a small garden, although it bears the largest flowers in the genus, reaching 27 cm across when ideally grown. The wide-open pink or red flower heads are filled with a cone of silvery hairs. It likes regular moisture at all times and does best in a warm situation. Quite large specimens may be transplanted. There are several forms of *P. cynaroides* and a miniature form is known. The foliage is easily recognisable as each leaf has a red stalk. (Illustrated Plate 53).

Protea eximia (P. latifolia)
RAY-FLOWERED PROTEA

Attractive when it is well-grown, this large shrub of 2 to 3 metres has large, wide open flowers, with narrow, spoon-shaped pink bracts. It blooms in the spring. (Illustrated Plate 53).

Protea grandiceps
OVAL-LEAVED OR PEACH PROTEA

A 2-metre bush with magnificent, 15-cm-long flowers, this is slow-growing but well worth having. The inward-curving, reddish-pink bracts are tipped with white hairs. The broad leaves are rimmed with red.

Protea laurifolia (P. marginata)
LAUREL-LEAVED OR FRINGED PROTEA

This has similar pink flowers to *P. neriifolia*, but these are fringed with black and white hairs and the centre is filled with yellowish hairs. It grows to almost 3 metres.

Protea longiflora
LONG-BUD PROTEA

The long slim buds of this species open wide to form a cup encircled with long pink or cream filaments in mid-summer. Unless very fresh and well-grown, however, it is apt to seem untidy. The large rounded bush grows to about 3 metres.

Protea longifolia
LONG-LEAVED PROTEA

Although the long flowers are not colourful, having white or pinkish bracts, they are attractive, being filled with white hairs culminating in a black spot. The leaves are very long and narrow and the bush is low and spreading.

Protea minor

GROUND-ROSE

The delicate colouring of this small flowerhead of about 10 cm in length makes it attractive. It has pale rose-coloured bracts and the centre of the cup is filled with pinkish-white hairs tipped with a brown or black central point. The flowers bloom in autumn, winter and spring. The leaves are very long and thin and the small bush has drooping branches that should be allowed to overhang rocks or a bank.

Protea nana (P. rosacea)

MOUNTAIN ROSE, SKAAMBLOM

A charming dainty 'shrub of 1 metre, this has soft, needle-like leaves and small, 6-cm, wine-coloured, drooping flowers that capture the imagination. This is not easy to grow in the summer rainfall area, often damping off after heavy summer rain and also succumbing to severe frost. It needs a well-drained, sandy, sunny situation. (Illustrated Plate 53).

Protea neriifolia

OLEANDER-LEAVED PROTEA

One of the best and easiest to grow, this quickly forms a rounded bush of 3 metres and flowers freely during winter. The 15-cm-long, narrow flowers are pink and there is a cream variety. Each bract is tipped with black fur and the centre is filled with purplish hairs. The narrow leaves resemble those of an Oleander (Illustrated Plate 53).

Protea obtusifolia

BREDASDORP SUGARBUSH

Similar to *P. repens*, this has greenish overlapping bracts, each tipped with deep rose, and may be recognised by its broader leaves. It grows in limestone soil in nature.

Protea pulchra (P. subpulchella, P. pulchella)

GLEAMING PROTEA

A spreading, winter-flowering bush that is generally low, but will grow to 2 metres, this has long, narrow buds in dusty pink or reddish shades and each bract tipped with fur. The leaves are narrow.

Protea repens (P. mellifera)

TRUE SUGARBUSH, WARE SUIKERBOS

This well-known, sticky Protea has pointed, hairless bracts in bright pink or red and there is a white variety. It drips nectar and the long narrow buds glisten. It blooms throughout winter. The leaves are narrow and the rounded bush grows to 3 metres. (Illustrated Plate 53).

Protea speciosa

BROWN-BEARDED PROTEA

Fairly rare in cultivation, this forms a bush of 1 metre and has rose pink, long flowers with overlapping bracts, each tipped with dark brown fur.

Protea susannae

This easily grown, 2-metre bush has 10-cm, rose-pink flowers in autumn, winter and spring. The 12-cm leaves have an unpleasant smell when cut but may be stripped for the vase. It grows in limestone soil in nature, and grows easily in gardens.

Prunus

Prunus (Rosaceae)

This very large genus includes Almonds, Cherries and Peaches as well as Plums. Apart from the orchard varieties that are grown for their fruit, the first three are cultivated for the beauty of their flowers, while the flowering Plums are grown mainly for their beautiful purple foliage. They are all deciduous trees that come from the temperate zones of the world and do very well in most parts of South Africa except in sub-tropical areas. They make a magnificent spring display. Unfortunately, the blooming period lasts only for three or four weeks and the foliage is rather ordinary during the summer, except for that of the Brown-leaved Plums, but they are well worth growing for the short glimpse of their exquisite blossoms.

They are hardy, grow easily and well, and require very little attention once they are established. They like an open, sunny position and a well-drained, light soil of a neutral or alkaline reaction. A mulch of well-rotted manure and, separately, an application of lime, is always beneficial. They should be watered at least once a week. They are grown as small trees and need no pruning, although the flowering sprays may be picked freely for the vase. The lower branches should not be removed higher than about 60 cm or the trunk may become sun-burned or scorched. The trees can be transplanted quite easily when a good size, in mid-winter. They are grown from cuttings which are grafted on to common stock, and named varieties should be bought from the nurseryman.

Prunus capuli

A small, tropical American tree of 8 metres, with light green, willow-like leaves, this is a useful small shade tree for a lawn. It is deciduous for a short period and grows moderately quickly. The flowers are insignificant, but it has drooping spikes of dark, cherry-like fruits, beloved by birds. It is hardy, fairly drought-resistant and grows from seed.

Prunus communis (Amygdalus communis)

This tree is grown for its well-known nuts and for the delicate tracery of its dainty, white blossom which appears before the leaves in the spring. The single blossoms are scattered all along the twigs, and the branches are beautiful in the vase. The light, fresh green leaves are smooth, oval and pointed, about 8 cm long, and cast a light shade. The tree grows very rapidly up to 5 or 7 metres in height, spreading across 5 metres, and bears almonds most profusely. These are formed in a pale-green, velvety case which splits open when the nut is ripe. The best form is *P. communis* var. *gracilis* which is the Soft or Paper-shell Almond, of which there are further varieties. It is always recommended that two trees be grown near one another for purposes of crosspollination. Closely matted or touching branches may be thinned out in winter. For the so-called double flowering Almonds see *Prunus glandulosa* and *P. triloba*.

Prunus cerasifera

BROWN-LEAVED PLUM OR CHERRY PLUM

These small, hardy trees have brownish-purple foliage that is excellent in the landscape throughout summer and autumn. They make magnificent back-grounds for perennials and bright annuals such as red Salvia. Their foliage is often picked for the vase and a small, dark-red plum often appears, which makes the branches even more valuable for picking. There are many varieties and hybrids which have different foliage and flowers. If the tree is wanted particularly for its blossom, it is best to buy it in bloom so that one may be sure of the type of flower obtained.

Prunus cerasifera var. *atropurpurea* (*Prunus cerasifera* var. *pissardii*)—This is one of the earliest flowering varieties of the Brown-leaved Plum, growing to 5 metres in height, with broadly spreading branches. It has broad, oval, purple-tinged leaves which drop quite late in the season. It has rich, pink, semi-double blossoms, which cover the tree in a cloud of bloom towards the end of winter or in spring. (Illustrated Plate 55).

There are several forms of this variety, some of which are listed as follows:

P. blireana—This hybrid has long, slender, spreading branches which grow up rapidly. It has very large, bronze-purple leaves, about 12 cm long, and single white flowers.

P. moseri var. *flore-pleno* is another hybrid with double pink flowers and bronze-purple leaves.

P. cerasifera var. *nigra*.—This is the best colour form of the Brown-leaved Plums. The leaves are a very dark purple, almost black, and have a rich, striking appearance. The tree is very compact and twiggy, growing fairly slowly into a well-rounded shape about 5 metres in height. The small, single flowers are very pale pink and daintily scattered along the thin twigs. They appear later than the flowers on the other Brown-leaved Plums and are not as floriferous.

Prunus glandulosa

FLOWERING ALMOND

A small, rounded, deciduous shrub of 1 to 2 metres, this is excellent in the shrub border, flowering in September and October. Although it is called Flowering Almond, and sometimes Flowering Plum, it belongs to the cherry group of *Prunus* and has richly double, tiny pompons of flowers similar to those of the Japanese Flowering Cherry. They are pink and white or pure white and wreathe the long straight stems from the base upwards. The leaves are narrow and pointed. This shrub suckers and may be multiplied by detaching stems at the root. It thrives in moist conditions and is hardy to frost. (Illustrated Plate 55).

It is often confused with *P. triloba*, which has similar, but larger, pink pompons of 4 cm across and grows to 3,5 metres in a tree-like shape, without suckering.

Prunus laurocerasus

CHERRY–LAUREL

A useful evergreen small tree of 5 metres, from Europe and Persia, this is grown for its shining, 15-cm, leathery foliage which makes a dense screen. It may be used for lawn shade. It has small spikes of white flowers in spring and the fruit is black. There are several leaf forms. It likes regular watering.

Do not confuse it with the Bay Laurel, *Laurus nobilis*, a tree of 10 metres with dark green, glossy, 10-cm, aromatic leaves, yellow flowers and black fruits. Laurel leaves were used to crown the heroes of ancient times.

Prunus mume

FLOWERING APRICOT

A small, deciduous, Chinese tree of 5 metres, this has semi-double, scented pink flowers in mid-winter. Pruning may be done after flowering if necessary, before the small narrow leaves appear in spring. There are also double white, single pink and white forms. It is referred to as "Plum" blossom (*ume*) in Japan and valued as the earliest blossom to appear in the new year.

Prunus pendula

WEEPING CHERRY, ROSEBUD CHERRY, SHIDARE–ZAKURA

Known as *Prunus subhirtella pendula* in England and America, this is a species from Japan, which is grown from seed and selected in the seedling stage for best shape and colour, as it does not always come true to form. They are also grown from cuttings. The best weeping forms are called *P. pendula* forma *pendula* and the more upright forms are known as forma *adscendens*. One variety *autumnalis* blooms in autumn, as well as at intervals in winter and spring.

Weeping Cherries form a cloud of rose-pink or pale pink, small blossoms, 2 cm across, on long drooping branches. They are usually single, but may also be semi-double. The tree is naturally tall, growing to 12 metres, but its long branches are often trained over an umbrella-like bamboo support in Japan, known as *shidare-zakura*. They are hardy and do best with cool winters and plenty of water, especially in late winter and spring. (Illustrated Plate 55).

Weeping Cherries do well in South Africa, but importation of new stock is strictly controlled because of the danger of introducing disease to the deciduous fruit industry.

Other early-flowering species of Cherries with single or semi-double blossoms are the Yoshino Cherry, *Prunus yedoensis*, and *Prunus sargentii*, which has larger, deep pink flowers and three horticultural forms. The leaves are reddish when young and rich red in autumn. (Also see *P. serrulata*).

Prunus persica var. flore-pleno

DOUBLE–FLOWERING PEACH

This is the most outstanding and showy tree of the whole genus. It has richly double flowers which are so thickly clustered together, right up against the branches of the tree, that they seem to wreathe the stems with pompons of blossom. The colours come in snow-white, rose-pink and cerise-red. Some trees have all three colours on the tree at the same time. This is known as a *chimera* and appears naturally. The leaves are like ordinary peach leaves, narrow, tapering and slightly curled. The tree grows fairly rapidly and reaches a height of 5 to 7 metres, with a well-rounded shape. There are also dwarf and weeping forms (Illustrated Plate 55).

Prunus serrulata

The flowers of the Japanese Flowering Cherries hang down in bunches in the same way as Cherries. Each flower is large, double and full, so that it is almost a ball. The pink and white, or pure white flowers come before the leaves or together with the first ones, and are very beautiful. They make great masses of bloom and are very profuse as the tree grows older. There are many named hybrids which have deep red, rose, white or green flowers. Some have 340 petals crowded into a ball, known as forma *sphaeranthe*. *Kanzan* is a popular hybrid which does well in this country. (Illustrated Plate 55).

There are many shapes and forms, ranging from tall, upright trees about 5 metres in height to more spreading, picturesque shapes and weeping forms. There are many wonderful named hybrids known as Lannesiana hybrids which are tall trees, about 10 metres in height. The large oval leaves of *P. serrulata* are from 10 to 15 cm long and 5 to 8 cm broad, with sharply toothed edges. They are green in summer and assume shades of red and yellow in autumn, especially during rainy weather. The tree is fairly slow-growing and needs plenty of moisture.

Pultenaea
(Leguminosae)

Pultenaea

AUSTRALIAN BUSH-PEA

Evergreen shrubs from Australia, these bloom in spring and early summer and usually have clusters of bright yellow pea-flowers. They require regular watering, but well-drained soil. Propagated by seed or cuttings.

P. daphnoides, with yellow flowers and broad, rounded leaves, grows to 2 metres and is possibly the best known.

P. foliolosa has tiny leaves, orange and red flowers and grows to 1 metre.

Punica
(Punicaceae)

Punica granatum

POMEGRANATE

This large shrub of about 4 metres comes from Southern Asia and is grown in the Mediterranean region. It is cultivated for its showy flowers and attractive fruits. The flowers are bright scarlet, very numerous and showy in the summer. The ruffled petals are arranged in the form of a half-open trumpet, about 5 cm long. The fruits are borne very freely and are large, hard-skinned globes, about 10 to 12 cm in diameter, containing hundreds of seeds covered with a juicy, crimson, edible pulp. They split open when ripe. The fruits turn scarlet in the autumn and are very decorative on the bush. They may be brought indoors and kept in a bowl for a long time.

The Pomegranate is deciduous and has shining, narrow-oval, green leaves about 5 to 8 cm long. The branches are twiggy and spiny and the shrub is sometimes grown and clipped as a hedge, but as it loses its leaves, should not be used on the boundary for privacy. Pomegranate is best grown as a single specimen and is extremely easy to grow. It is suited to all climates in South Africa, except the sub-tropical coast, and can withstand neglect, heat, drought and average frosts. It will thrive in well-drained soil and grows quickly. Its natural shape is bushy and rounded, but it can be well-shaped by pruning, which will also improve the size of the fruits. Five or six main stalks should be allowed to grow up from the base and all twiggy growth removed in winter to a height of about 1 metre, while the twiggy growth above that height should be thinned. This greatly improves the general appearance of the shrub and allows the branches which become heavily weighted with fruit to droop without trailing on the ground. Propagation is by seed, cuttings or layers.

There are also double-flowered varieties of Pomegranate (*P. granatum* var. *florepleno*) which are grown only for ornament and have scarlet or yellow flowers, and there is one particularly attractive variety (*P. granatum* var. *legrellei*) which is striped in vermilion and cream. *P. granatum* var. *nana* is a dwarf variety with tiny red flowers and ornamental fruits, which may be used in the rockery or as a tub-plant. (Illustrated Plate 54).

Pyracantha (Rosacea)

Pyracantha

FIRETHORN

Both the Red Firethorn (*P. coccinea*) and the Orange Firethorn (*P. angustifolia*) come from Asia and are extremely popular. They are hardy and can stand any climate from inland to the coast. They are easy to grow and spectacular in berry. *P. coccinea* var. *lalandi* is outstanding with its profuse and early orange-yellow berries, appearing in February.

Their white flowers appear in spring and their brilliant berries in the autumn. The red berries usually appear earlier than the orange. The berries are about 1 cm in diameter and cluster all over the branches. Both colours are extremely valuable for cutting for the vase and will last for at least a week. The orange berries are much brighter in their effect than the red, but the red is more graceful in its habit. The orange berries are much more vigorous and fast-growing than the red, reaching a height of almost 2 metres in 2 years. They both grow to a height of 4 to 5 metres.

Both the red and orange Firethorn are popular as hedges, both trimmed and untrimmed, on account of their strong growth, but the berries are lost on well-clipped hedges. The leaves are small and narrow. Those of the red Firethorn are dark-green and glossy, while those of the orange species are a duller green above and felted with white underneath. To obtain the best sprays of berries, the Firethorn should be grown as an individual untrimmed specimen, and the berries can be picked freely without fear of a set-back. The Firethorn grows easily from seed and seeds itself when the surrounding soil is damp enough. The roots grow rapidly, like Sweetpea roots, and the seedlings should therefore be transplanted only when 5 to 8 cm high, unless they are transplanted from tins. They are very strong, however, and will grow rapidly from small size. The soil should be trenched deeply for best results. (Illustrated Plate 56).

Pyrostegia (Bignoniaceae)

Pyrostegia ignea (Bignonia venusta)

GOLDEN SHOWER, FLAME VINE

This is one of the most popular of evergreen climbers, being very conspicuous and flowering for a long period in summer and at intervals throughout autumn and winter. It comes from Brazil, grows vigorously and will cover a large area. The flowers are a bright orange colour and hang in thick festoons all along the stems. Each flower is tube-like and has pointed petals that curl right back to reveal the stamens. It is called Cracker Vine in Hong Kong, referring to its explosion of colour, like fire-crackers. The smooth green leaves are oval, tapering in shape and make a thick screen. It is effective drooping from the height of a pergola and may be used as a ground cover on a sloping bank or a large rocky outcrop.

This climber does best on a warm, north-facing wall where it receives full sun. It is hardy to all but severe frosts. It grows most luxuriantly in moist soil, but, once established, seems to be able to withstand a drought, especially during winter. It is reproduced by cuttings. (Illustrated Plate 56).

Quercus (Fagaceae)

Quercus palustris

PIN OAK

This tall, deciduous tree comes from North America, and is grown for the beautiful autumn colouring of its attractive leaves as well as for shade. The long, distinctive, 15-cm leaves are deeply scooped out along the sides, so that they have many irregular points. They are a shiny, light-green all summer and turn a magnificent red before they fall, especially when there are autumn rains. Some trees turn a brownish-copper colour and they are all most attractive. There is no doubt that the leaf-colour is intensified when the tree is well-watered and has good, deep soil. The specific name of this tree means "of the marsh" in Latin, and this gives an indication of the fact that the tree likes moist, rich soil. It is a good idea to plant bulbs and other shade-loving plants beneath the tree so that it will benefit from the constant watering.

The Pin Oak is fast-growing when young and forms a shapely, symmetrical, pyramidal tree that grows up to about 30 metres in height or more. It has an erect trunk and horizontal branches that spread at least 20 metres across. The Pin Oak has fibrous roots and large specimens are transplanted quite easily. If one wishes to use this as a shade tree, the lower branches should be removed from time to time, to a height of at least 4 metres from the ground, as the branches sweep out and downwards, like an umbrella. This tree is hardy to frost and grows easily. It is not very happy in sub-tropical conditions. It is a useful landscape tree for a large garden and one of the loveliest of trees which are grown for their autumn foliage.

Some Pin Oaks have an idiosyncracy in that they retain their brown leaves all through winter, especially in warmer positions. This can be noticed when the trees are in their young stages in the nursery. Such specimens should not be planted near buildings where their copious falling leaves could be a nuisance or where one requires winter sunshine.

There are several other Oaks which have beautiful, red, autumn foliage such as *Quercus nigra*, the Water Oak.

Quisqualis (Combretaceae)

Quisqualis indica

RANGOON CREEPER

This evergreen, rambling shrub comes from Malaya. It has long, elegant, thin branches, richly clothed with soft, oval green leaves. The flowers hang down in clusters, like bunches of cherries at the ends of thin, tube-like calyces. They have 5 flat petals and are a dark crimson, some fading to pale-pink and white. They appear in profusion in summer and autumn and last well in the vase.

This shrub grows about 2 metres in height and spreads about 2 to 2,5 metres in diameter. It is useful for placing at the top of a terrace or bank, and is excellent at the top of a flight of steps. The Rangoon Creeper is very tender to frost and grows in sub-tropical areas. It needs a light soil well mixed with compost and a sunny position. Cut back the flowering stems severely after flowering in order to keep the plant within bounds. It grows rampantly in Durban. It may be propagated by cuttings and suckers freely.

Raphiolepis
(Rosaceae)

Raphiolepis

INDIAN HAWTHORN, YEDDO HAWTHORN

Evergreen shrubs with dense, dark green leathery foliage, these have sprays of pretty blossoms, like hawthorn, in late winter, spring or early summer, depending on the climate. All species like good, rich soil with plenty of water, disliking hot dry winds when flowering. They thrive in sunny situations at the coast, but prefer partial shade inland, while the Yeddo Hawthorn is particularly useful for a shady south wall in cold areas, as it is extremely hardy. They are slow-growing at first, but generally reach full size in about 5 years. Propagation is by seed, cuttings or layers. The four kinds that are available for gardens may be distinguished from one another by their leaves, although a certain amount of variation on some bushes makes this confusing.

Raphiolepis delacouri

PINK INDIAN HAWTHORN

A compact shrub of 2 metres, this has sprays of pretty pink flowers followed by blue-black berries. It is a hybrid between *R. indica* and *R. umbellata* and does not come true from seed so that it should be increased by cuttings or layers. The leaves are variable and combine the characteristics of both parents, being either pointed or broad at the tips and toothed along the margins.

Raphiolepis indica

INDIAN HAWTHORN

A well-known evergreen of 1,5 metres, from S. China, this has sprays of small, slightly fragrant flowers, about 2 cm across, with 5 pointed petals. They vary in colour, being pinkish or white, flushed or tipped with pink. The pea-sized fruits are bluish-black. The slender-oval leaves are pointed at the tip and taper to the base, with toothed margins. This species does best in areas with mild winters where it is sheltered from severe frost.

Raphiolepis umbellata

YEDDO HAWTHORN

Taller than the other kinds, this hardy Japanese and Korean species grows to 3 metres and forms a rounded evergreen that is laden with full sprays of large, pure white flowers with rounded petals and reddish-pink stamens. The leathery leaves are broad and oval, very slightly toothed on the edges and generally wider and rounded at the ends, tapering to the base, but they are variable and some are pointed. (Illustrated Plate 57).

The variety *ovata* has extremely broad, leathery leaves, almost rounded at the ends and the margins are smooth and thickened. This variety is grown frequently.

Reinwardtia
(Linacea)

Reinwardtia indica *(Linum trigynum)*

This showy, low-growing evergreen shrub comes from India and grows to a height of up to 1 metre. It belongs to the Flax family. It has pretty, open flowers, about 4 to 5 cm across, with 5 brilliant-yellow, rounded, overlapping petals. The buds grow in clusters at the ends of the twiggy, green stems, and open a few at a time throughout winter and early spring. The small, fresh-green leaves are smooth, narrow and oval.

This is a most cheerful little shrub, brightening the winter garden. It is tender to frost, although it will flower throughout the average Johannesburg winter if it is given some protection facing north or west. It is excellent for a warm corner in the rockery. It can also be grown in tubs or in pots or in the greenhouse. It must have winter sunshine in order to flower well, and requires a light soil well-mixed with compost as well as adequate watering. It is propagated by cuttings taken from the base, like suckers. (Illustrated Plate 57).

Rhigozum
(Bignoniaceae)

Rhigozum obovatum

A drought-resistant, slender, evergreen shrub of 3 metres, this is useful in dry areas with little rainfall and is native to the Karoo. It has showy, yellow, 4-cm-long Bignonia-like flowers in spring and tiny leaves on twiggy branches. Given very well-drained soil in a sunny rockery, it will grow in the summer rainfall area and is hardy to cold. It grows easily from seed sown in autumn. (Illustrated Plate 57).

Rhododendron
(Ericaceae)

Rhododendron *(Azalea)*

Azalea was previously kept as a distinct genus from Rhododendron by botanists, but this name has now been "sunk", so that all kinds are now classed under *Rhododendron*, Gardeners who are reluctant to change should regard AZALEA only as a common name. It will probably be found less confusing and simpler to refer to all kinds as *Rhododendron*, for this is a huge genus of about 500 wild species, with innumerable hybrids and varieties of these, so that even an expert has difficulty in distinguishing between them.

The three main groups that are grown in this country are described below, and, as there has been confusion about their names and characteristics, a few name changes have been noted. Rhododendrons originate mainly from Asia, with a few species found in North America. None occur wild in Africa or South America and very few in Europe, although they are grown in gardens throughout the world.

Rhododendrons are, without exception, the showiest of spring-flowering shrubs, while some remain in bloom for many months of the year. Their large and brightly coloured flowers almost cover the foliage, so that they make a vivid splash of colour from a distance or in a dark corner. They last well in the vase if the gardener can bear to break off their loveliness and pick them, with buds opening for weeks. The colours range from white, through pink, salmon and red to magenta and there is a race of yellow and orange-flowered kinds. There are both single and double forms of the flowers, the doubles sometimes being referred to as "hose in hose", while many are often beautifully streaked and marked with contrasting colours or deeper shades. Rhododendrons may be evergreen or deciduous and, while the evergreen types are most valuable in the landscape, the unusual colours of the deciduous types make them desirable.

Rhododendrons grow easily in moist or humid areas if the soil is of an acid nature, well-drained and peaty in texture. Unless they have very definite requirements they will not thrive and may even die. They have fine, fibrous surface roots and for this reason require light, loamy soil that will not dry out rapidly and will afford the delicate rootlets easy passage and growth. Do not plant them in competition with trees like Elms that have greedy surface roots. The hole which must be dug need not be very deep—about 50 cm—but should be at least 60 cm in diameter, as the roots spread and remain in the top soil. Drainage is extremely important and the hole should be filled with compost or peat mixed with good, light garden soil. A built-up bank on a foundation of rubble is excellent. Manure should not be used unless it is very well-rotted. Again, because these shrubs have fibrous surface roots, one should never dig or cultivate around them as they may die if the roots are disturbed and broken. Remove weeds by hand and keep the plants thickly mulched with compost, peat or pine-needles. This will help to retain moisture and keep the roots cool.

One of the most important requirements for Rhododendrons is that they need an acid soil. They will not thrive or flower in soil that contains any lime. Even well-established plants that are bought in flower will cease to bloom if brought into contact with lime and will die unless conditions are changed. Many things may be done to maintain the acidity of the soil (see chapter II). An occasional application of sulphate of iron or aluminium sulphate is beneficial. If it proves difficult to grow Rhododendrons in one's garden, try growing them in containers where one can control conditions more easily.

It is important to choose a suitable position. They like moist conditions and must be sheltered from the wind, especially when it is hot and dry. They do very well in shady spots, although they prefer to receive sunshine for part of the day. Filtered sunlight near deep-rooting trees like conifers is ideal and they do well under *Liriodendron* or *Liquidamber* in humid areas. They will thrive in full sunlight only in coastal areas or where humidity is high. They are hardy to frost in this country, but dislike cold winds and must be sheltered from wind by trees that will also provide shade. Shade is essential in warm, dry areas, where one must pay great attention to watering. The flowers will droop on the bush unless shaded, especially at midday. Spray the foliage with water to prevent wilting on a hot, dry day.

Pruning is not necessary, but the bushes will benefit from being freely picked or lightly sheared immediately after flowering in order to prevent seed-production. Do not prune after mid-summer or the following year's bloom will be sacrificed. Rhododendrons may be transplanted easily since they are shallow-rooted. Keep the ball of soil intact around the roots when moving the plants. Transplanting should be done on a rainy day during early summer or autumn.

Cuttings of the smaller-leaved hybrids will strike easily in moist climates and all species may be grown from seed, but both methods of propagation are too slow for the average gardener. Spreading plants may form new roots or may be layered, but this is also a slow method of propagation. One should buy established plants in containers from a nursery, preferably when in bloom so that one can make one's choice. They may be transplanted into the garden while in flower if handled carefully or immediately after flowering is over. Few pests attack

Rhododendrons that grow in good conditions, but Red Spider is sometimes troublesome and must be controlled. (See Illustrations, Plates 57 and 58).

I. EVERGREEN RHODODENDRONS (AZALEAS)

(i) *Large-leaved Rhododendrons*, which may grow into enormous bushes or small trees of about 5 metres, are not grown commonly in southern Africa, but do well in cool coastal or mountain areas with plenty of moisture. They generally have large clusters of bell-like flowers in many shades of rose, red, pink or white, backed by large, oval leathery leaves. One of the best-known hybrids is "Pink Pearl". Those with red flowers are generally derived from the Himalayan *R. arboreum*. (Illustrated Plate 58).

(ii) *R. simsii*

INDIAN OR EVERGREEN AZALEA

These showy evergreen shrubs grow up to 2 metres or more in height where conditions are favourable, such as in moist areas in the mountains or near the coast. They are the most popular kinds that are grown in this country, but have been erroneously known in the trade for many years as Indian Azaleas, under the name of *Azalea indica* or *R. indicum*. The correct name has now been established as *R. simsii* and the flowers may be recognised by the fact that they have from 8 to 10 stamens, as stated in the Royal Horticultural Society's Dictionary of Gardening. The name *R. indicum* is a correct one, but it refers to the hardy Japanese SATZUKI AZALEA which has only 5 stamens and mainly pink, salmon or white flowers, both single, double and variegated. This flowers in spring and is the species that most easily tolerates hard clipping.

R. simsii comes from China and is a little more tender than *R. indicum*, but tolerates the cold weather of Southern Africa, as well as the warm sub-tropical weather of coastal Natal. It has hairy shoots and much longer leaves, from 3–7 cm in length, than those of *R. indicum*, which grow only to 2 or 3 cm. The leaves of *R. simsii* are bristly on both sides. The flowers range in colour from pink and white to red and magenta, with variations. Those with white or magenta flowers grow taller than the pink or crimson shades and should be placed in the background. They often start blooming during winter in warm areas, but the chief flowering period is early spring. (Illustrated Plate 58).

(iii) *R. obtusum*

KURUME AZALEA, KIRISHIMA

This compact, evergreen species is most frequently cultivated for selling in pots and withstands hard pruning. It grows to about 1 metre in height and is the parent of many horticultural forms including most of the "KURUME AZALEAS". The small funnel-shaped flowers are about 3 cm across at the mouth and have 5 stamens. They bloom in spring and come in many colours from red, scarlet and crimson to salmon, pink, magenta and white (var. *album*). The small oval leaves are shining and glossy on the top surface, growing to 3 cm in length.

Hundreds of varieties have been raised in Japan, where the species grows wild, and the best known include var. *amoena* (*Hatsu-giri*) which is taller, growing to 1,5 metres, with rosy-purple flowers, and var. *kaempferi*, which is often semi-deciduous and grows even taller, with purplish-rose to rose-scarlet flowers. (Illustrated Plate 58).

II. *DECIDUOUS RHODODENDRONS (AZALEAS)*

(i) *R. japonicum (Azalea mollis)*

JAPANESE AZALEA

This beautiful dediduous species from Japan has been grown under the name of *Azalea mollis* for many years. It is the parent of many beautiful garden hybrids that have orange, salmon, rose or red flowers, each with 5 stamens. They bloom in large clusters on bare stems shortly before the fresh green new leaves that are smooth beneath and may be as long as 10 cm.

The shrubs grow from 1 to 2 metres in height, needing plenty of water and light, peaty soil in order to thrive. Thick mulches of pine-needles or compost will prevent the soil from drying out. They are very hardy and will thrive on the cold south wall of the house. (Illustrated Plate 57).

(ii) *R. molle (R. sinense)*

CHINESE AZALEA

This species has been very much confused in the past with *R. japonicum*, which is similar in its deciduous habit and size. It may be recognised by the colour of its flowers, which are in all variations of golden-yellow. They bloom in large clusters and each flower has 5 stamens that are shorter than the corona. Another distinguishing feature is to be seen on the leaves, which are soft and downy underneath, unlike those of *R. japonicum* which are smooth. *R. molle* grows wild in China and blends well in the garden in combination with *R. japonicum*. (Illustrated Plate 57)

Rhus (Anacardiaceae)

Rhus

SUMAC

This group of small trees or large shrubs, many of which are deciduous, assume brilliant autumn colours and are grown for their decorative foliage. These are usually hardy to frost and grow easily on ordinary soil. Unfortunately, some are poisonous. *R. toxicodendron* is the notorious Poison Ivy which is such a menace in America and should never be planted. Others are harmless, but have suckering habits which make them a nuisance in the garden. These suckers may be removed and growth may be thinned in the spring. Large specimens may be pruned back severely in late spring, if desired. These are many native species which are not poisonous. *Rhus erosa*, Besembos, is an upright shrub with narrow, scalloped leaves which remain evergreen. It comes from Lesotho and the Karoo. The Smoke-Bush, *Rhus cotinus*, is now *Cotinus coggygria*.

Rhus copallina

SHINING SUMAC

This large, American shrub grows from about 3 to 7 metres. It has compound leaves divided into narrow, shining leaflets that are hairy beneath. They are green in summer but deep crimson in autumn, falling rather early. This species suckers but is not poisonous.

Rhus glabra

SMOOTH SUMAC

This 5-metre American shrub has smooth leaves and branches. The large, compound leaves are divided into large, oval, tapering leaflets, about 8 to 12 cm long, with serrated edges. These turn the most magnificent, rainbow autumn colours, having crimson, yellow, orange, bronze and green on the leaves at the same time in early winter. This shrub is not poisonous and is spread by suckers. It is slightly tender to frost and grows well in hot climates—either dry or humid. It likes an open sunny position. It may be trained with a single main stem and has a graceful shape with spreading branches. It will grow in Durban as well as on the highveld.

Rhus succedanea

WAX TREE

This is probably the most beautiful of the Sumacs. It comes from Japan and China, and candles are made from the wax of its fruit in Japan. It has compound leaves about 20 cm long, which are divided into smooth, narrow leaflets from 5 to 10 cm in length. They arch gracefully on the branches and turn a most brilliant red in early winter. The tree is extremely graceful, with a short standard and spreading branches. (Illustrated Plate 59).

Rhus typhina

STAGHORN SUMAC

The large American shrub grows to about 7 metres. It has very hairy stems and branches. The long compound leaves measure up to 60 cm in length and are divided into numerous, tapering leaflets each up to 12 cm in length. They turn a brilliant red in the autumn, falling quite early. This shrub is not poisonous but suckers very freely from the base to form a thicket. If it is trained in the form of a tree it will be short-lived. This shrub is only suitable for a spacious corner of a large garden where its suckering will not be a nuisance. It grows very easily on the driest of soils.

Ricinus (Euphorbiaceae)

Ricinus communis

CASTORBEAN, CASTOR OIL PLANT

This showy, tropical shrub is believed to have come originally from Africa, but has naturalized itself in many parts of the world. In cultivation it grows to about 3 metres or more in height, with a spreading habit. It is ornamental where its exotic appearance is desired, and usually looks best against the background of a wall or hedge. It does well on a hot west wall. The large, decorative shiny leaves have 8 or 9 long points radiating from the centre and are attached by thick, fleshy red stems to the coloured main branches. The flowers are insignificant but the fruits are ornamental on the bush and in the vase. They are soft, red burrs which are clustered at the ends of stiff, upstanding stems. They harden and turn brown with age and contain beautiful mottled seeds from which Castor Oil is extracted. Unfortunately, these are very poisonous but the burrs may be removed before the seeds are formed if desired.

The ordinary Castorbean is decorative in the young stage when its leaves are reddish-brown, but the leaves turn greener with age. There are several variations, but the mahogany-coloured variety *purpureus* should be grown whenever possible. This Mahogany Castorbean retains its purple-red shiny foliage always and forms a daintier bush. It comes true from seed and is decorative even as a seedling.

The Castor Oil plant is evergreen in warm, frost-free areas but is killed by severe frost. It seeds itself so profusely in moist soil, however, that there are always new ones to spring up and grow rapidly to full height in a season. It may be treated as an annual. It likes a warm, sunny position and ordinary, well-drained soil, and should be planted facing north or west in cold areas. It will withstand drought in warm localities as well as brack soil. It may be used as a windbreak. (Illustrated Plate 56).

Robinia (Leguminosae)

Robinia hispida

ROSE–ACACIA OR LOCUST TREE

This is an attractive little deciduous shrub from North America, growing about 1 to 2 metres in height. The flowers, which appear in profusion in the spring together with the new leaves, are like large, pinkish-mauve sweetpeas and hang in full clusters like bunches of grapes amongst the branches. The stems of this shrub are covered with fine, reddish-brown hairs. The compound leaves are divided into smooth, oval leaflets, about 5 cm long.

This shrub is usually grafted on to a standard of *Robinia pseudacacia* and makes an attractive, formal subject like a large, standard rose-bush. Unfortunately the stock has bad habits of throwing up thorny suckers, and these should be carefully noticed and pulled up while small. Rose-Acacia is extremely hardy to frost and easy to grow. It likes an open, sunny position. It will do well in poor, dry, sandy soil and can be transplanted easily. It grows rapidly while young and needs no pruning. For best effect, when buying the grafted shrub, buy one with a standard of at least 1 metre.

R. kelseyi is a similar shrub with smooth branches.

Robinia pseudacacia

FALSE–ACACIA OR BLACK LOCUST

This tall, North American, deciduous tree grows to a height of about 13 metres or more. It has a black, irregular trunk and prickly branches. In spring it bears long sprays of white, pea-shaped flowers which hang down like Laburnum. The light-green, compound leaves are divided into oval leaflets. Although this tree has a certain woodland attraction, it should not be planted in cultivated gardens as it suckers freely and becomes a great nuisance difficult to eradicate. It is suited to parts of the country with hot, dry climates and poor sandy soil with very little rainfall, where it is difficult to grow less tolerant, flowering trees that will give shade.

Romneya (Papaveraceae)

Romneya coulteri

TREE–POPPY

This is really a sub-shrub which comes from California and Mexico. It is also called Matilija Poppy as it grows abundantly in the region of the Matilija Canyon in California. The flowers are stately and beautiful and bloom in spring and early summer. They are like huge Poppies, 15-cm across and pure white in colour. They have large centres of golden stamens and the petals are crinkled and papery like those of an Iceland Poppy. The flowers are borne in sprigs at the ends of the branches, opening one at a time, and make delightful picking for the vase. The shrub grows into a rounded, many-stemmed bush about 2 metres in height. The stalks are pale green and soft-wooded. The leaves are a smooth, pale, greyish-green and are daintily and irregularly cut.

The Tree-Poppy is grown very easily. It is difficult to transplant the whole bush, but suckers are produced freely and may be detached easily as they appear. The stems of the suckers should be cut back and the new bush grows up rapidly. On account of this suckering habit the Tree-Poppy should be grown in a roomy corner of a large garden where its spreading habits will not be a disadvantage. It is hardy to our average frosts and likes an open, sunny position. It will also grow in semi-shade and on any soil. It likes a rocky soil and will survive without water except that of the rainfall—either summer or winter. The Tree-Poppy may be cut down to the ground each winter if desired and is deciduous for a very short period.

Rondeletia (Rubiaceae)

Rondeletia

RONDELETIA

Tropical American, evergreen shrubs, these are grown in greenhouses in cold countries, but will grow out-of-doors in full sun in warm, frost-free, humid areas like the northern Transvaal and on the east coast. They could be grown in tubs on a sheltered varandah in cold areas. The small flowers are grouped in dense 15-cm heads at the ends of the branches and the leaves are oval and thick. Rondeletias like good soil, regular watering and may be grown from cuttings of half-ripened wood. *R. amoena* has soft rose-pink, yellow-throated flowers in spring, which have an old-fashioned air. It grows fairly slowly to 2 metres (Illustrated Plate 59).

Rondeletia odorata (*R. speciosa*) has orange-red, yellow-throated flowers and grows to 2 metres.

Rosmarinus (Labiatae)

Rosmarinus officinalis

ROSEMARY

This low-growing neat shrub comes from the Mediterranean region and grows about a metre in height. It is an old-fashioned favourite with sentimental associations such as "Rosemary for remembrance." It has many erect stems growing up from the base which are covered with small, narrow, deep-green leaves with rolled-back edges. They are strongly aromatic and are used as a herb. Oil of Rosemary is extracted from them. The small Salvia-like flowers are pale, lavender-blue with mauve markings, and grow between the leaves at the tips of the stems in spring and late summer.

Rosemary makes a useful, evergreen, low garden hedge or single specimen. It likes a well-drained, light soil and is hardy to frost. It will grow almost anywhere in South Africa, liking a neutral soil. It likes a sunny position but will grow in semi-shade. It may be trimmed each year if necessary and, if it grows too old and woody, may be cut back severely. Short cuttings, taken from the tips of the shoots in spring, grow easily and rapidly. The prostrate Rosemary, variety *prostratus*, is charming for overhanging a low wall. (Illustrated Plate 59).

Rothmannia (Rubiaceae)

Rothmannia (Gardenia)

ROTHMANNIA

Formerly grouped under *Gardenia*, these South African shrubs have been reclassified. They have cup-shaped flowers that are white and sweetly scented. Both are in cultivation.

Rothmannia capensis

An evergreen shrub that grows to 3 metres, this is covered with masses of creamy, scented flowers in mid-summer. They appear at intervals during the year if conditions are good. Each cup-shaped flower opens into 5 lobes. It is about 4 cm across and may have maroon spots in the throat. The glossy oval leaves are about 10 cm long. It grows wild in the Cape, Natal and the Transvaal.

This drought-resistant species thrives in a warm, sunny position with moisture during summer, tolerating dryness in winter. It grows from cuttings or seed. (Illustrated Plate 59).

Rothmannia globosa, SEPTEMBER BELLS, also has sweetly scented bell-shaped flowers in early spring and summer. The creamy flowers are felted with brown and there are faint pink lines along the 5 lobes. This needs a warmer climate than *R. capensis*, disliking frost. It grows wild in Natal and the eastern Cape.

Ruscus (Liliaceae)

Ruscus aculeatus

BUTCHER'S BROOM

A 60-cm, spreading, evergreen, European shrub, this is interesting as its stiff branches were said to be used for sweeping butcher's blocks. The female bushes bear small white flowers and red berries at the centre of the flattened stems, which resemble pointed leaves, along the branches. These are not showy but useful evergreens for growing in shade under trees. It is grown from seed, but females are best increased by division.

Ruspolia (Acanthaceae)

Ruspolia

RUSPOLIA

Small evergreen sub-shrubs, these were previously called *Pseuderanthemum* and are closely related to *Eranthemum*. The long-tubed, small, 5-petalled flowers are clustered at the tips of the stems, appearing during summer. The oval wrinkled leaves, narrowed at both ends, curve downwards. *R. seticalyx* grows to 60 cm, has deep salmon or brick-red flowers and grows wild in Southern Rhodesia and East Africa. *R. hypocraterifolius* grows almost to 2 metres and has scarlet flowers. It grows wild in Rhodesia and the Transvaal in the Soutpansberg area.

Ruspolia will grow in light loamy soil and needs moisture, especially during summer. It will need some protection from frost in cold areas and could be grown near a tree which provides morning shade. It grows easily from seed or cuttings.

Russelia (Scrophulariaceae)

Russelia equisetiformis (R. juncea)

RUSSELIA OR CORAL-BELL BUSH

This low-growing shrub from tropical America reaches a height of 1 metre and over. It has dainty, grass-like foliage and stems of a bright, lime-green colour that contrast effectively with the coral-coloured flowers. Each tube-like flower is about 3 cm long and opens at the tip into tiny, rounded petals. The flowers are borne on short stalks which grow up the thick, reedy main stems. The leaves are small, soft and insignificant. The whole appearance is very similar to that of the hardy border perennial commonly known as Coral Bells (*Penstemon barbatus*).

Russelia blooms almost perpetually and is very easy to grow, but is tender to frost. It grows in hot, frost-free and sub-tropical climates and will stand neglect and drought. It withstands the sea-air and wind and has been planted right on the sea-front in Durban. It is propagated by cuttings. (Illustrated Plate 59).

Russelia sarmentosa is another tender shrub, which has ordinary, rounded, darker green leaves and more thickly clustered flowers. Although the flowers are a brighter scarlet, they are half the size of the others and the shrub does not have such a bright effect.

Ruttya (*Acanthaceae*)

Ruttya fruticosa

RUTTYA, JAMMY-MOUTH

A 2-metre evergreen shrub from Kenya and Tanzania, this has arresting, 2-lipped, scarlet or brick-red flowers, marked with a conspicuous black patch at the throat in late summer and autumn. There is also a yellow colour form. This grows at high elevations in nature, up to 2000 metres, and can be grown in most parts of South Africa. Shelter from morning sun is advisable in cold areas. It needs good soil and plenty of moisture, especially during summer. It grows from seed and cuttings. Several other species are known, including one white-flowered species (*R. ovata*) which occurs on the east coast of South Africa, Mozambique and into Rhodesia. *Ruttya* belongs to the Acanthus family. (Illustrated Plate 60).

Salix (*Salicaceae*)

Salix

WILLOW

There are several small ornamental Willows which are worth growing, although the large Weeping Willow (*S. babylonica*) is not recommended for the average garden because of its invasive roots in their search for water. No Willow species should be planted near the walls of the house, but they will thrive in any garden which is watered regularly, especially during summer. Being deciduous, they can resist drought during winter. The botanical name is derived from the Celtic, meaning "near water" and this is where they thrive. Ideal for places with wet soil, they may be planted near a tap so that they benefit from the drips when the tap is used. They all grow easily from cuttings, growing roots in water in about 3 weeks. They are hardy and not suited to sub-tropical conditions.

Salix babylonica var. annularis.

CORKSCREW OR
RAMSHORN WILLOW

This is a slow-growing slender tree with graceful drooping branches covered with curled and twisted leaves that have a delicate appearance. It comes from China.

Salix bonplandiana var. fastigiata

MEXICAN WILLOW

An interesting tree because it is tall and slender, yet with a bamboo-like appearance, this is useful for the waterside or where an columnar accent is needed. This is the Willow made famous in the "floating gardens" of Mexico and it must be reproduced from cuttings. It is known as Xochimilco Willow in Mexico, where it grows wild.

Salix caprea

GOAT OR PUSSY WILLOW

This attractive, hardy deciduous tree comes from Europe and grows to a height of about 7 metres. It is valued for its ornamental catkins which form during the year and burst open in early spring, revealing the silky grey hairs which give it its name. Later these open up and are covered with powdery yellow pollen. The branches are popular for flower arranging and can be curved, by soaking in water. If the branches are cut as the catkins begin to open in the spring, they will continue to grow and open up in the vase, even producing their leaves. They will also grow roots after 2 or 3 weeks and this is the time to hand out cuttings to your friends to be planted right into the ground.

The Pussy Willow will grow in partial shade, but prefers an open sunny position. The effect of the sun shining on the silvery catkins is dazzling, and these also show up best if there is a dark green background. As these appear mainly at the top of the tree, keep it at a height of about 3 metres by pruning back long growths annually in spring.

The tree grows from a thick trunk and forms a compact shape as its branches all grow upwards at a light angle. It grows rapidly, reaching a height of 5 metres in 4 years and has a spread of over 2 metres at its widest parts. The leaves are a pretty, fresh green, oval in shape and ruffled at the edges. They are hairy and greyish-green on the underside. The roots are penetrating and the tree should not be planted nearer to the house than 7 metres. It is not suited to sub-tropical conditions.

Salix gracistyla

DWARF PUSSY WILLOW

A shrub from Japan and Korea that grows to 2 metres, this has large silvery catkins in spring before the leaves appear. These are greyish-green and silky, with numerous veins, and the shoots are downy. The Japanese prune this shrub annually so that it is cushion-like and one can look down on a ground-cover of catkins. It is attractive in association with large rocks at the side of a pool.

Sambucus (Caprifoliaceae)

Sambucus nigra var. aurea

GOLDEN ELDER

This is a variety of the European Elder which comes from the temperate zone of Europe. It is a large, deciduous shrub or small tree that grows about 4 to 5 metres in height. It has an irregular, picturesque habit of growth, and is grown for the colour of its foliage which remains golden yellow throughout the year until it falls in the winter. It is excellent against a background of dark trees such as the Brown-leaved Plum. The compound leaves have five or seven leaflets, which are each fully 10 cm long, oval and pointed. They are sometimes veined with green and some of the leaves revert to green. The branches droop downwards and the leaves cascade most gracefully. The Golder Elder has flat-headed sprays of tiny white flowers in summer followed by small black berries from which Elderberry wine is made in England. *S. nigra* var. *albo-variegata* has leaves which are variegated with white, and there are several other horticultural varieties.

The Golden Elder likes a rich, moist soil. It is hardy to frost and easily grown. It should be pruned back in spring to within two inches of the old wood, in order to encourage new, vigorous, non-flowering growth. It is propagated by seed or by cuttings. (Illustrated Plate 60).

Sanchezia (Acanthaceae)

Sanchezia nobilis var. glaucophylla

SANCHEZIA

A 2-metre, tropical evergreen shrub from Ecuador, with foot-long, narrow, bluish-green leaves, veined with yellow or white, this has 5-cm, narrow, yellow flowers, each with a red bract, arranged in spikes. Croton-like in appearance, it is suited to sub-tropical, humid climates and may be treated like *Codiaeum*. It is grown from cuttings. It should not be confused with *Aphelandra squarrosa* var. *louisae*, which has similar veined foliage, but different flowers. (Illustrated Plate 60).

Santolina (Compositae)

Santolina chamaecyparissus

LAVENDER-COTTON

A useful, low, silvery-grey shrublet for the mixed border, this has tiny heath-like leaves, crowded all over the bush. It grows to 60 cm and has bright golden-yellow button-like flowers, 2 cm across, in early or mid-summer. It comes from the Mediterranean area and is drought-resistant and easy to grow. It will grow from seed or cuttings. It needs replacing from time to time.

Schinus (Anacardiaceae)

Schinus terebinthifolius

BRAZILIAN PEPPER TREE

A small, spreading evergreen tree growing to 6 metres, this is laden with bunches of bright red berries in autumn, brightening the dark green foliage, which is divided into broad leaflets. This tree thrives in warm areas, disliking frost, and grows easily from seed.

It is more popular in gardens that the drought-resistant hardy PEPPER TREE from Peru (*S. molle*) that has been so overplanted in dry areas and generally neglected. This has drooping sprays of small rose-coloured berries.

Schizolobium (Leguminosae)

Schizolobium parahybum (S. excelsum)

TOWER TREE

An interesting Brazilian tree which is especially striking while young, with its slim green stem and "feather-duster" tuft of long, fern-like leaves, arranged palm-like at the top, this grows very rapidly into a tall tree. It flowers in early summer, when the old leaves fall for a short period, and has erect sprays of 5-petalled, bright yellow flowers with rounded petals that taper to a thin claw at the centre, similar to *Delonix*. This tree likes a moist sub-tropical climate, but is drought-resistant during winter. It will grow at altitudes of 1800 metres but needs a warm sheltered position. It grows from seed. (Illustrated Plate 60).

Schotia (Leguminosae)

Schotia brachypetala

TREE FUCHSIA,
WEEPING BOERBOON, HUILBOERBOON

Seen as a small tree in gardens, this grows from 10 to 13 metres in the warmer parts of the Transvaal and Natal, where it grows wild. Drooping clusters of deep crimson flowers spring from the bare old wood in October, for the leaves usually drop shortly before flowering. The compound leaves have glossy rounded leaflets. *Schotia* requires a warm sunny position with shelter from frost and will resist winter drought. Although it will withstand some frost when mature, it will not flower successfully unless given a warm, protected position in a cold garden. It grows fairly slowly, but responds to good soil with plenty of moisture and warmth. Propagation is by seed. (Illustrated Plate 60).

Scutellaria (Labiatae)

Scutellaria mociniana

SCARLET SKULLCAP

A Mexican sub-shrub that grows to 60 cm, this has thick clusters of brilliant scarlet flowers at the tips of the branches, which keep their colour in the shade. Each velvety vermilion flower is tubular, with a yellow lip, and lasts for several days, with new ones unfolding from the spike over a long period in summer and autumn. The large oval leaves are wrinkled and wavy. Propagation is by division of the root. (Illustrated Plate 60).

Securidaca (Polygalaceae)

Securidaca longipendunculata

VIOLET TREE

A small semi-deciduous tree of 4 metres, this has clusters of purple, pea-like, violet-scented flowers in early summer, appearing together with the small narrow leaves. The winged seeds do not germinate easily, but should be very fresh as the tree seeds freely in nature. This tree is drought-resistant in winter and grows in ordinary soil. It grows wild in Rhodesia and northwards and should prove an interesting addition to warm, frost-free gardens with dry winters.

Senecio (Compositae)

Senecio leucostachys

DUSTY MILLER

A soft, spreading shrub with very finely cut, silvery foliage, this has heads of pale creamy-yellow button flowers in early summer. It is useful in a sunny rockery or overhanging a bank. Cut it back periodically at the end of winter. It grows from cuttings and forms roots easily. It is also known as *S. cineraria* var. *candidissima*. Do not confuse this plant with *Centaurea cineraria*.

Senecio cineraria is more like a soft perennial than a shrub, which is useful in the front of a shrub border or rockery. It has woolly-white leaves and creamy or bright yellow daisy flowers.

Senecio petasitis

A shrubby Mexican perennial, this forms a rounded bush of 2 to 3 metres, with large velvety leaves and enormous heads of golden-yellow daisy flowers, fully 30 cm across. The flowers are spectacular in autumn. Cut back the whole bush at the end of winter or after flowering in mild districts.

S. petasitis grows easily in all parts of the country, but should be given shelter from frost by the overhanging branches of a tree. It will grow in full sun or semi-shade and is grown from cuttings.

Senecio tamoides

CANARY CREEPER OR CLIMBING CINERARIA

This semi-evergreen, South African, climbing shrub is found in the woods near Uitenhage and Albany and in parts of Natal. It has long, smooth green stems which support themselves on the shrubs in the woods and climb up into the tree. The flowers that appear in large clusters in the autumn are vividly showy and make a bright golden splash at a time when it is most noticeable and cheerful. Each cluster is about 12 cm across and made up of a mass of brilliant yellow tiny daisies, which can be seen from afar. The hairy seeds look like dandelions. The fleshy, green leaves of this climber are about 5 cm long and about 4 cm across. They have thin green stalks and are rounded at the base and pointed at the tip. They are irregularly cut and have many angled points.

The Canary Creeper, as it is commonly called, is a delightful climber which is deservedly popular. It is easily grown and will thrive in average, good, well-drained, light soil. It likes a sunny position but will also grow in semi-shade. The flowers develop best in the sun. It is delightful when allow to grow up into evergreen trees so that its great golden heads seem to spring from the tree itself. It can withstand slight frosts, but will be affected by a very severe frost. It should, therefore, be planted in a sheltered position in areas where severe frost is experienced. Propagation is by seed or by cuttings (Illustrated Plate 61).

The common name Canary Creeper is often loosely applied to yellow climbers, such as *Stigmaphyllon* or *Tropaeolum peregrinum*, an annual climber from Peru, which is really called the Canary Birdflower.

Serissa *Serissa foetida*
(Rubiaceae)

SERISSA

A dwarf evergreen shrub of about 60 cm, this has tiny, glossy, oval leaves and tiny white 1-cm flowers, usually solitary on the branches. The double-flowered variety is best, each flower resembling a miniature Camellia, and there is a variety with gold-margined leaves. The leaves have an unpleasant odour when bruised. This shrub is useful in the foreground of a shrub border or as a low, clipped hedge alongside paths and will grow in sun or shade. It comes from S.E. Asia and is hardy, needing good garden soil containing compost. It may be used as a pot plant. Propagation is by cuttings.

Serruria *Serruria florida*
(Proteaceae)

BLUSHING BRIDE

The genus *Serruria* belongs to the Protea family and comes from the South West portion of the Cape. It contains a number of small shrubs about 1 metre in height, but *Serruria florida*, the Blushing Bride, is a slender shrub of almost 2 metres in height. It is found in the mountains near the Berg River near Fransch Hoek in the Cape, and was not available to gardeners until recent years. It has such delightful and dainty flowers that it deserves a place in every garden. It has pretty drooping heads of flowers which measure about 6 cm across. Each head has petal-like bracts which are white, flushed with rosy pink, and the centres are filled with masses of small, pinkish hairy flowers which give it a very soft and feathery appearance. A number of pointed buds appear together with the open flowers and the whole effect is very graceful. The distinctive foliage is finely divided into smooth, narrow, hair-like segments. This shrub is attractive in the garden being particularly suited to the rockery, and provides excellent cut flowers which last for more than a week in water. It flowers throughout winter and in very early spring.

The Blushing Bride is easy to grow at the Cape, but requires careful attention elsewhere. The important thing to remember is that the plant requires water during winter. It should be planted in good, well-drained soil, well mixed with compost, and given an open, sunny position with protection from frost. Do not overwater in summer. Pruning is necessary in that faded flowers should be removed with a good length of stem. Leading shoots may be pinched back for the first two or three years of the shrub's life, in order to improve its shape. The plant drops its seeds on the ground before the flowers have dried, and these may be gathered from the ground. The seed germinates easily and well, taking about three weeks to come up. Best results are obtained if it is sown in autumn. Plants are now obtainable from specialist nurserymen. The Blushing Bride begins to flower in the second year and lasts for about seven years. It should be replaced every few years. (Illustrated Plate 61).

Sesbania (Leguminosae)

Sesbania punicea (Daubentonia punicea, Sesbania tripetii)

TANGO

Cultivation of this attractive, fast-growing South American shrub is now strongly discouraged by the Botanical Research Institute, Pretoria. Experiments at the Veterinary Research Institute, Onderstepoort, during 1974, proved that the seeds are poisonous to domestic birds, sheep and other livestock, while all other parts of the plant are toxic. This fact, coupled with the plant's tendency to seed freely, so that it has escaped from gardens and become a wide-spread weed in South Africa, with a threat of endangering birds and other animals, has prompted the opinion that it should no longer be cultivated by gardeners or offered for sale.

The shrub may be recognised by its drooping sprays of tangerine pea flowers in early summer, with dainty divided leaves and graceful branches. The seedpod is 4-angled. It is deciduous and grows to a height of 3 metres.

It is interesting to note that two other species are cultivated for fodder in the East, namely the prickly Egyptian Rattlewood, *S. bispinosa*, with pale yellow, brown-spotted flowers, and *S. grandiflora*, commonly called Sesban. This tropical Asian tree has long white pea-shaped flowers, large leaves and very long pods, and there is a red-flowered variety. The leaves are eaten as a salad, but not the ripe seeds. It is a short-lived tree and has become rare.

Solandra (Solanaceae)

Solandra nitida

CHALICE-VINE, CUP OF GOLD

A large, evergreen climber from Mexico, this has immense, golden trumpet flowers striped with purple, measuring about 15 to 20 cm across. They are redolent of cocoanut and bloom in the spring. The leaves are glossy. Cup of Gold is suitable for frost-free climates, requiring plenty of moisture during autumn and winter and a dry resting period in summer after flowering. It will grow in sheltered gardens on the highveld and does not mind mid-summer rainfall.

It should be given a sunny position in sandy loam. Propagation is by cuttings of young shoots, taken with a heel. It is frequently confused with *S. guttata*, which has creamy flowers and is not so fragrant (Illustrated Plate 61).

Solanum
(Solanaceae)

Solanum jasminoides

This deciduous climber comes from South America and grows vigorously and rapidly to a height of about 3 metres. It is related to the Potato and has large clusters of flowers in summer that are similar to Potato flowers. Each flower is about 5-cm across and the petals are joined into an open trumpet which is somewhat star-shaped. They are white, flushed with mauve, with yellow anthers grouped into a point in the centre. The flowers close up at night and are at their best in full sunlight. The leaves are smooth, pale green and pointed. The top leaves are simple and the lower leaves divided into three leaflets. This creeper grows very easily in all conditions. It will stand light frost and does best on a warm, sunny wall. It will also grow in partial shade. It may be pruned back in the spring if desired, and is grown from cuttings.

Solanum wendlandii

MAUVE POTATO CREEPER

This is a much larger climber which comes from Costa Rica. It is much showier than the white Potato Creeper. It has similar clusters of flowers that are altogether a deep mauve and are very conspicuous from a distance. It grows magnificently in warm, frost-free areas, and has heads of flowers which spread about 22 cm across, flowering in summer and autumn. It should be given a warm, sunny, north-facing wall in areas which have cold winters, and will flower in partial shade in warm places. It requires a rich soil and plenty of water in the summer. It grows very easily from cuttings. A young plant will grow up to 5 metres or more in a single season. (Illustrated Plate 62).

Solanum macranthum

POTATO TREE

This tree comes from Brazil and is one of the few tree forms of the Potato family. It is a very striking tree, reminding one of a giant Yesterday, Today and Tomorrow, for the flowers change from deep purple to pale mauve and white before they fade and, as new buds open continuously, the three colours appear together. The flowers are borne in large clusters at the ends of the branches, backed by the dark foliage. Each flower is about 5 cm across and star-shaped, with a protruding yellow centre. The petals are joined together for about two-thirds of their length. The tree grows about 7 metres in height and has an erect trunk with spreading and drooping, soft-wooded branches. The dark green, oblong-oval leaves are about 20 cm long, and rough in texture.

This tree is tender to frost and will thrive only in hot, frost-free localities. It may be grown from cuttings and grows easily and quickly in the right conditions. It prefers a position that is sheltered from strong winds, and likes a fairly rich, warm soil. It will grow in full sun or in semi-shade. (Illustrated Plate 62).

Solanum mammosum

PIG'S EARS

A prickly shrub of 1 to 2 metres, this has numerous large golden seed-pods which are pear-shaped with ear-like knobs at the top. They persist on the branches from May throughout winter and are prized as dried material for the vase. The prickly leaves generally drop off in winter except in very hot climates. *S.*

mammosum grows easily from seed, reaching maturity in one season if conditions are warm. It needs full sun and moisture in summer, with dryness in winter. It should be protected from frost but can be treated as an annual (Illustrated Plate 62).

Solanum rantonnettii from the Argentine, forms a soft bush of 2 metres with numerous clusters of violet, 5-cm flowers in summer. It needs some protection from frost.

Solanum pseudo-capsicum, Jerusalem-cherry, is a 1-metre shrub with scarlet or yellow globular fruits. It is often grown in pots.

Sollya
(Pittosporaceae)

Sollya heterophylla
BLUEBELL CREEPER

Clusters of small, bright-blue, bell-like flowers appear on this evergreen, twining, Australian shrub during summer. It needs well-drained soil and is suitable for banks, low fences or a sunny rockery. It grows to 2 metres and may be clipped to keep it tidy. It is propagated by seed or cuttings.

Sophora
(Leguminosae)

Sophora japonica
PAGODA TREE

A small tree of 20 feet to 30 feet, which grows rapidly only in good, moist soil and a sunny position, this has a spreading crown, dainty foliage and small drooping sprays of creamy white pea-flowers in summer. It is deciduous, hardy and comes from China. It makes an excellent shade tree or street tree. (Illustrated Plate 61).

Sophora microphylla, WEEPING KOWHAI, is a small New Zealand tree, growing to about 6 metres, that has a weeping habit while young. It has clusters of yellow pea-flowers about 3 cm long and tiny leaflets.

Sophora tetraptera, NEW ZEALAND LABURNUM or YELLOW KOWHAI, is a slender evergreen tree that grows to 10 metres and bears yellow flowers in spring. The leaflets are small and rounded and the foliage becomes sparse shortly before flowering-time. This hardy quick-growing tree likes moisture and comes from New Zealand and Chile.

Sophora davidii (*S. vicifolia*) A deciduous hardy shrub from China, growing to almost 3 metres, this has drooping sprays of bluish-white flowers in early summer. The narrow leaflets are silky-hairy beneath.

Sorbaria
(Rosacea)

Sorbaria tomentosa
FALSE-SPIREA

A 3-metre, deciduous Asian shrub with finely divided foliage reminiscent of ferns, this makes a luxuriant background to a water-garden. It has white sprays of flowers in summer. It suckers and should be given room to spread. Prune it back at the end of winter. It is hardy and likes moisture, especially during summer.

Sparmannia
(*Tiliaceae*)

Sparmannia africana

SPARMANNIA, AFRICAN HOLLYHOCK, STOKROOS

This large, soft, evergreen shrub grows from 3 to 7 metres and spreads in proportion. The huge leaves, 22 cm, are reminiscent of Catalpa and make this a decorative pot-plant. Clusters of white flowers with a puff of crinkled yellow stamens appear in spring. *Sparmannia* grows in the open sun at the coast, but may be grown in the shade under trees inland, where it is both sheltered from frost and the hot sun. It needs loamy soil and regular watering. This South African shrub grows easily from cuttings.

Spartium
(*Leguminosae*)

Spartium junceum

SPANISH BROOM

This Broom is common in cultivation in South Africa, and comes from the Mediterranean region. It produces masses of clear yellow, 5-cm long, pea-shaped flowers in spring and early summer, which are valued as much for their sweet scent as for their colour. It is pleasant to plant this Broom near the house for it richly perfumes the night air. The stems resemble the bristles of a broom, for they are stiff, smooth and cylindrical. The sparse leaves are tiny, about 1 cm long and narrow. They drop off in winter, but the bush retains its evergreen appearance, for it develops a thick mat of green twigs.

Spanish Broom requires a sunny position, well-drained soil and a reasonable amount of moisture. It is surprising how much neglect this Broom will survive, however, and it withstands drought. It will grow on sandy or stony soil, in windy situations and is hardy to frost. Broom is difficult to transplant unless it is quite young, but is propagated easily from seed and seeds itself in gardens. It can also be grown from cuttings. Many people are disappointed because Broom becomes woody and leggy with age, and seems to flower only at the top. One way of preventing this is by trimming in order to keep the bush compact. Clip it back after flowering, cutting into the old wood, and remove all seed pods. This means also that the bright, fragrant flowers can be picked freely for the vase. It is best to replace the bushes from time to time, using the young seedlings as new stock. Broom grows rapidly in the early stages and reaches a height of about 3 metres, with a narrow, compact shape. It can be used as a hedge. There is said to be a double-flowered form and also a white-flowered variety. (Illustrated Plate 62).

The name Broom is also used for two other genera, namely *Cytisus* and *Genista*, which are allied to *Spartium*. There are small botanical differences between the three, and there are numerous species and hybrids of both *Cytisus* and *Genista* which are frequently confused.

Spathodea
(*Bignoniaceae*)

Spathodea campanulata

FIERY-TORCH, NANDI FLAME,
AFRICAN FLAME, AFRICAN TULIP TREE

This magnificent, tall, evergreen tree, growing up to 20 metres in height, comes from tropical Africa. It flowers for a long period in autumn and winter. The flowers are large and very conspicuous from a distance. They look like great, inverted, scarlet lamps glowing against the dark-green, glossy foliage. Each single cup-shaped flower is about 10 cm long and opens into 5 points at the top. The frilly edges are bordered with gold. The flowers light up very brightly when the sun shines through them. The closed buds are attractive, for they look like khaki-coloured, velvety bunches of bananas. The half-open flowers are always full of liquid, making children at play give the tree the rather ugly name of Squirter Tree. The buds and flowers are clustered at the end of long stalks that stand well up above the foliage. The compound leaves are about 35 cm in length and are divided into long, oval leaflets about 8 cm in length.

The Spathodea is very tender to frost and grows well only in sub-tropical conditions. It is one of the loveliest trees around Pietermaritzburg and Durban. The tree is also suited to hot, dry climates up to 1200 metres and does well in Rhodesia and the lowveld. It likes a rich, well-drained soil and adequate moisture during the growing season, especially when it is young. It is easily raised from seed, cuttings or from suckers which form at the base of the tree, and grows rapidly. (Illustrated Plate 63).

A sport with golden-yellow flowers has now been cultivated and is propagated by root cuttings.

S. nilotica is similar, but grows only to about 7 metres in height.

Spiraea (Rosacea)

Spiraea

SPIREA OR MAY

There about 70 species of Spirea found in the temperate regions of Europe and America, while numerous hybrids are of garden origin. It is generally acknowledged that many of them are very similar in appearance and very much confused. The Spireas have showy and dainty flowers in white, pink and red, and are extremely easy to grow. They are hardy to frost and like areas which have cool winters. The spring-flowering varieties are not happy in sub-tropical conditions. At the same time, they dislike drought. They need a moist, though well-drained soil, which is neutral or slightly acid. They should be planted in a sunny position, although some will grow in semi-shade. Propagation is by seed, cuttings or division of the root.

The Spireas are divided into 2 classes for pruning purposes. The types that flower in winter and early spring are separated from those which flower in summer and autumn. The spring-flowering types should have the old wood removed immediately after flowering—as well as crowed growths thinned—so that the shrub will make new long shoots that will bear flowers in the following spring. The summer flowering types should be hard pruned in winter so that they will grow new flowering wood which will bear flowers later in the season.

Spiraea arguta

GARLAND MAY

This extremely dainty shrub is a garden hybrid, one of the parents being *S. thunbergii* from Japan, which has a very similar habit. It is deciduous and grows to about 1 or 2 metres in height. It has tiny, single white flowers barely 1 cm across, with the scooped out petals much longer than the stamens. The flowers are freely borne in small sprays all along the leafless branches in early spring. The foliage is the daintiest of all the Spireas. The tiny, narrow tapering leaves, only about 3 cm long, are bright green and thickly clustered along the thin, graceful, waving stalks which bush out from the base. The effect is feathery and dainty. In early winter these leaves turn to red and russet colours.

Spiraea bumalda var. Anthony Waterer

Spiraea bumalda is a garden hybrid, of which *Anthony Waterer* is the best variety. It is a dwarf, deciduous, compact bush about 60 cm to 1 metre in height. In the summer it has large, flat heads of tiny deep crimson flowers. The long stamens give the flowers a very soft, dainty appearance. If the flowerheads are removed as they fade, the blooming period will be lengthened. The foliage is green with an occasional pure yellow stalk and leaves. The tapering leaves are about 5 to 8 cm long with serrated edges. They are shaded yellow, red and bronze in the autumn. (Illustrated Plate 63).

Spiraea cantoniensis (*S. reevesiana*)

REEVES SPIREA OR CAPE MAY

This deciduous shrub comes from China and Japan and is the popular May which is most commonly grown in South African gardens. It makes a well-rounded shrub of about 1 to 2 metres in height, with spreading, arching branches that are laden with flowers in the spring, brilliantly white like thick snow. The flowers are tiny, single and thickly clustered in small flat heads about 4 cm across. The heads appear all along the top surface of the branches and side-twigs. The branches make good cutting material for the vase, and if mixed with blossoms from the Double-Flowering Peach, seem to be the very essence of spring. The leaves are oval and tapering, from 3 to 6 cm long, and have serrated edges. They are deep green on the top surface and a light, bluish-green underneath. They remain green until the end of autumn, falling in early winter. *S. cantoniensis* var. *lanceata* has double flowers which are even more effective. The leaves are narrower and slightly longer, but the shrub has a similar habit of growth. (Illustrated Plate 63).

Spiraea menziesii var. triumphans

PINK MAY

This is a hybrid of *S. douglasii*. It comes from North America and is an upright, yet rounded shrub, growing about 1 to 2 metres in height. In the summer it has long, 12-cm, feathery plumes of closely packed, pale pink flowers. The stamens are longer than the flowers and give a soft, dainty effect to the mass. Faded sprays should be removed in order to prolong the flowering period. The leaves are about 5 to 7 cm long and oval in shape with rounded tips and serrated edges. They remain green in autumn, not falling until the beginning of winter.

Spiraea prunifolia var. plena

BRIDAL-WREATH MAY

This graceful shrub comes from China and reaches a height of about 2 metres. It is distinctive, for it flowers in winter and very early spring. The tiny white flowers appear on delicate bare stalks in small sprays. Each 1-cm flower is double and has several rows of tiny petals, resembling a miniature, double Camellia. This shrub has a snowy effect from a distance and makes a delightful contrast to the Japanese Flowering Quince which flowers at the same time. They are beautiful when planted side by side. The leaves of this May are small, oval, shining, dark-green above and slightly hairy beneath. They turn orange and fall very early in autumn. This is a dense, twiggy, upright bush but the thin branches curve outwards at the top. The original species has single flowers and a similar habit (Illustrated Plate 63).

Stemmadenia (*Apocynaceae*)

Stemmadenia galeottiana (S. bella)

WHITE-BELL TREE

This small, evergreen tree comes from Mexico and grows to a height of about 3 to 4 metres. It has a crooked, picturesque habit of growth and bears large, waxy, white trumpet flowers for a long period in summer and autumn. The deep tube of the flower is yellow inside, and opens into 5 pure-white petals. The flowers measure about 6 cm across at the mouth. They grow singly or in clusters. The leaves are bright green and large, about 20 cm long. They are not very luxuriant, however, and cast a light shade. This tree is very tender to frost and grows in hot, sub-tropical areas. It requires no pruning and grows from cuttings. There are two beautiful specimens in the Durban Botanical Gardens.

Stenocarpus (*Proteaceae*)

Stenocarpus sinuatus

FIREWHEEL TREE

When the flowers finally appear in late summer on this evergreen Australian tree, after about 10 years, they are excitingly spectacular, being scarlet and shaped like a 10-cm catherine-wheel. The large deeply cut, glossy leaves are attractive and the tree has a neat upright habit, growing fairly slowly to about 10 metres or more. It needs shelter from severe frost while young. (Illustrated Plate 62).

Stephanotis (*Asclepiadaceae*)

Stephanotis floribunda

STEPHANOTIS

Fragrant, white, waxy flowers appear in masses during late spring and summer on this large evergreen climber from Madagascar. The long-lasting flowers are prized by florists. It has thick, oval leaves. It needs a warm wall in cold areas and will also grow in semi-shade. It may be grown in a large pot and coiled around a central column for support. *Stephanotis* grows very well out-of-doors in hot, humid places and may be grown in greenhouses in cold areas. Propagation is by cuttings. (Illustrated Plate 63).

Stereospermum (*Bignoniaceae*)

Stereospermum kuntheanum

AFRICAN OR PINK JACARANDA

Pretty, pinky-mauve bignonia flowers appear in clusters in early spring on this deciduous tropical African tree, which grows to about 10 metres, but is generally seen about half the size. The leaves are divided into broad oval leaflets. Fairly drought-resistant, this will grow at elevations of 1800 metres, but is best suited to warm climates in the summer rainfall area with mild dry winters. It grows from seed.

Stifftia (*Compositae*)

Stifftia chrysantha

STIFFTIA

This large leafy evergreen shrub or small tree from Brazil grows to about 3 metres. The interesting flowers consist of a puff of golden-orange or saffron hairs forming a rounded mass about 10 cm across. They are borne at the tips of the branches throughout summer. The tapering leaves grow to about 15 cm.

This shrub likes a warm climate suitable for citrus and will thrive in sub-tropical districts. It needs moisture during summer, but is fairly drought-resistant. The soil should be deep and contain compost. It is grown from seed. (Illustrated Plate 64).

Stigmaphyllon (Malpighiaceae)

Stigmaphyllon ciliatum

GOLDEN VINE

This medium-sized, evergreen climber from Brazil is suitable for trellis work or fences, and climbs by twining. It has pretty, bright-yellow flowers with petals that have thin stalks at the centre and flare out into wide, ruffled edges that resemble the wing feathers of a canary. Each flower is about 4 cm across and they are grouped in clusters against the foliage. The leaves are heart-shaped and Begonia-like, about 10 to 12 cm long. They have long stalks attached to the twiggy, notched branches, and are a soft, lime-green colour. The leaves have hairy edges that look like tiny thorns but are soft to the touch. The young growth is pink. There is a narrow, long fruit that is shaped like a 6-ribbed, small cucumber and has a pungent smell.

This vine is very tender and grows rapidly in warm, frost-free localities. It likes an open, sunny position with a good soil, but will also grow in semi-shade. It stands up to the winds on the coast but needs protection from hot, dry winds. It is usually grown from cuttings taken in autumn. (Illustrated Plate 64).

Stransvaesia (Rosacea)

Stransvaesia davidiana

STRANSVAESIA

A hardy Chinese evergreen shrub valued for its pea-sized orange-red berries which appear in autumn and winter, this has white flowers and large glossy leaves. It is suited to growing in a tub, where it grows to about 1 metre, but becomes much larger in the garden. It is propagated by seed or cuttings.

Strelitzia (Musacea)

Strelitzia reginae

CRANE-FLOWER

This is strictly not a shrub, but can be treated as a small shrub for the rockery. It is native to the eastern Cape and grows about 1 metre in height. The thick, stiff stalks branch from the base and unfurl into large, veined, evergreen leaves similar to those of Cannas. The spectacular orange and blue flowers resemble a bird's head and grow to 20 cm across, blooming in autumn, winter and spring. The Crane Flower, also known as Bird-of-Paradise, thrives in mild climates and should be protected from severe frost. It will grow in full sun or semi-shade. Drought-resistant, especially at the coast, it enjoys good soil and regular water. Propagation is by division of the root or by seed, but seedlings may take 5 years or more before flowering. (Illustrated Plate 64).

The SMALL-LEAVED STRELITZIA, S. parvifolia, has similar flowers, but small, blade-like leaves at the tips of stiff stalks, while the variety juncea is rush-like, forming a spiky tuft of stems without leaves. These may be grouped as forms of S. reginae in the future.

Strelitzia nicolai, BLUE-AND-WHITE STRELITZIA, has huge blue and white flowers. It is a palm-like tree which grows to 10 metres and has banana-like leaves. It has a tropical appearance and is effective near a house or patio. It is suited to coastal areas or warm, protected gardens inland. It grows slowly from seed. (Illustrated Plate 64).

Streptosolen
(Solanaceae)

Streptosolen jamesonii

MARMALADE BUSH

A small, evergreen shrub that grows to a height of about 1,5 metres, this comes from Columbia and Peru. The brilliantly showy flowers cover the bush in spring and early summer. They are clustered at the ends of the branches and are various shades of vivid orange and yellow. A pure golden-yellow form is cultivated. Each flower has a narrow trumpet opening out into a flat, 5-petalled shape like annual Phlox. The leaves are small, oval and rough-textured.

This shrub is tender to frost and requires a warm, sheltered position against a north wall in areas with cold winters, but may be grown in the open sun in warm, frost-free localities. The soil should be rich, light and well-watered. This shrub may be grown as a pot-plant in cold areas. It may be pruned to shape and trained as a standard. It grows easily from cuttings (Illustrated Plate 65).

Strongylodon
(Leguminosae)

Strongylodon macrobotrys

JADE VINE

The unusual metallic jade green pea flowers, closely arranged in a pendant spray about a metre or more in length, make this a spectacular vine for pergolas in tropical and sub-tropical climates. This vigorous climber, with pinnate leaves, comes from the Philippine Islands and blooms in spring, summer and autumn in areas of high humidity with copious summer rains, such as Durban. The soil should be rich and well-drained and the plant should have shade at the root, which would be provided by its own coverage if it is grown over a pergola. It may be grown in large hot-houses in areas with cold winters, in temperatures which suit Vanda orchids. Propagation is by cuttings or by seed. The plants bloom in about 18 months from seed, but the first year's buds tend to drop. (Illustrated Plate 65).

The so-called Scarlet Jade Vine will be found under *Mucuna*.

Strophanthus
(Apocynaceae)

Strophanthus speciosus

CORKSCREW FLOWER

This rambling shrub becomes a vine when it has the opportunity of climbing to the tops of surrounding trees or is given a support in a greenhouse. It has curious flowers with 5 twisted petals, each extending into long streamers that spiral as they hang down. *S. speciosus* has yellow flowers with red spots near the mouth and grows wild in the eastern districts of South Africa. *S. petersianus*, from the northern Transvaal and Mozambique, has red lines in the tube and on the tails.

Strophanthus is popularly grown, but it should be noted that all parts of the plants are poisonous. It grows easily in warm, protected positions and needs watering in summer, enduring winter drought. The soil should be light and well-drained. Propagation is by seed or cuttings. (Illustrated Plate 65)

Sutera
(Scrophulariaceae)

Sutera grandiflora

SUTERA OR WILD PHLOX

This dainty South African sub-shrub is an attractive plant for the rockery and grows to a height of about 1 metre. It has long, waving, woody stalks completely clothed with small, grey-green, wrinkled leaves. The flowers grow in spread-out heads at the tips of the branches and the side-twigs, resembling Phlox in shape and size. The flowers are a pretty, clear bluish-lilac and vary in the intensity of the colour. The plant flowers most of the year, particularly in the autumn and throughout winter in sheltered places. Dead flowers should always be removed together with a length of branch, in order to prolong the flowering period. Cut back the whole plant at the end of winter and new stems will grow up to flower in the following summer.

Sutera will grow almost anywhere in South Africa and comes from the mountains of the eastern Transvaal and Swaziland. It withstands average frosts and likes a sunny position and well-drained, light soil. It likes fairly dry conditions, but if the soil is well-drained, benefits from twice-weekly watering. If one has any criticism of Sutera, it is that it is a sparse plant with only 5 or 6 stalks growing up at a time from a matted base. For best effect, therefore, one should grow several plants close together. Sutera is grown very easily and rapidly from seed, but must be transplanted when only about 3–4 cm in height. Better still, the seed may be broadcast in the open ground. Bigger plants may be transplanted if they have been grown individually in tins, but as they grow to full size in a season, this is hardly necessary. The plants flower for several years, but one must be prepared to replace them after a time (Illustrated Plate 65).

Sutherlandia (Leguminosae)

Sutherlandia frutescens

BALLOON-PEA OR GANSIES

This evergreen, South African shrub grows to a height of about 1 to 2 metres and is a lovely plant for the rockery. The flowers appear in winter and early spring in drooping sprays. They are bright-red, curved tubes, similar in shape to the flowers of the Kaffirboom, but only about 3 cm in length. They are followed by decorative seedpods that are greenish and papery, about 5 cm long and puffed out like ballons. The leaves are pale-green and dainty. They are about 5 cm long and divided into numerous 7 mm oval leaflets. The reed-like woody stems branch out from the base. It is also known by the rather unattractive name of Cancer Bush. There is a dwarf form growing to 60 cm, but this may be the effect of drought.

Sutherlandia is not really a permanent shrub as it gets rather straggly after a few years and one must be prepared to replace it. It grows so easily and rapidly from seed and sows itself so readily in gardens, however, that can be treated as an annual and transplanted quite easily into the garden when large. It will flower in the first year. The shrub likes a sunny position in good, well-drained soil. It will stand severe frosts and drought and may be grown in all parts of the country (Illustrated Plate 66).

Swainsona (Leguminosae)

Swainsona galegifolia

SWAINSONA

A low shrub of about 1 metre, with sprays of pink pea-flowers almost throughout the year, this should be cut back at the end of winter to improve its shape. The pinnate foliage is said to be poisonous to stock. There are many other Australian Swainsonas with red, white, blue or pink flowers. They grow from seed.

Symphoricarpos (Caprifoliaceae)

Symphoricarpos albus (S. racemosus)

SNOWBERRY

This low-growing, deciduous American shrub grows up to about 1 metre in height. It has insignificant flowers but is grown for its attractive, snow-white, puffy pea-sized berries which appear in autumn, clustered along the delicate stalks. The leaves are small and oval, growing neatly and symmetrically in wing-like pairs up the stems. This shrub is very useful since it can be grown in any soil, from clay to gravel, and will grow under trees, in sun or in shade, but it likes moisture. It is hardy to frost. Propagation is by seed, cuttings or division.

Symphoricarpos orbiculatus

INDIAN-CURRANT OR CORAL-BERRY

This is another deciduous, American, low-growing shrub which has purplish-red berries in autumn and winter. These berries are crumpled and look like clusters of red currants all along the branches between the dainty leaves. The branches droop over gracefully with the weight of the berries and make interesting material for the vase. This shrub is also very hardy and suited to any position in the garden. It spreads by means of suckers and is able to hold the soil on a steep bank.

S. orbiculatus var. variegatus has decorative variegated leaves—green, outlined with yellow, and arranged symmetrically in pairs along the stems. (Illustrated Plate 64).

Syncarpia (Myrtaceae)

Syncarpia glomulifera

TURPENTINE-TREE

A broad, evergreen, Australian tree of 13 metres, this may be used as a shade tree in warm areas, as it is tender to frost. It has dark green, laurel-like leaves and flowers like creamy fluffy "balls". It is drought-resistant and said to resist white ants.

Syringa (Oleaceae)

Syringa

LILAC

This genus must not be confused with the locally-named Syringa Tree which is *Melia azedarach*. The *Syringa* is the true Lilac which is so popularly grown in Europe for its scented and beautiful sprays of flowers in the spring, and is a magnificent florist's flower. It likes cool climates, and does not do very well in South Africa. Lilacs have been grown in parts of the Cape and the Transvaal, but are not as successful as they are overseas. They like rich, moist soil and cold situations and are suitable for a south-facing wall. They must be pruned immediately after flowering, for if they are pruned in winter the new flowering sprays will be damaged. Lilac must not be severed across the top but pruned to shape from the ground.

The Common or English Lilac (*Syringa vulgaris*) comes from Europe and has many beautiful varieties in lilac, white, pink and red, but has comparatively poor flowers in this country. It is a large, deciduous, upright shrub with notched and woody stems. The leaves are large, heart-shaped and light-green. If it is grown on its own roots, many suckers will form rapidly. Remove most of these at ground level, leaving 2 or 3 young suckers, together with new strong shoots from old stumps which can be removed in rotation each spring. Many modern varieties are grafted on to Privet stock, and any growths from the stock must be removed immediately. (Illustrated Plate 66).

There are several species that are said to do better in this country than the English Lilac. One is *Syringa villosa*, which flowers while quite small. It is quite a pleasing lilac, though not as full or pretty as the English Lilac. The flowers are a pale fleshpink and grow in open, slender sprays. They are very faintly perfumed. Each 2-cm long flower is more tube-like and not as starry as the flowers of the English Lilac. The stems are thick, sturdy and upright in growth. The leaves are oval and pointed at both ends, growing to about 10 cm. They are dull green above and light green beneath. (Illustrated Plate 66).

Tabebuia
(Bignoniaceae)

Tabebuia

TRUMPET TREE, TABEBUIA

Beautiful in flower, the Tabebuia trees form a group of about 150 species, mainly evergreen, from Central and South America. They have trumpet-shaped flowers in pinks, lilacs and yellow. Many are useful street trees in sub-tropical coastal areas or protected positions in warm, inland districts. Some flower when young and are exciting when they bloom, mainly in early spring.

They need ordinary well-drained soil and somewhat dry conditions during winter, with moisture during summer. They have proved to be disease and pest-free in cultivation and grow easily from seed. The names of the different but similar species are often confused.

Tabebuia chrysotricha

YELLOW TABEBUIA

The brilliant yellow, large clusters of flowers on this small, semi-deciduous tree from Brazil make this one of the most outstanding of the yellow-flowered Tabebuias. Each wide-open trumpet flower is about 10 cm long and grouped to make a rounded mass, gorgeous in full bloom. Hot spring winds will shrivel the delicate flowers in dry areas, so that the flowering may be brief, but it remains spectacular nevertheless. The oval pointed leaves are grouped in fives, springing from one point, and the tree has a lacy open-branched habit. The cinnamon-coloured seedpods are long and rough to the touch. This species grows quickly from seed and blooms while young and only 2 or 3 metres in height. It will grow on the highveld in a sunny, warm position, sheltered from frost against a wall. (Illustrated Plate 66).

Several other species have similar yellow flowers. *T. argentea* forms a small rounded tree with silvery-grey leaves and grows well at the coast, but is said to withstand low temperatures. *T. donnell-smithii*, a tall tree called Primavera in the Caribbean, is acknowledged to be one of the showiest, flowering on bare branches, and is now placed in the genus *Cybistax*.

Tabebuia ochracea differs from *T. chrysotricha* in its more elongated inflorescences, which are sulphur yellow or ochre in colour.

Tabebuia ipe (*T. avellanedae*)

This delightful small semi-evergreen tree from South America grows to about 5 metres and bears clusters of bright pink or lilac flowers with a yellowish throat on bare branches in early spring. It may flower during winter in mild districts. It flowers when quite small and is used as a street tree in Pretoria and in Durban. (Illustrated Plate 66).

Tabebuia pallida (*T. triphylla*)

CUBAN TRUMPET TREE

A large rounded evergreen tree from the West Indies, this has long been grown as a useful ornamental for sea-side localities as it withstands coastal wind and salt spray. It grows to a height of about 13 metres. It has lilac trumpet flowers with a yellow or whitish centre, similar in shape to a Bignonia. The flowers appear freely in spring and at intervals during summer and autumn, blooming while the tree is small. The deep green leaves have 1–3 oval leaflets. It is widely planted as a street tree in Durban and is suitable for large gardens on the east coast.

Tabebuia pentaphylla (*T. rosea*)

MEXICAN PUE

A medium-sized rounded tree that is spectacular from a distance, this is covered with large clusters of pink trumpet flowers in autumn, although some appear during winter and spring. The flowers may vary from pink to white and have a yellow or white throat. The glossy leaves have 5 leaflets that are much larger than those of *T. pallida*. The flowers sometimes appear before the new leaves although the tree is more or less evergreen. It is evergreen at the sub-tropical coast, where it thrives, but will also grow in warm inland districts, needing a mild dry winter and rain during summer. It comes from Mexico and Central America. (Illustrated Plate 66).

Tamarix (*Tamaricaceae*)

Tamarix

TAMARISK

There are several Tamarisks which come from the Mediterranean region and are extremely hardy to drought or frost. They are found in Mexico and in all hot, dry countries. In Australia, *T. aphylla* is being used successfully to combat soil erosion. The Tamarisk can also grow in sandy and brack soil, so that it will grow in the Karoo as well as on the wind-blown coast sands such as are found at Port Elizabeth. It resists salt spray and will grow on the beach. Apart from its hardy qualities, the Tamarisk is very beautiful and is popular in moist and even sub-tropical districts. It has dainty, Cypress-like foliage which is very short and fine, giving the whole tree a feathery appearance. Probably its only requirement is that the soil should be well-drained. It is reproduced by cuttings taken in early spring. Tamarisk species are difficult to identify, but all are worth growing.

Tamarix aphylla

ATHEL TREE

This North African tree is interesting as it has no noticeable foliage, for the leaves are minute scales. Pink flowers are borne in sprays and it grows to 10 metres.

Tamarix parviflora

This deciduous, small tree, about 3 to 4 metres in height, has bright-green foliage. The tiny flowers appear all along the dark-red stems in early spring, looking like small, pink beads. Later, these beads burst open into tiny, feathery pink masses, and the whole tree becomes most conspicuous, for it is altogether pink-stemmed and feathery. The branches are numerous and graceful and the effect is very dainty. After three or four weeks, the tiny leaves begin to grow and the tree remains green for the rest of the season. It grows in a bush shape but should be trained with a single stem, unnecessary growths being cut back from time to time. It can be trimmed as desired (Illustrated Plate 67).

T. gallica, French Tamarisk, is similar, but flowers in summer and is rarely seen in gardens.

Tamarix pentandra (*T. hispida*)

This Tamarisk has a more bluish-green foliage than the spring-flowering variety. It is a small deciduous tree, but its flowers are produced in early summer. The flowers are much fuller and come in large, graceful sprays which fall in cascades all over the bush. They are a pretty lilac pink, almost cyclamen. This is a most delightful addition to any garden. This Tamarisk must be pruned back hard each winter, to within 5 to 8 cm of the old wood. It flowers on new growth which grows rapidly. This can also be shortened after flowering. (Illustrated Plate 67).

Taxodium (*Pinaceae*)

Taxodium distichum

A tall, pyramidal tree form the southern United States, this has attractive foliage even in the young stages, with its light green "ostrich-feather" leaves in spring, that turn every shade of gold, bronze or red before becoming cinnamon-brown in winter.

The Swamp Cypress is useful for boggy places, growing as it does in the swamps of the Everglades, where it develops "knees" or hollow protuberances that emerge around the trunks of trees standing in the water. It will also grow in ordinary good soil in gardens, where it should be watered regularly. Although it thrives in a sub-tropical climate, it experiences cold nights in nature and is hardy in places with severe winters. It does well on the highveld and in the Pieter-maritzburg area. Propagation is by seed or cuttings. (Illustrated Plate 67).

Taxodium mucronatum, the Montezuma Cypress from Mexico, is slightly less hardy and forms a broader, large tree with larger, feathery leaves. Ancient trees dating from Aztec times are still said to be standing in the park in Mexico City.

Tecoma (*Bignoniaceae*)

Tecoma garrocha

A graceful evergreen shrub of nearly 2 metres, this has drooping sprays of showy, 5-cm, trumpet flowers in summer. They are yellowish-red or salmon with a scarlet tube. It needs a warm, sunny position with shelter from severe frost and grows from seed or cuttings. It comes from Argentina.

Tecoma stans (*Stenolobium stans*)

This large, vigorous shrub grows wild in Yucatan, Florida and the West Indies where it is called Yellow Elder, and grows about 5 metres high and more. The flowers are bright, canary yellow trumpets, about 4 cm long, which are clustered together in huge heads up to 22 cm in length. They are extremely showy against the soft green serrated leaflets and appear in autumn for quite a long period. The young growth is bronze-coloured. Long green seed-pods hang down conspicuously all over the shrub. It seeds itself freely in moist ground.

Tecoma stans is evergreen and fast-growing. The foliage becomes sparse during cold winters. It will survive frost if it is given some protection against a wall or other shrubs, and likes a warm, sunny spot in the garden as well as a moist soil. It is magnificent in hot or sub-tropical districts where it grows luxuriantly (Illustrated Plate 67).

Tecomanthe (*Bignoniaceae*)

Tecomanthe dendrophylla

A medium-sized climber from New Guinea, this has large clusters of pendant funnel-shaped flowers on the old wood in summer. Each flower is about 8 cm long, red on the outside and white inside. The leaflets are in threes, the central one being longest.

T. venusta is similar, with shorter, rosy-purple flowers that are creamy within. There are from 5 to 7 leaflets.

Both species are tender and suitable for frost-free, warm gardens, with plenty of moisture in summer. Propagation is by cuttings or seed.

Tecomaria (*Bignoniaceae*)

Tecomaria capensis

This is a rambling shrub that has its origin in the eastern Cape, South Africa, and grows to a height of about 2 to 3 metres. The fiery bright orange flowers are massed together in bunches on the ends of upstanding branches. There is also a light yellow-flowered variety, which is slower growing. Selected colour forms have been developed at Longwood Gardens, U.S.A. and hybrids with deep orange-red flowers are now obtainable. These are propagated by cuttings and division of the root. (Illustrated Plate 67).

Each separate flower is shaped like a narrow, curved tube with turned-back lips like a Snapdragon and his protruding stamens. They make a conspicuous splash of colour in the autumn against the small, dark-green, shiny leaflets, and continue to flower during winter if conditions are warm enough. This shrub is evergreen in warm localities and deciduous during cold winters.

Cape Honeysuckle is very easy to grow in ordinary garden soil in full sun. It can stand dry conditions quite well. Frost will burn this shrub in exposed places, but it will come on again in the spring. It needs the support of a low wall or fence, but can be grown as a single specimen if it is kept in shape by clipping. Long branches grow out flat against the ground from the base, but these can be cut back and trimmed in the spring. If it is untrimmed, the bush forms a lower, more spreading shape, requiring a space of about 3 metres in diameter. It makes an excellent subject for a bank or large rockery. Cape Honeysuckle grows very easily from seed or from cuttings and forms roots where it spreads along the ground, so that these layers may be severed and planted (Illustrated Plate 67).

Telopea
(Proteaceae)

Telopea speciosissima

WARATAH

If one can grow Proteas, one should be able to grow the Waratah, an exciting Australian member of the Protea family. It has a showy cone-like red flower-head, about 10 cm across, produced in spring. It is an evergreen shrub of 3 metres, with deeply toothed leaves. Full sun, excellent drainage and some protection from frost are necessary requirements. It grows slowly but successfully at the Cape. It is propagated by seed, which should be sown in autumn (Illustrated Plate 68).

Tetrapanax
(Araliaceae)

Tetrapanax papyriferum (Fatsia papyrifera)

RICE–PAPER PLANT

Huge, round, deeply serrated, velvety leaves, growing to 70 cm in diameter, make this ornamental evergreen shrub useful against a wall where a dramatic accent is needed. The woolly white flower-balls come in large sprays. It grows to 3 metres and forms suckers which may be detached to make new plants, so that it is best planted in a large garden in a shrub border or at the water-side, but it also makes a good tub-plant for a patio. It comes from Taiwan and the pith was used to make rice-paper by the Chinese.

Tetrapanax grows easily in ordinary soil, but needs moisture in dry climates, especially during summer. It will grow in full sun or light shade and should have shelter in areas with severe frost (Illustrated Plate 68).

Teucrium
(Labiatae)

Teucrium fruticans

GERMANDER

A spreading evergreen shrub of over a metre in height, from southern Europe, this is a useful grey-foliaged plant, for it has long whitish stems covered with small oval leaves, overlaid with white hairs. The pale lilac salvia-like flowers appear singly near the tips of the branches in summer. It is suitable for a rockery or a sunny bank in front of shrubs with contrasting foliage. It is fairly drought-resistant and grows easily with little attention. It will grow from seed or cuttings.

Thevetia
(Apocynaceae)

Thevetia peruviana (T. nereifolia)

YELLOW OLEANDER

A large, evergreen shrub of 5 metres from Tropical America, which is suited to warm areas with mild winters, this is rounded and dense, so that it is used as a hedge in sub-tropical districts. It has very long narrow leaves. The bright yellow trumpet flowers appear in spring, summer and at intervals throughout the year. It will grow in sandy soil near the coast and is grown from cuttings. (Illustrated Plate 68).

T. thevetioides, from Mexico, has flowers which are three times as big and showy. It will grow from seed.

Thunbergia
(Acanthaceae)

Thunbergia

TRUMPET VINE

There are about 100 species of *Thunbergia*, which may be climbers or bushy perennials, natives of tropical Africa and Asia. They are named after the famous Swedish botanist Karl Thunberg. The following are popular in gardens.

Thunbergia alata

BLACK-EYED SUSAN

This popular climber which grows to a height of 2 to 3 metres comes from the eastern Cape, Natal and eastern Tropical Africa. It grows to this height in a season and flowers in late summer. It is covered with small, flat-faced trumpet flowers which have five rounded petals. They are a vivid orange with a black centre which gives them their common name. The stems are thin and hairy and the leaves are bright green, soft in texture and triangular or heart-shaped. It needs the support of a fence or trellis.

This climber is suited to all climates with warm summers. It is cut down by frost every winter, but grows up again in the spring. It should be pruned back if the frost does not kill it. It sows itself freely and it is often the new plants that grow up in the spring. It is usually treated as an annual.

Thunbergia grandiflora

BENGAL TRUMPET VINE

This large, vigorous, evergreen climber comes from Bengal. It flowers in autumn and has large, pale, bluish-mauve trumpet flowers like a Bignonia. There is also a white-flowered variety *alba*. Each flower has wide, turned-back petals and measures about 6 cm in width and 8 cm in length. The flowers grow singly on long stalks and lie in front of the luxuriant, dark green foliage. The leaves are large, oval, somewhat heart-shaped and rough to the touch. This twining climber is very quick-growing and needs the support of a fence or tree.

This climber is tender to frost and is suited to low frost-free elevations. It does very well on the east coast, but may be grown against a warm wall in cooler climates. It requires a rich soil with adequate root-room. It should have a sunny position and lots of water in summer. Pruning is inclined to spoil free flowering, so that the vine should rather be given a large space in which to spread. It can be increased by seed, cuttings or layers formed during the summer. (Illustrated Plate 69).

Thunbergia mysorensis

MYSORE TRUMPET VINE

This magnificent evergreen climber grows to 5 metres and is best grown on a pergola so that its long pendant sprays of flowers may hang downwards freely. They bloom in profusion in early spring and at intervals throughout the year, beneath a curtain of luxuriant foliage. The sprays grow to at least 40 cm in length with the flowers, each 5 cm long, unfolding continuously from the top down and shedding on the ground. Each golden, hooded flower opens wide and the outer lobes are a rich mahogany or Indian red. The effect is striking and unusual. The deep green glossy leaves are oval and about 15 cm long.

This climber from India grows well in a sub-tropical climate and is popular in Durban, but will bloom in warm gardens on the highveld if it is protected from frost. It is drought-resistant in winter and needs moisture in summer. The soil should be well-drained and contain compost. This plant needs a sunny position although the flowers emerge in the shade under the leaves. Propagation is by seed or cuttings. It blooms in about 18 months in the right conditions. (Illustrated Plate 69).

Thuya
Thuya
(Pinaceae)

ARBOR–VITAE

Thuyas are neat, hardy, evergreen members of the Pine family, prized in gardens for their slow, compact growth which makes them suitable for pots and formal accents in the landscape. They are particularly useful in cold countries which have few hardy evergreens. They have stiff, flattened branches, scale-like leaves and bear long cones.

Very few are obtainable in this country, chiefly those which are raised from seed, but they will grow from cuttings. Avoid planting a collection of differing shaped, sizes and colours in one bed, but use several of one kind in groups or plant them singly, to contrast with other plants. They make an excellent background to bright-flowering plants like *Rhododendron simsii* or Japanese Rhododendrons.

Thuya orientalis, ORIENTAL ARBOR-VITAE, is a tall tree with numerous varieties. Variety *aurea*, GOLDEN THUYA, forms a golden pyramid of 2 metres, at its brightest in spring, which makes a good accent. The best golden forms are selected in the seedling stage. (Illustrated Plate 68).

Tibouchina
Tibouchina
(Melastomaceae)

GLORY TREE

There are about 250 species of Tibouchina that come from S. America and especially from Brazil. Some are trees that grow to 25 metres, but most are small evergreen trees and shrubs.

Tibouchina semidecandra (Lasiandra macrantha)

BRAZILIAN GLORY BUSH

This is a large evergreen shrub from Brazil, growing from 2 to 3 metres in height, with a number of long, graceful stems growing out from the base. The rich purple flowers are about 8 cm wide and are enhanced by the velvety pink buds. They are prolific from mid-summer to autumn. The velvety leaves are deeply ribbed, with about 3 to 5 veins.

Not as tender are most other species, this popular shrub may be grown in areas with cold winters with protection from frost against a warm sunny wall. It does not like wind which breaks the little branches, but severe cutting back will keep it in shape and prevent breakage. It may be increased by cuttings taken in early spring. It likes acid soil as do all Tibouchinas. (Illustrated Plate 70).

Tibouchina elegans

SMALL–LEAVED GLORY BUSH

A dainty small tree or large shrub that grows to about 2 or 3 metres, this is distinguished by its tiny, oval, pointed leaves, each about 4 cm in length, which are glossy green above, with 2 or 3 nerves. The large single flowers, almost 8 cm wide, are a rich violet when mature, emerging white and becoming deep pink, so that several colours are present on the bush. It blooms in early summer and autumn and is native to S. Brazil. It should be given a warm sheltered position in cool areas. (Illustrated Plate 70).

Tibouchina granulosa

This is one of the most spectacular landscape trees that have been introduced into Natal from Brazil. It grows to a height of about 10 metres, with a rounded shape, flowering while quite small. The masses of gorgeous violet-purple flowers, about 6 cm across, cover the entire surface, reminiscent of a Rhododendron in flowering splendour. The seeds give rise to pink or violet forms, including a vibrant cyclamen-purple (var. *cianea*) and a clear, rich rose-pink, which is known as var. *rosea* (Illustrated Plate 70). They may be reproduced by cuttings. The trees bloom in late summer and autumn, as well as in spring. They need sun and do best in acid soils. They are tender to frost and thrive in sub-tropical places. (Illustrated Plate 70).

Tibouchina holosericea
SILKY GLORY BUSH

A small evergreen Brazilian shrub of 1 to 2 metres, this has very large silky leaves. Its upright, branched spikes of smallish purple-violet flowers, 4 to 5 cm in diameter, distinguish it from most other Tibouchinas. It blooms in late summer, prefers the sub-tropics, and its neat size makes it suitable for the smallest garden.

Tibouchina pulchra is a medium-sized tree from Brazil that has flowers which change from white to rose and then lilac, with all three colours appearing at the same time. There are several other species with flowers that change colour on the same plant, notably *T. mutabilis* from Brazil.

Tipuana
(Leguminosae)

Tipuana tipu (T. speciosa)
TIPUANA

A large, spreading, deciduous tree, this bears clusters of 3-cm, golden-yellow pea flowers, together with the pale green leaves in summer. The long leaves are divided into about 13 pairs of oblong, 5-cm leaflets. The branches grow out at all angles, forming a flattened crown, but the tree should be trained to form a standard when young.

Tipuana grows fairly rapidly in ordinary garden soil without special attention. It stands up to the average cold winters of Johannesburg and will grow up again if it is cut back by frost. Seed should be soaked and sown in spring. *Tipuana* is native to South America (Illustrated Plate 68).

Trachelospermum
(Apocynaceae)

Trachelospermum jasminoides (Rhyncospermum jasminoides)
STAR-JASMINE

This evergreen, climbing shrub may be allowed to climb or may be grown as a low, spreading shrub about 1 metre in height. It comes from China and has clusters of fragrant white flowers similar to those of the white Jasmine, which are freely borne in spring or early summer. The flowers are different from Jasmine in that each of the 5 petals twist to one side and has rolled-back edges. The leaves are dark green, leathery and very glossy on the top surface. They are oval, pointed and about 6 cm long. The branches are thick and whip-like and need a support upon which to twine.

The Star-Jasmine is easy to grow, but grows slowly, especially at the beginning. It likes a warm, sunny position, but will also grow in semi-shade. It can stand our average frosts and can be grown almost everywhere. It enjoys lots of moisture. The plant is propagated by cuttings or by division of the root (Illustrated Plate 71).

Trichilia (Meliaceae)

Trichilia emetica

THUNDER TREE

A spreading evergreen South African tree of 13 metres, this has glossy leaves divided into large leaflets. The creamy flowers are not showy, but are followed by berries which split to reveal striking orange seeds marked with a black patch. This tree is useful for coastal gardens as it is wind-resistant, but it is suited only to mild, moist areas as it is tender to frost.

Uncarina (Pedaliaceae)

Uncarina sakalava

UNCARINA

A large soft evergreen shrub from the drier parts of Madagascar, this grows to 3 metres. It has large, yellow, Hibiscus-like trumpet flowers, about 10 cm across, with a maroon throat. The broad, soft leaves have notched leaves like a mallow. It has prickly, hooked seed pods. The specific name refers to a tribe in the north of the island.

Uncarina will grow in full sun in warm frost-free areas or in partial shade, so that it may be grown in a large greenhouse in cold climates. It must be kept fairly dry and endures a long period of drought in winter. The soil should be light and well-drained and it must not be given much moisture. Propagation is by seed. (Illustrated Plate 71)

Viburnum (Caprifoliaceae)

Viburnum

SNOWBALL BUSH

There are many hardy species of *Viburnum* from America, Europe and Asia. *V. opulus* var. *sterile* is the most spectacular in bloom and has been grown most freely, but several recent introductions are well worth growing, particularly in the large garden. They grow easily in well-watered gardens, the deciduous types preferring cold climates. A situation facing east or south is most suitable. They are propagated by seed or cuttings.

Viburnum burkwoodii

BURKWOOD VIBURNUM

An evergreen, hybrid shrub of 2 metres, with *V. carlesii* as one of its parents, this has 10 cm clusters of fragrant white flowers which are pink-tinged in bud. The narrow, pointed leaves are shiny above.

Viburnum carlesii

A deciduous shrub that grows to almost 3 metres, this may be recognised by its dense clusters of fragrant white flowers, about 6 cm across, in early spring. The leaves are oval, pointed and irregularly toothed. They are dull green above and downy beneath, while the shoots are also downy. This hardy species from Korea has black fruits and grows easily in loamy well-watered soil. It will grow in full sun or partial shade. (Illustrated Plate 71).

Viburnum opulus var. sterile

This deciduous shrub comes from the Netherlands and grows to about 2 metres in height. It is one of the loveliest of white spring-flowering shrubs with its 10-cm "balls" of florets festooned gracefully all over the bush. They last for 3 or 4 weeks and are most spectacular. In the original species the heads of white flowers are smaller, but are followed by red berries, which are not present in the sterile but showier variety. (Illustrated Plate 71). The leathery, maple-shaped leaves turn russet before falling.

The Snowball Bush is happiest in cold districts where it thrives in an open position, being very hardy to frost. In places with a hot dry spring, it is best to give it semi-shade with some morning sun. It will grow in light shade under trees or on a cold south wall. It needs plenty of moisture during flowering time in spring. It does not need regular pruning but old growths may be thinned out and the bush trimmed back after flowering if necessary. It can be transplanted easily during winter (Illustrated Plate 71).

Viburnum rhytidophyllum
LEATHER-LEAF VIBURNUM

A robust, Chinese, evergreen shrub of about 3 metres, this has distinctive, decorative leaves which are 15 cm long, leathery and deeply wrinkled, dark green above and grey-felted beneath. Flat, 20-cm heads of dull flowers open in summer and are followed by scarlet berries which turn black with age. This makes an interesting background shrub.

Viburnum sargentii

A large, deciduous shrub of 4 metres from Asia, this has long-stalked sprays of white flowers followed by scarlet berries. The large lobed leaves assume autumn tints.

Viburnum tinus
LAURESTINUS

An old-fashioned evergreen shrub which grows fairly slowly to 3 metres or more, this is extremely useful as it is so hardy and flowers towards the end of winter. It can be grown on a cold south wall and forms a useful screen. The tiny, pinkish-white flowers are clustered in posy-like heads, about 8 cm across. The foliage is dark green. There are several horticultural varieties.

Viburnum tomentosum
DOUBLE-FILE VIBURNUM

Gorgeous in flower and seen at its best from above, the Double-File Viburnum bears its heads of white flowers in rows on either side of the branches, forming a neat and attractive sight in spring. Each flower-head measures about 9 cm across, with large flat sterile flowers ringed around small dainty fertile flowers at the centre. Tiny bright red fruits in summer turn black later. The toothed oval leaves taper to a point and are deeply veined and rough to the touch, up to about 15 cm in length. They are light green at first and deepen in colour with age, assuming golden autumn tints. This shrub comes from China and Japan and grows fairly quickly from cuttings to a height of 3 metres. It does well in cold gardens with good, well-watered soil in summer and does not like sub-tropical conditions. (Illustrated Plate 71).

The variety *Mariesii* is a more spreading bush with larger flowers.

The variety *plicatum*, Japanese Snowball, has ball-like clusters of white sterile flowers, spectacular in bloom.

Viminaria (*Leguminosae*)

Viminaria denudata

AUSTRALIAN BROOM

A small Australian tree of about 4 metres, this has almost leafless, drooping, rush-like branches with long sprays of small yellow pea-flowers for a short period in early summer. It is suitable as a background shrub for a large pond. It needs sunshine and well-drained soil with similar treatment to *Chamaelaucium*. It can be given regular watering, but is fairly drought-resistant and hardy and should be given a warm situation in cold areas. It is grown from seed or cuttings.

Virgilia (*Leguminosae*)

Virgilia oroboides (*V. capensis*)

KEURBOOM

The Keurboom is one of the quickest-growing evergreen trees in cultivation when conditions are favourable. It forms an upright rounded tree of about 10 metres, which is valued for its clusters of sweetly-scented, mauve-pink pea-flowers which cover the tree and are conspicuous from a distance, making this an outstanding flowering tree. The short, deep green leaves are divided into narrow leaflets, about 3 cm long.

Some trees flower profusely in spring and others only commence flowering in early summer, remaining in bloom until the autumn. This variable habit of flowering led botanists to believe that there were two distinct species and the name *V. divaricata* was suggested for the spring-flowering tree in 1936. As the other differences between the trees are so very slight, many people believe that they are only two forms of the same species, *V. oroboides*. The spring-flowering species however, continues to produce trees that flower in spring. The Keurboom comes from the Cape, extending from the Peninsula to the forests near Knysna and Uitenhage.

The Keurboom grows easily, but does best in deep good soil with plenty of moisture throughout the year, so that it helps to grow other plants around it. It should not be exposed to strong prevailing winds as it has shallow roots and may be blown over. It likes a sunny position and is fairly hardy to frost when mature, but must be protected from frost for the first 2 or 3 winters. A low-branching tree, this should not be grown with a standard, nor should the lower branches be removed to shape it as a shade tree. Unfortunately, the Keurboom is not long-lived, dying back after about 12 or 15 years. As it grows easily and rapidly from seed sown in spring, this should not be a deterrent to planting it. (Illustrated Plate 71).

Vitex (*Verbenaceae*)

Vitex agnus-castus

CHASTE TREE

Upright, Buddleia-like sprays of lilac, fragrant flowers appear in spring and late summer on this hardy deciduous shrub which grows to about 3 metres in height. The greyish leaves are divided into 5 to 7 narrow leaflets. It comes from the Mediterranean area and grows easily in ordinary soil in full sun. It is propagated by cuttings and seed.

Wagatea (Leguminosae)

Wagatea spicata

CANDY CORN VINE

This fascinating evergreen climber from India has large, graceful trusses of long flower-spikes at the ends of long branches in late summer. Each tapering spike is about 30 cm long and has numerous orange and scarlet buds, opening into pea-shaped flowers. The leaves are divided into large, glossy leaflets, about 5 cm long.

This very large, billowing vine should be supported over a wall or on a strong trellis, so that the branches can sweep downwards to reveal the flower sprays near the ground. It should be allowed to flower in sunshine, although the plant itself will flourish in partial shade. This is a vine for warm, sub-tropical places, thriving in areas of high humidity. It may be grown from seed. (Illustrated Plate 72).

Weigela (Caprifoliaceae)

Weigela

FAIRY TRUMPETS OR WEIGELA

There are about 10 species of Weigela which come from Asia. They were formerly included in the genus *Diervilla* which comes from America, but are now separated. They are deciduous and have very showy flowers in spring and early summer. They grow up to 2 metres in height, requiring about 2 metres in which to spread, and do best when they have space around them.

These shrubs are all easy to grow and will thrive in most conditions. They are hardy to frost and dislike hot, dry air and wind, disliking sub-tropical conditions. They like a moist, partially shaded or sunny position and do well facing east. They should be planted in soil which is generously mixed with compost, and should be well and frequently watered. Propagation is best by cuttings. Pruning is important in order to improve the flowering sprays and to avoid the untidy appearance of twiggy growth in the winter. Pruning must not be done in winter or the spring flowers will be spoilt. Remove faded flower twigs and cut out the old wood almost at the base after flowering. This will encourage long new growths to shoot up ready to flower in the following spring.

Weigela florida is the hardiest and the most beautiful of the genus. Each funnelshaped flower is about 4 cm long. It is very narrow at the base and flares out into an open trumpet at the mouth. The flowers are pale pink, opening from rosepink buds, and thickly clustered all the way up the spreading branches, in between the leaves. Long branches last for several days in the vase. The leaves are oval, wrinkled and large—up to 12 cm in length. There is also a variety with variegated foliage. (Illustrated Plate 72).

Weigela hybrida is the collective name given to all the different hybrids of the different species of Weigela which are now most popularly cultivated. The flowers come in many delicately-tinted shades of white, pink and crimson, and there are many named varieties. Perhaps the most popular are *W. Eva Rathke*, which is a deep crimson (Illustrated Plate 72). and *W. styriaca*, which has pink flowers changing to red. They are all as thickly clustered as *W. florida* and are extremely beautiful.

Wigandia
(Hydrophyllaceae)

Wigandia caracasana (*W. macrophylla*)

This large, deciduous shrub comes from South America and Mexico. It grows to a height of about 3 metres, with several thick, woody stems which branch upwards in a spreading fashion. It has large, spectacular plumes of purple flowers which are up to 25 cm in length. These plumes are made up of clusters of small, 5-petalled flowers in a pure violet colour with white centres. They drop off, carpeting the ground with purple, while new flowers open continuously for several weeks in the spring. The heart-shaped leaves are very arresting in appearance for they are huge. Some are about 35 cm in length and about 20 cm wide, and they have a rough, soft texture reminiscent of grape leaves.

Wigandia has a very tropical appearance, sometimes thought to be a little coarse, and is best suited to a roomy corner in a large garden. It seeds itself in moist soil and may also be grown from cuttings and suckers. It grows easily and rapidly in warm, sheltered situations, reaching about 2 metres in a season. It enjoys moisture and humidity and thrives at the coast, but is also very drought-resistant. (Illustrated Plate 72).

Wisteria
(Leguminosae)

Wisteria sinensis (*W. chinensis*)

This strong, deciduous climber comes from China and grows to a great size and age. It is one of the most beautiful and graceful climbers and the flowers make the loveliest of spring displays. They resemble large, lavender-blue bunches of grapes hanging down in masses and remain showy for two or three weeks before the leaves appear. The individual flowers are pea-shaped and the sprays grow to about 30 cm in length. The fresh green compound leaves have about 11 oval, pointed leaflets, each from 5 to 8 cm long, with slightly ruffled edges. Velvety green seedpods form at the end of the season. The strong, woody branches climb by twining and need support in the form of a trellis or wires when grown against a wall. It will spiral around a strong down-pipe and climb rapidly to the top of a double-storey house. It is grown on slanting bamboo trellises in Japan, to form arbours in a garden, so that one may admire the blooms in spring.

Wistaria is hardy to frost and easily grown. It likes a sunny position and good soil. It should be watered very well when young if it to grow rapidly. As it grows older, its penetrating roots find moisture well below the surface, if the soil is deep, and it then becomes drought-resistant. Pruning is essential in order to increase the number of blooms, as well as keep the plant in check. It may be cut back to spurs or to a single stem that is trained along the top of a fence, so that the flowers festoon it like a fringe. The vine develops a woody stem that is like the trunk of a tree and it may be grown in the shape of a small tree or rounded shrub by careful training. It must be clipped back ever year in late winter, until it has formed a thick trunk that is strong enough to support the mass of flowers and foliage. This makes a beautiful standard shaped like an umbrella. It is also used to form Bonsai in Japan.

Wistaria is grown from cuttings as the seeds do not always reproduce the horticultural forms. Although named after Professor Caspar Wistar, the botanical name was inadvertently spelt with an "e", so that *Wisteria* must be spelt thus when used botanically, but it may be spelt as Wistaria when using it as a common name. (Illustrated Plate 72).

Wisteria sinensis var. *alba* is a white-flowering form.

Wisteria floribunda (*W. multijuga*) is the Japanese Wistaria, which has very much longer, more slender sprays and comes in white and pink as well as violet.

Wisteria floribunda var. *violacea-plena* has double violet flowers.

INDEX

Botanical names are in *italics*. Common names are in roman type.
Numbers in **heavy type** refer to the main description.